Public School Integration of Severely Handicapped Students

Public School Integration of Severely Handicapped Students

Rational Issues and
Progressive Alternatives

edited by

Nick Certo, Ph.D.
Department of Special Education
University of Maryland

Norris Haring, Ed.D.
Department of Special Education
Washington Research Organization
University of Washington

Robert York, Ph.D.
Community Integration Program
State of Wisconsin
Department of Health and Social Services

·P A U L·H·
BROOKES
PUBLISHING C?

Baltimore • London

Paul H. Brookes Publishing Co.
Post Office Box 10624
Baltimore, Maryland 21204

Typeset by Brushwood Graphics, Baltimore, Maryland.
Manufactured in the United States of America
by the Maple Press Company, York, Pennsylvania.

Library of Congress Cataloging in Publication Data

Main entry under title:

Public school integration of severely handicapped students.

Bibliography: p.
Includes index.
1. Mainstreaming in education—United States. 2. Handicapped
children—Education—United States. I. Certo, Nick, 1949–   . II.
Haring,   Norris   Grover,   1923–   .   III.   York,   Robert,
1948–   . [DNLM: 1. Education, Special. 2. Handicapped. 3.
Education of mentally retarded. LC 4019 P976]
LC4019.P8   1984   371.9'046   83-15212
ISBN 0-933716-35-4

Contents

Contributors

Diane Baumgart, Ph.D.
Department of Special Education
Room 113
University of Idaho
Moscow, ID 83843

Felix F. Billingsley, Ph.D.
Associate Professor, Special Education
EEU/CDMRC, WJ-10
University of Washington
Seattle, WA 98105

Lou Brown, Ph.D.
Department of Studies in Behavioral
    Disabilities
University of Wisconsin-Madison
432 N. Murray Street, Room 305
Madison, WI 53706

Nick Certo, Ph.D.
Department of Special Education
University of Maryland
1308 Benjamin Building
College Park, MD 20742

Daniel J. Donder, Ph.D.
School Association for Special Education
    in DuPage County
Century Hills Education Center
6 South 331 Cornwall
Naperville, IL 60540

Dvenna Duncan, Ph.D.
School of Education
Buckley Center
University of Portland
Portland, OR 97203

Alison Ford, Ph.D.
Division of Special Education and
    Rehabilitation
Syracuse University
805 South Crouse Avenue
Syracuse, NY 13210

Robert J. Gaylord-Ross, Ph.D.
Department of Special Education
San Francisco State University
1600 Holloway
San Francisco, CA 94132

Susan Hamre-Nietupski, Ph.D.
Department of Special Education
University of Northern Iowa
150 A Education Center
Cedar Falls, IA 50614

Norris Haring, Ed.D.
Professor, Special Education
Director, Washington Research
    Organization
205 Parrington Hall, DC05
University of Washington
Seattle, WA 98195

Dawn Hunter, M.Ed.
Department of Special Education
University of Maryland
1308 Benjamin Building
College Park, MD 20742

Ginny Salce Iverson, M.Ed.
Center for Developmental Disabilities
499C Waterman Building
University of Vermont
Burlington, VT 05405

Frances L. Kohl, Ph.D.
Department of Special Education
University of Maryland
1308 Benjamin Building
College Park, MD 20742

Ron Kowalski, M.A.
Special Education Programs
U.S. Department of Education
Donohoe Building
400 Maryland Avenue, S.W.
Washington, DC 20202

Ruth Loomis, M.A.
Division of Specialized Educational
 Services
Madison Metropolitan School District
545 W. Dayton
Madison, WI 53703

Lucy G. Moses, M.Ed.
Regional Inservice Training Project
Portland Public Schools
Portland, ME 04301

John Nietupski, Ph.D.
Department of Special Education
University of Northern Iowa
150 A Education Center
Cedar Falls, IA 50614

Jan Nisbet, Ph.D.
Syracuse University
Division of Special Education and
 Rehabilitation
805 South Crouse Avenue
Syracuse, NY 13210

Margaret M. Noel, Ph.D.
Department of Special Education
University of Maryland
1308 Benjamin Building
College Park, MD 20742

Valerie Pitts-Conway, B.A.
Marin County Office of Education
1111 Las Galinas Avenue
P.O. Box 4925
San Rafael, CA 99913

Ian Pumpian, Ph.D.
Department of Special Education
San Diego State University
San Diego, CA 92182

Dave Rostetter, Ph.D.
Special Education Programs
U.S. Department of Education
Donohoe Building
400 Maryland Avenue, S.W.
Washington, D.C. 20202

Judy A. Schrag, Ed.D.
Assistant Superintendent for Special
 Services & Professional Programs
Division of Special Services
Washington State Department of
 Education
7510 Armstrong Street, S.W.
Turnwater, WA 98504

Jack Schroeder, M.S.
Division of Specialized Educational
 Services
Madison Metropolitan School District
545 W. Dayton
Madison, WI 53703

Richard P. Schutz, Ph.D.
Center for Developmental Disabilities
499C Waterman Building
University of Vermont
Burlington, VT 05405

Susan Stainback, Ed.D.
Department of Special Education
University of Northern Iowa
150 A Education Center
Cedar Falls, IA 50614

William Stainback, Ed.D.
Department of Special Education
University of Northern Iowa
150 A Education Center
Cedar Falls, IA 50614

Frances Stetson, Ph.D.
Consultant, Programs for Severely
 Handicapped Students
Region IV Education Service Center
P.O. Box 863
Houston, TX 77001

Barbara A. Stettner-Eaton, M.Ed.
Department of Special Education
University of Maryland
1308 Benjamin Building
College Park, MD 20742

Luanna Meyer Voeltz, Ph.D.
Special Education Programs
Department of Educational Psychology
University of Minnesota
Burton Hall
178 Pillsbury Drive, S.E.
Minneapolis, MN 55455

Wes Williams, Ph.D.
Center for Developmental Disabilities
499C Waterman Building
University of Vermont
Burlington, VT 05405

Robert York, Ph.D.
Community Integration Program
State of Wisconsin
Department of Health and Social Services
1 West Wilson Street
P.O. Box 7851
Madison, WI 53707

Preface

This edited volume, compiled under the authorization of The Association for the Severely Handicapped (TASH), has been written to provide a factual, conceptual, and economic counterpoint to the many negative myths, alarmist exaggerations, and opinions often based on incomplete information that have effectively blocked many severely handicapped students from receiving their education in the same settings as their nonhandicapped peers, not to mention usurping their rights as citizens.

The volume includes 14 chapters, written by TASH members, that form a comprehensive, multifaceted treatment of public school integration for severely handicapped students. The first chapter begins with a review of the history of educational services for severely handicapped students and concludes with a strong statement regarding what education should be, namely, integrated education for all students. The second chapter presents a thorough review and analysis of the factual research basis for integration which clearly supports the following simple conclusion: If you want severely handicapped students to interact with nonhandicapped individuals, they have to spend a little time together. Once again, severely handicapped students demonstrate that they cannot learn a skill without direct instruction, and that systematic direct instruction with nonhandicapped peers is the only remedy to the interaction deficits that result from segregated education.

Following the presentation of the book's position of what education should be, and the factual basis for this position, the third chapter presents the reality. This chapter reports on the frustrating experiences of four families who have attempted to secure an education for their severely handicapped children in integrated settings. It reviews obstacles presented by school administrators and compromises of questionable legal validity families were encouraged to accept. It demonstrates the type of commitment and perseverance families often must have to secure integrated services for their children. When one compares the ample legal and empirical support for integration against the stories of these four families, a sense of outrage at the callous manipulation of children by some school officials emerges.

The following four chapters describe the process of transition from segregated to integrated services. These chapters deal with this transition from a variety of perspectives that range from long term planning and systematic statewide change, to building-level facility and staff preparation strategies. The next five chapters provide concrete strategies for determining interaction instructional content and for facilitating interactions once severely handicapped students begin receiving their education in integrated regular school settings.

The final two chapters present both a state department of education and federal department of education perspective on the integration of severely handicapped students. Of the two, the federal perspective particularly is noteworthy both for its strong, clear position in support of integration for all severely handicapped students and for the unique perspective it provides for analyzing the potential points of contention between constituent groups who inevitably are involved in the development of new educational options.

By maintaining a consistent balance between philosophical information, practical techniques, and empirical validity, we believe the contributors to this latest TASH volume have provided a valuable resource to families and practitioners attempting to provide severely handicapped students with an equal and meaningful education—one that does more than simply occupy 5 hours a day for 9 months of a school year at public expense.

N.C.
N.H.
R.Y.

Public School Integration of Severely Handicapped Students

1

Integration of Students with Severe Handicaps

*Daniel J. Donder
and Robert York*

Historically most children and youth with severe handicaps have been excluded from public educational services on the assumption that their disabilities made efforts to teach them not only fruitless but a waste of scarce resources (Donder, Hamre-Nietupski, Nietupski, & Fortschneider, 1981). Most of these individuals resided within their natural communities and were cared for by parents or other family members. Occasionally, determined educational efforts were made, with results that ranged from modest to extraordinary (Buck, 1930; Hunt, 1967; Keller, 1955; Killilea, 1962). As these individual instances of successful educational efforts accumulated, many parents and charitable groups began private school programs to educate children who were excluded from the public schools. These services were often sketchy and incomplete, operating across ages and disability levels. The personnel who staffed such "educational programs" frequently were uncertified and received salaries that were much lower than teachers in the community public schools. Facilities were literally "church basements" and older, abandoned schools that had been phased out of service by the community public schools. Despite the limitations of such schools, most parents felt fortunate to have some type of services for their severely handicapped child (Guess & Horner, 1979). Eventually some programs became so large that "progressive" communities developed the necessary resources to build their own private schools. These private educational systems still were forced to be separate from the public educational system, however.

1

In addition to the children with severe handicaps who remained with their families, a significant number were placed in large public institutions. Although institutional placement was a difficult and painful process for most families, these families were following what they sincerely believed to be the best course for their child. After all, they were acting on the advice of professionals who indicated that these state facilities contained the expertise and programs needed by their child. Unfortunately, services provided at these institutions were often woefully inadequate, and their living conditions can only be described as inhumane (Blatt & Kaplan, 1966; Ferleger & Boyd, 1979; *Halderman* v. *Pennhurst State School and Hospital*, 1977; *Wyatt* v. *Stickney*, 1972).

Perhaps most incomprehensible of all the institutional practices was the discrimination practiced against those residents with severe handicaps. Despite the state "mandated missions, specialized expertise, and specially designed facilities," individuals with severe handicaps were often isolated from other residents and excluded from educational and other habilitative services (*Garrity* v. *Gallen*, 1981). Families frequently followed professional advice and institutionalized their child, only to be filled with horror at the dismal quality of educational and habilitative efforts expended by the state (Ferleger & Boyd, 1979). Thus, the history of institutional educational services for individuals with severe handicaps is also one of exclusion and isolation.

Fortunately, it is now generally recognized that individuals with severe handicaps can and do benefit from educational services. Numerous studies have been published in journals, monographs, and texts demonstrating this fact. Perhaps the more pressing need now is to address the arguments of those who believe that educating individuals with severe handicaps is an unproductive use of limited resources. First it is important to recognize that resources are always finite and that the uses to which those resources can be applied are therefore necessarily limited. In the end, decisions as to how resources are to be used depend upon what is valued as important by those in decision-making positions. Clearly, politics plays a major role in determining the values that are ultimately supported (Weintraub, 1976).

Arguments supporting the authors' view that resources should be used to educate individuals with severe handicaps reflect values that are simple and direct. First, individuals with severe handicaps have the same rights to life, liberty, and the pursuit of happiness as anyone else. The presence or absence of a disability is irrelevant when considering an individual's basic humanity and the rights to which he or she is entitled. Second, education is a critically important and frequently essential component for successful functioning in society. To deny educational access to an individual may seriously limit that individual's future. This is especially true for individuals with disabilities who may have difficulty acquiring new skills. In fact, the denial of educational services may lead to a compounding set of circumstances that, when accumulated, lead to unnecessary idleness, suffering, and a shortened lifespan (Gilhool, 1973). Third, society as a whole is directly affected by its treatment of each of its members. How a society chooses to treat its least advantaged members is an important measure of the humanity of that society and is ultimately a determinant of the society's respect for all of its members (Martin, 1976).

Ed Martin, speaking as the director of the Bureau of Education for the Handicapped of the U.S. Office of Education, synthesized these issues eloquently in a presentation he made in 1976 to the American Association for the Education of the Severely/Profoundly Handicapped (now The Association for the Severely Handicapped):

> There are many reasons for not educating the severely and profoundly handicapped. Educating these children is often enormously costly. The class sizes have to be small. In traditional education terms, the gains may be small as well. I have heard the argument that such programs are not fair to the majority. They rob resources: many more "normal" or even mildly handicapped children could be educated with the same dollars. The only protection a severely handicapped child has against such thinking is a government of laws which is fiercely devoted to the intrinsic rights of a given individual. . . . To my mind, what has made this country great, and what holds our promise for the future, is the preservation of our commitment to the individual even if, as with our commitment to the profoundly handicapped, it is expensive or unpopular. . . . Many will not understand. They will see only a profoundly damaged organism. . . . They will speak of higher priorities.
>
> What you know, however, is that equity for these citizens is essential to our national security. It is essential for our fidelity to our Bill of Rights. If we violate these persons, we violate our commitment to the principle which protects us all (pp. 9–10).

Other authors provide support for this same premise. Wolfensberger (1981), in reviewing the history of pre–World War II Germany, argues that the devaluation and extermination of individuals with handicaps can lead to the devaluation of an ever-expanding group of individuals. Since all criteria for devaluation are arbitrary points on a continuum of human characteristics, the selection of an increasing number of criteria for devaluation, such as pigmentation and religious/cultural heritage, are only logical extensions of an illogical practice.

The above perspectives on history and values have been provided here as a backdrop against which the reader may judge the authors' recommendations. Too frequently the integration of students with handicaps into age-appropriate regular public schools has been viewed as the legal legacy of Public Law 94-142. The fundamental rights and exemplary educational practices from which this law evolved often are overlooked, as is the evolutionary and universal nature of integration efforts. That integration versus segregation is a fundamental principle guiding services for individuals with handicaps is recognized worldwide is evidenced by the position of the Catholic church on this matter:

> The principle of *Integration* opposes the tendency to isolate, segregate and neglect the disabled; but it also goes further than an attitude of mere tolerance. It includes a commitment to make the disabled person a subject in the fullest sense, in accordance with his or her capacities, in the spheres of family life, the school, employment, and more generally, in the social, political and religious communities (Document of the Holy See for the International Year of Disabled Persons, 1981, p. 4).

The narrow and myopic view espoused by both advocates and opponents of public school integration in the United States frequently disregards the larger issues and international efforts at integration.

SCHOOLS FOR HANDICAPPED STUDENTS ONLY

After many years of efforts by parents, advocates and professionals, public school districts began to assume responsibility for educating children with severe handicaps. Largely owing to past practices, the majority of parents and special educators believed it was not possible for the regular schools to provide educational situations in which children with severe handicaps could learn and thrive. It was assumed that neither severely handicapped students nor nonhandicapped children could benefit from shared public school education. Few considered the possibility that these students might coexist and interact positively with each other (Brown, Branston, Hamre-Nietupski, Johnson, Wilcox, & Gruenewald, 1979). Thus, isolating students with severe handicaps in separate schools was thought the best way to educate them. In cases where separate facilities were built they were frequently constructed in undeveloped suburban areas because of the reduced cost of land. Similarly, when existing facilities were used, the special education program was often located in an equally remote area: A school in an area of declining enrollment would be designated as the "special needs" school, and the nonhandicapped students would be transferred to surrounding schools. Since all of the students with severe handicaps in a school district were to be bused to one school, the location of that school was considered relatively unimportant to many districts.

The "clustering" approach to providing services was believed to be the most favorable means of meeting the educational needs of students with severe handicaps, primarily because of the presumed advantages of staff proximity and of administrative convenience. It was felt that the proximity of special education personnel to each other would allow them to collaborate to a greater degree; moreover, by sharing common problems they would avoid feelings of isolation, of "being the only person in the world" with such instructional problems (Sontag, Burke, & York, 1973). Support staff (e.g., communication specialists, developmental therapists) might also be used more effectively, since they could be scheduled for more contact time with students and teachers and would expend less time traveling between several locations. This concept of grouping expertise could be extended, as well, to health and medical services, so that almost all services needed by students with severe handicaps would be available within one building. Administratively, the one-building concept has, in fact, proved convenient for arranging inservice training, curriculum development projects, and transitions between classrooms. The need to interact with a number of principals and regular school staff is eliminated, as is the need to concern oneself with several physical plants.

Despite these reasons for maintaining a special school, the pivotal consideration remains whether or not the model itself is successful in meeting the needs of students with severe handicaps. Proponents of the model have consistently expressed the fear that the integration of nonhandicapped and handicapped students may be harmful to one or both parties. They have argued that students with severe handicaps need the shelter and protection of the special school; under a segregated system, students without handicaps can proceed with their education unencumbered by their less able peers.

SEGREGATED ADULT ENVIRONMENTS AND SERVICES

As long as it was generally assumed that adults with severe handicaps could function only in highly sheltered post-school environments, any impetus for integrated school programs was muted. Educational preparation in self-contained school environments seemed the logical precursor for postschool functioning in work activity centers and sheltered workshops—which are themselves typically available only to individuals with handicaps and are organized in such a way that contacts with other workers and community members are infrequent. Few individuals leave such adult services and those that do depart within the first few months after placement (Bellamy, Sowers, & Bourbeau, 1983). Thus, prior to passage of PL 94-142,attempts to provide severely handicapped individuals with opportunities to obtain the skills and experiences required to function effectively in their communities with nonhandicapped people have often been viewed as both unrealistic and unnecessary. Likewise, there frequently appeared no justification for providing nonhandicapped community members with the skills and experiences necessary to interact effectively with severely handicapped persons as neighbors, coworkers, employers, or service providers (Brown et al., 1979). As long as individuals with severe handicaps spent their time at home or engaged in highly supervised work, recreation, and living situations that were separate from those containing nonhandicapped individuals, separate educational settings could be rationalized.

PROGRESSION FROM SEGREGATED
SCHOOLS TO SEGREGATED ADULT SERVICES?

The usual pattern of "progression" from segregated educational programs to similar segregated adult services has come under extensive attack from numerous quarters, perhaps the most devastating attacks coming from two fronts: the philosophical bankruptcy of the position and its demonstrated limited effectiveness in improving the quality of life for individuals with severe handicaps.

Philosophically the assumed movement from segregated schools to segregated adult services hardly qualifies as a progression at all, but may be more appropriately described as a "doctrine of limitations" (Sontag, Certo, & Button, 1979). Can individuals with severe handicaps be considered so limited in their prospects that they must be educated throughout childhood for a separate, colorless, and unproductive life? Vastly more appealing and philosophically sound are the approaches falling under the general rubric of "normalization" (Wolfensberger, 1981) and "functional skill development" (Brown, Branston, Hamre-Nietupski, Pumpian, Certo, & Gruenewald, 1979). These approaches recognize the essential humanness of individuals with severe handicaps and the fact that their wants and needs follow the same pattern as all other people. Rather than emphasizing differences between people these strategies focus upon commonalities. Thus, such views hold that there is no need to create a separate world to which those with severe handicaps must be relegated; instead, the common world that all people share serves as the basis for determining educational goals and the criteria for judging the success of such education.

The limited effectiveness of the progression from segregated school to segregated adult services has been demonstrated in several ways, perhaps the most direct measures having been follow-up studies of individuals with moderate and severe handicaps following their school years. In general these studies show that these graduates lead isolated and rather unproductive lives (Pumpian, Baumgart, Shiraga, Ford, Nisbet, Loomis, & Brown, 1980; Stanfield, 1973). On the other hand, when severely handicapped persons have been involved in an educational program providing training in functional life skills in integrated school settings, at least economic measures of adult productivity have improved significantly (Pumpian, et al., 1980). Data have yet to conclusively demonstrate the superiority of such a philosophical approach in producing a higher quality of life for individuals with severe handicaps. However, the steadily accumulating pieces of hard data, combined with the authors' own experiences as service providers, observers, and evaluators, provide, in the authors' opinion, convincing evidence of the superiority of a philosophy emphasizing normalization and functional skill training.

SCHOOLS SERVING BOTH
HANDICAPPED AND NONHANDICAPPED STUDENTS

A commitment to a philosophy that stresses the essential similarity of all individuals and their need to acquire skills relevant to the community in which they live, work, recreate, and interact forces an unavoidable conflict with the practices of segregation. If individuals with severe handicaps are to function within normal community social, vocational, residential, and recreational settings, then it is imperative that the educational environments those individuals experience as children provide the necessary preparation. In other words, these educational settings must provide daily and longitudinal interactions between handicapped and nonhandicapped students (Brown, Branston, Hamre-Nietupski, Johnson, Wilcox, & Gruenewald, 1979; Brown, Ford, Nisbet, Sweet, Donnellan, & Gruenewald, 1982). Segregation of students with severe handicaps impedes the development of the requisite interactional skills and experiences that facilitate their appropriate functioning as adults in diversely populated community environments. Severely handicapped persons can hardly learn to interact appropriately with their nonhandicapped peers without being exposed to them. Of course, exposure alone does not ensure the development of such interactions, but lack of exposure guarantees their absence (Brown et al., 1979).

MOVEMENT TOWARD EDUCATION IN
THE LEAST RESTRICTIVE ENVIRONMENT

Despite notable improvements, the restrictive segregationist point of view is still prevalent in schools and communities. Educational services for severely handicapped students often do not promote the type of heterogeneous community in which handicapped and nonhandicapped community members interact with each other in schools, in social activities, and in the course of their employment. The predominant educational model continues to be the cluster approach, which isolates and segregates severely handicapped students in self-contained schools. This is borne out by a study conducted by Kenowitz, Zweibel, and Edgar (1978) to determine present and future placement opportunities for students with moderate and severe handicaps. According to 81 public school district administrators surveyed in a nationwide, representative sampling of large and small districts, 70% of these students were receiving educational services in segregated schools, with 88% of the administrators noting that the facilities had been built within the 5 years between 1973 to 1978. Even though 12% of the administrators indicated plans to close the segregated facilities, 20% were planning to build additional segregated facilities for students labeled as severely handicapped, trainable mentally retarded, or educable mentally retarded.

PLACEMENT—ONLY ONE ASPECT OF LRE

As several authors have indicated (Kenowitz et al., 1978; Nietupski, Hamre-Nietupski, Schuetz, & Ockwood, 1980; Thomason & Arkell, 1980), the concept of least restrictive environment, (LRE) for educating severely handicapped students is often considered by both special educators and the public to deal with physical placement alone (e.g., special school versus self-contained classroom within a regular public school). In this context, *where* students are placed seems to be primary criterion for determining the least restrictive environment, rather than considering what transpires after a placement is complete. Of equal importance, however, is whether consistent opportunities for interaction between handicapped and nonhandicapped students are provided (Bricker, 1978; Guralnick, 1976; Snyder, Apolloni, & Cooke, 1976). With this expanded concept in mind, Brown, Nietupski, and Hamre-Nietupski (1976) defined a less restrictive environment for students with severe handicaps to include both placement in age-appropriate public schools and a *maximization* of interactions between students with handicaps and their nonhandicapped peers.

Using the definition of less restrictive environment given by Brown et al. (1976), Thomason and Arkell (1980) have provided a model for educating severely handicapped students in the least restrictive environment. These authors state that school districts should disperse clusters of classes for severely handicapped students throughout the district's schools, and, in order to eliminate segregated wings and/or floors in these public schools, administrators should disperse classrooms throughout the school buildings. This "side-by-side" approach to educating handicapped and nonhandicapped students encourages frequent interactions between students, teachers, and staff within the school.

A parallel can be drawn between the integration of students with severe handicaps and the integration of students of different races. Hoben (1980) reports that in the 1960s educators learned that to desegregate racially unbalanced schools was much easier to accomplish than to generate integrated interactions among students. Hoben states that educators quickly realized that "desegregation and integration are not the same" (p. 100). Desegregation can be mandated, whereas integration must be viewed as an ongoing process of interactions that cannot be expected to occur spontaneously. Moreover, in order to facilitate integration, once severely handicapped students are placed in an age-appropriate public school, continual efforts must be made to encourage positive interactions between such students and their nonhandicapped peers.

INTEGRATING SEVERELY HANDICAPPED STUDENTS

Hamre-Nietupski, Branston, Ford, Stoll, Gruenewald, and Brown (1978), Hamre-Nietupski and Nietupski (1981), and Nietupski et al. (1980) present several strategies for training persons who will be involved in developing interactions between severely handicapped students and others. Since the integration of severely handicapped students will be a new experience for many people, these authors stress the importance of preparing all appropriate individuals, including special and regular educators, both handicapped and nonhandicapped students, and parents. (Considerations for readying a school system for integrating severely handicapped and nonhandicapped individuals are presented in several other chapters of this text.)

Special educators in the public school should realize that it is their responsibility to provide opportunities for positive interactions between students. Nietupski et al. (1980) stress that the special education teacher is, to a large extent, the major person responsible for integration. The manner in which a special education teacher interacts with other staff members and students will influence the degree to which severely handicapped students are integrated and accepted in the school. Stated another way, if special education teachers make no attempt to involve themselves and their students in daily school activities, few positive integration experiences are likely to occur. Nietupski, Hamre-Nietupski, Schuetz, & Ockwood (1980), in addressing teachers of severely handicapped students in public schools, state: "we believe that you will want to make integration as important a priority as self-care, social, domestic living, communication, community functioning and functional academic skills instruction . . ." (p. 27). If teachers fail to comprehend the importance of interactions between handicapped and nonhandicapped students, neither group of students may experience the positive aspect of an integrated educational setting.

Other authors have offered strategies for preparing nonhandicapped students to interact positively with their severely handicapped peers (Brown, Hamre-Nietupski, Lyon, Branston, Falvey, & Gruenewald, 1978; Glazzard, 1979; Gottlieb, 1980; Hamre-Nietupski et al., 1978; Hamre-Nietupski & Nietupski, 1981; Stainback, Stainback, & Jaben, 1981). If students with severe handicaps are to become an integral part of their schools and communities, educators need to incorporate training about handicapping conditions into the curriculum for nonhandicapped students. These units of study might be a revision of or an addition to an already existing health, social studies, or child development curriculum.

Curriculum units that focus upon individual and cultural differences could also easily be modified to include such information. Donder (Note 1), Litton, Banbury, and Harris (1980), and Nietupski et al. (1980) provide references for magazines, movies, kits and filmstrips available to special and regular education teachers that might prove helpful in planning activities to better acquaint nonhandicapped students both at the elementary and secondary level with their handicapped peers.

Special education teachers should set aside time for nonhandicapped students in order to discuss such topics as: 1) pros and cons of having students with handicaps integrated into the schools and community, 2) basic information on philosophical, legal, and educational approaches for interacting with students with severe handicaps, and 3) preconceived notions that nonhandicapped students may have about students with handicaps. By making themselves accessible for this type of discussion, special educators provide important opportunities within the school setting to clarify inaccurate perceptions and present worthwhile information. Such discussion sessions may also provide a chance for the special educator to determine which nonhandicapped students might be interested in becoming involved in integration activities.

EXAMPLES OF EFFORTS TOWARD INTEGRATION

Despite the continuing need for more research, several studies have begun to substantiate the effectiveness of integrated settings for students with severe handicaps, indicating positive results in terms of benefits to both handicapped and nonhandicapped populations. Ziegler and Hambleton (1976) studied two classes of students with severe handicaps who were transferred from a segregated facility to an integrated public school that allowed for interactions with nonhandicapped students. After the transfer the handicapped students were compared to a matched group of students still attending the segregated facility. Ziegler and Hambleton found that interactions involving only handicapped students at both schools were predominantly positive, and added that fewer acts of aggression and considerably more teaching and helping interactions were reported in the integrated public school. It also was found in the integrated public school setting that a large number of the nonhandicapped students knew the handicapped students individually by name. Ziegler and Hambleton (1976) concluded that ''there [could] be little doubt that the placement of the special classes in a regular school was extremely effective in promoting interaction between the retarded and nonretarded students, thus providing a more normal environment for the retarded children'' (p. 460).

In two similar studies McCarthy and Stodden (1979), and Poorman (1980) reported on the outcomes of a peer tutoring strategy for involving nonhandicapped and handicapped students in interactions throughout the school day. It was found in both elementary and secondary school settings that peer tutoring resulted in an attitude of acceptance and understanding of the severely handicapped students by both their peers and faculty. For most of the nonhandicapped students involved in the studies, the peer tutoring situation was their first interactive opportunity with a handicapped person. McCarthy and Stodden (1979) stated that "indications [were] that these accepting experiences and attitudes [would] carry over into the community and [would] facilitate postschool adjustment" (p. 163).

In their report of another peer-tutoring program, Almond, Rodgers, and Krug (1979) described results that indicated not only a demonstration of understanding and support for handicapped students on the part of both faculty and non-handicapped peers, but also increased achievement in academic skills by handicapped students, an improvement that was attributed to the success of the peer tutoring program. In addition, it was found that the increased opportunity for contact between handicapped and nonhandicapped students on the playground made more appropriate social models available to the handicapped students. Furthermore, the nonhandicapped students developed a sense of responsibility as they left their classroom each day to go to "work" in the special education classroom. The nonhandicapped students and teachers alike expressed positive attitudes about the experiences they had gained, as well as an understanding of the handicapped student's abilities.

Russo and Koegel (1977) investigated the feasibility of using behavior management techniques to integrate an autistic student into a class of 20 to 30 nonhandicapped students within a public school. A special educator conducted a 10-week training session in which behavior management techniques were taught to the regular educator who would be conducting playground activities with the severely handicapped children. In addition the nonhandicapped student volunteers who participated in the program indicated that their involvement was reinforcing in that it provided them with enjoyable playground activities in which to interact with the handicapped children during recess.

More recently, researchers have begun to study the attitudes of non-handicapped and less handicapped students toward severely handicapped students. Voeltz, Kishi, Brown, and Kube (1980) surveyed 2,392 regular education students (1,217 boys, 1,175 girls) in grades two through seven to determine their attitudes toward severely handicapped peers who had begun to attend some of the regular public schools in their district. It was found that most nonhandicapped students expressed accepting attitudes toward their severely handicapped peers. Upper elementary-age students, girls of all ages, and students in the schools that had been integrated with severely handicapped students exhibited the most accepting attitudes.

McHale and Simeonsson (1980) studied nonhandicapped students' "under-standings" or knowledge of their autistic school peers. Thirty elementary-age nonhandicapped students were divided into five small groups of six students each. Each group of six students engaged in 1 week of play (five sessions) with the six autistic students. During these play sessions, the nonhandicapped students' "job" was to teach the autistic students how to play. Interviews were held with each nonhandicapped student both before and after the play sessions. It was found that the nonhandicapped students' "understandings" of their autistic peers improved significantly after interactions, although it was noted that their perceptions were considered adequate before interactions occurred.

In conclusion, some of the latest research suggests that nonhandicapped students tend to have positive attitudes about severely handicapped students. In addition, such research suggests that increased interactions between nonhandicapped and severely handicapped students increases nonhandicapped students' positive attitudes about their severely handicapped peers.

CONCLUSIONS

Historically, the predominant educational placements for severely handicapped students have been in the home, in state or private institutions, and in segregated public schools. The successful groundwork laid by advocates of the civil rights movement has done much to enable parents, professionals, educational organizations, and advocates of the severely handicapped students to lobby effectively for the integration of severely handicapped students into regular public schools. Because of their efforts, as well as the passage of PL 94-142, placement of severely handicapped students within age-appropriate regular attendance public schools is becoming a reality.

The concept of least restrictive educational environment should not be viewed in terms of placement options alone. If this were the case, severely handicapped students might remain segregated from their nonhandicapped peers and from the community, though placed within the same public school building. When severely handicapped students are placed within an integrated public school, a significant amount of time must be spent with the handicapped student, nonhandicapped students, parents, faculty, and building staff to prepare them for the integration process and to encourage them to provide opportunities for interactions between handicapped and nonhandicapped students.

Implementing this type of heterogeneous school program for severely handicapped students is a critical issue facing not only special educators but the entire educational community.

REFERENCES

Almond, P., Rodgers, S., & Krug, A. Mainstreaming: A model for including elementary students in the severely handicapped classroom. *Teaching Exceptional Children*, 1979, *11*(11), 135–139.

Bellamy, G.T., Sowers, J.A., & Bourbeau, P.E. Work and work-related services: Post school options. In: M. E. Snell (ed.), *Systematic instruction of the moderately and severely handicapped* (2nd ed.). Columbus, OH: Charles E. Merrill Publishing Co., 1983.

Blatt, B., & Kaplan, F. *Christmas in purgatory: A photographic essay on mental retardation*. Rockleigh, NJ: Allyn & Bacon, 1966.

Bricker, D.D. A rationale for the integration of handicapped and non-handicapped preschool children. In: M.J. Guralnick (ed.), *Early intervention and the integration of handicapped and non-handicapped children*. Baltimore: University Park Press, 1978.

Brown, L., Branston, M., Hamre-Nietupski, S., Johnson, F., Wilcox, B., & Gruenewald, L. A rationale for comprehensive longitudinal interactions between severely handicapped students and non-handicapped students and other citizens. *AAESPH Review*, 1979, *4*(1), 3–14.

Brown, L., Branston, M., Hamre-Nietupski, S., Pumpian, I., Certo, N., & Gruenewald, L. A strategy for developing chronological age appropriate and functional curriculum content for severely handicapped adolescents and young adults. *Journal of Special Education,* 1979, *13*(1), 81–90.

Brown, L., Ford, A., Nisbet, J., Sweet, M., Donnellan, A., & Gruenewald, L. Opportunities available when severely handicapped students attend chronological age appropriate regular schools in accordance with the natural proportion. In: L. Brown, J. Nisbet, A. Ford, M. Sweet, B. Shiraga, & L. Gruenewald (eds.), *Educational programs for severely handicapped students,* Vol. 12. Madison,WI: University of Wisconsin and the Madison Metropolitan Schools, 1982.

Brown, L., Hamre-Nietupski, S., Lyon, S., Branston, M.B., Falvey, M., & Gruenewald, L. (eds). *Curricular strategies for developing longitudinal interactions between severely handicapped students and others and curricular strategies for teaching severely handicapped students to acquire and perform skills in response to naturally occurring cues and correction procedures,* Vol. 3, Part I. Madison, WI: Madison Metropolitan School District, 1978.

Brown, L., Nietupski, J., & Hamre-Nietupski, S. The criterion of ultimate functioning. In: M.A. Thomas (ed.), *Hey, don't forget about me! Education's investment in the severely and profoundly handicapped.* Reston, VA: The Council for Exceptional Children, 1976.

Buck, P. *The child who never grew.* New York: John Day, 1930.

Document of the Holy See for the International Year of Disabled Persons. *For all those who work for the disabled.* Vatican City: Canadian Conference of Catholic Bishops, 1981.

Donder, D., Hamre-Nietupski, S., Nietupski, J., & Fortschneider, J. Integrating moderately and severely handicapped students into regular schools: Problem solving and strategy development. In: R. York, W. Schofield, D. Donder, & D. Ryndak (eds.), *Organizing and implementing services for students with severe and multiple handicaps.* Springfield, IL: Illinois State Board of Education, 1981.

Ferleger, D., & Boyd, P.A. Anti-institutionalization: The promise of the Pennhurst Case. *Stanford Law Review,* 1979, *31*(4), 717–752.

Garrity v. *Gallen,* 522 F. Supp. 171 (D.N.H., 1981).

Gilhool, T.K. Education: An inalienable right. *Exceptional Children,* 1973, *39*(8), 597–609.

Glazzard, P. Simulation of handicaps as teaching strategy for preservice and inservice training. *Teaching Exceptional Children,* 1979, *11*(3), 101–104.

Gottlieb, J. Improving attitudes toward retarded children by using group discussion. *Exceptional Children,* 1980, *47*(2), 106–111.

Guess, D., & Horner, D. The severely and profoundly handicapped. In: E. Meyer (ed.), *Basic readings in the study of exceptional children and youth.* Denver: Love Publishing Co., 1979.

Guralnick, M.J. The value of integrating handicapped and nonhandicapped preschool children. *American Journal of Orthopsychiatry,* 1976, *46,* 236–245.

Halderman v. *Pennhurst State School and Hospital,* 446 F. Supp. 1295 (E.D.Pa. 1977).

Hamre-Nietupski, S., Branston, M., Ford, A., Stoll, A., Gruenewald, L., & Brown, L. Curricular strategies for developing longitudinal interactions between severely handicapped and nonhandicapped individuals in school and nonschool environments. In: L. Brown, S. Hamre-Nietupski, S. Lyon, M.B. Branston, M. Falvey, & L. Gruenewald (eds.), *Curricular strategies for developing longitudinal interactions between severely handicapped students and others and curricular strategies for teaching severely handicapped students to acquire and perform skills in response to naturally occurring cues and correction procedures,* Vol. 8, Part 1. Madison, WI: Madison Metropolitan School District, 1978.

Hamre-Nietupski, S., & Nietupski, J. Integral involvement of severely handicapped students, within regular public schools. *Journal of The Association for the Severely Handicapped,* 1981, *6, 30*–39.

Hoben, M. Toward integration in the mainstream. *Exceptional Children,* 1980, *47*(2), 100–105.

Hunt, N. *The world of Nigel Hunt: The diary of a mongoloid.* New York: Garrett, 1967.

Keller, H.A. *Teacher: Anne Sullivan Macy—A tribute by the foster-child of her mind.* Garden City, NY: Doubleday, 1955.

Kenowitz, L., Zweibel, S., & Edgar, E. Determining the least restrictive educational opportunity for the severely and profoundly handicapped. In: N.G. Haring & D. Bricker (eds.), *Teaching the severely handicapped,* Vol. 3. Columbus, OH: Special Press, 1978.

Killilea, M. *Karen.* New York: Prentice-Hall, 1962.

Litton, F., Banbury, M., & Harris, K. Materials for educating nonhandicapped students about their nonhandicapped peers. *Teaching Exceptional Children,* 1980, *13*(1), 39–43.

McCarthy, R., & Stodden, R. Mainstreaming secondary students: A peer tutoring model. *Teaching Exceptional Children,* 1979, *11*(4), 162–163.

McHale, S., & Simeonsson, R. Effects of interactions on nonhandicapped children's attitudes towards autistic children. *American Journal of Mental Deficiency,* 1980, *85,* 18–24.

Martin, E.W. On Justice Douglas and education for the severely/profoundly handicapped. *Journal of Special Education,* 1976, *10*(2), 123–126.

Nietupski, J., Hamre-Nietupski, S., Schuetz, G., & Ockwood, L. *Severely handicapped students in regular schools.* Milwaukee, WI: Milwaukee Public Schools, 1980.

Poorman, C. Mainstreaming in reverse with a special friend. *Teaching Exceptional Children,* 1980, *12*(4), 136–142.

Pumpian, I., Baumgart, D., Shiraga, B., Ford, A., Nisbet, J., Loomis, R., & Brown, L. Vocational training programs for severely handicapped students in the Madison Metropolitan School District. In: L. Brown, M. Falvey, I. Pumpian, D. Baumgart, J. Nisbet, A. Ford, J. Schroeder, & R. Loomis (eds.), *Curricular strategies for teaching severely handicapped students functional skills in school and nonschool environments.* Madison, WI: University of Wisconsin—Madison and Madison Metropolitan School District, 1980.

Russo, D.C., & Koegel, R.L. A method for integrating an autistic child into a normal public-school classroom. *Journal of Applied Behavior Analysis,* 1977, *10,* 579–590.

Snyder, L., Apolloni, T., & Cooke, T.P. Integrated settings at the early childhood level: The role of nonretarded peers. *Exceptional Children,* 1976, *43,* 262–266.

Sontag, E., Burke, P.J., & York, R. Considerations for serving the severely handicapped in the public schools. *Education and Training of the Mentally Retarded,* 1973, *8,* 20–26.

Sontag, E., Certo, N., & Button, J.E. On a distinction between the education of the severely and profoundly handicapped and a doctrine of limitations. *Exceptional Children,* 1979, *45,* 604–616.

Stainback, W., Stainback, S., & Jaben, T. Providing opportunities for interactions between severely handicapped and nonhandicapped students. *Teaching Exceptional Children,* 1981, *13,* 72–75.

Stanfield, J.S. Graduation: What happens to the retarded child when he grows up? *Exceptional Children,* 1973, *39,* 548–552.

Thomason, J., & Arkell, C. Educating the severely/profoundly handicapped in the public schools: A side-by-side approach. *Exceptional Children,* 1980, *47*(2), 114–122.

Voeltz, L., Kishi, G., Brown, S., & Kube, C. *Special friends trainer's manual: Starting a project in your school.* Honolulu: Hawaii Integration Project, Department of Special Education, University of Hawaii, 1980.

Weintraub, F. J. Politics—The name of the game. In: F. J. Weintraub, A. Abeson, J. Ballard, & M. L. LaVor (eds.), *Public policy and the education of exceptional children.* Reston, VA: The Council for Exceptional Children, 1976.

Wolfensberger, W. The extermination of handicapped people in World War II Germany. *Mental Retardation,* 1981, *19*(1), 1–7.

Wyatt v. *Stickney,* 344 F. Supp. 387 (M.D.Ala. 1972).

Ziegler, S., & Hambleton, D. Integration of young TMR children into regular elementary school. *Exceptional Children,* 1976, *42*(8), 459–461.

REFERENCE NOTE

1. Donder, D. *Interactions between moderately/severely mentally retarded and non-handicapped school peers: Toward a less restrictive educational environment.* Champaign, IL: University of Illinois, 1980.

2

Social Integration of Severely Handicapped Students

Richard P. Schutz,
Wes Williams, Ginny Salce Iverson,
and Dvenna Duncan

The provision of services to severely handicapped citizens in this country is changing markedly. Perhaps nowhere in the field of human services is the contrast between past and present service delivery more striking, the implications for the provision of services more wide-ranging, and the task of responding to human needs more complex than in special education services to severely handicapped students.

Owing to recent litigation, legislation, and the work of parent and professional advocates, the trend to integrate severely handicapped individuals into the mainstream of society has increased dramatically (Novak & Heal, 1980). The major philosophical impetus of community integration is embodied in the principle of normalization, which stresses the delivery of services in environments and

This chapter was developed through federal contract #300-81-0413, "Integrated Educational Service Delivery Models for Severely Handicapped Children and/or Youth," from the U.S. Department of Education, Office of Special Education and Rehabilitation Services, Washington, D.C.

Opinions expressed in this chapter do not necessarily reflect the position or policy of the U.S. Department of Education, Office of Special Education and Rehabilitation Services, and no official endorsement by that office should be inferred.

under circumstances that are as culturally normal as possible (Nirje, 1969; Wolfensberger, 1972). Recent interpretation of this principle includes expanding programs for severely handicapped persons to encompass the broad array of services and activities available to most residents of a community (Rusch & Schutz, 1981). It is projected that in the near future the majority of severely handicapped individuals will receive educational, recreational, domestic living, vocational, and general community living services in community-based settings (Brown, Branston, Hamre-Nietupski, Johnson, Wilcox, & Gruenewald, 1979), instead of in large institutional or segregated settings.

The community integration process is multifaceted, involving much more than the physical removal of individuals from segregated settings and their placement in community-based settings. To facilitate the success of severely handicapped persons in integrated community settings, it is essential that they be provided opportunities to learn functional skills to help them participate as independently as possible in a variety of settings (Schutz, Vogelsberg, & Rusch, 1980). It is equally important that both handicapped and nonhandicapped individuals acquire skills and the longitudinal experience to enable them to socially interact in integrated community environments (Brown, Branston, Hamre-Nietupski, Johnson, Wilcox, & Gruenewald, 1979).

The philosophical change regarding the locus of services for severely handicapped individuals has far-reaching implications for our public schools. In the not too distant past, school-age severely handicapped persons spent their developmental years in large residential facilities (institutions), segregated private schools, or confined to their own homes. Following the enactment of Public Law 94-142 in 1975 there has been a movement toward providing services for this population within the regular public school system. Consequently, the task of preparing severely handicapped persons to function adaptively in complex, community-based settings is increasingly becoming the responsibility of local public school systems.

A number of recent texts have detailed the application of basic principles of instruction and behavior management to the education of children with severe handicaps (e.g., Sailor, Wilcox, & Brown, 1980; Snell, 1983; Wilcox & Bellamy, 1982). This chapter does not attempt to duplicate the procedural detail available in these texts. Rather, it addresses several critical issues associated with the educational integration of severely handicapped students. The initial section presents an overview of several conceptual and theoretical issues. The second section presents several definitions of social interaction skills and types of activities. This is followed, in the third section, by an overview of research concerning physical and social integration. The concluding section discusses some of the implications of model educational integration program demonstrations.

EDUCATIONAL INTEGRATION:
AN OVERVIEW OF CONCEPTUAL ISSUES

According to the National Advisory Committee on the Handicapped (*Education of the Handicapped Today,* 1976), all but two states had legislative statutes in 1976 that made education for handicapped children mandatory; however the timetables for implementation extended well into the future for many states. While the specifics of these legislative acts differed from state to state, the basic intent common to all was the inclusion of all school-age children, regardless of degree of handicap, within the realm of public education.

The importance of state legislative initiatives was bolstered by the passage of the Education for All Handicapped Children Act (Public Law 94-142) and Section 504 of the Rehabilitation Act of 1973 (PL 93-112). This federal legislation served to codify the philosophy of providing services to persons with handicaps in least restrictive settings. The following section reviews several interpretations of these legislative mandates for educational integration.

A Rationale for Integrated Educational Settings

The Education for All Handicapped Children Act and Section 504 of the Rehabilitation Act require state and local agencies to follow a policy of providing services in the least restrictive setting. However, this legislation does not specifically define the least restrictive standard, other than stating that handicapped children should be educated with nonhandicapped children to the maximum extent possible. While the issue of appropriate special education placement typically focuses on the assignment of children with learning and behavior problems to regular classes with assistance provided from special education resource teachers (mainstreaming), the question assumes a different form when applied to the placement of severely handicapped students. Here, the general guideline of least restrictive placement subsumes two primary issues: 1) placement of severely handicapped students in self-contained classes within regular, chronologically age-appropriate public schools (Sontag, Burke, & York, 1973), and 2) direct provision of services by local education agencies rather than subcontracting for services with other organizations.

Professional opinion increasingly favors integration efforts, such as the dispersal approaches provided by some public school systems (e.g., Bricker, 1978; Brown, Branston, Hamre-Nietupski, Johnson, Wilcox, and Gruenewald, 1979; Sailor & Haring, 1977). Gilhool and Stutman (1978) provide the following rationale for such an integration imperative:

> The fabric of the legislative history . . . shows three congressional judgments lay behind this integration imperative:
> 1. Integration is important in the education of all handicapped children, because whatever the severity of their disability, modelling is a crucial mechanism in their learning.
> 2. Given that the education of handicapped children is intended to be education for a lifetime lived in integrated fashion in the community, integrated education is important so that handicapped and nonhandicapped children may truly know each other, as children and as adults.
> 3. Given the long history of prejudice and stereotype, of consigning . . . . the disabled to inferior facilities and inferior services, integration, i.e., the education of handicapped children with nonhandicapped children, is a necessary and felicitous and more or less self-executing insurance that handicapped children will receive their equal due (p. 39).

Sontag, Certo, and Button (1979) also concluded that a legislative mandate requires placement of severely handicapped students in integrated public school settings and, conversely, that the continued practice of providing segregated services to this population violates constitutional guarantees.

Brown and his colleagues have offered a similar argument to suggest that the public schools should represent the standard for the least restrictive educational placement. They argue that the neighborhood public school provides the only environment that allows for daily and longitudinal interaction between severely handicapped and nonhandicapped students (Brown, Branston, Hamre-Nietupski, Johnson, Wilcox, & Gruenewald, 1979). Brown, Wilcox, Sontag, Vincent, Dodd, and Gruenewald (1977) further stated that

> Long-term, heterogeneous interactions between severely handicapped and non-handicapped students facilitate the development of the skills, attitudes, and values that will prepare both groups to be sharing, participating, contributing members of complex, post-school communities. Stated another way, separate education is not equal education (p. 198).

Proponents of integration do not dispute the fact that severely handicapped students require special educational services; it is the separate, segregated nature of the provision of these services that they question. Inherent in the above arguments is that the segregation of severely handicapped students from their nonhandicapped peers greatly reduces their personal growth and development. Consequently, while discussions of less restrictive educational placements have typically focused on the characteristics of the physical placement (see, for example, Aloia, 1978; Kenowitz, Zweibel, & Edgar, 1978), physical integration, alone, does not meet the educational integration imperative.

Physical Versus Social Integration

Once a local school district has decided to integrate severely handicapped students into classrooms within regular public schools and to provide community-based training, one might contend that the least restrictive placement has been achieved. However, the mere physical transfer of an individual from a segregated, self-contained facility to a classroom in a regular educational setting does not constitute what many professionals believe to be a least restrictive educational environment (Brown, Branston, Hamre-Nietupski, Johnson, Wilcox, and Gruenewald, 1979; Hamre-Nietupski, Branston, Gruenewald, & Brown, 1978; Kenowitz et al., 1978). In many cases, severely handicapped persons are integrated into public schools, but remain socially segregated from nonhandicapped peers. Forms of social segregation that take place within integrated settings include the following:

1. Housing classrooms for severely handicapped students in segregated wings of public school buildings
2. Requiring severely handicapped students to eat lunch in their classroom or a separate section of a school cafeteria
3. Providing separate, segregated extracurricular activities such as dances and "special" swimming times at local pools

4. Providing separate transportation to severely handicapped students
5. Excluding severely handicapped students from school activities such as assemblies
6. Providing separate, segregated bathrooms for severely handicapped students

A major expected benefit of physical integration has been that it should provide opportunities for longitudinal social interactions between severely handicapped and nonhandicapped students (Apolloni & Cooke, 1978; Bricker, 1978; Brown, Branston, Hamre-Nietupski, Johnson, Wilcox, & Gruenewald, 1979; Stainback & Stainback, 1980). While physical integration is clearly the initial step, research indicates that it does not necessarily lead to social interactions (e.g., Goodman, Gottlieb, & Harrison, 1972; Guralnick, 1980; Johnson & Johnson, 1980; Porter, Ramsey, Tremblay, Iaccobo, & Crawley, 1978). It follows that innovative and systematic efforts on the part of special and regular educators must be made in order to bring about positive interaction experiences. A critical component of severely handicapped students' appropriate education in the least restrictive environment is not merely the presence of nonhandicapped students in the same school, but the way in which interactions between these students are systematically guided and encouraged (Stainback & Stainback, 1982).

Accordingly, the concept of a least restrictive environment requires not only placement into chronologically age-appropriate schools, but also, and perhaps more important, continual efforts to promote positive interactions between severely handicapped students and nonhandicapped peers and adults (Donaldson, 1980; Kenowitz et al., 1978). Brown and his colleagues have argued that if nonhandicapped students have an opportunity to grow up with severely handicapped learners, they will be more adequately prepared to interact with them in a variety of integrated community environments (Brown, Branston, Hamre-Nietupski, Johnson, Wilcox, & Gruenewald, 1979).

Educational Programming Beyond the Classroom

The educational integration of severely handicapped students transcends the issue of regular school versus special, segregated school placement. Crowner (1975) contended that public school resources should be available not only within classrooms, but in all settings where they may be required. It has been well documented (e.g., Stokes & Baer, 1977; Wehman, Abramson, & Norman, 1977) that severely handicapped students do not readily generalize skills taught in one setting (e.g., classrooms) to other settings (e.g., recreational, vocational, domestic, and general community environments). A number of authors have suggested that instruction that occurs exclusively in the classroom, or that exclusively involves simulation activities, is clearly inadequate for severely handicapped individuals who are expected to ultimately function in heterogeneous community settings (Brown, Nietupski, & Hamre-Nietupski, 1976; Certo, Brown, Belmore, & Crowner, 1977; Stainback, Stainback, Raschke, & Anderson, 1981). Consequently, there is a need to provide functional skills instruction in the community-based environments where the skills will ultimately be performed (Brown, Branston, Hamre-Nietupski, Johnson, Wilcox, and Gruenewald, 1979).

Wehman and Hill (1982) suggest several reasons, in addition to skill generalization, for implementing instruction in the local community. They argue that severely handicapped students will never be aware of the reinforcing aspects of community facilities (e.g., a local restaurant) unless they are systematically exposed to them. They also suggest that instruction in the community on high-utility functional tasks may elevate teacher and parent expectations because skill performance would take on more relevance and significance of purpose. A final compelling rationale for community-based instruction has been offered by Voeltz (1980), who states that local citizens (e.g., bus drivers and shopkeepers) will respond more positively to severely handicapped individuals if they are exposed to them on a frequent basis, over time.

The preparation of severely handicapped persons for the fullest possible participation in society suggests not only that the center of educational services should be shifted from segregated, self-contained facilities to local public schools, but that direct instruction and skill performance evaluations should be conducted in a variety of integrated community settings. Consequently, it appears that public schools and community settings, in general, should be considered jointly as less restrictive settings for the provision of appropriate educational services to severely handicapped individuals.

In summary, this section discussed several issues related to integrating severely handicapped students into regular public schools. It has been suggested that physical integration, alone, does not meet the educational integration imperative. Total educational integration of severely handicapped students must involve efforts to maximize opportunities for interactions with nonhandicapped peers in a variety of school and community settings. The following section reviews some of the common definitions of social interaction skills and accompanying activities that have been featured in the literature.

DEFINITIONS OF SOCIAL INTERACTION SKILLS AND ACTIVITIES

During the last decade, the study of social interaction has become extremely popular among psychologists, zoologists, anthropologists, and educators. Despite a proliferation of cross-disciplinary studies, there continues to be a lack of conceptual clarity regarding the meaning of social interaction (Lamb, 1979; Menzel, 1979). A recent analysis of interaction research concerning mildly handicapped students (Gottlieb, 1978) concluded that researchers have produced a series of unrelated research that has delayed both theoretical and procedural development, and has resulted in a body of literature that defies meaningful generalization.

Difficulties in defining, teaching, and measuring skills associated with social interactions are due largely to the complexity of social activities. Social interaction has been described as a process of interpersonal reinforcement (Strain & Timm, 1974; Whitman, Mercurio, & Caponigri, 1970). This definition assumes some form of sensory exchange between two or more people; such an exchange may be visual (e.g., eye contact), auditory (e.g., speaking), or tactile (e.g., touching) in nature. While this definition appears straightforward and comprehensive, it is inadequate to measure the frequency and quality of social interactions and, consequently, does not provide a conceptually concrete base for the development of programmatic interventions. Accompanying this definition, then, must be a focus on the participants and the social context of an interaction. Few would disagree that a behavioral expression can be socially appropriate when directed toward one person but not another, and, similarly, appropriate in one context but not another.

Partially because of the problems associated with defining and assessing social interactions, severely handicapped students are typically not provided with social interaction skills training in a systematic manner. Usually, such training is circumscribed to include only language training, play/leisure skills training, or the teaching of isolated interaction skills (e.g., shaking hands).

Interactive Behaviors Restricted to Language Training

People communicate for many reasons, such as to transmit information and feelings, and to evoke approving responses from others (Argyle, 1969). Social interactions between nonhandicapped individuals often involve verbal communication skills. Unfortunately, severely handicapped persons are often so deficient in verbal communication skills that poor interpersonal communication abilities is a defining characteristic of such persons (Grossman, 1973). Severely handicapped persons frequently exhibit no verbal expression capabilities and at best limited speech capabilities. They also often communicate through signing and communication boards. These augmentative modes of communication may inhibit the quality and quantity of communication between severely handicapped and nonhandicapped people.

However, severely handicapped individuals are often at an unnecessary disadvantage in communication situations, not simply because of deficit verbal skills, but also because few augmentative language programs for them emphasize training in the use of these skills in social interactions. Symbolic and semisymbolic forms of communication (e.g., signing, gestures, communication boards) training are often presented in isolated situations. It is not unusual to find language comprehension and expression training limited to pointing at or labeling specific objects placed on a classroom worktable. This practice does not train the individual to apply language skills to "everyday" social interaction situations (e.g., indicating a selection from a menu).

The selection of certain alternative methods of communication may also limit a severely handicapped person's ability to communicate with others (Schepis, Reid, Fitzgerald, Faw, van den Pol, & Welty, 1982). For example, many severely handicapped persons are being taught sign language. Regardless of how competent the person becomes in the use of sign language, communication with nonhandicapped people in community settings will tend to be limited because nonhandicapped persons typically do not understand signs. While signing may be a functional means of communicating with people who understand signs, it must be supplemented by another communication system (e.g., picture cards) to be effective in communicating with the general public.

Interactive Behaviors Restricted to Leisure and Recreational Skills Training

Interactive behavior assessment and training is frequently structured around acquiring recreational and leisure activities (e.g., Hill, Wehman, & Horst, 1982; Hopper & Wambold, 1976; Paloutzian, Hasazi, Streifel, & Edgard, 1971; Wehman, Karan, & Rettie, 1976; Whitman et al., 1970). While leisure activities provide an excellent vehicle for facilitating social interactions (Wolfensberger, 1972), there are several limitations to relying solely upon these types of activities for social skills training. One limitation relates to the fact that the types of recreational programs typically available to severely handicapped individuals traditionally have focused on simple, repetitive arts and crafts activities (Amary, 1975) and simplistic, often age-inappropriate skills such as block play, bead stringing, and ball rolling. One could certainly question how acquired competence in such skills will facilitate age-appropriate interactions in integrated community recreational, educational, vocational, and domestic environments.

Opportunities for age-appropriate leisure skills training must be provided, along with community-based programs, that reflect opportunities for severely handicapped individuals to interact with nonhandicapped peers. Unfortunately, community recreation programs, when used at all, are typically limited to the provision of segregated access to severely handicapped people—for example, "handicapped-only" swimming times at a local health center. Simply allowing access to community facilities falls short of the integration imperative.

A final limitation of focusing interactive skills training on leisure activities relates to skill generalization concerns (Strain & Kerr, 1980). Researchers have noted the difficulty severely handicapped persons have in generalizing social skills outside of the actual teaching situation (e.g., Guralnick, 1978). Consequently, it cannot be assumed that social interaction skills acquired through leisure/recreation activities will generalize, or even be relevant to, other activities such as eating in a restaurant.

Interactive Behavior Training Limited to Severely Handicapped Persons

Another belief that has restricted the focus of social interaction skills training is the assumption that severely handicapped persons should be the sole recipients of training. While improvement in the interactive behavior and social skills of severely handicapped students is imperative and can be accomplished, it may not be possible in all instances for these individuals to become highly competent in these skills and socially astute (Guralnick, 1978; Stainback & Stainback, 1982). However, if these students were to be excluded from integrated activities and experiences until they demonstrate "acceptable" levels of social skills, they may never have an opportunity to participate. A logical alternative is to train non-handicapped students to interact with severely handicapped students who may exhibit "different" behaviors in social situations.

Toward an Inclusive, Functional Definition of Social Interaction

The vast majority of daily living activities involve some form of social interaction. Consequently, providing social skills training as an isolated curriculum area is a questionable practice. While it may be justifiable that specific time periods be designated for working on functional skills related to curriculum domains such as communication, self-care, recreation, vocational skills, and domestic living, an isolated period devoted to social skills training is less generalizable to everyday situations. Since social skills are an integral part of school and community activities throughout the day, it would appear more appropriate to consider social skill training opportunities as they relate to these activities. Training of social skills and appropriate interactive behavior also should focus on skill clusters rather than isolated, splinter skills. This approach to addressing social interaction programming in a natural context is advocated because of the nonsegmented nature of interactions and the need to generalize appropriate social behavior across a variety of settings, people, and activities.

Classification of Social Interactions   When educators assume the responsibility for developing opportunities for social interactions between severely handicapped students and other people, it becomes important to consider the types of interactions that can be generated. Brown and his colleagues have delineated four types of social interactions (i.e., proximal, helping, service, and reciprocal) that may be utilized for this purpose (Hamre-Nietupski, Branston, Ford, Stoll, Sweet, Gruenewald, & Brown, 1978). The authors define the four types of interactions as follows:

a. *Proximal interaction* refers to an interaction in which a severely handicapped student is in physical proximity to a nonhandicapped person.
b. *Helping interaction* refers to an interaction in which a nonhandicapped person provides direct and discernible assistance or instruction to a severely handicapped student.
c. *Service interaction* refers to an interaction between a nonhandicapped citizen and a severely handicapped student in which the nonhandicapped person enters into the interaction as a result of his or her employment responsibilities.
d. *Reciprocal interaction* refers to an interaction between a severely handicapped and nonhandicapped person in which the exchange results in mutual, but not necessarily similar, benefits (pp. 40–43).

The category of proximal interaction does not actually denote a type of social interaction, but presents an opportunity for social interactions to occur. In order for a social interaction to take place, individuals must be in close enough physical proximity to establish visual, auditory, or tactile contact. Proximity must be established prior to any type of social interaction. However, as previously articulated, severely handicapped and nonhandicapped individuals are often segregated and have no opportunity to interact.

It is important to consider physical proximity for several reasons. First, the frequency and duration of proximity between severely handicapped individuals and nonhandicapped peers can be used as a measure of social integration. Physical proximity is fairly easy to assess. In school settings, one can analyze severely handicapped students' daily schedules to determine where and the amount of time they are in proximity with nonhandicapped peers. It follows that an initial step for increasing social interactions would be to increase and maximize proximity. Restructuring programs to enable severely handicapped students and their non-handicapped peers to have an opportunity to eat lunch together, have recess together, or get together for other activities on a regular basis provide the foundation for social interaction skills programming. In other words, proximal situations can be structured to facilitate social interactions.

Helping or instructional interactions refer to situations in which one person attempts to teach or assist another person. An example of this type of interaction would be a situation where a severely handicapped student opens a door for a book-laden nonhandicapped peer. Conversely, a nonhandicapped student may assist a nonambulatory, severely handicapped student to negotiate a doorway. Instructional interactions typically involve a nonhandicapped student tutoring a severely handicapped student (i.e., peer tutoring systems).

As defined above, service-related interactions refer to interactions that take place as part of an individual's job or assigned task. For example, school cafeteria workers may interact with severely handicapped students while serving food because it is part of their job. Similarly, a severely handicapped student may interact daily with the school secretary because the student is assigned the task of bringing the class roll to the office. A severely handicapped student being trained as a food services worker in the school kitchen may also frequently interact with nonhandicapped coworkers as part of the job.

The final type of interaction is of a reciprocal or interpersonal nature. This category refers to social interactions that occur outside the context of a job or of attempting to assist or teach someone. Examples of interpersonal interactions include engaging in "small talk" while waiting in line for a movie, greeting others, and participating in recreational activities with others.

Structuring Social Skills Training While the four types of social inter-actions discussed above provide a conceptual framework to aid in the development of interactions, they are insufficient for the analysis or structuring of social skills training. However, Williams, Hamre-Nietupski, Pumpian, McDaniel-Marx, and Wheeler (1978) described a five-component social interaction model that may be utilized for these purposes. The five components are: 1) recognition of the appropriate time and place for an interaction; 2) initiating interactions; 3) receiving requests for interactions; 4) sustaining interactions; and 5) terminating inter-actions. This general framework for social interactions may be utilized to structure social skills training and to dovetail them with associated activities of daily living instruction.

Typically, activities of daily living are task analyzed, student performance of component skills are assessed, and instruction is then provided to perform skills correctly and in sequence. Unfortunately, this process usually does not incorporate the social skills integral to the activity. Employing the social interaction model suggested by Williams et al. (1978) enables teachers to transcend basic task performance training. For example, if students were to be taught to play Frisbee, a task analysis of the activity and direct instruction concerning component skills (i.e., appropriate methods to catch or throw a Frisbee) could be augmented with related social skills training. In such a way, students would not only learn how to play Frisbee, but would acquire such additional skills as:

1. *Recognition* of appropriate times and places to play Frisbee
2. *Initiation* of the activity by asking someone to play with them
3. *Reception* by appropriately accepting or rejecting an invitation to play Frisbee
4. *Sustaining* by appropriately playing Frisbee with others as delineated in a task analysis
5. *Terminating* by appropriately concluding the activity when they, or others engaged in Frisbee play, want to stop

As suggested by the above example, the five-component model delineates classes of social interaction skills, but not specific social interaction behaviors that students must acquire. The specific behaviors targeted for instruction can be individualized, based upon a student's current functioning level and individual needs. For example, an interaction can be initiated, responded to, or terminated through such behaviors as gestures, signs, and pointing to communication board symbols. Consequently, specific behaviors can be selected on the basis of the individual's mode and level of communication. Severely handicapped students can be taught to sustain interactions through any activity involving two or more people (i.e., catching and throwing a Frisbee in the example above).

In summary, educational integration of severely handicapped students must involve efforts to maximize opportunities for interactions with nonhandicapped peers in a variety of school and community settings. Accordingly, interactive behavior and social skills training should be conceptualized as integral components of most daily living activities. The types of interactions that may occur include proximal, helping/instructional, service-related, and reciprocal interactions. For each type of interaction it can be noted whether a severely handicapped or nonhandicapped person initiated the contact and who terminated the interaction. Similarly, appropriate acceptance of requests to interact and the duration of interactions can be monitored. Taken together, the four types of interactions and the five-component interaction model provide a basis for observing and assessing severely handicapped/nonhandicapped interactions in any setting.

OVERVIEW OF RESEARCH ON PHYSICAL AND SOCIAL INTEGRATION

As indicated in the previous section, research concerning the educational integration of exceptional children and resulting peer relations has become a favorite line of inquiry. The vast majority of this research has focused on "mainstreaming" and its effects on the acceptance of mildly handicapped children by nonhandicapped peer groups (see, for example, Strain, 1981). However, a number of educators have cautioned that it is probably inaccurate to generalize data involving mildly handicapped children to the educational and social integration of severely handicapped children (Voeltz, 1980). Fortunately, researchers are beginning to address issues specific to the educational integration of children with severe handicaps. While many recent innovations in instructional methodology (e.g., Falvey, Brown, Lyon, Baumgart, & Schroeder, 1980; Snell, 1983; Wehman & Hill, 1980; Wilcox & Bellamy, 1982) and administrative procedures (e.g., Hurd, Costello, Pajor, & Freagon, 1981; Stetson, Chapter 4, this volume) have been developed, this section specifically focuses on research related to integration outcomes and strategies to promote social interactions.

Social Outcomes of Integration

As students with severe handicaps are integrated into regular school programs, the social interaction behaviors that occur between severely handicapped and nonhandicapped peers are becoming a critical, and often controversial, issue. A primary assumption held by proponents of educational integration for severely handicapped children is that contact with nonhandicapped children will produce improvement in social relationships between the two groups (e.g., Brown, Branston, Hamre-Nietupski, Johnson, Wilcox, & Gruenewald, 1979). However, some professionals have voiced concern that integration may be detrimental to the educational progress of both severely handicapped and nonhandicapped students (e.g., Burton & Hirshoren, 1979; Kauffman & Krouse, 1981).

Hambleton and Ziegler (1974) provide some of the most pertinent data on the social impact of integrating severely handicapped students into regular public schools. As part of a systematic case study of educational integration in the Toronto Metropolitan Schools, they monitored and compared both positive social initiations and aggression directed toward 25 moderately/severely handicapped students in an integrated school setting with that of a matched group of students who remained in a segregated setting. Their analysis of over 30 hours of naturalistic observation of recess activities indicated that "trainable" students in integrated sites were involved in integrated (handicapped and nonhandicapped) activities on more than 50% of the coded observations. Comparisons of data from matched groups of students in segregated and integrated sites revealed that: 1) more positive interactions occurred in the integrated setting (755 versus 262), 2) target students were more socially responsive in the integrated setting, and 3) the frequency of aggressive behavior toward target students was higher in the segregated setting, and, perhaps most interesting, aggression in the integrated setting toward target students was overwhelmingly likely to be initiated by their handicapped peers.

Preliminary data related to potential academic and social "hardships" for both regular and severely handicapped students are also encouraging. Existing evidence provided by Hambleton and Ziegler (1974) and Fink (1979) suggests that severely handicapped students in segregated settings do not achieve significantly better on instructional objectives than their counterparts in integrated settings. These findings of "no difference" contradict the argument of some educators (e.g., Kauffman & Krouse, 1981) that integration would in some way be detrimental to the education of those integrated. Currently, similar data addressing the impact of educational integration on the academic performance of regular education students do not exist. However, this is really a moot issue because educational integration of severely handicapped students does not imply the academic integration of such students into regular classroom instruction.

While the above research results appear promising, other investigations indicate that nonhandicapped students prefer to interact with other nonhandicapped or mildly handicapped students more than severely handicapped students (Guralnick, 1980; Porter et al., 1978). It should be noted however, that because nonhandicapped students demonstrate a higher preference for interacting with nonhandicapped and mildly handicapped students, it does not necessarily follow that severely handicapped students are actively rejected. Instead, many educators interpret the data regarding nonhandicapped students' preferences (attitudes) as documentation of a need for systematically guided interactions (e.g., peer tutoring or buddy arrangements) between nonhandicapped and severely handicapped students (Donaldson, 1980; Stainback & Stainback, 1982).

The results of several investigations concerning the social impact of integrating severely handicapped students tend to support the strategy advocated above. For example, Voeltz (1980) examined the attitudes of over 2,000 elementary-age nonhandicapped students toward their severely handicapped peers. The students had varying degrees of contact with severely handicapped students in public school settings. The results of this investigation indicated that students from schools that included classrooms of severely handicapped students were likely to have more positive attitudes toward interactions than students from schools without such integration. These findings indicated that contact with severely handicapped students can influence nonhandicapped students' attitudes toward their severely handicapped peers in a positive direction.

In another investigation, McHale and Simeonsson (1980) studied the influence of interactions between severely handicapped and nonhandicapped students during play sessions on the attitudes and "understandings" of nonhandicapped students toward severely handicapped peers. The results suggested that nonhandicapped students held positive attitudes toward severely handicapped students before and after contact with them. In addition, McHale (Note 1) recently reported the results of additional data collected during the previously mentioned study, but not reported in the 1980 article. This analysis of direct observational data collected during the play sessions indicated that the frequency of interaction between severely handicapped and nonhandicapped students is influenced by time. Specifically, McHale (Note 1) found that the more time the two groups spent together, the more they tended to interact.

Clearly, there is a need for additional research concerning the social outcomes of educational integration. Nevertheless, initial evidence is promising.

While social interactions between severely handicapped and nonhandicapped students may not occur spontaneously, the research literature does suggest that physical proximity can influence the attitudes and behaviors of those involved positively. Furthermore, no detrimental findings associated with educational integration have been reported for either severely handicapped or nonhandicapped students.

Strategies to Promote Social Interactions

Initial research concerning the social outcomes of integration indicate that promoting interactions between severely handicapped and nonhandicapped students is a feasible educational objective that can produce benefits for both groups. As investigations conducted by Voeltz (1980) and McHale and Simeonsson (1980) suggest, one strategy that can promote positive social interactions is the implementation of attitudinal change interventions. In both of these studies structured contact was found to produce attitudinal change. Other attitudinal change interventions that have met with some success include the provision of information on disabilities (Donaldson, 1980; Sandler & Robinson, 1981) and provision of opportunities for nonhandicapped peers to reduce discomfort through unobtrusive or socially sanctioned staring (Donaldson, 1980).

Despite these findings, there is a paucity of research to suggest that measured attitudes correspond with actual social interaction behavior. Two methods that have been used to directly influence social interaction behavior are organizing and structuring integrated social groups and providing direct training on social interaction skills.

Social Integration Group Structures Nietupski, Hamre-Nietupski, Schuetz, and Ockwood (1980) indicate that dividing students into small heterogeneous groups facilitates interactions between students of varying degrees of handicaps to a greater degree than attempting to obtain interactions with larger groups. This implies that in order to promote interactions between severely handicapped and nonhandicapped students, it would be more advantageous to establish groups of 1 severely handicapped student with 5 regular students, than one large heterogenous group of 30 students. Furthermore, Johnson and Johnson (1980) have stressed that the specific type of small group structure requires careful consideration. These authors have described three group structures that may be employed in integrated activities: 1) "cooperation" or positive goal interdependence, 2) "competition" or negative goal interdependence, and 3) "individualistic learning" or no interdependence (Johnson & Johnson, 1980).

Two investigations utilizing group structure interventions have been attempted with severely handicapped students. In both studies, adolescents labeled trainable mentally retarded were integrated into a recreational activity with nonhandicapped peers. In the first study (Johnson, Rynders, Johnson, Schmidt, & Haider, 1979), direct observational measures of social interactions between handicapped and nonhandicapped students under conditions of cooperative, competitive, and individual goal structures were compared. The results indicated that cooperative conditions were associated with more positive social interaction than were either of the other two structures. The results of this investigation were later replicated by Rynders, Johnson, Johnson, and Schmidt (1980) with a similar population. These findings, together with similar research conducted with mildly handicapped and regular students (Johnson & Johnson, 1980) suggest that cooperative goal structuring (e.g., a group is assigned a common goal and everyone is encouraged to work together to reach the goal) may be useful in promoting positive social interactions between severely handicapped and nonhandicapped students.

Direct Training Strategies Another approach to promoting positive social interactions has emphasized the importance of training individuals directly to engage in specific social behaviors. The vast majority of this research has focused on demonstrations that severely handicapped students can learn interaction and other social skills (e.g., Gable, Hendrickson, & Strain, 1978; Ragland, Kerr, & Strain, 1978; Wambold & Bailey, 1979; Whitman et al., 1970). One specific strategy that has been utilized successfully is referred to as peer social initiation (Strain & Kerr, 1980). When employing this strategy, a nonhandicapped peer prompts a severely handicapped student to engage in social interactions by initiating social bids (interactions), with teacher involvement kept at a minimum. Specifically, Strain and his associates trained selected peers to make social bids, with the purpose of increasing severely handicapped children's rate of social responding and social interactions (Ragland et al., 1978; Strain & Kerr, 1980; Young & Kerr, 1979).

The use of peer modeling strategies as a means of improving social interactions has also been empirically validated in a number of studies conducted in preschools serving children with severe handicaps (Cooke, Cooke, & Apolloni, 1978; Guralnick, 1976; Peck, Apolloni, Cooke, & Rauer, 1978). Specific interventions that have been used to increase imitation of nonhandicapped peers have included prompting and reinforcement from a teacher (Peck et al., 1978), peer prompting and reinforcement (Nordquist, 1978), and vicarious reinforcement (Guralnick, 1976). The results of these investigations indicate that severely handicapped children can be trained to imitate the social, verbal, and material use behavior of nonhandicapped peers.

Other behaviorally based methods have been employed to train social skills to severely handicapped students, but a comprehensive review is beyond the scope of this chapter. Such methods include behavioral rehearsal, verbal instruction, and corrective feedback. The reader is referred to Bates (1980) and Bornstein, Bach, McFall, Miles, Friman, and Lyons (1980) for a description of these and other techniques, as well as empirical data concerning their effectiveness.

Interestingly, no well-organized, widely accepted, or empirically validated procedures for training nonhandicapped students to interact with severely handicapped peers have emerged. However, a number of professionals have recently advocated the development of such procedures (e.g., Stainback & Stainback, 1980). In this light, it is encouraging that materials have been developed to acquaint regular education students with various handicapping conditions (e.g., Bookbinder, 1978; Edrington, 1978; Nietupski et al., 1980).

In summary, based upon the initial results of research on the educational integration of severely handicapped children and the resulting interactions with nonhandicapped peers, educators can be optimistic. It has been pointed out that while handicapped/nonhandicapped interactions may not occur spontaneously, physical proximity does appear to exert a positive influence on the attitudes and behaviors of the individuals involved. The research literature also suggests that interactions can be enhanced by systematic educational programs to promote interactions and by the careful structuring of environments. Finally, no detrimental findings associated with educational integration have been reported for either severely handicapped or nonhandicapped students.

MODEL PROGRAM DEMONSTRATIONS: IMPLICATIONS FOR THE PRACTITIONER

Local school districts throughout the country are providing educational services to severely handicapped students. In many districts, educational integration has included dispersing classrooms for children with severe handicaps throughout regular public school buildings (e.g., Brown et al., 1979; Hamre-Nietupski & Nietupski, 1981; Thomason & Arkell, 1980; Voeltz, Kishi, Brown, & Kube, 1980; Williams, Iverson, Schutz, Duncan, & Holbrook, 1982). Other school districts have also attempted to integrate severely handicapped students into extracurricular and other nonacademic activities such as assemblies, cafeterias, dances, physical education classes, and field trips. In several regular schools, severely handicapped students perform a variety of school jobs such as acting as cafeteria helpers and attendance monitors (e.g., Nietupski et al., 1980). Other communities have extended educational integration to include instruction related to such community activities as playing pinball at a local arcade (Hill et al., 1982) and participation in Boy Scout and Girl Scout groups (Wehman & Hill, 1980).

Accompanying educational integration efforts has been the publication of numerous program reports and manuals. While much of this literature does not contain supportive research data, many authors have suggested practical, experience-based strategies to facilitate educational integration and to promote severely handicapped/nonhandicapped peer interactions (e.g., Almond, Rodgers, & Krug, 1979; Brown, Hamre-Nietupski, Lyon, Branston, Falvey, & Gruenewald, 1978; Poorman, 1980). This section reviews a number of these strategies separately; however, the reader is reminded that many of these strategies are typically utilized together.

Fundamental Approaches to Promote Social Interactions

The educational service base for developing longitudinal interactions between severely handicapped and nonhandicapped peers and other citizens typically is a special education classroom within a regular, chronologically age-appropriate public school. From this base, specific strategies to bring severely handicapped students into contact with others in school or general community settings are associated with one of two fundamental approaches: integration and reverse integration.

Integration Approaches As stated previously, contrary to typical usage, the educational integration of severely handicapped students is not synonymous with mainstreaming (see, for example, Blankenship & Lilly, 1981). Due to the severity of the handicapping conditions of many students, consistent participation in regular classrooms during academic instruction is probably not feasible. However, a number of strategies have been developed to facilitate opportunities for social interactions during other times in selected activities such as lunch, recess, and riding a school bus (Brown, Hamre-Nietupski, Lyon, Branston, Falvey, & Gruenewald, 1978; Hamre-Nietupski & Nietupski, 1981; Thomason & Arkell, 1980).

Reverse Integration In addition to integrating severely handicapped students into a variety of general school activities (e.g., assemblies) and community activities (e.g., scouting groups), social interactions with nonhandicapped peers can be facilitated through a reverse integration approach. Strategies within this category refer to integrating nonhandicapped students into classrooms for children with severe handicaps. Examples of the reverse integration approach include the regular involvement of nonhandicapped students in such activities as recreation/ leisure, art, and music, or in assisting with functional academic instruction in a classroom for severely handicapped students (e.g., Almond et al., 1979; Poorman, 1980).

In-School Integration/Social Interaction Strategies

While the two basic approaches to social integration presented above may appear simple and straightforward, successful integration is never haphazard. Initial considerations in the integration process are careful preparation and planning at the school and classroom levels. Several authors have described the methods they used in preparing to integrate students with severe handicaps into public school activities (e.g., Brown et al., 1978; Hamre-Nietupski & Nietupski, 1981; Voeltz et al., 1980). These methods often include: 1) assigning a faculty member and/or consultant the primary responsibility for planning interaction activities; 2) conducting inservice sessions for regular and special educators to explain integration efforts; 3) arranging meetings with administrators to discuss integration issues; and 4) involving parents in the planning process. In addition to outlining integration methods prior to implementation, several authors have suggested that the integration process should be gradual and should progress through planned stages (e.g., McCarthy & Stoddin, 1979).

Well-conceived plans for integration often include a number of formal and informal strategies for promoting social interactions between severely handicapped students and their nonhandicapped peers. Some of the more widely used strategies address: 1) classroom location, 2) organization of the school day, 3) equal access to educational facilities, 4) peer buddy/tutor systems, and 5) informational presentations to the general school population.

Classroom Location Preliminary research regarding the educational integration of severely handicapped students suggests that physical proximity affects to a positive degree the attitudes and social behavior of those involved. Consequently, to encourage beneficial results, the public school environment should be manipulated to facilitate contact between nonhandicapped and severely handicapped students. An initial manipulation that may be effective concerns the location of "special" classrooms in regular school buildings. All too frequently, classrooms for students with severe handicaps are isolated at the end of hallways or in basements, are clustered with other special education classrooms, or are placed without regard for the chronological ages of the nonhandicapped students in the area. In order to promote social interactions, classrooms for severely handicapped students should neither be segregated from the rest of the school nor surrounded by classrooms of regular education students who differ significantly in chronological age.

Organization of the School Day   Another environmental manipulation strategy that is basic to maximizing opportunities for social interactions concerns the organization or scheduling of a school day (Wilcox, 1979). For example, efforts should be made to schedule starting and dismissal times for severely handicapped students to coincide with those for nonhandicapped students. Similarly, the organization of the school day should be patterned after the system in effect for nonhandicapped students. If elementary students receive all of their instruction in a self-contained classroom, then a similar arrangement is justified for severely handicapped elementary students. However, since high school students typically travel throughout a school building, taking classes in different settings, the educational environment for severely handicapped secondary students should provide similar opportunities to move through the school setting.

Equal Access to Educational Facilities   In order to maximize interaction opportunities, it is also important that severely handicapped students be provided opportunities to use the same school facilities at the same time as nonhandicapped students (Brown et al., 1977; Hamre-Nietupski & Nietupski, 1981). For example, requiring severely handicapped students to have lunch in their classroom does little to enable opportunities for interactions with nonhandicapped peers. In addition to regularly scheduled school activities such as lunch periods and recess, efforts should be made to include students with severe handicaps in intermittently scheduled school activities (e.g., assemblies and pep rallies). Again, educational integration should focus on maximizing opportunities for possible interactions, and not on seeking reasons or methods to minimize these opportunities.

Peer Buddy and Tutor Systems   Another strategy frequently utilized to promote social interactions involves establishing peer buddy or peer tutor systems (e.g., Almond et al., 1979; Fenrick & McDonnell, 1980; McCarthy & Stodden, 1979; Poorman, 1980). The term "peer buddies" typically refers to situations in which nonhandicapped students volunteer to socially interact with severely handicapped students, without emphasizing an instructional role. Peer buddies may be utilized in both integration and reverse integration situations. For example, nonhandicapped students can be recruited on a voluntary basis to eat lunch or serve as a companion during recreational/leisure activities with a "special" friend. Peer buddy systems may also be extended to include after-school and community activities such as Boy Scouts and Girl Scouts (Wehman & Hill, 1980).

Peer tutors are also recruited on a voluntary basis, but they function in a role similar to a classroom aide. Typically, a teacher of severely handicapped students will recruit peer tutors, provide them with a specific assignment, teach them to perform the assignment, and supervise their performance. Peer tutors may implement specific self-care, communication, or motor programs with severely handicapped students. Two important aspects of successful peer tutoring systems are efforts on the part of teachers to assure that the experiences are pleasant and that peer tutors are reinforced for their efforts.

Presentation of Information to the School Population   A final strategy for promoting educational integration and appropriate social interactions involves the systematic presentation of information regarding children with severe handicaps to the general school population. It has long been realized that anxiety, fear, and general apprehension that many people feel toward severely handicapped persons is due to a lack of exposure and experience with this population and a paucity of information concerning their capabilities. The educational integration of severely handicapped students is helping to alleviate the exposure part of the problem. However, exposure alone will not necessarily promote the type of intentional, longitudinal interactions that are the ultimate goals of educational integration. Consequently, some school districts are beginning to conduct sensitization sessions in social studies, health, English, human relations, and other classes in an attempt to provide regular education students with information regarding severely handicapped students (e.g., Hamre-Nietupski et al., 1978; Nietupski et al., 1980). Inservice training programs for regular education teachers and administrators that provide relevant and current information about handicapping conditions have also been developed for implementation prior to providing nonhandicapped students with similar information (e.g., Nietupski et al., 1980).

Community Integration/Social Interaction Strategies

A number of educators have argued that instruction that occurs exclusively in classrooms or that only employs simulation activities is inadequate for severely handicapped students who are expected to function in heterogeneous community environments (Brown et al., 1976; Certo et al., 1977; Stainback & Stainback, 1980). Considering what educators know about the difficulty this population has in acquiring and generalizing skills across environments, community-based instructional programming appears to be essential. In addition, community-based instruction provides students with access to a wide variety of natural reinforcers (Kazdin, 1980). The presence of numerous nonhandicapped models also provides opportunities for observational learning (Egel, Richman, & Koegel, 1981). Finally, community-based training provides an opportunity to change community attitudes toward handicapped individuals.

Despite an increasing number of reports addressing instruction outside of the classroom (e.g., Freagon, Pajor, Brankin, Galloway, Rich, Karel, Wilson, Costello, Peters, & Hurd, 1981; Wehman & Hill, 1980; Wheeler, Ford, Nietupski, Loomis, & Brown, 1980), the methodology for providing instruction focused on, and delivered in, the community is still emerging. However, three strategies have been reported that appear germane to community instruction: 1) ecological inventories, 2) utilization of community resources, and 3) educating the local community.

Ecological Inventory Strategy The first step in the utilization of community resources for educational programming involves the identification of functional skills (i.e., skills frequently required in community settings) and performance criteria related to the demands and expectations of the local community. The strategy basic to developing educational programs that are referenced to the community is an ecological, or environmental, inventory process along the lines described by Brown and his colleagues (Brown, Branston-McClean, Baumgart, Vincent, Falvey, & Schroeder, 1979; Brown, Branston, Hamre-Nietupski, Pumpian, Certo, & Gruenewald, 1979; Brown, Falvey, Vincent, Kaye, Johnson, Ferrara-Parrish, & Gruenewald, 1979). The ecological inventory requires the direct inspection of leisure, vocational, domestic, and general community environments to which a student has, or might be expected to have, access. These settings are then analyzed to delineate such information as the performance demands, naturally occurring cues and consequences, and environmental arrangements present in specific settings. Finally, the information is used to design instructional programs to develop the identified requisite skills.

Community referencing of curricular content serves not only to validate objectives but also to assign priority to objectives. Rather than selecting instructional objectives according to their relative position on a "developmental sequence" or based on whether or not a student demonstrates necessary "prerequisite skills," educational priorities are based upon the frequency and importance of particular behaviors in specific environments.

Numerous authors have stated that community-referenced curricula should lead to instruction in the community (e.g., Bellamy & Wilcox, 1980; Brown, Nietupski, & Hamre-Nietupski, 1976). Despite these views, instruction is typically provided in simulated settings within public schools (e.g., Lynch, 1979; Potter, Biacchi, & Richardson, 1977). However, recent research suggests that skills acquired in simulated situations do not generalize to targeted settings in the community until training is initiated in the natural environment (e.g., Bates, 1980; Coon, Vogelsberg, & Williams, 1981). Consequently, it would appear that, at a minimum, skill performance probes must be conducted in the community settings requiring a specific skill. Depending upon performance, it may also be necessary to provide instruction in local community settings.

Utilization of Community Resources The environments that are appropriate for community-based programming can be identified through the environmental inventory process. Environments that appear logical to consider for community-based training include restaurants, grocery stores, department stores, swimming pools, and shopping malls. In addition to employing these settings to assess skill generalization, it is important to note that many adaptive skills necessary in the community are largely contextual; they are timely only in selected situations and cannot be programmed easily into a simulated classroom setting. For example, appropriate bus riding behavior, acceptable ways of looking through racks of clothing, selecting grocery items off shelves, or rolling a bowling ball down a lane may be taught most effectively in the community setting that calls for the specific behavior.

Severely handicapped students need to be taught how to interact with people, materials, and equipment in community settings. Consequently, if adaptive or prosthetic equipment is required by a student, it must be developed in a manner that allows for interactions with unfamiliar, nonhandicapped persons, as well as teachers and parents. For example, communication boards or books used by some students with limited verbal communication skills should be understandable to service personnel (e.g., waitresses) in the community. In addition, students may need to be taught appropriate means of using alternative methods of communication with the general public.

Educating the Local Community Since community-referenced services for severely handicapped students represent a significant departure both from regular and traditional special education, some professionals and the general community may harbor misconceptions that undermine successful program operation (Hurd et al., 1981). For example, superintendents, school boards, and building principals may be concerned that classroom space is not being fully utilized when significant time is spent away from the school building. Members of the community may also be surprised to see students in the community during school hours. Moreover, shopkeepers may be overly accommodating to severely handicapped students learning to use their facilities. Consequently, special educators are beginning to develop public relations and information strategies such as inservice training for educators and administrators, local media exposure, and civic presentations (Hurd et al., 1981; Nietupski et al., 1980).

In summary, this section has reviewed a number of strategies to facilitate the integration of severely handicapped students into school and community settings. While a number of formal and informal methods have been promoted, the goals of school and community integration currently appear to be more clearly defined than the strategies to attain them. Additional efforts to develop, implement, and document strategies to facilitate positive interactions between severely handicapped and nonhandicapped persons are needed to ensure total school and community integration.

SUMMARY

The integration of students with severe handicaps into public schools and other community settings is a relatively recent service delivery development. As a result, there is currently a dearth of literature that documents or validates strategies that efficiently promote integration and social interactions between severely handicapped and nonhandicapped individuals. However, the emerging literature in this area does indicate that the physical placement of students with severe handicaps into integrated settings is only an initial step in encouraging appropriate social interactions with nonhandicapped individuals. Systematic efforts must be made to maximize opportunities for social interactions in integrated settings.

The literature reviewed in this chapter suggests that educational integration of severely handicapped students may be regarded as a process consisting of advance planning and preparation, development of facilitative administrative policies, and carefully planned strategies to promote positive social interactions. A variety of promising strategies were described that may be employed to facilitate appropriate social interactions. These strategies include:

1. Increasing the amount of time students spend in integrated settings and activities
2. Implementing attitudinal change strategies
3. Structuring integrated group activities to include cooperative group goals
4. Providing social skills training to students with severe handicaps in integrated settings
5. Providing social skills training to nonhandicapped peers in integrated settings
6. Using reverse integration techniques
7. Employing peer tutor and buddy systems
8. Providing information to the entire school and the local community on integration

It is inappropriate, however, to view integration solely in terms of strategies and technical matters. For example, despite documentation of no detrimental findings associated with integration, as well as several reports of positive outcomes, many administrators, teachers, and parents continue to oppose integration efforts because they fear a "negative impact." In the authors' experience, successfully integrated programs are distinguished by a commitment to the philosophy of educating severely handicapped students with their chronologically aged peers and preparing them for the fullest possible participation in society.

Social integration of severely handicapped students in public school and community settings is a new and exciting frontier in service delivery. The challenges for the future are to have all students with severe handicaps receive their education in integrated settings and to further document both the benefits of integration, as well as strategies that effectively promote social interactions.

REFERENCES

Almond, P., Rodgers, S., & Krug, D. Mainstreaming: A model for including elementary students in the severely handicapped classroom. *Teaching Exceptional Children,* 1979, *11,* 135–139.

Aloia, G. Assessment of the complexity of the least restrictive environment doctrine of Public Law 94–142. In: *LRE: Developing criteria for the evaluation of the least restrictive environment provision.* Washington, DC: U.S. Office of Education, Bureau of Education for the Handicapped, Division of Innovation and Development, 1978.

Amary, I. *Creative recreation for the mentally retarded.* Springfield, IL.: Charles C Thomas, 1975.

Apolloni, T., & Cooke, T. Integrated programming at the infant, toddler, and preschool age levels. In: M. Guralnick (ed.), *Early intervention and the integration of handicapped and nonhandicapped children.* Baltimore: University Park Press, 1978.

Argyle, J. *Social interaction*. London: Methuen & Co., 1969.

Bates, P. The effectiveness of interpersonal skills training on the social skill acquisition of moderately and mildly retarded adults. *Journal of Applied Behavior Analysis, 1980, 13*, 237–248.

Bellamy, G.T., & Wilcox, B. Secondary education for severely handicapped students: Guidelines for quality services. In: B. Wilcox & A. Thompson (eds.), *Critical issues in the education of autistic children and youth*. Washington, D.C.: U.S. Office of Education, 1980.

Blankenship, C., & Lilly, M.S. *Mainstreaming students with learning and behavior problems: Techniques for the classroom teacher*. New York: Holt, Rinehart & Winston, 1981.

Bookbinder, S. *Mainstreaming: What every child needs to know about disabilities*. Boston: Exceptional Parent Press, 1978.

Bornstein, P., Bach, P., McFall, M., Miles, E., Friman, P., & Lyons, P. Application of a social skills training program in the modification of interpersonal deficits among retarded adults: A clinical replication. *Journal of Applied Behavior Analysis, 1980, 13*, 171–176.

Bricker, D. A rationale for the integration of handicapped and nonhandicapped preschool children. In: M. Guralnick (ed.), *Early intervention and the integration of handicapped and nonhandicapped children*. Baltimore: University Park Press, 1978.

Brown, L., Branston-McClean, M., Baumgart, D., Vincent, L., Falvey, M., & Schroeder, J. Using the characteristics of current and subsequent least restrictive environments in the development of content for severely handicapped students. *AAESPH Review, 1979, 4*, 407–424.

Brown, L., Branston, M., Hamre-Nietupski, S., Johnson, F., Wilcox, B., & Gruenewald, L. A rationale for comprehensive longitudinal interactions between severely handicapped students and nonhandicapped students and other citizens. *AAESPH Review, 1979, 4*, 3–14.

Brown, L., Branston, M., Hamre-Nietupski, S., Pumpian, I., Certo, N., & Gruenewald, L. A strategy for developing chronological age-appropriate and functional curricular content for severely handicapped adolescents and young adults. *Journal of Special Education, 1979, 13*, 81–90.

Brown, L., Falvey, M., Vincent, B., Kaye, N., Johnson, F., Ferrara-Parrish, P., & Gruenewald, L. Strategies for generating comprehensive, longitudinal and chronological age-appropriate individual education plans for adolescents and young adult severely handicapped students. In: L. Brown, M. Falvey, D. Baumgart, I. Pumpian, J. Schroeder, & L. Gruenewald (eds.), *Strategies for teaching chronological age-appropriate functional skills to adolescents and young adult severely handicapped students*. Madison, WI: Madison Metropolitan School District, 1979.

Brown, L., Hamre-Nietupski, S., Lyon, S., Branston, M., Falvey, M., & Gruenewald, L. *Curricular strategies for developing longitudinal interactions between severely handicapped students and others and curricular strategies for teaching severely handicapped students to acquire and perform skills in response to naturally-occurring cues and correction procedures*, Vol. 8, Part 1. Madison, WI: Michigan Metropolitan School District, 1978.

Brown, L., Nietupski, J., & Hamre-Nietupski, S. Criterion of ultimate functioning. In: M. Thomas (ed.), *Hey, don't forget about me! Education's investment in the severely and profoundly handicapped*. Reston, VA: The Council for Exceptional Children, 1976.

Brown, L., Wilcox, B., Sontag, E., Vincent, B., Dodd, N., & Gruenewald, L. Toward the realization of the least restrictive environments for severely handicapped students. *AAESPH Review, 1977, 2*, 195–201.

Burton, T., & Hirshoren, A. The education of severely and profoundly retarded children: Are we sacrificing the child to the concept? *Exceptional Children 1979, 45*, 598–602.

Certo, N., Brown, L., Belmore, K., & Crowner, T. A review of secondary level educational service delivery models for severely handicapped students. In: E. Sontag, N.

Certo, & J. Smith (eds.), *Educational programming for the severely and profoundly handicapped*. Reston, VA: The Council for Exceptional Children, 1977.

Cooke, T., Cooke, S., & Apolloni, T. Developing nonretarded toddlers as verbal models for retarded classmates. *Child Study Journal*, 1978, *8*, 1–8.

Coon, M., Vogelsberg, T., & Williams, W. Effects of classroom public transportation instruction on generalization to the natural environment. *Journal of The Association for the Severely Handicapped*, 1981, *6*, 46–53.

Crowner, T. A public school program for severely and profoundly handicapped students: Zero exclusion. In: L. Brown, T. Crowner, W. Williams, & R. York (eds.), *Madison's alternative for zero exclusion: A book of readings*. Madison, WI: Madison Public Schools, 1975.

Donaldson, J. Changing attitudes toward handicapped persons: A review and analysis of research. *Exceptional Children*, 1980, *46*, 504–514.

Edrington, M. *Friends*. Monmouth, OR: Instructional Development Corporation, 1978.

Education of the Handicapped Today. Washington, D.C.: U.S. Department of Health, Education and Welfare, U.S. Government Printing Office, June, 1976. (Reprinted from 1976 annual report of National Advisory Committee on the Handicapped.)

Egel, A., Richman, G., & Koegel, R. Normal peer models and autistic children's learning. *Journal of Applied Behavior Analysis*, 1981, *14*, 3–12.

Falvey, M., Brown, L., Lyon, S., Baumgart, D., & Schroeder, J. Strategies for using cues and correction procedures. In: W. Sailor, B. Wilcox, & L. Brown (eds.), *Methods of instruction for severely handicapped students*. Baltimore: Paul H. Brookes Publishing Co., 1980.

Fenrick, N., & McDonnell, J. Junior high school students as teachers of the severely retarded: Training and generalization. *Education and Training of the Mentally Retarded*, 1980, *15*, 187–194.

Fink, W. *Evaluation of the rural model program for severely handicapped students*. Salem, OR: Programs for Mental Retardation and Developmental Disabilities, 1979.

Freagon, S., Pajor, M., Brankin, G., Galloway, A., Rich, D., Karel, P., Wilson, M., Costello, D., Peters, W., & Hurd, D. *Teaching severely handicapped students in the community*. DeKalb: Northern Illinois University, 1981.

Gable, R., Hendrickson, J., & Strain, P. Assessment, modification, and generalization of social interaction among severely retarded, multihandicapped children. *Education and Training of the Mentally Retarded*, 1978, *13*, 279–286.

Gilhool, T., & Stutman, E. Integration of severely handicapped students: Toward criteria for implementing and enforcing the integration imperative of P.L. 94–142 and Section 504. In: *LRE: Developing criteria for the evaluation of the least restrictive environment provision*. Washington, D.C.: U.S. Office of Education, Bureau of Education for the Handicapped, Division of Innovation and Development, 1978.

Goodman, H., Gottlieb, J., & Harrison, R. Social acceptance of EMRs integrated into a nongraded elementary school. *American Journal of Mental Deficiency*, 1972, *76*, 412–417.

Gottlieb, J. Observing social adaptation in schools. In: G.P. Sackett (ed.), *Observing behavior, Vol. 1: Theory and applications in mental retardation*. Baltimore: University Park Press, 1978.

Grossman, H. *Manual on terminology and classification in mental retardation*. Washington, DC: American Association on Mental Deficiency, 1973.

Guralnick, M. The value of integrating handicapped and nonhandicapped preschool children. *American Journal of Orthopsychiatry*, 1976, *42*, 236–245.

Guralnick, M. *Early intervention and the integration of handicapped and nonhandicapped children*. Baltimore: University Park Press, 1978.

Guralnick, M. Social interactions among preschool children. *Exceptional Children*, 1980, *46*, 248–253.

Hambleton, D., & Ziegler, S. *The study of the integration of trainable students into a regular elementary school setting.* Toronto: Metropolitan Toronto School Board, 1974.

Hamre-Nietupski, S., Branston, M., Ford, A., Stoll, A., Sweet, M., Gruenewald, L., & Brown, L. Curricular strategies for developing longitudinal interactions between severely handicapped and nonhandicapped individuals in school and nonschool environments. In: L. Brown, S. Hamre-Nietupski, S. Lyon, M. Branston, M. Falvey, & L. Gruenewald (eds.), *Curricular strategies for developing longitudinal interactions between severely handicapped students and others and curricular strategies for teaching severely handicapped students to acquire and perform skills in response to naturally occurring cues and correction procedures,* Vol. 8, Part 1. Madison, WI: Madison Metropolitan School District, 1978.

Hamre-Nietupski, S., and Nietupski, J. Integral involvement of severely handicapped students within regular public schools. *Journal of The Association for the Severely Handicapped,* 1981, *6,* 30–39.

Hill, J., Wehman, P., & Horst, G. Toward generalization of appropriate leisure and social behavior in severely handicapped youth: Pinball machine use. *Journal of The Association for the Severely Handicapped,* 1982, *6,* 38–44.

Hopper, C., & Wambold, C. An applied approach to improving the independent play behavior of severely retarded children. *Education and Training Center,* 1976, *2,* 1–18.

Hurd, D., Costello, D., Pajor, M., & Freagon, S. Administrative considerations in changing from a school-contained to a community-based program for severely handicapped students. In: S. Freagon, M. Pajor, G. Brankin, A. Galloway, D. Rich, P. Karel, M. Wilson, D. Costello, W. Peters, & D. Hurd (eds.), *Teaching severely handicapped students in the community.* DeKalb: Northern Illinois University, 1981.

Johnson, D., & Johnson, R. Integrating handicapped students into the mainstream. *Exceptional Children,* 1980, *47,* 90–98.

Johnson, R., Rynders, J., Johnson, D., Schmidt., B., & Haider, S. Interaction between handicapped and nonhandicapped teenagers as a function of situational goal structuring: Implications for mainstreaming. *American Educational Research Journal,* 1979, *16,* 161–167.

Kauffman, J., & Krouse, J. The cult of educability: Searching for the substance of things hoped for; the evidence of things not seen. *Analysis and Intervention in Developmental Disabilities,* 1981, *1,* 53–60.

Kazdin, A. *Behavior modification in applied settings.* Homewood, IL: Dorsey Press, 1980.

Kenowitz, L., Zweibel, S., & Edgar, E. Determining the least restrictive educational opportunity for the severely and profoundly handicapped. In: N. Haring & D. Bricker (eds.), *Teaching the severely handicapped,* Vol. 3. Columbus, OH: Special Press, 1978.

Lamb, M. Issues in the study of social interaction: An introduction. In: M. Lamb, S. Suomi, & G. Stephenson (eds.), *Social interaction analysis: Methodological issues.* Madison: University of Wisconsin Press, 1979.

Lynch, K. Toward a skill-oriented prevocational program for trainable and severely mentally impaired students. In: G.T. Bellamy, G. O'Conner, and O.C. Karan (eds.), *Vocational rehabilitation of severely handicapped persons: Contemporary service strategies.* Baltimore: University Park Press, 1979.

McCarthy, R., & Stodden, R. Mainstreaming secondary students: A peer tutoring model. *Teaching Exceptional Children,* 1979, *11,* 162–163.

McHale, S., & Simeonsson, R. Effects of interactions on nonhandicapped children's attitudes toward autistic children. *American Journal of Mental Deficiency,* 1980, *85,* 18–24.

Menzel, E. General discussion of the methodological problems involved in the study of social interactions. In: M. Lamb, S. Suomi, & G. Stephenson (eds.), *Social interaction analysis: Methodological issues.* Madison: University of Wisconsin Press, 1979.

Nietupski, J., Hamre-Nietupski, S., Schuetz, G., & Ockwood, L. (eds.), *Severely handicapped students in regular schools*. Milwaukee, WI: Milwaukee Public Schools, 1980.

Nirje, B. The normalization principle and its human management implications. In: R. Kugel & W. Wolfensberger (eds.), *Changing patterns in residential services for the mentally retarded*. Washington, D.C.: President's Committee on Mental Retardation, 1969.

Nordquist, V. A behavioral approach to the analysis of peer interactions. In: M. Guralnick (ed.), *Early intervention and the integration of handicapped children*. Baltimore: University Park Press, 1978.

Novak, A., & Heal, L. *Integration of developmentally disabled individuals into the community*. Baltimore: Paul H. Brookes Publishing Co., 1980.

Paloutzian, R., Hasazi, J., Streifel, J., & Edgard, C. Promotion of positive social interaction in severely retarded children. *American Journal of Mental Deficiency*, 1971, *75*, 519–524.

Peck, C., Apolloni, T., Cooke, T., & Rauer, S. Teaching retarded preschool children to imitate nonhandicapped peers: Training and generalization effects. *Journal of Special Education*, 1978, *12*, 195–207.

Poorman, C. Mainstreaming in reverse with a special friend. *Teaching Exceptional Children*, 1980, *12*, 136–142.

Porter, R., Ramsey, B., Tremblay, A., Iaccobo, M., & Crawley, S. Social interactions in heterogeneous groups of retarded and normally developing children: An observational study. In: G.P. Sackett (ed.), *Observing behavior*, Vol. 1: *Theory and applications in mental retardation*. Baltimore: University Park Press, 1978.

Potter, J., Biacchi, A., & Richardson, E. Simulating real-life situations in a classroom setting: The Montgomery County training module. In: E. Sontag (ed.), *Educational programming for the severely and profoundly handicapped*. Reston, VA: The Council for Exceptional Children, 1977.

Ragland, M., Kerr, E., & Strain, P. Behavior of withdrawn autistic children: Effects of peer social initiations. *Behavior Modification*, 1978, *2*, 565–579.

Rusch, F., & Schutz, R. Vocational and social work behavior research: An evaluative review. In: J. Matson & J. McCartney (eds.), *Handbook of behavior modification with the mentally retarded*. New York: Plenum Publishing Corp., 1981.

Rynders, J., Johnson, R., Johnson, D., & Schmidt, B. Effects of cooperative goal structuring in producing positive interaction between Down's Syndrome and non-handicapped teenagers: Implications for mainstreaming. *American Journal of Mental Deficiency*, 1980, *85*, 268–273.

Sailor, W., & Haring, N. Some current directions in education of the severely/multiply handicapped. *AAESPH Review*, 1977, *2*, 67–87.

Sailor, W., Wilcox, B. & Brown, L. *Methods of instruction for severely handicapped students*. Baltimore: Paul H. Brookes Publishing Co., 1980.

Sandler, A., & Robinson, R. Public attitudes and community acceptance of mentally retarded persons: A review. *Education and Training of the Mentally Retarded*, 1981, *16*, 97–103.

Schepis, M., Reid, D., Fitzgerald, J., Faw, G., van den Pol, R., & Welty, P. A program for increasing manual signing by autistic and profoundly retarded youth within the daily environment. *Journal of Applied Behavior Analysis*, 1982, *15*, 363–379.

Schutz, R., Vogelsberg, T., & Rusch, F. A behavioral approach to integrating individuals into the community. In: A. Novak & L. Heal (eds.), *Integration of developmentally disabled individuals into the community*. Baltimore: Paul H. Brookes Publishing Co., 1980.

Snell, M. *Systematic instruction of the moderately and severely handicapped*. Columbus, OH: Charles E. Merrill Publishing Co., 1983.

Sontag, E., Burke, P., & York, R. Considerations for serving the severely handicapped in the public schools. *Education and Training of the Mentally Retarded*, 1973, *8*, 20–26.

Sontag, E., Certo, N., & Button, J. On a distinction between the education of the severely and profoundly handicapped and a doctrine of limitations. *Exceptional Children*, 1979, *45*, 604–616.

Stainback, W., & Stainback, S. Some trends in the educating of children labeled behaviorally disordered. *Behavioral Disorders*, 1980, *5*, 240–249.

Stainback, W., & Stainback, S. Nonhandicapped students' perceptions of severely handicapped students. *Education and Training of the Mentally Retarded*, 1982, *17*, 177–182.

Stainback, W., Stainback, S., Raschke, D., & Anderson, R. Three methods of encouraging interactions between severely retarded and nonhandicapped students. *Education and Training of the Mentally Retarded*, 1981, *16*, 188–192.

Stokes, T., & Baer, D. An implicit technology of generalization. *Journal of Applied Behavior Analysis*, 1977, *10*, 349–367.

Strain, P., (issue editor). Peer relations of exceptional children and youth. *Exceptional Education Quarterly*, 1981, *1*, 1–115.

Strain, P., & Kerr, M. Modifying children's social withdrawal: Issues in assessment and clinical intervention. In: M. Hersen, R. Eisler, & P. Miller (eds.), *Progress in behavior modification*, Vol. 2. New York: Academic Press, 1980.

Strain, P., & Timm, M. An experimental analysis of social interaction between a behaviorally disordered preschool child and her classroom peers. *Journal of Applied Behavior Analysis*, 1974, *7*, 583–590.

Thomason, J., & Arkell, C. Educating the severely/profoundly handicapped in the public schools: A side-by-side approach. *Exceptional Children*, 1980, *47*, 114–122.

Voeltz, L.M. Children's attitudes toward handicapped peers. *American Journal of Mental Deficiency*, 1980, *84*, 455–464.

Voeltz, L., Kishi, G., Brown, S., & Kube, C. *Special friends training manual: Starting a project in your school*. Honolulu: University of Hawaii, 1980.

Wambold, C., & Bailey, R. Improving the leisure-time behaviors of severely/profoundly retarded children through toy play. *AAESPH Review*, 1979, *4*, 237–250.

Wehman, P., Abramson, M., & Norman, C. Transfer of training in behavior modification programs: An evaluative review. *Journal of Special Education*, 1977, *11*, 212–231.

Wehman, P., & Hill, J. *Instructional programming for severely handicapped youth: A community integration approach*. Richmond: Virginia Commonwealth University, 1980.

Wehman, P., & Hill, J. Preparing severely handicapped youth for less restrictive environments. *Journal of The Association for the Severely Handicapped*, 1982, *7*, 33–39.

Wehman, P., Karan, O., & Rettie, C. Developing independent play in three severely retarded women. *Psychological Reports*, 1976, *39*, 995–998.

Wheeler, J., Ford, A., Nietupski, J., Loomis, R., & Brown, L. Teaching moderately and severely handicapped adolescents to shop in supermarkets using pocket calculators. *Education and Training of the Mentally Retarded*, 1980, *15*, 105–112.

Whitman, T., Mercurio., J., & Caponigri, V. Development of social responses in two severely retarded children. *Journal of Applied Behavior Analysis*, 1970, *3*, 133–138.

Wilcox, B. Severe/profound handicapping conditions: Administrative considerations. In: M.S. Lilly (ed.), *Children with exceptional needs*. New York: Holt, Rinehart and Winston, 1979.

Wilcox, B., & Bellamy, G.T. *Design of high school programs for severely handicapped students*. Baltimore: Paul H. Brookes Publishing Co., 1982.

Williams, W., Hamre-Nietupski, S., Pumpian, I., McDaniel-Marx, J., & Wheeler, J. Teaching social skills. In: M. Snell (ed.), *Systematic instruction of the moderately and severely handicapped*. Columbus, OH: Charles E. Merrill Publishing Co., 1978.

Williams, W., Iverson, G., Schutz, R., Duncan, D., & Holbrook, L. *Burlington's making special friends project: Model overview*, Vol. 2. Burlington, VT.: Center For Developmental Disabilities, University of Vermont, 1982.

Wolfensberger, W. *The principle of normalization in human services*. Toronto: National Institute on Mental Retardation, 1972.

Young, C., & Kerr, M. The effects of a retarded child's social initiations on the behavior of severely retarded school-aged peers. *Education and Training of the Mentally Retarded,* 1979, *14,* 185–190.

REFERENCE NOTE

1. McHale, S. *Social interactions of autistic and nonhandicapped children during free play.* Manuscript submitted for publication, 1981.

3

Securing
Integrated Services
Four Histories

Margaret M. Noel

Research, program development, and professional commitment notwithstanding, parents have provided significant impetus for the major changes that have occurred in special education for severely handicapped students over the past two decades. One has only to review the history of parent advocacy organizations during this period to recognize the changes in educational policy that have been initiated through parent lobbying and, in some instances, litigation.

The area of integration of severely handicapped students has been no exception. Parent groups and individual parents have been responsible for much of the progress toward realizing this educational ideal. Achieving the integration of severely handicapped students with nonhandicapped peers has been a primary goal in the education of severely handicapped learners. Guided by such concepts as "normalization" and the "criterion of ultimate functioning," the rationale for educating severely handicapped students in programs that allow involvement and interaction with nonhandicapped peers has received much support in the professional literature (Brown, Branston, Hamre-Nietupski, Pumpian, Certo, & Gruenewald, 1979; Brown, Wilcox, Sontag, Vincent, Dodd, & Gruenewald, 1977; Guralnick, 1976; Larsen, 1976; Stainback & Stainback, 1981).

The progress that has been made in securing integrated service delivery has not come easily and, in many cases, is a direct result of strong parent advocacy. Supported by the protections and guarantees of PL 94-142, parents have used the courts as well as administrative due process to gain educational programs for their children that are "free and appropriate" and "within the least restrictive environment."

This chapter presents the case histories of four families who have been involved in securing integrated educational services. The intent of these histories is to provide readers with a sense of the practical reality of the integration movement. For despite the evident professional commitment, the philosophical and empirical bases for integration, and direct federal support for program development, many local school districts have not readily implemented integrated educational programs. Often, parental willingness to force the issue in the schools has been the deciding factor in effecting change in school systems.

These histories underscore the role that parents, aided by professionals, have played in translating educational ideals into reality. Parents have taught local policymakers the importance of quality educational programs for severely handicapped children. They have encouraged an awareness of the need both to set relevant, long-term educational goals for their children and to develop specific yet comprehensive educational programs focused on developing skills that allow for the maximum independent functioning in the adult community.

The narratives presented were derived from structured interviews and, in two cases, from written histories prepared by the parents. The interviews sought to describe not only the process parents underwent to secure integrated educational services, but also why they chose paths of great resistance in order to intervene in the educational process. In addition, parents were asked to recommend strategies for professionals and parents for effecting change. Parents were asked to contribute their histories based on the age of their handicapped child, their geographic location, and the specific ways in which they attempted change. The four children are Aaron, a 6-year-old boy; Coolidge, a 19-year-old young man; 12-year-old Andrew; and 16-year-old Gina. The story of Aaron, who is labeled trainable mentally retarded, traces the intensive lobbying efforts of his parents in the local public schools before they were forced to file for due process in order to gain quality educational services for their son. Coolidge's mother resorted to threatening school officials with what she calls "professional embarrassment" in order to obtain a new integrated placement for her son who has cerebral palsy and is mentally retarded. Andrew's parents, after years of dissatisfaction and compromise with special schools for mentally retarded youngsters, finally invoked due process to enable their son to be placed in a regular public school. Finally, the history of Gina, who is now in an integrated educational setting for mentally retarded children, recounts years of parental activism and, ultimately, litigation.

Following the presentation of the case histories, the recommendations for change made by the participating parents are included, as well as conclusions and observations drawn from the interviews.

A CASE FOR PERSISTENCE

Background

Aaron, 6 years old, currently attends a multihandicapped class in a regular public school 2 miles from his home. His father is a junior-high public school teacher and his mother is a self-described "part-time tutor [public schools] and full-time mother and advocate." Aaron has a younger brother, Tommy. They live in a medium sized midwestern city.

Aaron's handicap was not immediately apparent to his parents during the first months of his life. However, at 9 months, when he failed to develop basic motor skills, was not reaching for objects, could not raise his head, and made few sounds they knew something was wrong. He also cried incessantly. At this point, the parents were referred to a pediatric neurologist who, while finding nothing physically wrong with Aaron, told the parents that their son was "far below normal" and to expect that he would probably "always be in special schools."

Aaron's mother describes the next few months as a time of great guilt and intense loneliness. "I just kept wondering how I had caused this mysterious problem that had no cure and could not even be identified. I would hold Aaron close on nights when we both could not sleep and think about moving to an isolated mountain where we could love him and not have to worry about people staring at him or kids making fun of him. Aaron was just so dear, so wonderful, I didn't want him ever to have to suffer anything."

The parents' fears for their son continued to occupy their thoughts. They were afraid he would never walk, play, have friends, or be happy; and that he would be forever helpless and dependent. During this time, Aaron's mother read "fiercely," looking for some new operation or cure. She read studies on Down's syndrome and on children in orphanages and underprivileged environments. She also read books on child development, most of which she says covered her son's 10 to 12 months of development in three sentences. "We really did not understand the implications of 'always being in special schools.' Looking back . . . it would have helped to have been told that Aaron was mentally retarded."

At 13 months, Aaron was enrolled in an infant stimulation program for handicapped children. His mother describes her reaction to the first day in the program as "shock." "As I walked through the program that day it was as if I couldn't see the smiles and bright faces of the children. I ignored, too, the dedication of the volunteers and colorful toys and surroundings. All I saw were children who *could not* . . . could not walk, could not talk, could not run. I was shocked. Nothing in my life had prepared me for this experience. I kept wondering how it was that I have lived in neighborhoods, gone through school, watched TV, traveled, gone shopping in the community, and never had a single firsthand experience with a person who had mental retardation. I really feel I missed a vital educational experience . . . an experience that could have helped me to not only be a more complete person, but, more importantly, as it turned out, adjust to my son's handicap."

As Aaron adjusted to the infant program, his mother gradually became used to having a handicapped child. In conversations with other mothers, she learned more about her son's limitations and about mental retardation in general. The more she learned, the more she began to focus on expectations and goals for Aaron. Despite the fact that Aaron's general development was described as being in the "lowest one percent of the population," his mother became committed to the goal that he would use all of his talents. She began to concentrate on "what is left, rather than what was lost."

The Search for an Appropriate Program

Aaron continued in the private infant program and made the transition to the preschool program where he stayed until he was 3. At 3, he moved to a special preschool run by the county for moderately to severely handicapped children. His mother began to explore the available special education programs in her state. What she found distressed her. "Many of our children are bused 1½ hours each way to a school in the middle of a cornfield or an industrial park. Many have no chance to be around nonhandicapped children. They are being taught skills they will never use in the real world. Many children 'graduate' from our special schools at age 21 and have little or no vocational training or skills for the next 50, 60, 70 years of their lives. There is no continuum of services."

In the state in which Aaron lives, programs for severely mentally retarded children are not included within the special education system, but are run in separate schools under the department of mental health and mental retardation. These separate schools have their own standards, programs, and buildings. In the past 5 years, according to Aaron's mother, three of these schools have been constructed in one metropolitan area alone. Each is actually a complex consisting of a school, a sheltered workshop, and a group home. The programs are designed for total education so that a child can stay in the same facility from infancy through adulthood. Though programs do offer a variety of services, they are, nevertheless completely segregated, and students can spend their entire school career, from preschool to adulthood, without interacting with nonhandicapped peers.

A general dissatisfaction with these programs forced Aaron's parents to look elsewhere. Thus, 3 years ago, while on vacation in Washington, D.C., Aaron's mother decided to telephone the (then) U.S. Office of Education to obtain information about programs for mentally retarded children. By luck, the operator connected her to a project officer in the (then) Bureau of Education for the Handicapped (now Special Education Programs in the U.S. Department of Education). Aaron's mother obtained the information she was seeking, but, equally important, she was given the names of several professionals in special education to contact. In discussions with these people and their referrals, she began to "define the dream" she had for her son. She began to realize what a quality educational program could be, and to understand that, with education, her son's life could be positive, productive, and fairly independent. From the "dream plan" she developed for Aaron's life came commitment. She began to get in touch with other parents and professionals in her state and, collectively, they started to define common problems and goals.

The Process

At about the time that Aaron's mother began her active search for programs, another parent in the same city filed suit against the local public school district. At issue was the right of severely handicapped students to be educated in the public schools. The plaintiff was a severely handicapped boy a year older than Aaron. Consequently, when Aaron's parents began to talk to the local public schools about placement options, the school officials knew about integration and the issues involved.

In spring 1980, when Aaron was 5 and officially school-age, his parents began to formally seek public school placement. Initially, they were determined to stay out of the courts. Because they both were employed by the public schools, they preferred that the school district spend its money on teacher salaries and not on attorneys' fees. They also had observed the process the other parents were going through, and they hoped to avoid a legal confrontation. Aaron's mother therefore first went to the neighborhood school and met with the principal. She discussed her goals for Aaron, which included not only quality education, but education in the least restrictive environment. From this meeting came other appointments and numerous phone calls, each of which she logged, including name, date, and notes about the content. At every meeting she would pass out copies of *A Rationale for Comprehensive Longitudinal Interactions between Severely Handicapped Students and Nonhandicapped Students and Other Citizens* (Brown, Branston, Hamre-Nietupski, Johnson, Wilcox, & Gruenewald, 1979).

In late spring, Aaron had the required evaluation. His parents requested that the school psychologist recommend programmatic activities or objectives only, and not specify a placement, as they wanted to discuss this at the placement meeting. At this time they also discovered that the local public schools did not employ occupational or physical therapists, who would normally do an assessment of Aaron. Fortunately, both parents had health care insurance that covered the cost of these evaluations, as well as the audiological, vision, and speech and language assessments. The subsequent placement meeting was held in July, 1980. Aaron's entire family, as well as his babysitter, attended the meeting. The parents stated that they purposely did not bring a lawyer or advocate. Aaron played with his brother and babysitter and, in his mother's words, "became a real live person and not just a name on a report." The various assessment reports were distributed, including two pages of recommendations prepared by Aaron's parents.

The recommendations, written by Aaron's parents, were concise statements of what they wanted for Aaron. Major program areas were addressed, including: length of school day; pupil–teacher ratio; need for education with same-age peers, both handicapped and nonhandicapped; and specific skill training. The reasons for including the report were to assist the parents in presenting their position, to ensure that their views could become part of the official placement decision, and to assist a judge or lawyer if the need arose.

Despite what the parents feel was a calm and reasonable meeting in which all issues were addressed, the team recommended placement in the special school. Aaron's parents responded by filing for due process immediately, and an administrative review was scheduled for mid-summer. Expecting confrontation, the parents invited two local parent advocates and two individuals from the state's protection and advocacy agency. The schools were represented by the superintendent, the assistant superintendent, and two lawyers from the city solicitor's office. There was no confrontation; all issues were thoroughly discussed, and the superintendent, despite some serious reservations, agreed to try placing Aaron, on an experimental basis, in an existing class for multihandicapped youngsters in a local public school. Because the public schools had no occupational therapy or physical therapy services available, the parents agreed to obtain these services—which were covered by their health insurance—privately. The individualized education program (IEP) meeting was held a month later, the day before Aaron was to begin school.

The Integrated Setting

According to Aaron's mother, there are really three major issues involved in integration: placement, appropriateness of the educational program, and the quality of the interactions with nonhandicapped peers. She regards placement as only the first step.

Aaron was enrolled in the special class for multihandicapped children, but his mother regarded the quality of the overall program as questionable. The contrasts between the multihandicapped program and the preschool program were great. For one thing, the physical setting of the integrated program was not optimal. The school in which the multihandicapped class was housed was an old, three-story "fort-type" building. Because of the existing architectural barriers, the multi-handicapped classroom was located in a converted teachers' lunchroom on the first floor, along with the cafeteria, gymnasium, and boiler room.

Regarding Aaron's educational program, Aaron's mother initially felt that the principal and special education teacher made a sincere effort to make Aaron's placement work; however, they both readily admitted that they were learning on the job. Aaron's mother soon found that she knew the community resources better than the public school staff. She contacted the local university and the special education regional resource center. With the financial assistance of the resource center, she was able to arrange several large workshops involving both parents and professionals, featuring several national leaders in the education of severely handicapped children. Aaron's mother feels that these workshops motivated the other parents to think about ways to improve the program. Through a call to the university, Aaron's mother also obtained a student teacher for the multi-handicapped class. The student teacher's supervisor at the university helped with Aaron's home program, worked with Aaron's teacher, and used the class as a training laboratory for the university students. Said Aaron's mother, "the university's presence is what made Aaron's year a step forward instead of a disaster." Aaron was the most severely involved student in the class. Most of the other children were considered mildly handicapped; in fact, one child was returned to a regular first-grade, full-time class after less than a year in the special education class.

Aaron's parents had made the decision to forego a segregated school with an OT, a PT, a teacher for trainable mentally retarded (TMR) children, buildings that were new and accessible, and classes with children on their son's own developmental level, in favor of a public school that would allow Aaron to pass non-handicapped children in the hall, eat lunch with them, go to assemblies, and engage in recess with them—a least restrictive environment. Despite the trade-offs, however, the staff, the children, and the parents at the public school were very accepting of Aaron and his classmates. Parents from the parent-teachers association (PTA) volunteered to serve as classroom aides, and the older children took turns taking Aaron to the restroom and helping him on to the school bus and at recess.

The summer after his first year in the integrated program, Aaron participated in a new demonstration school program at the local university. The program was designed to facilitate interactions among handicapped and nonhandicapped children. In his mother's words, Aaron made "excellent progress." As of this writing he is in his second year in the public school multihandicapped classroom. Nevertheless, the school recently reevaluated Aaron and is once again considering moving him back to the special school. Subsequent to the date of this interview, the school district attempted to move Aaron back to the special school. The parents filed for due process and won the right for Aaron to remain in the public school and to have physical therapy. He was transferred, however, to another class, 13 miles from his home, in order to be with "developmental peers."

Aaron's mother acknowledges that their struggles are not over; however, she and her husband see themselves as part of a chain of parents and professionals. She has no doubts about the course they took and would do it all again if necessary. However, she does wonder sometimes if they are sacrificing their son—"philosophy over reality." She feels, however, that the links in the chain are getting stronger, and that the end result will be improved education for all children. As she says, "It's just scary to be one of the first."

A CASE FOR "PROFESSIONAL EMBARRASSMENT"

Background

The second history involves a parent who resides in a metropolitan area in the northwest and has been a successful lobbyist and advocate for special education within her state. She has taken an active part in securing major state legislation guaranteeing education for handicapped persons, and is now drafting a policy document defining standards for quality educational programs, including integration, that she hopes will become an amendment to existing legislation. "Over the past 10 years, we advocates have lobbied for hundreds of thousands of dollars each biennium, but the programs have not improved . . . . nearly all of the handicapped children in our state are in school now, and the public school system is used to a zero reject policy. However, the program quality has not changed measurably."

Her experience with special education is long and extensive. Coolidge, her 19-year-old son, is brain damaged, with cerebral palsy, significant problems in language and speech, and moderate retardation. Coolidge's major problem, however, has been his severe maladaptive behavior, which has resulted in exclusion from certain programs. Given the skills Coolidge has been able to acquire, it could be assumed that integration would have been easily secured. However, his case history is indicative of the public schools' general resistance to integration.

Coolidge's handicap was identified as cerebral palsy when he was less than a year old. During his first year he had some medical problems from which he recovered completely. His general development, however, was described as "atypical" and "slow." At about age 2, Coolidge began to exhibit severe behavior problems, specifically hyperactivity. According to his mother, "He rocked two cribs to matchsticks during his preschool years. On one occasion, at age 2½, he climbed out of his bedroom window at midnight, climbed on the roof, and fell off into a bush."

The parents' major source of information during their son's first 3 years was their family pediatrician. While the pediatrician did refer Coolidge to specialists to treat some existing orthopedic problems, she offered no other advice or reassurance. Said Coolidge's mother, "I could tell that the pediatrician felt sorry for us, but she never really discussed the handling of a handicapped child." The pediatrician finally did mention, when Coolidge was 3, a preschool for spastic children; Coolidge's mother promptly enrolled him. However, she was chagrined to find out that Coolidge could have been attending this school from infancy.

The preschool program was heavily therapeutic. The staff was unaccustomed to dealing with behavior problems, and there was no behavior management program. Because of Coolidge's intense hyperactivity, the staff referred him to a psychologist for evaluation. The major outcome of the evaluation, however, was a recommendation that the parents put their son's name on a waiting list for a state school so that he could be institutionalized when he reached 6 years old. This only increased Coolidge's parents' frustration with the program's failure to provide concrete, useful information or advice. No one had suggested a prognosis or plan; there was no mention of a behavior management program or suggestion of an alternative educational program. The parents were certain of one thing, however: they were determined not to institutionalize their son.

Coolidge continued at the preschool through age 5, despite numerous threats from the director that the child would have to be removed because of his behavior. The mother credits the teacher and the occupational therapist with keeping Coolidge enrolled because they "liked him and worked with him, and didn't get over-excited about his behavior." During this 2-year period, the only interaction Coolidge had with nonhandicapped peers was within his own family.

The Search for an Appropriate Program

When Coolidge was 5, and eligible for placement in a public school special education program, the district special education director visited the preschool to determine which children would be accepted into the program. While Coolidge's mother contends that her son was not as severely handicapped as many of the children at the preschool, he was not accepted into the public schools because of his hyperactivity.

Earlier that year, 1967, Coolidge's mother had heard about a new program at a local center for retarded children. She had visited the center, but had rejected the notion of sending Coolidge there because she felt that most of the children were far more severely handicapped than he. Meanwhile, however, the mother's guild at the center became dissatisfied with the existing program, which was staffed by public school teachers, because a number of children were being excluded or expelled owing to their so-called "unique problems" or "behavior problems." With funding from diverse sources, the mothers managed to launch a separate, highly structured educational program with non-public-school staff.

Coolidge entered this latter program at age 6, and in the course of the next two years became, according to his mother, a manageable child. He continued in this program until he was almost 12, at which time he was placed in a special school within the local public school system. The program within this segregated school setting consisted of preacademics, speech and language instruction, physical education, and shop courses. When Coolidge was enrolled in the school, his mother was told that it was the only placement available; during the 5 years that he remained there, no one mentioned "integration" or the possibility of transferring him to a less restrictive program.

The Process

Coolidge's mother first became aware of the concept of integration of handicapped children with the nonhandicapped in 1977, when she enrolled in a master's degree program in special education and took a course that analyzed PL 94-142. "I had never thought of integrated programs before that date because there was such difficulty finding *any* program, and because I had never seen any programs that were not segregated. Other parents and I had received nothing but negative vibrations from the general public and from medical and social systems for years, and the idea of my child being able to participate in a more normalized environment without penalty was foreign."

Coolidge was now 15, and his mother was not at all pleased with his program or progress at the special school.

Both as a result of her dissatisfaction and her own increasing knowledge of special education, she was determined to find out what Coolidge *could* do. She therefore obtained a copy of the regular education K–6 curriculum summary, which contained very specific and detailed learning objectives. She then requested that the special education staff assess Coolidge's mastery of these objectives. When it became apparent that he had, in fact, mastered some of the regular primary academic skills, his program was changed, and he was assigned to teachers who began to concentrate on functional reading and mathematics skills.

A year later, an important event in Coolidge's life prompted his mother to begin thinking of integration as a possibility for him. The special education staff at Coolidge's school requested his mother's permission to teach him to ride the city bus to school. (Until then, he had been provided portal-to-portal transportation.) His mother described the training program as "excellent," and reported that Coolidge quickly mastered getting to and from school on the city bus. He then began to learn to use the bus system to go to other places in the city. After about 6 months, his parents and teachers began to notice a major improvement in Coolidge. He became, in his mother's words, more "mature" and more "self-assured," changes that she attributes to learning to ride the bus.

Between the ages of 16 and 18, the parents' dissatisfactions with Coolidge's program increased. During this time, Coolidge, too, began to comment negatively about his placement. For several years he had been participating in recreational programs at the center for retarded children. At age 17, he refused to attend any more of these programs, and began to personally express dissatisfaction with his school. His mother felt that he was "bored" because so much of his instruction was repetitious. Convinced that his special school program was inadequate, his mother finally began to look for other programs and, to her dismay, found a self-contained program for moderately retarded students that had been operating for "years at one of the district high schools." Despite Coolidge's progress over the past 3 to 4 years, no one at his school had ever mentioned the possibility that he could, in fact, be moved to this less restrictive program.

The Integrated Setting

In spring 1980, Coolidge's mother decided to try to change his placement. After discussing her son's progress and attitude with the principal at the special school, it was decided that Coolidge could enroll in special education classes at the high school on a part-time basis. He would receive basic academic skill instruction in the mornings in the regular high school and then return to the special school for vocational training. Soon after, and without any orientation, Coolidge was placed in the high school program. Almost immediately, the teachers at the high school complained that Coolidge could not function socially in the secondary school environment, and that he did not know how to relate to nonhandicapped students—even though he was adjusting well to the academic program. The teachers also felt Coolidge's size (6′5″) to be threatening to the other students and were afraid that he would "get into trouble with some of the regular students who did not know how to deal with him." However, Coolidge remained in the dual program for the remainder of that school year.

The next fall, Coolidge was back in the special school with a promise that a "better program would be developed." For several months he was in a "holding" program that his mother described as "inadequate" and "babysitting." He spent three periods a day in a shop class where he counted and sorted nails and similar items, and spent the rest of the time in music or physical education. His mother was continually reassured by the principal that the school district was working on a plan to move a number of similar students to the high school and that a transition plan was being developed that would teach them "social skills."

Finally, tired of waiting, Coolidge's mother wrote a lengthy and, in her words, "scathing" letter to the assistant superintendent of the district, in which she stated her position regarding her son's program and threatened to lobby against the district's entire budget in the state legislature because of the district's failure to provide appropriate services to its secondary handicapped student population. The letter prompted an immediate meeting of the district's director of special education, key administrators and staff at the special school, and Coolidge's mother for the purpose of discussing Coolidge's placement and an IEP. The IEP that was drafted by the special school staff in preparation for the meeting, however, was totally unacceptable to Coolidge's mother. It did include placement at the district high school but did not contain a transition plan, nor did the mother feel that the goals and objectives were appropriate or well stated. She therefore rewrote the IEP and drafted a transition plan for Coolidge's transfer to the high school. After 3 weeks of negotiation, the IEP was approved, and in February 1981, Coolidge was back in the half-day program at the high school, still spending the afternoons at his old school in order to receive vocational training. Not one of the other students who were supposed to be moved to the high school with Coolidge was moved.

In fall 1981, Coolidge began a new full-day special education placement in a regular high school that he was transferred to under the school district's racial desegregation plan. Coolidge entered the program at his new school without a new IEP; however, a one-month program was negotiated to include basic functional skills such as reading and computation, as well as physical education. Initially, no vocational program existed; Coolidge's mother was hopeful that one would be started soon, but recognized the school district's limitations. Several months into the program, the school district began its first community-based vocational program.

Coolidge's program now includes language arts and mathematics at the high school. He then travels by city bus to an unpaid work experience site where he services cars at a car rental agency. He has the support of a vocational counselor and has demonstrated that he can learn specific work routines, follow directions, and stay on task with little supervision. His progress has surprised everyone, according to his mother. Coolidge, she says, is now more mature, actively seeks greater responsibility for himself, and even has definite ideas about his program. She feels that he has some "unrealistic" expectations about a career, such as becoming a pilot, but she feels that with good vocational training these expectations will become more realistic and he will be able to become a reasonably independent, functioning member of society.

Coolidge's mother is gratified with her son's progress. She is also pleased with the fact that the school district "came around." She is convinced that his integrated high school program exists largely because of her work and that of a few other parents.

A CASE FOR DUE PROCESS

The third case history is that of Andrew, 12 years old and described in official school records as moderately to severely retarded. Andrew is currently in a special education class in a regular middle school located in a large West Coast city. His placement is the result of an administrative due process. Andrew has been in this class less than a year, and his mother "trusts" that the program will work. The program focuses on cooking and other domestic skills, and community living skills such as shopping, eating in restaurants, and some vocational skills. It does not include grooming or personal hygiene, which his mother feels are Andrew's biggest needs right now. "They teach him how to go to the store, how to make his own lunch, and how to go into a restaurant and buy his own food, but I think grooming is important, too. It [the program] is not doing everything, but it is the best that I can find."

Background

Andrew's handicap was not immediately identified. Despite what his mother describes as a "complicated delivery," doctors assured her that Andrew would not be retarded. At 9 months, when he was not sitting up or crawling, and had a "big head," his mother expressed concern to her doctor, who agreed to have Andrew hospitalized for tests. She was then told that the tests were inconclusive and Andrew was "just slow." The slow development continued, but his mother felt that she should not worry because doctors had said Andrew was not retarded.

When Andrew was 4, his mother tried to enroll him in a preschool for low-income children. The preschool refused Andrew because they clearly felt that he was "retarded." His mother then returned to the pediatrician and insisted that he determine if Andrew was retarded. Andrew was referred to a child development clinic at a local hospital and was given a full evaluation. The diagnosis was returned as "brain damaged," but again his mother was given no real indication of Andrew's developmental level nor were program recommendations made. The clinic staff did, however, refer Andrew's mother to the local headquarters for the Association for Retarded Citizens. There Andrew was enrolled in a special preschool and began receiving speech therapy and other educational services. Because the preschool was only half-day, Andrew spent the afternoons in a neighborhood day-care center.

Andrew attended this special preschool until he was 6, at which time his mother contacted the local school district to discuss placement possibilities. She was not sure how or where she got the idea that Andrew needed contact with nonhandicapped children. She says she just "knew" that he would do better if he could be with normal children. Therefore, she requested that Andrew attend a special education class in a regular neighborhood school. She says that the school psychologist agreed to this placement on a trial basis with the understanding that if it did not work out, Andrew was to be placed in a segregated special school.

The regular school, however, never gave Andrew the trial placement. According to his mother, on the first day of school, the school bus picked up Andrew at his babysitter's house, and took him to the special school. When his mother protested, the psychologist denied the original agreement; however, school officials assured the mother that the special school placement was on a trial basis, although they also reportedly told her that "this is where Andrew belongs, and he is not going anyplace else." After "some time," the school told Andrew's mother that they had determined that the segregated placement was appropriate, and that Andrew was to remain there.

The Search for an Appropriate Program

One day during Andrew's first year in the special school, his mother saw a little girl on the playground at a regular neighborhood school. She noticed that the girl looked retarded. After inquiring about the child, she found out that the child was in a regular education class. "I figured if teachers were willing to try with a child like that, you had nothing to lose. I figured it wasn't right. They refused to give [Andrew] that break; just because he had brain damage didn't mean that he couldn't learn." From that point on, Andrew's mother was determined to have her son moved out of the special school.

Yet, over her continuous objections, Andrew remained in the special school for 3 more years. During this time, Andrew's mother felt that he received little educational assistance or skill development, and that he was not learning. He was also becoming a severe behavior problem. "Everytime I went to school, it didn't seem that they were doing anything. They complained about Andrew. I told them, if he isn't listening, and he can't learn here, let's do something about it. We have to transfer him to a better school." During this 3-year period, Andrew's mother was given little information on what Andrew could do or what kind of education he needed. Nevertheless, she sensed that he needed more structure and a systematic instructional program.

At age 10, Andrew was still not dressing himself, nor was he learning appreciably. At this time, he was attending an after-school program for retarded children, sponsored by the local Association for Retarded Citizens. At his mother's request, the Association arranged for an evaluation of Andrew, and it was determined that not only was he functioning at the level of a 3-year-old, but he had made only minimal progress since his last evaluation at age 4. For the first time Andrew's mother began to wonder if Andrew could learn, and if he could not, why she was fighting the system. She decided to try to find out on her own, and started to work with Andrew at home on the recognition of simple shapes. When Andrew did in fact learn these shapes, she felt she had proven to herself that her son was capable of doing more. She then demanded a change in placement for him.

The Process

The school district refused to move Andrew because, according to his mother, they had no place for him. There were simply no options for mentally retarded students.

Undeterred, Andrew's mother, with direct assistance and support from a local advocacy organization, engaged the school district in due process and won. The decision not only specified a structured educational program for Andrew that provided community living and self-help skills, but included placement within an integrated setting.

The local school could not provide such a program. However, it agreed to a trial placement—a self-contained class for mildly handicapped adolescents in one of the district's middle schools. The special education officials polled teachers in the special education classes for mildly handicapped children to determine who would be willing to take Andrew. Only one teacher agreed to give Andrew a try. His mother enrolled him. But while she says Andrew's behavior problems disappeared, he was "babied" by the students, who were much older. In addition, the educational program was inappropriate. Andrew's mother therefore requested another placement.

School district officials told her that they would try to find another placement for Andrew within a regular school. In the meantime, however, they wanted him to remain in the segregated school. His mother refused. "I told them that whenever they found a school, Andrew would go to school." Andrew consequently remained at home for a year and a half, attending only the afternoon program sponsored by the local Association for Retarded Citizens. A stalemate resulted.

During the due process hearing, the psychologist who was retained by the advocacy organization had recommended a self-contained program in a regular elementary school in a neighboring district. After a year and a half of waiting, Andrew's mother visited the program and found that, except for a lack of emphasis on personal grooming and self-care, the requirements for an appropriate educational program for Andrew were met. Accordingly, Andrew's mother returned to her school district and requested out-of-district placement. The school district agreed.

The Integrated Setting

Andrew was placed in the middle school. However there was no transition period. More importantly, the receiving teacher had no prior introduction to Andrew and little information on him; in fact, she delayed writing Andrew's new IEP for 3 months in order to obtain a better understanding of him.

Initially, Andrew had some adjustment difficulties involving increased fighting and aggression—problems his mother had anticipated and had discussed with the new teacher. For the first time, Andrew's mother felt that his new teacher listened to her, from the start. A behavior management program was instituted, and the teacher kept his mother informed of Andrew's progress.

After almost a year in the new program, his mother feels that Andrew is improving. The behavior problems have diminished, due to a structured behavior management program. Also, Andrew is much quieter at home. "He doesn't fight as much. He knows how to act when we go out. I think he also really wants to learn now."

Ultimately, Andrew's mother regards an appropriate placement as one that more closely approximates the schedule and activities of Andrew's non-handicapped peers, as well as one that allows for more contact with them. The current program does neither, but it is an improvement over what has been offered Andrew over the past 6 years.

A CASE FOR ACTIVISM

Background

The final case history, that of Gina, a 16-year-old young woman, is somewhat different. While Gina's parents have waged a long and arduous campaign to secure quality educational services for their daughter, they did not focus solely on integration. Gina, who is severely mentally retarded with no verbal language, lives with her parents in a major northeastern city.

The emphasis on providing Gina a "quality" program is reflected in her parents' long association with both public and private educational systems. Gina's handicap was apparent, though not labeled, at birth. She had several serious health problems, including lack of immunological defenses, and was considered very "fragile." Despite obvious evidence of a handicap, the medical professionals did not provide Gina's parents with any support or information. "They treated the medical problems and that was about it."

The Search for an Appropriate Program

Gina's mother said that she knew immediately that Gina would not develop normally, and that she had to do "something" to help her. In desperation, she found out about patterning, and began a program with Gina to provide stimulation.

At age 3, Gina was enrolled in a special Saturday program for young handicapped children that was run in a parochial school in the city. According to Gina's mother, "The program wasn't much help for Gina. It was actually better for me. It provided me with an opportunity to meet other parents of handicapped children." This gave her much-needed support and information. After one year in this program, Gina entered a private, church-run day-care/preschool for handicapped children. At this time, she was given her first major diagnostic evaluation (state-required in order for the parents to receive funds for support services such as special camping programs). The evaluation, which Gina's mother regards as thorough, suggested that the parents consider institutionalization as a future option, and also ruled out placement in any existing public school program.

When Gina was almost 6, the financial burden of the private preschool became excessive, and the parents sought another program. The public schools offered nothing for severely handicapped students, so the parents transferred her to a preschool program run by a private nonprofit agency for handicapped children. The program was described by Gina's mother as the worst experience in her daughter's school history. Gina had 17 "teachers" in 2 years. There was no supervision and no program. After 2 years in the program, Gina was still not toilet trained. During this time, her mother was offered placements for Gina in what was described as an "integrated" setting in the public schools. However, these programs were essentially special classes of lower functioning mentally retarded students from 6 to 18 years old. Because of the lack of any structured program, Gina's mother refused these placements.

When Gina was 8, her mother moved her to a trainable mentally retarded class in a special center in the public school system. Gina was the lowest functioning child in the class, and during her first year, she reportedly spent most of her day in timeout. She still was not toilet trained, nor was she receiving any self-help instruction. In disgust, Gina's mother began looking at private schools, but could find nothing beyond "babysitting" programs. Faced with the decision that if Gina's education was to improve, it would have to come from the public schools, her mother began to take steps toward that end.

The Process

At about the time that her mother's dissatisfaction with the special center program was peaking, Gina attended a private, summer day camp program. The teacher in the program was "excellent" according to her mother, and within 2 weeks after starting camp, Gina was toilet trained. In addition, Gina, who had no communication skills, began private speech therapy. Within 6 weeks, she had acquired words in sign language that she began to use to communicate. These experiences convinced her mother that her daughter could progress and that she could profit from an educational program. In her mother's words, "It strengthened my commitment in what I was doing. I knew that Gina could learn, and that I would have to work toward changing the system."

Through a local university program, Gina was given a complete multi-disciplinary evaluation, and an educational program was defined. With report in hand, Gina's mother—and her lawyer—met with local public school administrators to discuss a proposed IEP. Six weeks later, the school district informed them that their proposed program was unacceptable; they termed it unrealistic and said they could not provide such a program. Gina's parents then filed for due process.

The due process hearing was lengthy and detailed, but resulted in what Gina's mother calls "a decent decision." It clearly outlined a program for Gina—to be conducted at the special center—that specified class size, daily schedule, materials, and how various services such as occupational and physical therapy were to be combined with the total program. In addition the decision listed necessary staff qualifications, suggested home activities, and called for regular team meetings to discuss and identify instructional strategies and to ensure continuity in approach among all staff involved with Gina. The hearing decision was returned in August, 1976.

Gina's parents spent the next 3 years trying to get the program implemented. Gina's education during this time was described by her mother as "less than adequate," and the classroom as "out-of-control." "I felt real sympathy for the teacher. She was really trying to learn, but she was under great pressure from the administration because of the decision, and no one was providing leadership or coordinating the total program." Gina's mother spent the 1976–77 school year hoping for changes that for the most part never occurred. She wrote letters and visited the schools involved, but while a few minor recommendations were implemented, Gina's program remained unchanged, and by the end of the next school year, Gina had had two new teachers. Finally, at the end of the 1977–78 school year, Gina's parents wrote an eight-page letter detailing their frustrations and the lack of responsiveness on the part of the schools. They sent copies of the letter to their governor, the (then) U.S. Office of Special Education, and state and local school officials. According to Gina's mother, after the letter "things began to happen." The recommendations began to be implemented, and Gina's program began to improve. However, Gina was still in the class at the special center, and was still having no contact with either higher functioning students or non-handicapped children.

These program improvements did not come without cost to Gina's parents. In her mother's words, "I stayed on top of the school for 3 years to keep things going. There was no monitoring or coordination by the school district, and no one took authority for the program. In 3 years, Gina had three teachers. Each time a new teacher came, the administration would warn him or her about me. It made for very bad relations with the school. The teachers were well meaning, but they didn't have the skills and didn't know what to do. The last teacher was not responsive at all. She had a poor attitude toward the kids and didn't want parents involved. The more I intervened, the more she took it out on the kids." At this point, Gina's mother removed herself from the situation. She said that she needed to relieve the tension, and the animosity created by her involvement was not worth whatever improvements she was getting in her daughter's program.

The Integrated Setting

Finally, a new program, a special class for severely involved students housed within a regular middle school, was created, and Gina's mother agreed to place her daughter there. As of this writing, Gina is in her second year of the program, which focuses on life skills and, according to Gina's mother, is "supposed" to include some vocational training. The nonhandicapped students in this school are 2 to 3 years younger than Gina, but as she is small for her age, her parents do not see this age difference as a problem. Gina's contact with these children is "minimal" and somewhat structured; there is a "buddy system" through which nonhandicapped students assist handicapped students to participate in classroom activities and social or recreational activities. In addition, Gina is involved in an after-school cooking class with nonhandicapped students. She is currently the only severely handicapped student in the school district involved in a program such as this—a direct result, said her mother, of the parents' long history of aggressiveness toward the school system.

Gina's mother is "minimally satisfied" with the current program, but is quite pleased with the teacher. She feels that there is a lack of individualization in the program, and that neither the activities nor the teaching environment closely approximate the natural environment. In terms of the nature and degree of Gina's contact with nonhandicapped students, her mother is reasonably satisfied. She feels that both the students and parents have been accepting and supportive. A larger problem, however, has been Gina's parents' attempts to provide their daughter with contact with higher functioning mentally retarded students, attempts that have been met with great resistance by the parents of these children.

The current program is Gina's first experience in an integrated educational setting. Her mother agreed to the placement because she felt that the program represented a great improvement over Gina's former special school. "I placed Gina in this program because the teacher was good. Her attitude was positive, and she worked well with the students. The principal also had a helpful attitude. I was less concerned about [obtaining] an integrated setting. I was even a little fearful of integration. The primary issue was the quality of the program." Although Gina was given no transition to the new program, this was not a problem according to her mother. "She is really much happier because she learns more; she sees more appropriate behavior, and she really doesn't consider herself different from these kids."

Integration is important, according to Gina's parents, but only in the context of an overall quality program. Furthermore, they feel, a quality program can happen only if the attitudes of all involved are positive. Gina's mother realizes that such attitude changes take time, and will not happen if handicapped children are pushed out of sight or are not challenged. Gina's parents fought a long battle to improve educational opportunities for their daughter. They worry sometimes, they say, about perhaps having made things worse for her becaue of their activism. However, they emphatically stated that if they had to start over, and had to face the same options, they would not do things differently.

PERSPECTIVES ON THE CHANGE PROCESS

The final portion of each interview concerned parents' perspectives on change. Specifically, each of the four parents was asked to state what he or she regarded as the greatest obstacles to obtaining quality educational services, as well as to make recommendations on how such obstacles can be overcome.

In response to the first question regarding obstacles, there was unanimity. Parents identified lack of services as the major problem. All four parents stated that within their school districts, there were no alternatives for the moderately to severely handicapped. Programs tended to be developed to accommodate a label, and children were placed in these programs not because of specific educational needs, but because they were labeled trainable mentally retarded, severely impaired, and so on. All of the parents also mentioned the lack of adequately trained teachers and other service providers as a concomitant impediment. In all cases, teachers were cited as the critical variable in a program's success, even in instances where a specific placement was not necessarily optimal. In addition to expressing the need for specific teaching skills, all of the parents mentioned the importance of teacher attitude. Comments such as "She really wanted to make the program work," "She accepted my son," or "She was cooperative" frequently prefaced comments regarding the good programs the children had experienced.

Administrators, particularly principals, were viewed as playing a significant role in the entire educational process. Each of the parents gave examples at some point during the interview of how a principal had pressured their child's teacher not to cooperate or had provided no support or leadership. However, when a principal was supportive and had a good attitude toward special education, the parents reported that the whole program inevitably improved. Without the principal's support, parents felt that integration could not be accomplished.

Other obstacles cited by parents included lack of written school district policies on goals and objectives for special education programs, and lack of curricula. Two parents noted that the absence of policies forced parents to negotiate for programs on an individual case basis, and that each change in placement or program entailed a major meeting or confrontation.

In addition to the lack of policy, all parents expressed concern over the fact that their school districts did not inform them of available services, regardless of their appropriateness. One parent stated that she felt she was "at the mercy of the staff, who can tell you what they want you to know." This control over information seemed to be the largest factor in the parents' mistrust of the school system and led parents to feel that they had to act as monitors and watchdogs. In fact, three of the parents felt that if the schools had been more honest and open during the early contacts, later confrontations might have been avoided.

With respect to options for change, all of the parents were asked to respond to questions regarding what teachers, administrators, and parents could do to facilitate the integration of severely handicapped students into the public schools. The unanimous response was, "become educated!" Parents felt that teachers and administrators need to become aware of what severely handicapped students can learn as well as how to facilitate this learning. Parents, too, they said, must become knowledgeable about a variety of educational alternatives. In addition, two parents noted that it is crucial for school personnel and parents to have information regarding national exemplary programs. As one parent commented, "We all need exposure to a visionary, to someone who can show what can be done."

The role of the visionary, said the two parents, is that of university researcher or program developer. Such professionals should provide guidance and information to school districts and parent groups regarding innovative programs and their implementation. Parents and professionals in general need access to greater knowledge regarding education of severely handicapped students in integrated settings. Universities, said the parents, need to become more involved and take more leadership in providing this knowledge.

The parents felt that if such knowledge could filter into the school districts, it would serve two purposes. First, it would stimulate development of new programs and improve teachers' skills. Second, and equally important, it would encourage more parents to "take a chance" and give their child an opportunity to prove that he or she can learn and that integration is not a dangerous idea. All four parents stated that if large-scale change is to occur, parents must overcome their fears about integration and the feeling that they are "sacrificing" their child. They felt that this could only be accomplished by making parents aware of the current successes in the education of the severely handicapped.

A second unanimous parental response with respect to facilitating integration was to try to avoid litigation. Litigation, they said, should be a last resort, the foremost reason cited being that it creates enemies and effectively destroys whatever cooperation exists with the schools. Parents felt that litigation put them in an adversary position with the school, causing the school to resist compromise and negotiation. The consensus was to engage in litigation only when *all* other options for working within the system have been exhausted.

A final unanimous recommendation for facilitating integration was the necessity to build formal working relationships between *teachers* and parents. The general feeling was that teachers have been excluded from the decision-making process; yet, some of the most crucial issues involved in integrated service delivery are directly related to the classroom and include such things as teaching load, availability of support services, and social adjustment. As one parent stated, "The teacher and I are the ones who really have to implement the program." Another parent suggested that while teachers may not understand the pressures on parents who have lifetime responsibility for their son or daughter, parents often also do not appreciate the day-to-day problems faced by teachers. This same parent recommended that the system provide for formalized communication through regularly scheduled forums or meetings so that teachers and parents can share concerns and information and engage in cooperative planning. In general, all parents believed that teachers and parents are in the best position to develop programs that are sound and appropriate to the needs of their children.

CONCLUSION

In the course of the four case histories, several issues emerged that, while not specifically addressed by parents, deserve discussion. The first is best described as the element of fatigue. The general tone of each interview suggested that these parents had expended great emotional effort and would continue to do so in monitoring their child's education. Parents spoke of the need for support from other parents; the need to unite; and to remain active, persistent, and determined. Yet, there was an element of resignation rather than crusader's zeal in their comments. Two parents spoke of "the emotional costs" to them and to the rest of their family.

There was, in addition, an element of doubt as to the course of action taken. Three of the parents expressed concern that they might have sacrificed their child's education for an ideal, or that perhaps they could have chosen a less difficult path. These feelings were more evident among those parents who had been involved in due process. Also, as might be expected, there was a sense of frustration on the part of parents about having to "fight" for their child's educational rights, only to be ostracized by the school district when they had succeeded.

Despite the sense of fatigue and the overall comments cautioning against due process, all of the parents stated, with conviction, that they would not hesitate to continue their work, or, if confronted with the same choices, do it all again. From each of the narratives came a feeling of accomplishment at having succeeded in improving the educational services for their own son or daughter. What parents did not fully acknowledge was their contribution to the education of other severely handicapped youngsters.

On one level, the actions of these parents and the other advocates they represent have educated public schools to what can be done for severely handicapped children. Such advocacy thus creates a critical link between theory and development and grass-roots implementation. A more obvious contribution, however, has been the establishment of the legal right of the severely handicapped population to services. Without parental commitment and determination, basic laws would not have been enacted or, equally important, implemented. After all, the four cases presented in this chapter provide examples of outright violations by public schools of PL 94-142 including, for example, refusal to provide public school financed physical therapy, occupational therapy, or vocational education. The histories also illustrate the often arbitrary and questionable nature of the decision-making used by public schools. One must acknowledge the work of these parents in keeping the public schools honest.

The fact that parents have, through the exercise of their rights, been the prime instigators of progress to date, should serve to reinforce the importance of the parent-professional partnership. However, it should also call into question the role of professionals in the change process. It is unfortunate that changes such as those described have not generally resulted from comprehensive planning but, rather, have been episodic and scattered reactions to individual activism. Professionals can be grateful to parents who have helped pave the way for public school integration of severely handicapped students. Certainly the parents in the case histories described remain optimistic that positive change can continue. But they feel strongly that it will occur only if parents assume responsibility for becoming informed, not only about their children's educational rights, but their needs as well—and, just as important, if schools adopt specific procedures that allow and encourage parents to work with them to develop educational programs.

REFERENCES

Brown, L., Branston, M.B. Hamre-Nietupski, S., Johnson, F., Wilcox, B., & Gruenewald, L. A rationale for comprehensive longitudinal interactions between severely handicapped students and nonhandicapped students and other citizens. *AAESPH Review,* 1979, *4*(1), 3–14.

Brown, L., Branston, M.B., Hamre-Nietupski, S., Pumpian, I., Certo, N., & Gruenewald, L.A. A strategy for developing chronological age-appropriate and functional curricular content for severely handicapped adolescents and young adults. *Journal of Special Education,* 1979, *13*(1), 81–90.

Brown, L., Wilcox, B., Sontag, E., Vincent, L., Dodd, N., & Gruenewald, L. Toward the realization of the least restrictive educational environments for severely handicapped students. *AAESPH Review,* 1977, 2(4), 195–201.

Guralnick, M.J. The value of integrating handicapped and non-handicapped preschool children. *American Journal of Orthopsychiatry,* 1976, *46*, 236–245.

Larsen, L.A. Community services necessary to program effectively for the severely/profoundly handicapped. In: E. Sontag, J. Smith, & N. Certo (eds.), *Educational programming for the severely and profoundly handicapped*. Reston, VA: The Council for Exceptional Children, 1976.

Stainback, W., & Stainback, S. A review of research on interactions between severely handicapped and nonhandicapped students. *Journal of The Association for the Severely Handicapped,* 1981, *6*(3), 23–29.

4

Critical Factors That Facilitate Integration
A Theory of Administrative Responsibility

Frances Stetson

Within the past decade, the right of this nation's eight million handicapped students to be educated, to the greatest extent appropriate, beside their non-handicapped peers has been affirmed through the courts, strengthened through legislation, and now rests in the hands of the public school administrators to be implemented. The least restrictive environment (LRE) doctrine, as this concept is called, has generated more interest and emotion than any other provision contained within Public Law 94-142, the Education for All Handicapped Children Act (Aloia, Note 1). As Sarason and Doris point out, this provision "puts back on the discussion table the question of how we want to live together" (1979, p. 10).

The question that Sarason and Doris refer to has yet to be answered with conviction with regard to one segment of the handicapped student population—severely handicapped students. Although schools have made important strides in providing services to mildly and moderately handicapped students in appropriate educational environments, the predominant educational settings for severely

---

The content of this chapter was drawn from Stetson, F.E., *Critial administrative factors which facilitate the successful inclusion of severely handicapped students in the least restrictive environment.* Unpublished doctoral dissertation, University of Maryland, College Park, 1979.

handicapped children and youth continue to be "the isolated and segregated educational programs offered in self-contained schools or in schools located at or operated by institutions" (Brown, Branston, Hamre-Nietupski, Johnson, Wilcox, & Gruenewald, 1979, p. 6). Recent estimates (Certo, in press) indicate that this pattern of exclusion continues.

Why then, 8 years after the passage of PL 94-142, do a significant number of severely handicapped students still await the realization of their right to be educated within the least restrictive environment? Perhaps, as Sarason and Doris suggest, we have "misjudged the gulf between theory and practice, between legislative intent and everyday practice" (1979, p. 9).

GUIDANCE FROM FIELD-BASED RESEARCH

To assist in narrowing this gulf between intent and practice, the Education Department (formerly U.S. Office of Education) and the Office for Civil Rights jointly funded and administered a recently completed research and technical assistance effort designed to explore the role of the public school administrator in the implementation of the LRE mandate. (This contract, #300-80-0935, was awarded to JWK International Corporation, Annandale, Virginia, on October 1, 1978 and was completed July 30, 1982.) One of the central questions addressed during the research phase of the contract was as follows: What are the critical administrative factors that facilitate the successful inclusion of severely handicapped students in the least restrictive environment?

This question was asked of 122 district-level personnel (superintendents, directors of special education, directors of regular education, and support personnel), building-level personnel (principals and teachers), and parents from six sites involved in the provision of public education to severely handicapped students. Four of the sites were school districts, one was an intermediate education unit, and one offered a statewide model of service delivery to severely handicapped students. Each site was selected on the basis of its reputation for innovative strategies for meeting the educational needs of severely handicapped students. The six sites varied, however, in geographic location, population density, and service delivery model. This variation helped to assure that all aspects of each administrative factor related to the education of severely handicapped students in the least restrictive environment would emerge.

From the interview responses obtained, seven critical administrative factors emerged. It should be noted that although the individual sites varied considerably, these same factors were repeated again and again from interview to interview. The resulting field-based perspective of issues that administrators must address if severely handicapped youngsters are to be successfully served represents a theory of administrative responsibility. The results of the interviews underscored that the concept of least restrictive environment must be defined as a right guaranteed to each handicapped child, in other words, a right that must not be compromised by administrative convenience, limited resources, or opposing philosophies. For the LRE concept to be translated into an effective experience for each severely handicapped student, for the student's family, and for the school, an implicit set of administrative responsibilities must be recognized and carried out.

SEVEN CRITICAL ADMINISTRATIVE FACTORS

Seven administrative factors were identified as critical in facilitating the successful inclusion of severely handicapped students in the least restrictive environment. They are as follows: 1) organizational support for the LRE concept; 2) an appropriate service delivery model; 3) personnel assigned to provide administrative assistance and instructional leadership to those involved in the education of severely handicapped students; 4) a responsive staff development program that prepares personnel to assume their roles in the implementation of the LRE concept; 5) a positive attitude on the part of regular education teachers and students toward severely handicapped students; 6) community acceptance of the LRE doctrine; and, 7) parental acceptance of the LRE concept for their severely handicapped children.

Although these factors would appear basic to any program, they are rarely considered formally and systematically by public school administrators and are therefore addressed most often by chance or on an informal and infrequent basis. Their haphazard application may lead to dysfunctions within the system—such as teacher burnout, parental dissatisfaction, and isolation of severely handicapped students within an integrated setting—dysfunctions that could well have been avoided given proper administrative attention to one or more of the factors listed above. Fortunately, a vast array of practical strategies exists in relation to each factor to help improve the status of special education in general and encourage the inclusion of severely handicapped students in the least restrictive environment in particular.

The remainder of this chapter describes in detail these seven administrative and clarifies the relationship of each to the successful provision of educational services to severely handicapped students within the least restrictive environment.

Organizational Support for LRE Concept

> In influencing the learning climate of the school, no other individual is potentially as powerful as the school administrators. . . . Whether an administrator is a school superintendent, school principal, or some other official in the school system, especially if in the line of authority, the administrator's relationships are reflected in the effectiveness of the organization, in the ways in which teachers work with children, and ultimately in the personalities of the children themselves (Newell, 1978, p. 11).

The superintendent, who articulates district-wide goals, and the principals, who set the climate within each school building, are central forces in the effort to educate severely handicapped students in positive and accepting environments. Individuals in both of these administrative positions are responsible for allocating time, energy, money, personnel, and many other resources necessary to the system's effort to educate severely handicapped students in the least restrictive environment. In addition, both the superintendent and building principals are in positions to strengthen the commitment of regular educators to be accepting, flexible, and creative in meeting their responsibilities to severely handicapped students.

It has been noted that without the visible and verbal support of the superintendent, isolated examples of excellence may exist in individual school buildings or in individual classrooms, but the system as a whole will not adequately attend to the rights and educational needs of the severely handicapped student population. Similarly, the support that principals are capable of providing (e.g., shaping the attitudes of the regular education faculty and student body; demonstrating a willingness to make necessary and often unique accommodations for severely handicapped students; and recognizing the intense physical and emotional nature of the responsibility to educate severely handicapped students) is highly valued by the special education faculty. Such support sets the stage for a natural acceptance of severely handicapped students in the regular education environment, as well as a building-wide philosophy of shared responsibility for all children, regardless of their unique needs and characteristics. Positive intervention on the part of the district superintendent and the building principal is significantly more effective if it ceases to be casual and incidental and becomes formal, systematic, and on going.

In addition, the elevation of the director of special education to a position and status equal to that of the director of regular education is an important strategy for dismantling a segregated system and creating a single system dedicated to addressing the needs of all children. When the director has line authority over building principals, decisions regarding the appropriate placement of severely handicapped students are not dependent upon individual principal receptivity to the notion. As Newell (1978) reminds us, "systems theory suggests that an important task of an administrator is to provide leadership in the integration of the system, both internally and with external and superordinate systems" (p. 40). Cabinet-level representation for special education enables the director to address this task directly and with authority.

An Appropriate Service Delivery Model

The selection of appropriate service delivery patterns for the provision of educational services to handicapped students in the least restrictive environment is crucial to every school system's efforts to address the LRE mandate. Each school district, responding to its own unique characteristics, to the needs of its school population, and to varying geographic and political constraints, selects patterns for the delivery of services to handicapped students. At their worst, such patterns develop randomly, in response to available space or to other factors not related to student need. At best, the selection of appropriate service delivery patterns for severely handicapped students occurs after a consideration of the appropriateness, location, and accessibility of the educational environment. Public school administrators must establish clear and objective program planning criteria to assist in this task. The number of severely handicapped students, their location throughout the district, and the system's particular characteristics must be considered.

Commitment to a Larger Planning Base   Just as administrators have relied on a continuum of placement options to enhance the provision of services in the least restrictive environment at the student level, the emerging notion of a continuum of planning bases serves this same purpose at the system level. The standard for determining the most appropriate planning base for the delivery of services to a mildly handicapped student is the student's neighborhood school. This is an important reference point when considering the least restrictive environment for any student. Yet, as the severity of the handicapping condition increases and the incidence of the population decreases, school systems may select from a number of service delivery options that extend beyond the neighborhood school. These options include, for example, classrooms on selected regular education campuses throughout the district; a cooperative or consortium model between districts; and regional, statewide, and multistate models. Often the rural nature of a district requires that it seek creative alternatives for addressing the needs of low-incidence populations—such as severely handicapped students—within the least restrictive environment. All of the above options can be used within the context of an integrated setting, however, despite the fact that many of them, for example, regional models, are often automatically equated with a segregated setting.

Administrators must select from a continuum of planning bases, typically utilizing two or more to achieve delivery of appropriate services to handicapped students in appropriate settings. The determination of the most appropriate planning base(s) should be predicated upon the intensity of the services required, the incidence of the student population requiring these services, and the size and sophistication of the district. Single, segregated settings, still common in many school districts across the country, should be discouraged as representing a move toward a larger planning base that fails to consider the need for opportunities for integration, that disregards age-appropriate settings, and that ignores the rights of severely handicapped students to be free from unnecessary restriction and segregation.

The decision regarding the appropriate planning base is further complicated by the importance of maintaining a constructive balance between the ratio of the handicapped population to the nonhandicapped population assigned to a single building. As Wolfensberger (1972) cautioned:

> in regard to size of a facility or client group, it is important not merely to consider the ability of the surrounding social systems to absorb . . . [the handicapped] . . . , but also the size of the grouping that tends to create clannishness, exclusiveness, and inward-centeredness. Members of small groups tend to gravitate toward and to interact with other social systems; as group size increases, this tendency diminishes (p. 37).

If the number of severely handicapped students assigned to a regular education campus becomes too large, their opportunities to interact with their peers in regular education may become limited (due to the system's inability to accommodate the range of needs presented by the group), and their school building may become identified as a "special education" building. On the other hand, if the number of severely handicapped students assigned to a regular education campus is too small, the severely handicapped students may become insular and the likelihood of frequent and meaningful interaction between the two groups will be diminished.

The selection of an appropriate planning base is a prerequisite to the provision of services to severely handicapped students in the least restrictive environment. When the decision is made regarding the most appropriate school sites to accommodate classrooms for severely handicapped students, administrators can turn their attention to the remaining critical factors.

Appropriateness and Location of the Educational Environment This issue refers to the suitability of the educational setting in which severely handicapped students receive instructional and related services and the extent to which the setting facilitates positive interactions between severely handicapped students and their nonhandicapped peers.

For the setting to enhance rather than inhibit interactions and acceptance, severely handicapped students should be educated with their chronological-age peers. This standard requires that the system identify at least one building at the elementary, middle, and high school levels to house classrooms for severely handicapped students. In addition, services should be provided in service appropriate settings. For example, self-care skills should be taught in both the school and home environments; and prevocational skills should be taught in both the classroom and community. Clearly, this notion requires a closer working relationship with parents and with community members. Finally, the design of the educational facility must be considered. One need not look far to find programs for severely handicapped students that are housed either in portable buildings removed from the regular education campus, in separate wings of a regular education building, or in separate buildings adjacent to regular education buildings. Without careful attention to the appropriateness and location of the educational environment, severely handicapped students can easily be as segregated from their nonhandicapped peers, while paradoxically in close proximity to them, as would be the case if they were placed in separate facilities.

Accessibility of the Educational Environment The removal of transportation and architectural barriers is a primary administrative concern when providing educational services to severely handicapped students in the least restrictive environment. As these low-incidence students make the transition from segregated schools to selected regular education buildings throughout the district, the distance between the child's home and school may decrease or increase. Due to the isolated location of many segregated schools, severely handicapped students frequently attending these schools are required to spend more time on buses than their peers attending neighborhood schools. However, in those cases where attending integrated schools will increase travel time, administrators must work to ensure that creative transportation strategies are utilized, including more advantageous routing techniques, to provide the most direct access to school for these students.

There is, moreover, evidence to suggest that a number of school administrators have become more concerned with the cost and the extent to which architectural barriers must be removed from school buildings than is actually warranted (Sontag, Certo, & Button, 1979). As more than one innovative school system has noted, costly structural changes frequently are not required if simple programmatic changes are followed. The accessibility of the educational environment relates to the implementation of the LRE provision to the extent that transportation or architectural barriers must not be allowed to inhibit attainment of the goal of integrating severely handicapped students in appropriate settings.

In sum, the provision of services to severely handicapped students in the least restrictive environment relies heavily upon the utilization of an appropriate service delivery model. A commitment to a larger planning base for this low-incidence population and concern for the suitability and the accessibility of the educational environment are important issues that must be resolved.

Personnel Assigned to Provide
Administrative Assistance and Instructional Leadership

Almost without exception, school systems throughout the United States employ professionals to provide administrative assistance and instructional leadership to principals and teachers who serve severely handicapped and other handicapped students. These professionals, whether known as instructional supervisors, master teachers, consultants, or coordinators, all have similar responsibilities: They typically provide assistance in developing individualized education programs (IEPs), in selecting appropriate instructional materials and strategies, and in addressing parental concerns and student problems. The individuals in these positions offer schools their best opportunity for developing programming excellence and enhancing the success of efforts to educate severely handicapped students within regular education buildings.

It is apparent, however, that administrators often fail to free such professionals from additional tasks and mushrooming paperwork responsibilities that restrict their availability to teachers, principals, and parents. The predictable result of this lack of assistance and support may be administrative resistance, teacher "burnout," and parental dissatisfaction. Administrators must, instead, support and protect such professionals and appreciate their vital role in ensuring that the unique requirements imposed upon educational programs serving severely handicapped students are recognized and addressed.

A Responsive Program of Staff Development

A comprehensive staff development program that prepares administrative and instructional personnel for their roles in educating severely handicapped students in the least restrictive environment is a critical factor in the success of this effort. Public school administrators must evaluate the existing staff development models and reject those that do not respond to the training goals and technical-assistance needs of integration.

The trend toward building-based staff development is evident throughout the nation and reflects a growing reliance on designating midmanagement personnel to provide more responsive training to special education teachers. Although teachers interviewed in connection with the JWK contract consistently reported that this approach is effective and appreciated by them, they also expressed a desire for opportunities to meet with all teachers of severely handicapped students from across their district in order to share and discuss common goals and concerns. Such meetings could form the basis for longitudinal planning for severely handicapped students from birth through graduation—a necessary component of a comprehensive program development effort.

In addition, teachers of severely handicapped students typically require training in options and techniques that have little or no relevance for their colleagues who teach regular education students or mildly handicapped students. Demonstration teaching techniques and opportunities for hands-on experimentation with specific teaching strategies, followed by critique, are some of the most effective staff-development strategies for teachers of severely handicapped students. The unique and fairly intensive nature of these preferred training techniques further sets teachers of severely handicapped students apart from their regular education colleagues.

Throughout the above-mentioned study, teachers expressed frustration that the staff development program offered did not always address their information and training needs, in spite of the fact that their school systems utilized structured needs-assessment instruments to gather data on preferred staff development topics. Administrators must thus review their present strategies for determining the training needs of personnel and for establishing priorities based on district goals, and must revise these plans, when necessary, to assure that their staff development program responds to both sets of needs.

These unique requirements for providing effective inservice offerings for teachers of severely handicapped students challenge the flexibility and responsiveness of many traditional staff development programs. Yet the creation of a comprehensive, longitudinal staff-development program that can effect change, reinforce skills, introduce new ones, and provide positive reinforcement for professionals involved in educating severely handicapped students is a critical component of any serious effort to provide this education in the least restrictive environment.

Positive Attitude Toward LRE Concept within the School

The successful inclusion of severely handicapped students in educational environments with their nonhandicapped peers depends, to a considerable degree, upon the extent to which students and school personnel have been prepared for the experience. The combined attitudes of building principals, regular education teachers, special education teachers, and regular education students will form a climate that either accepts or rejects severely handicapped students within the school.

Student Acceptance of LRE Concept In the language of Public Law 94-142, (Education of Handicapped Children . . .), it is the intent of the LRE provision that "to maximum extent appropriate, handicapped children . . . are educated with children who are not handicapped" (Section 300a.400). In order for the inclusion of severely handicapped students in the least restrictive environment to be successful, both severely handicapped and nonhandicapped children must be prepared for the new relationship. Severely handicapped students, particularly those coming from segregated facilities, should not be placed in situations that are overwhelming, but should be carefully and systematically introduced to the regular campus environment and to their fellow students. Regular education students also should be prepared for the entry of severely handicapped students into the school setting—by providing them factual information about handicapping conditions, by answering their questions, and by helping them to recognize the important role they can play in assisting their handicapped peers to learn and develop socially.

Regular education teachers in this chapter's study reported that many school children have inadequate and incorrect information regarding children with handicaps—particularly regarding severely handicapped children. The two questions that regular education students ask most frequently at the elementary level, according to their teachers, are: "Is it contagious?" and "When will he [or she] (a severely handicapped student) get well?" Teachers suspect that many of these misconceptions are carried into high school and adult life.

The development of nonhandicapped students' acceptance of their severely handicapped peers must not be left to chance or to individual teacher interest. One promising strategy engages parents of severely handicapped students, parents of regular education students, principals, teachers, and community members in the development of instructional modules designed to prepare students to understand and accept the wide range of differences and similaritites that exists in any given group of individuals. Such an approach should be thoughtfully conceptualized, should offer supporting materials, and be presented in small-group or classroom sessions with opportunities for students to discuss issues and raise questions. As Bookbinder (1978) reminds teachers and parents:

> [The inclusion of handicapped students in regular school settings] places a tremendous burden of responsibility on nondisabled school children to welcome and understand their disabled classmates in order to make the broader social aspect of mainstreaming work. Without a systematic program to help children handle such a responsibility, disabled newcomers often experience school as an unfriendly, lonely place—or worse, as a place where they are teased or ignored by other children (pp. 48–49).

A systematic program designated to provide information and enhance understanding is essential in order to eliminate fears, prejudices, and stereotypes and promote appreciation and acceptance of individual differences. Administrators who are forced to wrestle with community rejection of handicapped students must come to recognize that the most powerful and yet the most subtle mechanism for developing a more informed, accepting community is through a sensitive program that prepares regular education students to enter into positive relationships with their handicapped peers.

Teacher Acceptance of LRE Concept   Positive teacher acceptance of the LRE concept for severely handicapped students may be viewed as a measure of the extent to which the earlier-discussed critical factors are implemented within the district. In other words, if the planning base is viable, if the organization strongly supports special education and its responsibility to implement the LRE mandate, if the system provides administrative assistance and instructional leadership to those responsible for carrying out the program, and if a staff development program is offered that is responsive to personnel needs for continued learning, it is quite likely that teachers' attitudes toward all students will be positive and accepting. If, however, these crucial factors are not in place and are not aggressively maintained, one could predict a decline in school personnel acceptance of and commitment to the least restrictive environment concept.

Community Acceptance of LRE Concept

The community setting increasingly is being utilized as the most relevant "classroom" for severely handicapped students who must learn daily living, travel, and recreation/leisure skills. The involvement of community members as partners in the educational process for these students greatly facilitates the building of a basis for community support, which is critical to ensure that resources necessary to meet the educational goals established for severely handicapped students are provided.

The community, as a whole, may be unaware that the public schools are providing educational services to severely handicapped students. Furthermore, few community members have had the opportunity to become acquainted with severely handicapped children or adults. Although most citizens have had some acquaintance with mildly handicapped individuals—such as those who have speech problems, learning disabilities, or are mildly retarded—they have seldom known individuals who had no speech, were nonambulatory, or were unable to care for their basic physiological needs. Given such lack of knowledge and experience, community members are often unaware of the contributions they can make toward furthering integration of severely handicapped individuals into the community.

Nevertheless, this chapter's study noted that in cases where there has been a successful history of including severely handicapped students within public school settings with their nonhandicapped peers, school officials have reported that the once-difficult task of identifying work-study and vocational placement sites in the community has become somewhat easier over time. In addition, as the students who shared their educational environment with their severely handicapped peers become adult community members, the degree of positive community acceptance and understanding of severely handicapped citizens will likely increase. These responses to an integrated school and community setting that incorporates community-based instruction and the construction of group homes, serve as an excellent barometer of present and future public attitudes toward severely handicapped individuals.

Parental Acceptance of LRE Concept

The full implementation of the least restrictive environment concept requires tremendous dedication from both the family and the school on behalf of the severely handicapped student and a willingness to work as partners to achieve common goals. Public school administrators must develop training programs that are responsive to the needs of parents and that recognize the talents and capabilities of parents to assist the schools in successfully addressing the educational needs of severely handicapped students. Parents, moreover, must be active participants in their child's education and must be encouraged to recognize the ultimate benefits of integration.

In all sites visited during the research phase of this chapter's study, it was clear that parents had worked diligently to obtain services for their severely handicapped children and, in many cases, had waited a long time for these services to be provided. In almost every instance, the first victory of these parents and their children had been that of securing entry into a segregated educational facility, and it was often difficult to "let go" of something that was not easily won.

Three specific parental concerns were common across all programs: concern that their severely handicapped children would be ridiculed; concern that they would be harmed; and concern that the instructional and related services to be provided in the integrated setting would not be as comprehensive or as available as they had been in the segregated setting.

School personnel suggest that these worries are legitimate and that administrators must take measures to ensure that such concerns do not become a reality. The study found, for example, that careful preparation of regular education students for the entry of severely handicapped students into the educational environment, (i.e., a systematic program of nonhandicapped student preparation and training), reduced ridicule. In addition, administrators must utilize an appropriate service delivery model that guarantees that adequate numbers and kinds of instructional and related service personnel are assigned to the new programs serving severely handicapped students in integrated settings.

Throughout the study, school personnel reported that a growing number of parents of severely handicapped children, although far from a majority of the parents, were either unable or unwilling to care for their children, therefore necessitating foster home or group home placement. The reasons for this divestment of responsibility should be identified and mechanisms strengthened to support the continued care of the severely handicapped child within its nuclear family. Procedures for effectively involving foster parents and group home parents in programming efforts will be crucial responsibilities for public school administrators now and in the future.

It has been documented that a carefully planned and coordinated parent training program can increase parental acceptance of and participation in the implementation of the LRE mandate. This basic notion was supported almost three decades ago by a study conducted by Yepsen and Cianci (1946) that showed that the number of parents who wanted to place their severely handicapped child in an institution decreased significantly after receiving training to deal more effectively with their child. The implications for administrative action are obvious. Public school administrators must develop and support training programs for parents of severely handicapped children that are designed to prepare them to meet the physically and emotionally demanding needs of their children, and are further designed to foster the parent-professional partnership.

A final concern frequently expressed by parents was that the school had not adequately endeavored to explain the legal and educational rationales for the least restrictive environment provision. As severely handicapped students are moved from institutions to separate facilities to regular education campuses, school administrators must find better ways to communicate to parents the concept behind this practice.

As public school administrators are able to identify the parameters of this new and challenging responsibility to develop appropriate programs for severely handicapped students within the least restrictive environment, it is hoped that their decisions and actions will become more effective. The section following briefly describes some of the information collected in a study by Stetson, Elting, and Raimondi (1982) related to the recurring theme of cost savings associated with decisions designed to enhance a district's compliance with the LRE mandate.

COST-EFFECTIVE SERVICE DELIVERY

Many public school administrators who continue to provide educational programs for severely handicapped students in segregated facilities express the conviction that these segregated settings are less expensive than one or more integrated settings located throughout the district or consortium. Typical arguments for separate educational environments for severely handicapped students include the belief that fewer instructional and related service personnel are required, that costs are more easily controlled, and that fewer resources are necessary to maintain the program.

Yet, during the technical assistance phase of the JWK contract, when teams of administrators from over 50 public school systems from across the country attended training sessions to examine current programs (which typically included one or more segregated schools for severely handicapped students) and to develop plans for addressing each of the seven critical factors presented earlier in this chapter, many administrators noted a cost savings associated with integration. Savings identified particularly were those in transportation costs as severely handicapped students were bused shorter distances from their homes to their neighborhood schools or schools within the vicinity; in reduced contracting costs as programs were created in home districts to serve a population previously served by an out-of-district program; and in reduction of administrative and other expensive resources necessary to maintain separate school programs. Summaries of the service changes and related costs reductions from four of the districts that participated in the JWK contract follow. (The descriptions are excerpted from a technical report submitted to the U.S. Department of Education, in partial fulfillment of contract #300-80-0935.)

Riverside Unified School District
Riverside, California
Respondent: Dr. Nancy Marley, Assistant Superintendent for Instruction

In the early spring of 1981, an administrative team from the Riverside Unified School District initiated comprehensive planning activities to enable them to critically review the current service delivery patterns in place in the district and to determine changes that would be required to assure that all students were educated in the least restrictive environment. The analysis revealed that previous patterns of student assignment in special education programs did not reflect consideration for each student's neighborhood school, and thus many handicapped students were bused to distant schools for instruction. Their analysis further revealed that a number of handicapped students throughout the district who were educated in segregated facilities could benefit from the opportunity to receive their education in integrated settings nearer their homes.

As a result of the plans laid by the administrative team during the summer of 1981, the following changes have been made throughout the Riverside Unified School District during a single year:

A resource program has been established on every regular education campus, and a special day-class has been established on a regular education campus in each of five cluster areas—administrative areas that comprise the district. Thus, when appropriate, the district was able to reassign each handicapped student to his neighborhood school or to a school close to his home for instruction.

Fifteen emotionally disturbed students who were previously educated in a nonpublic school setting have been returned to appropriate programs in regular education buildings within the district. To accomplish this, two SED programs were created; one in an elementary school, another in a middle school.

Eight students, residing in and receiving their education in the State School for the Deaf in Riverside, have returned to live with their families, although their education continues to be provided on the State School campus. These students are profoundly deaf and are now at the secondary level; thus, the district elected to continue their instruction in the familiar and more segregated setting.

A three-year effort to close one of the two separate facilities in the district has been initiated. The number of handicapped students educated in a separate facility in the Riverside Unified School District has dropped from 125 to 70 in the last year.

The following are cost savings documented by Riverside U.S.D. as a result of the changes in service delivery:

Seventy-six thousand dollars has been saved in transportation costs as excess time and mileage have been eliminated through an increased reliance on the neighborhood school as the primary service delivery model for handicapped students. Fewer students require transportation services and those who do are typically transported shorter distances.

The return of fifteen students from the nonpublic school for emotionally disturbed students eliminated the requirement for the district to pay tuition costs. The creation and operation of the two SED programs on regular campuses did not equal or surpass the former figure.

Administrative costs and building maintenance costs [will be] reduced [because] one of the two separate facilities will be closed.

Spokane Public Schools
Spokane, Washington
Respondent: Dr. Rob Knox, Director of Special Education

The Spokane Public Schools in Spokane, Washington, have for a number of years operated separate facilities for over 10% of the 2,500 special education students in the district. Within the past 5 years, this district has been cited for failure to comply with LRE provisions of Public Law 94-142 and Section 504 by the Washington Department of Public Instruction, the [U.S.] Office of Special Education, and the [U.S.] Office for Civil Rights. The Spokane Public Schools recognized and responded to this concern by making significant changes in student placement during the past year. A preliminary review at the district level revealed that over 1,000 students, or 40% of the special education population, were bused away from their neighborhood school and that transportation costs for 1 year for special education exceeded $100,000.

Working with a multidisciplinary team from the University of Washington, the district evaluated the instructional and related service needs of all students who were educated in separate facilities in the districts. Each neighborhood school's capacity to provide appropriate services for the majority of these students was analyzed, and the decision was made to return almost all handicapped students in the district to their neighborhood schools. All educational programs in each building were placed under the direct control and supervision of the principal, and special education became a support system rather than a separate system in the Spokane schools. Special education personnel were redistributed throughout the district, and a range of placement options was created at each building level.

Music, physical education, library science, and art are now available to all students in the district. These services were previously not available to special education students. Related service personnel are now assigned on an itinerant basis to provide services to handicapped students in their assigned regular education building. In the past, students requiring these services were either placed in separate facilities or district programs, or they were bused for part of the day to a location where these services were available. The funds that were previously expended to support transportation costs have been redistributed to enhance the quality of the special education program. District administrators feel that these changes have resulted in a system that is much closer to its goal of providing an appropriate educational opportunity to handicapped children in the least restrictive environment. Thus, the cost savings that were realized as a result of the broad programmatic changes have been reinvested in the special education program.

Exeter-West Greenwich Regional School District
Exeter, Rhode Island
Respondents: Dr. John Eldridge, Superintendent
               Robert A. Hicks, Supervisor
               Special Education Department

The Exeter-West Greenwich Regional School District in Rhode Island serves two rural communities in the western central portion of the state. Within the past year, this district created an administrative planning team to direct district-wide efforts to implement LRE provisions.

During the summer of 1981, the administrative team conducted an analysis of the needs of the 21 special education students who are served in out-of-district programs such as private day schools, programs in other districts on a tuition basis, and in state institutions. The long-range goal of this planning effort was to begin to develop local capability to provide appropriate services to the majority of the population in their home district. As a result of this preliminary analysis, the team identified the need to develop a preschool program for the handicapped in the district. Six of the 21 students were returned to Exeter-West Greenwich schools, 4 of whom were to be served in the newly created preschool program. In the words of the superintendent, John Eldridge, "We found this to be much more cost-effective and appropriate.'' The tuition costs were applied to the salary of a teacher, and the team expects that the program will continue to grow in the coming years as additional students are returned to the community and as others are identified.

Greensville County Public Schools
Emporia, Virginia
Respondent: Joseph Jones, Director of Pupil Personnel Services

The Greensville public schools have initiated a number of system-wide changes within the past two years that are designed to improve service delivery to handicapped students in the LRE. The primary change involved the closing of the Learning Center, a separate facility that served over 300 mentally retarded students from Greensville County. This number represented nearly 10% of the total school enrollment. With the conviction that all handicapped students in the county could benefit from interaction with their non-handicapped peers, the administrators and school board members accelerated their plans to close the separate facility and to create new programs and improve existing programs in the regular education buildings.

The following specific changes have recently been implemented:

Four new programs for mentally retarded students have been created—three at the elementary level and one at the senior high school level. The population of students served at the existing junior and senior high programs more than doubled with the closing of the learning center.

Two new programs for multi-handicapped students have been created on regular education campuses.

A preschool program, the first in the county, has been created on the Emporia Elementary School campus. This program provides early intervention services to handicapped students, ages 2 to 4.

The Learning Center complex is now being used for administrative office space and for school board meetings.

Cost savings as a result of these changes were noted by the district. These savings were primarily noted in significantly reduced transportation costs, [because] most handicapped students were reassigned to their neighborhood schools. Better use of existing building space and personnel were also noted.

From the experience of these four districts and other districts that implement specific changes to enhance the congruence of their program with the dictates of the least restrictive environment mandate, it appears, therefore, that there is a positive relationship between cost-effective service delivery and the implementation of services to severely handicapped students in the LRE. However, documentation of this relationship must be a future research priority as federal, state, and local budgets or education are closely examined and challenged.

CONCLUSION

The responsibility for assuring that each handicapped student—regardless of severity of condition—receives an appropriate education within the least restrictive environment rests in the hands of the nation's public school administrators. It is an obligation that extends far beyond an appropriate placement decision. It requires the creation of a positive and accepting environment; visible and consistent organizational support; an appropriate service delivery model; a comprehensive staff development program; and attention to the integration concerns of students, parents, and community members. Critical administrative factors, as identified through a field-based method of inquiry and described in this chapter, offer distinct advantages to administrators seeking to improve service delivery to severely handicapped students in the least restrictive environment.

The theory of administrative responsibility outlined in this chapter provides a framework against which current service delivery systems can be analyzed and dysfunctions that may restrict the severely handicapped student's opportunity to be educated in the least restrictive environment can be diagnosed and corrected. A source of power is thus available to public school administrators to enable them to establish and meet the often-illusive goal of programming excellence for severely handicapped students.

Formal and systematic attention to these administrative factors may result in an increased capacity to respond successfully to an array of programmatic challenges. Capacity-building must be seen as a significant goal of administrative behavior. In this way, the system can be viewed as proactive, rather than reactive, and can be significantly more responsive to the rapidly changing demands of public education. In a proactive system, administrators have increased time, energy, and resources to address new challenges. Conversely, a reactive system, by attending little to the essential administrative factors described in this chapter, proves unable to move beyond crisis management to planning for the future.

Therefore, the factors presented here must be considered and aggressively implemented in order to facilitate the successful inclusion of severely handicapped students in educational environments that maximize their opportunity to interact with their normal peers. If the service delivery model is viable, if the organization provides strong support for the goals and ideals of special education, if individuals are assigned to provide instructional leadership to personnel responsible for serving severely handicapped students, if a responsive staff development program is in place, if school personnel, parents, and community members are supportive of the LRE concept, it can be predicted that both the letter and the spirit of this mandate will be met. If, however, these critical factors are not in place and are not conscientiously maintained, it is likely that the potential for a realization of the LRE mandate for severely handicapped students will be limited. The power of the theory of administrative responsibility is that through formal, systematic attention to each factor, the quality of education for severely handicapped children may be enhanced, and the gulf between intent and practice may be bridged.

REFERENCES

Bookbinder, S. Mainstreaming: What every child needs to know about disabilities. *The Exceptional Parent*, 1978, *8*, 48–49.

Brown, L., Branston, M., Hamre-Nietupski, S., Johnson, J., Wilcox, B., & Gruenewald, L. A rationale for comprehensive longitudinal interactions between severely handicapped students and nonhandicapped students and other citizens. *AAESPH Review*, 1979, *4*, 3–14.

Certo, N. An analysis of selected characteristics of educational services for severely handicapped students. In: M. E. Snell (ed.), *Systematic instruction for the moderately and severely handicapped,* Vol. 2. Columbus, OH: Charles E. Merrill Publishing Co., in press.

Education of Handicapped Children, Implementation of Part B of the Education of the Handicapped Act. *Federal Register,* August 23, 1977, 42 (163). Washington, DC: U.S. Department of Health, Education, and Welfare.

Newell, C.A. *Human behavior in educational administration.* Englewood Cliffs, NJ: Prentice-Hall, 1978.

Sarason, S.B., & Doris, J. *Educational handicap, public policy, and social history: A broadened perspective on mental retardation.* New York: Free Press, 1979.

Sontag, E., Certo, N., & Button, J.E. On a distinction between the education of the severely and profoundly handicapped and a doctrine of limitations. *Exceptional Children,* 1979, *45,* 604–616.

Stetson, F.E., Elting, S.E., Raimondi, S.R. *Report on project impact with regard to cost effectiveness of service delivery to handicapped students in the least restrictive environment.* JWK International Corporation, Annandale, VA: Report submitted to U.S. Department of Education, July, 1982.

Wolfensberger, W. *The principle of normalization in human services.* Toronto: National Institute on Mental Retardation, 1972.

Yepsen, L. N., & Cianci, V. Home training for mentally deficient children in New Jersey. *Training School Bulletin,* 1946, *43,* 21–26.

REFERENCE NOTE

1. Alioa, G.F. *Assessment of the complexity of the least restrictive environment doctrine—Public Law 94-142.* Paper presented at BEH National Conference on the "Concept of the Least Restrictive Environment," Washington, D.C., April, 1978.

5

Systems-Change Strategies to Ensure the Future of Integration

*Norris Haring
and Felix F. Billingsley*

A major factor in the successful integration of severely handicapped individuals into society is the preparation of personnel who are committed to such integration and who are competent in training severely handicapped persons to adapt to a natural community. The placement of severely handicapped individuals in natural settings less structured than the classroom has many implications for the education of professionals. This chapter explores these implications.

Traditionally, teachers and others who work with severely handicapped youngsters have themselves adjusted to the restricted world of the special education classroom or institution. The goal of "new integration" teachers, however, is to teach severely handicapped students to adapt to the natural world. This requires that teachers identify those responses that severely handicapped students must make in natural settings—responses that will be the basis for curricular changes not only in educational programs for students, but also in preparation programs for teachers and other professionals. Professional training must occur more often in such natural settings as the classroom and community; it is furthermore essential that firsthand experience in teaching necessary behaviors to severely handicapped students accompany or immediately follow didactic training.

The teacher also should be trained to provide opportunities for community members who may be uninformed or apprehensive about severely handicapped individuals to learn about and become more understanding toward this group. In addition, teachers must become practiced in eliciting cooperation from various agencies so that the usually sluggish bureaucracy works together, with all relevant agencies doing their part.

In essence, our professional programs must train the integration teacher to lead the way in defining and implementing comprehensive plans to serve severely handicapped people in their own communities.

STATE EDUCATION AGENCY AND UNIVERSITY COOPERATION

A great variation in the extent and quality of services to severely handicapped students exists among local education agencies (LEAs). To ensure that the availability of services to handicapped students is uniform throughout the state, state education agencies (SEAs) often create statewide systems whose goal is to develop and implement comprehensive plans.

One frequent discrepancy, for example, is in the provision of integrated educational services for handicapped students. To reduce this discrepancy, an SEA may adopt a statewide systems-change model aimed at training teachers and other personnel in integrated educational services. By using a model that includes intensive training, demonstration, and research, LEAs and their staffs can improve the quality of their services. These trained personnel and the models they develop can then be used to train others in the local district.

A cooperative program between the University of Washington and the Washington state education agency, funded in part by Special Education Programs, Office of Special Education and Rehabilitation Services, illustrates this process. This program assists the state in providing personnel competent in integrating severely handicapped students and is involved, as well, in developing a long-range plan to assess the state's needs for professional preparation. As the latter plan is developed and current skills are assessed, the systems-change project identifies new areas or levels of competency for which training is needed. Now in its second phase, the systems-change project has initiated a number of integrated demonstration programs throughout Washington State. The model thus offers a network of sites that both provides effective communication among special educators and demonstrates the most up-to-date administrative, management, and intervention strategies.

Systems-Change Plan

The systems-change strategy seeks to alter the nature, extent, and quality of services for handicapped students in a community through the following activities:

1. Identifying the generic systems, agencies, and persons in the community capable of providing necessary services to handicapped individuals
2. Assessing the status of services provided by related systems, including the

amount, quality, and completeness of services and the target populations to be served
3. Determining the changes needed in the current system and developing a time line for them
4. Establishing change objectives for each agency in the system
5. Implementing change strategies that motivate people and create circumstances to effect change
6. Evaluating progress made by agencies so as to refine change strategies and increase the agencies' effectiveness
7. Monitoring activities of community agencies to ensure the successful implementation and maintenance of change strategies

The above systems-change activities will help to ensure integration of handicapped individuals into the community (Haring & Lynch, 1981).

Integrating Classroom and Vocational Settings

In the past, severely handicapped students have been educated in segregated classrooms. They often have been placed on the basis of such variables as availability of staff, classroom space, the severity or nature of their handicaps, and the wishes of the parents. Frequently, these segregated classrooms have been situated in special schools for handicapped persons. Thus, many students have had virtually no contact with normal children (Sontag, Smith, & Certo, 1977). However, Public Law 94-142 mandates that handicapped children should be taught with their nonhandicappd peers to the maximum extent possible and that all handicapped children should be educated in the least restrictive environment (PL 94-142, 1975).

One part of the systems-change model surveys existing opportunities for severely handicapped students to engage in normalizing activities. For example, a critical consideration for the school setting is the percentage of time handicapped students spend with less handicapped or non-handicapped peers. The change model also addresses options available in the community for severely handicapped pupils to engage in leisure activities with less handicapped or nonhandicapped peers.

Comprehensive Team Assessment and Management

Because of the complex disabilities of many severely handicapped children, assistance from a wide spectrum of professions may be needed. Too often, individual professionals are isolated from one another because of the manner in which they provide services (Reynolds & Birch, 1977). For example, the language specialist may take a pupil to his or her laboratory room three times a week, the occupational therapist may work with a child during recess each day, and the nutritionist/nurse may be in contact with the parent about a feeding program. Although these professionals may provide the teacher with formal and informal reports on the child's progress, there may be little true coordination of services. The comprehensive educational team approach (Haring, 1977) establishes a wide-ranging and coordinated program of services for each child.

Comprehensive assessment is crucial to the success of programming for severely handicapped students. The number of goals for any severely handicapped child is so large that all goals cannot be addressed simultaneously. Therefore, the team must cooperate to set priorities for the kind and extent of goals and to assess the child's progress toward them. Since the change in rate (frequency) of response is typically very slow, without this careful, direct, and continuous team assessment, the special education teacher can neither determine the child's progress nor make necessary modifications in the instructional program. An additional benefit of such assessment is that the team derives a sense of accomplishment from the student's gains.

Comprehensive teams that are based on behavioral principles, that practice systematic instruction and use direct measurement and applied behavior analysis as the essential strategies for assessing behavior change are found to be very effective. Such procedures provide reliable evidence of the progress produced by intervention and enable team members to communicate clearly among themselves and with parents and other professionals who need ongoing information on the status of individual students.

Composition of the Transdisciplinary Team   A team concept has been in use for some time, but team members traditionally have worked in isolation. Hart (1977) points out that previously, when the *multidisciplinary* team model was popular, specialists saw the child individually, did not consult, and sent separate recommendations to the classroom teacher for implementation. The multidisciplinary model was replaced by the *interdisciplinary* team model, whose members discussed their findings and devised a single set of recommendations. Nevertheless, many professionals still carried out their own programs, although some recommendations were passed on to the teacher for implementation. Often, however, these recommendations did not take into account the existing educational environment, and coordination of a child's program was difficult. In addition there was frequently little provision for team follow-up or feedback in either model.

In contrast to the above models, the *trandisciplinary* team model contains the following principles:

1. The make-up of the team is based on the needs of the particular child.
2. Professionals on the team trade skills with and learn from one another.
3. Accountability is built into the model through staff meetings and cross-skill training.

A typical team may consist of medical personnel, a physical therapist, an occupational therapist, a communications specialist, an audiologist, a paraprofessional aide, and, of course, the special education teacher and parents or other family members. The actual team make-up will vary, but the way in which the team functions remains the same. The comprehensive educational team has the following goals:

1. To assess the current developmental level of functioning and the functional skills of each pupil

2. To develop pupil goals and objectives
3. To determine most appropriate pupil placement
4. To plan and implement appropriate programs according to team-established objectives
5. To provide continuous evaluation of pupils' functioning
6. To provide ongoing communication among all members of the team to ensure continuity and coordination of services
7. To provide inservice training to team members so that they can conduct programs for other disciplines in their own instructional environments

The family and the special education teacher have the most frequent contact with the child, and are the most intimately involved in implementing the team's recommendations. They are exposed to many more opportunities and settings— such as leisure activities and meals—in which they can not only carry out the program, but also observe the child and obtain data for the team's program decisions. However, the transdisciplinary model also ensures more direct care for and interaction with the child by individual team members than did earlier models.

One member of the team, usually the special educator, acts as an "educational synthesizer" (Bricker, 1976). This person seeks information and techniques from the team members, develops effective intervention strategies, and coordinates their implementation. Preparation programs must ensure that special education teachers have the broad conceptual background necessary for this synthesizing activity. Special education teachers are the major recipients of the team's cross-disciplinary skill sharing, and they must be trained to teach not only handicapped individuals, but also parents and other primary caregivers.

A survey of professional programs for teachers of severely handicapped students at the University of Kansas, the University of Washington, the University of Wisconsin, and San Francisco State University shows that all four institutions include training in transdisciplinary teaming. This training includes:

1. Experiences in planning the total program for the classroom
2. Development of instructional plans in the context of a comprehensive management plan
3. Utilization of professionals
4. Work with parents and parent instruction (Haring, 1980)

As Iacino and Bricker (1978) point out, special education teachers must be trained to synthesize both information and the efforts of a transdisciplinary team. Only with a trained and competent manager can the barriers among specialists be transcended, can parents and paraprofessionals be involved, and can the skills of all team members be used to the fullest.

State of the Art in Programming Because students with severe handicaps vary widely in ability and may require different types of programs to make optimum progress, it is important that field personnel share a common educational approach. A process approach, which can be used with whatever materials or curricula are most appropriate to a particular child, provides the common base required for coordination of services. Such an approach (Lynch, McGuigan, & Shoemaker, 1977) includes the following steps:

1. Assessment of general and specific skills (by the comprehensive educational team)
2. Establishment of long-term goals for each skill area or behavior of concern
3. Establishment and sequencing of short-term objectives
4. Development and writing of an instructional plan
5. Development and writing of measurement procedures for each behavior
6. Implementation of the instructional plan and measurement procedures
7. Modification of the plan based on data collected
8. Periodical evaluation of overall pupil progress

By using this system, teachers optimize the learning environment for each pupil while providing parents, administrators, and funding agencies with meaningful and accurate documentation of each learner's progress toward objectives and goals. This last point is especially important to a systems-change project staff, because the staff uses data on child change to determine the effectiveness of staff inservice training and of systems-change strategies.

Ultimate Functioning Education professionals must attend to the exit skills necessary for competent functioning in community environments. For example, the ultimate goal for a severely handicapped adolescent may be employment in a supervised job station in industry and placement in a community-based group home. The success of this transition depends upon coordination among the school, family, and receiving agencies and upon the skills taught. Research shows that generalization is enhanced if instruction takes place in a number of settings beyond the original environment (Schreibman & Koegel, 1975).

Coordination among home, school, and community can help ensure that the school and family teach those skills necessary for success in the group home and on the job and that the student is provided information and technical assistance for dealing with his or her unique needs in adult environments. In turn, the severely handicapped student's performance in adult environments can indicate to the school areas where additional staff training is needed.

Social Impact Social impact is related directly to the ultimate functioning of severely handicapped students in the community. A major goal of the cooperative systems-change model is to explore methods for changing professional and community attitudes about severely handicapped students. Regarding professional attitudes, sometimes it is difficult to convince school personnel, even teachers, that severely handicapped students can develop skills that will enable them to live more self-sufficiently (Bellamy, Peterson, & Close, 1975). "State-of-the-art" training assists school staff to realize that appropriate programming can release previously untapped potential in their pupils. Thus the perennial problem of lowered expectations for severely handicapped students is minimized (Reynolds & Birch, 1977).

In the community, agencies and the general public are frequently unaware that, with appropriate training and support, severely handicapped individuals can be effective, productive, and useful citizens (President's Committee on Mental Retardation, 1976; Smith & Smith, 1978; Sternat, Messina, Nietupski, Lyon, & Brown, 1977). Those who work with such students can promote local appreciation for the potential of handicapped persons by speaking to local community groups and inviting local residents into the schools to observe severely handicapped programs. Parents, too, can become effective advocates for changing negative public attitudes about handicapped individuals (Bronfenbrenner, 1974).

The systems-change model identifies, implements, and evaluates techniques for promoting positive changes in attitudes toward severely handicapped students. Some observable indicators of social impact include individual actions, modifications in community services planning, increased financial support for services and programs, and increased coordination and cooperation among agencies. Others are the development of vocational or residential placements and expanded opportunities to interact in the community.

Cooperation and Coordination For a statewide systems-change model to succeed, the project must have the full support and cooperation of the SEA, the LEA network, state institutions of higher education, and a wide variety of local resource providers. Contacts with a broad range of service providers can help local professionals build strong school-based programs for children and meet needs that extend beyond the school system, such as independent living skills and mental health monitoring. Since the ultimate result of all educational services for severely handicapped students must be functioning within the community (Brown, Nietupski, & Hamre-Nietupski, 1976), the schools must coordinate with businesspersons, adult services agencies, and other groups interested in adult services.

Inservice Training and Staff Development In order to develop and maintain a "best practices" systems-change project, the staff must have a method for continuing education. Once developed, this method can be disseminated to the staffs of replication sites as well as to other interested individuals and groups.

Parent Services Encouraging parent involvement in the design and implementation of the systems-change process is necessary to the success of the model. Parent participation in the model's design ensures that services viewed by families as necessary to the success of their children are incorporated. Parents are keenly aware of any lack of services or lack of continuity in or inaccessibility to services; they are, moreover, an excellent source of relevant information. Also, the child's home has been most often viewed as the least restrictive residential environment. To help parents keep their child in the home, however, parents/caregivers must be provided the support they need, including information on the management of physical, medical, health, and behavioral concerns; assistance in the generalization of *appropriate* classroom programming to the home; peer support from other families of severely handicapped individuals; and assistance in becoming advocates for their children in the community.

PREPARATION FOR SYSTEMS-CHANGE LEADERSHIP

If educators are to act as change agents they must understand systems-change theory and have firsthand exposure to the systems-change process. An example of the importance of systems-change strategies can be found in the area of integration.

It is entirely possible to "integrate" a school and maintain a deg.ce of segregation approaching that which exists in institutions or training centers for severely handicapped students. This situation is most readily observed in schools that include a "handicapped wing" (or building), as well as in those that practice a cosmetic "side-by-side" approach. Although classrooms for severely handicapped students in "side-by-side" facilities may, in fact, be distributed throughout the school, contact with regular program elements and pupils is minimized or nonexistent; thus, in the absence of physical integration, the desired social integration cannot be accomplished.

The maintance of such restrictive policies reflects stereotypical attitudes concerning the educational goals for and needs of severely handicapped students. If severely handicapped individuals are, in fact, to be excluded from school activities with normal peers, and are to remain the life-long, passive recipients of care provided by parents and/or residential staff, then it is unnecessary for them to have integrated experiences or to develop functional skills for adapting to the community. However, the evidence is undeniable that severely handicapped individuals are capable of learning skills far beyond those required for the receipt of care and stimulation. It is equally clear that "they have the right to be visible, functioning citizens integrated into the everyday life of complex public communities" (Brown et al., 1976). If the integration is to be realized, educational personnel must be trained to recognize restrictive systems and to modify those systems.

Educational Needs of Handicapped Individuals

Successful integration requires that the classroom, traditionally considered the central focus of educational activity, be viewed as a staging area from which to implement programs in the broader community. As stated in the beginning of this chapter, effective systems-change, therefore, requires that curricula be developed that identify needs of severely handicapped individuals in natural settings. In order to implement such an approach to curriculum development, the teacher must be trained to deviate substantially from commonly used developmental scales and checklists in order to determine those skills that will facilitate pupil functioning in current and subsequent least-restrictive environments (Brown, Branston-McClean, Baumgart, Vincent, Falvey, & Schroeder, 1979). Educators must also become proficient in identifying and analyzing innovative instructional targets for severely handicapped individuals. In addition, since pupils are exposed to environments that differ in response requirements, curricula must be individualized. The standard curriculum, applicable across pupils, has become a thing of the past.

Teaming

To implement training in the community as well as in the classroom, the functioning of educational teams also requires modification. As noted earlier in this chapter, educators of severely handicapped students must become familiar with the skills of other professionals and practiced in working within transdisciplinary teams (Crowner, 1979; Stainback, Stainback, & Maurer, 1976). Members of such teams are likely to require "reeducation" in the requirements of functional curricula, and must learn from multiple disciplines the information that is most useful in teaching functional skills in the natural environment. Instruction within the community will also require the cooperation of individuals who form the community's public service base.

Educational teams in integrated settings may from time to time include nontraditional members such as school janitors, members of the school safety patrol, bus drivers, managers of fast-food restaurants and convenience stores, church ushers, department store sales personnel, optometrists, and supermarket managers. The involvement and cooperation of such individuals can be of tremendous assistance in developing and implementing functional programs as well as in facilitating the provision of longitudinal services within the community. Training programs can aid systems change, therefore, by providing educators with the skills necessary to gain the cooperation of, and synthesize information from, individuals from diverse backgrounds who may be participating for the first time in educational service delivery.

Coordination

Finally, a community-based orientation to education requires the coordinated efforts of community agencies that provide specialized services for handicapped individuals. Crowner (1979) has noted that because severely handicapped students must cope with their handicap around the clock in all settings, schools must be involved in the activities of agencies that serve individuals outside of school. Ideally, this involvement should occur within an interagency network (Crowner, 1979). Such networks, however, are rare indeed, and services tend, rather, to be provided in an isolated, haphazard manner (Larsen, 1977). Given the early contact of school personnel with handicapped individuals, and the experience acquired by educators in the development of precise, systematic, and transdisciplinary educational plans, graduates of systems-change training programs are in a logical position to assert leadership in coordinated interagency planning and accountability. Training, therefore, should acquaint the professional with the nature of services provided by various community agencies, the means by which services are delivered, agency funding sources, formal and informal relationships among agencies, legal and political barriers to interagency cooperation, group dynamics, and those needs of severely handicapped students that most clearly require coordination of community services. (See Kenowitz, 1979, for a discussion of community-based services critical to the maintenance of severely handicapped individuals in noninstitutional settings.)

CONTINUING COMMUNITY SERVICES AND DEINSTITUTIONALIZATION

Once the moral and practical value of integrating severely handicapped persons into the natural environment is accepted, it is up to society to provide the post-school services that severely handicapped persons require. Community involvement and advocacy is of course necessary to ensure that these basic services are fully provided to severely handicapped adults. But, as Scheerenberger (1974) has noted, most communities have a long way to go toward making these services available. The following components should be included in developing a post-school plan:

1. Local and regional boards to plan and coordinate services
2. An independent monitoring agency separate from the local planning board
3. High-quality technical assistance available to planning boards and agencies
4. Adequate financial support
5. Representation by responsible advocates for handicapped persons as they interact with the service delivery systems

Inclusion of the above elements helps to ensure that services are identified and coordinated and that a third party is available to monitor and evaluate the system.

Transition from School to Community

One of the most crucial periods in a severely handicapped student's post-school experience occurs when the school releases its responsibility. Since the school uses age rather than performance level as its criterion for the end of training, students who complete public education have varying degrees of skill and require a wide range of services. Agencies that might assume responsibility at this time include the departments of mental health or vocational rehabilitation. In some states, however, no agency has direct responsibility for ensuring that handicapped individuals have the necessary services within their communities. In the past, young handicapped adults integrated into the community may not have received necessary services because the agencies in charge were not clearly designated. For example, professional preparation programs in higher education, vocational and technical training institutions, or vocational rehabilitation agencies have variously assumed responsibility.

Clearly, considerable improvement is needed in services to severely handicapped adults, and particularly immediately after their school years, when abruptly they must learn to function in the adult world. Secondary-level programs are needed, such as that conducted by Madison, Wisconsin's Metropolitan School District, which utilizes community training extensively to build necessary skills such as maintaining a checkbook, shopping for clothing and groceries, and using public transportation. Transitions programs are most successful if staff not only teach the skills necessary to function independently but cooperate with family and adult service providers in planning for such transitions.

Continuum of Services

A huge problem in the transition from school to community is the provision of additional services the severely handicapped individual requires to live in community environments. Communities typically say that they will deal with this problem by providing a continuum of services. However, as Galloway (Note 1) has observed, the concept of a continuum of services translates too often into providing the individual with a listing of the facilities and programs that already exist in the community, arranged from most to least segregated. A continuum of services should consist, rather, of a variety of community agencies that offer those broad and individualized services necessary for all severely handicapped individuals to function within their home communities. Scheerenberger (1975, 1976, 1978) reports that a major reason for more than 50% of readmissions to public residential facilities is the inadequacy of community services, including the failure to follow up on the progress of handicapped individuals placed in the community.

Most adults with severe handicaps, no matter how independent, require services from community agencies. Obviously, it is preferable for handicapped individuals themselves to be able to identify the proper agencies to contact. However, it is often difficult even for nonhandicapped persons to discriminate among a maze of governmental agencies. Therefore, personnel who work with severely handicapped individuals must be able to identify relevant community agencies, the agencies' responsibilities in serving handicapped persons, and methods of obtaining these services. Efforts should then be made to teach these information-acquiring skills to severely handicapped students or their parents/ primary caregivers at the secondary level.

Communities must eventually act on the need for an effective advocacy system to guarantee that individual agencies perform optimally for all handicapped citizens in the community. Until such a system is functioning, however, it is up to teachers to provide the information and experience necessary for handicapped individuals to obtain services.

Alternate Residential Settings

Since the major move in the 1960s toward deinstitutionalization, more options for residential settings have become available. Several factors govern the desirability of alternatives. Certainly, the best residential setting for children is the natural home (Stedman & Eichorn, 1964). The next most desirable placement is a foster-home setting that can provide a caring environment similar to the natural home (Adams, 1970). For adults, well-managed adult foster-care and small-group homes can provide a community setting with a good quality of life and a great amount of normalization (Baker, Seltzer, & Seltzer, 1977). In fact, in some cases small-group homes appear to have a better success rate that all other placements (Wyngaarden, Freedman, & Gollay, 1976).

A more recent alternative is a supervised apartment setting in which two or three handicapped adults live together and have substantial independence (Schulman, 1980). For the more severely handicapped person, regular supervision of apartment settings may be required. However, many of the apartment settings developed for moderately and mildly handicapped persons in the Seattle area, for example, are succeeding with only limited supervision. Properly organized and supervised, apartment settings can provide highly satisfactory natural residences for large numbers of handicapped individuals.

Community-Based Vocational Adaptation

One of the most important aspects of integration is training to adapt to community and vocational environments. Training for community adjustment has been shown to increase successful community placement (Bell, 1976; Gollay, Freedman, Wyngaarden, & Kurtz, 1978), while unmet training needs may increase re-institutionalization (Baker et al., 1977). With training, handicapped persons can hold a variety of unskilled and semi-skilled jobs, such as those in the human services, food and lodging, and manufacturing and packaging industries. Cuvo, Leaf, and Borakove (1978) demonstrated that handicapped individuals can successfully learn to perform janitorial tasks, while other authors have documented handicapped persons' success in food service occupations (Sowers, Thompson, & Connis, 1979).

Educators working with severely handicapped students at the secondary level must make a major effort to identify potential vocational positions in the community and use them as basic vocational training sites. Building this kind of cooperation between secondary programs and employers, both large and small, is a primary function of special education at this level. Almost all teaching can be done at actual vocational sites and can be supported and strengthened by the involvement of handicapped peers who have already become competent at special tasks while on the job. It has been shown that a training team of teachers and students can enable a vocational training teacher to coordinate and supervise up to six trainees at one time (F. R. Rusch, personal communication, 1977).

Integration and community involvement make new demands on professional preparation strategies. Professionals must examine closely the requirements of the setting while evaluating the performance level demanded of the trainee, in order to develop more efficient and systematic training methods.

PRACTICUM EXPERIENCES IN INTEGRATED SCHOOL SETTINGS

Practica: Why?

The importance of extensive, field-based experience in the preparation of personnel to serve severely handicapped students in integrated settings cannot be overstated. Practica conducted in the field accomplish at least three crucial functions: they provide practice in the development of professional skills; they provide a means by which skill acquisition may be verified; and, they offer a means by which students may confirm their professional goals.

Skill Development

Ruch (1967) relates a story concerning an attempt by Eli Culbertson, the bridge expert, to learn to play golf through conceptualization. Culbertson engaged in extensive analysis and mental rehearsal of the game, but no actual practice. Unfortunately, his initial attempts to transfer his knowledge to the realities of fairway, green, and sand trap met with failure. The point, of course, is that conceptualization alone is inadequate to develop behavioral fluency. There is simply no substitute for overt practice corrected by feedback.

Many of the general competencies required of teachers of severely handicapped students in integrated settings are the same as those required of educators in more restrictive, segregated settings. Educators in either setting must:

1. Organize the learning environment in a manner that ensures training opportunities appropriate in quality and quantity
2. Provide effective programming (including assessment, writing of goals and objectives, task analysis, proper teaching procedures, and ongoing, precise assessment and evaluation) within a variety of curricular areas
3. Respond to the needs of physically handicapped and medically fragile individuals
4. Work productively within a transdisciplinary team
5. Exhibit behaviors that reflect ethical responsibility and professionalism

Even with segregated settings, it has become clear that knowledge related to such competencies gained in didactic coursework does not automatically transfer to actual teaching situations. It is much less likely, however, that automatic transfer will occur in integrated settings, where instruction is undertaken in natural, less predictable environments. In other words, the specific skills required to achieve proficiency in general educational competency areas are different, and possibly more numerous and complex, in integrated settings than in segregated ones. In addition, achieving integration requires that educators develop skills in a competency area—that is, the maintenance of instructional gains in the natural environment—that is foreign to educators practicing in segregated facilities. Several examples of teacher skills that might be considered essential for maintaining gains in integrated settings are: informing the public of significant educational outcomes; engaging in advocacy for normalization, least restrictive alternative, and community integration; referring students to appropriate educational and community agencies; evaluating education and social service delivery systems; conducting inservice training and providing training for paraprofessionals, parents, siblings, volunteers, and peer tutors; and instructional programming for generalization and maintenance in the natural environment (Wilcox, 1977).

A knowledge base upon which to build competency may certainly be developed within university and college classrooms. As stated, though, it is difficult to envision classroom-based activities that could provide the diversity of experience and intensity of practice necessary to equip educators of severely handicapped students with even a minimally acceptable behavioral repertoire. Practicum experience, therefore, must be considered a primary mode of skill development rather than merely an adjunct to didactic coursework.

Studies dating from Thorndike (1927) have supported the contention that feedback during learning is a fundamental condition affecting performance. In order to facilitate skill development within practica, then, teachers in training should receive frequent feedback regarding their progress. The authors agree with

Wilcox (1977) who stated that because public school teachers may not possess skills consistent with those required in a specific training program, trainee supervision and feedback should be supplied by personnel *directly associated with the program*. Primary supervision responsibility should be given to faculty members or, perhaps, to advanced graduate students acting under the direct supervision of faculty.

Skill Verification

Brown et al. (1976) have suggested that a *zero-degree inference strategy* be adopted in relation to the instruction of severely handicapped individuals. Because criterion-level performance on any task in a given situation does not necessarily ensure satisfactory performance on the same task in similar but different situations, zero-degree inference strategy requires that empirical verification of skill acquisition be undertaken each time an environmental situation changes. We suggest that a similar strategy be undertaken with regard to the preparation of educational personnel. If the degree of inference is not zero, it should at least be very low. Just as it is insufficient to assume that transfer will automatically occur from didactic coursework to practical teaching situations, it is inappropriate to attempt to evaluate the attainment of practical competence solely on the basis of coursework performance. In addition, the precision and instructional consistency required of personnel serving severely handicapped students render unsuitable those evaluation instruments that rate trainee performance in relation to global skills. Adequate evaluation consists not in rating a teacher in training according to ambiguous criteria along a five-point scale on his or her abilities to "demonstrate genuine enthusiasm for teaching" and "maintain a physical atmosphere conducive to learning," but in verifying the trainee's acquisition (and use) of specific skills according to clearly defined standards.

Skill verification procedures will undoubtedly vary from program to program; however, a comprehensive evaluation system should provide for assessment within at least three basic performance areas:

1. Generic teaching behaviors relevant to instruction regardless of pupil population or setting. Such behaviors include: selection of appropriate instructional programs; pre-instruction organization; consistency of instruction (i.e., *procedural reliability*); level of control in program settings; fluency of transition between programs; and quality of verbal interactions in nonprogram settings.
2. The ability of the teacher in training to operate within the parameters of the instructional environment as established by the field teacher and support staff. As trainee behaviors in this area are likely to occur outside the direct observation periods undertaken by the program field supervisor (e.g., trainee input to nonprogram activities, cooperation with the instructional staff), the major portion of this data base would consist of information provided by the field teacher.

3. Behaviors critical to the education of severely handicapped students in integrated settings. Instruments designed to access such behaviors frequently consist of lists of sequential skills in competency areas that reflect the acquisition of increasing degrees of instructional expertise, instructional responsibility, and knowledge of the educational system across time. The University of Washington personnel preparation program in the severely handicapped specialty, for example, employs a Student Competency Assessment Form to evaluate attainment of competencies across three academic quarters: first quarter competencies address major components of systematic instruction; second-quarter competencies focus on assessment, evaluation, professional meetings, and communications; and third-quarter competencies emphasize materials selection, administrative tasks, and the effective utilization of support services and personnel. Skills are verified as they are demonstrated; however, student trainees are continually checked for skill maintenance throughout the practicum sequence.

Goal Confirmation

In the absence of adequate prior field experience, it is probable that many program graduates will eventually find that the attitudes and abilities required to serve severely handicapped students in integrated settings conflict with their own personal goals and expectations (Stainback et al., 1976).

Consider the following examples: It is one thing to learn about exciting new developments in instructional and classroom evaluation technology and quite another to assume the responsibility for applying that knowledge to make decisions that affect the quality of life of another human being; it is one thing to be told about self-destructive and stereotypical behaviors and another to interact effectively with a pupil who ruminates more than 100 times a day; it is one thing to understand the need to involve parents in the educational process and another to ensure the active participation of a parent who views education primarily as respite care. Such examples point to the need for considerable practica, not only because practica contribute to the development of appropriate abilities and attitudes but because they permit trainees to confirm empirically that they do, in fact, desire to pursue their initial interests.

The "Ideal" Experience

Based on the functions practica serve, as discussed above, it is possible to generate a picture of the "ideal" training experience.

First, practica would be conducted in integrated settings in which systems-change activites are being undertaken. As noted earlier, teaching skills required in integrated settings are likely to differ markedly from those required in segregated settings, and generalization should not be taken for granted.

Second, primary responsibility for trainee supervision would lie with program personnel, and supervisor-trainee contacts would be frequent. The instructional precision required of graduates should be such that feedback is frequent.

Mid-term and final evaluations appear insufficient to effect numerous, fine-grained changes in trainee behavior. It is thus recommended that on-site observation and feedback occur at least once every 2 weeks and more often where persistent problems are noted.

Third, trainees would be placed under the partial supervision of program graduates who are now teachers in the field. Such teachers would provide the most appropriate role models and could assume some degree of responsibility for trainee supervision without compromising the goals of the program (Wilcox, 1977).

Fourth, practicum experiences would be integrated with didactic coursework. Wilcox (1977) has noted that simple correlation is insufficient; rather, the knowledge base for competencies displayed in practicum settings should be traceable to specific information provided within specific courses.

Finally, practica would be extensive and sequential. The skills required to serve severely handicapped students are far too numerous and complex to coalesce in a single half-day (or even full-day) "practice-teaching" experience. Data indicating the optimal amount of time that should be spent in field settings are unavailable. The authors' experience, however, suggests that at least one academic year of continuous, partial-day placement, followed by one academic quarter of full-day work, will permit training to proceed in a systematic, sequential, and effective manner.

Although real-world contingencies frequently preclude achievement of the ideal, a commitment to the provision of quality field experiences demands continuous effort to approximate the ideal as closely as possible. Graduates of personnel preparation programs must *know,* but the critical test is what they have been trained to *do*. The nature of practica will, in large part, determine trainees' performance on the "real-world test."

DIDACTIC REQUIREMENTS

Although the on-the-job experience obtained within a practicum setting is necessary to the professional development of trainees, it is by no means sufficient. In the absence of a conceptual base, skills gained in the field may consist largely of a "bag of tricks." As Baer, Wolf, and Risley (1968) have noted, collections of "tricks" are difficult to expand systematically and, when the number of tricks is large, difficult to learn. It is through relevant didactic coursework, then, that trainees are exposed to the principles that will enable them to be flexible and to generate new "tricks" required to meet the needs of severely handicapped learners.

Although the concept of integration must be woven throughout the total fabric of personnel preparation programs, five areas of didactic preparation are especially shaped by the concept. Instruction must be provided in: methods for promoting positive interactions between handicapped and nonhandicapped persons, methods for effecting behavior changes within the natural environment, parent education, curriculum development, and the scientific approach to instruction.

Promoting Positive Interactions

Hamre-Nietupski, Nietupski, Stainback, and Stainback (this volume) argue persuasively for the advance and continued preparation of regular public school staff and students in order to facilitate ongoing, positive interactions between severely handicapped pupils and other persons in the regular school environment. If special educators are to contribute meaningfully to such preparatory activity, they should possess a cluster of communication and training skills that differ from those required in segregated environments. Based on procedures recommended by Hamre-Nietupski et al. (this volume) that skill cluster might include, for example:

1. The ability to share accurate information—on both the nature of handicapping conditions and the needs of severely handicapped pupils—with regular education staff (and students) in both formal and informal contexts
2. The ability to plan and structure integrated activities between handicapped and nonhandicapped pupils
3. The ability to select, train, and use peer tutors

The skills noted above have not been included in competency lists developed within personnel preparation programs that assume segregated placement for severely handicapped pupils. Where successful public school integration is the goal, however, such skills must no longer be excluded.

Behavior Change in Natural Environments

The elements of a systematic approach to the instruction of severely handicapped students do not change when pupils are educated in integrated as opposed to restrictive settings. Thorough assessments must still be conducted, objectives must be determined, instructional and evaluation procedures must be developed and implemented, and changes must be based on pupil performance data. Considerations involved in the application of each element, however, may differ considerably and the content of successful personnel preparation programs must reflect those differences. The elements of assessment, instructional methods, and evaluation of pupil progress illustrate some of the modifications in traditional thought and practice that may be necessary as a function of integration.

Assessment   Educational assessments of severely handicapped persons of all ages have often been conducted with instruments that provide an indication of performance in relation to the normal developmental sequence. An unfortunate outcome of this practice is that a 16-year-old adolescent, for example, whose developmental level has been found to be that of a 4-year-old, may be exposed to a curriculum appropriate to a 4-year-old normal child. But since the skills required by a 16-year-old to adapt to integrated community settings differ considerably from those required of a 4-year-old, such an assessment will severely limit the 16-year-old's exposure to instructional experiences that facilitate adaptation to adult settings. While developmental inventories will continue undoubtedly to play a significant role, the assessment of functional skills required in current and subsequent least restrictive environments (Brown et al., 1979) becomes increasingly important to appropriate programming as pupils grow older. Graduates of personnel preparation programs, therefore, must be trained to assess functional skill levels and, because the functionality of any given skill depends on the environmental circumstances of specific pupils, to develop appropriate assessment tools.

Instructional Methods To date, our instructional efforts have been focused largely on applying methods to ensure that severely handicapped students acquire skills. We have been much less concerned with whether pupils become fluent in those skills, maintain them, generalize them, and adapt them as necessary (Haring & Pious, 1976). The emphasis on acquisition is understandable if severely handicapped learners are to reside, work, and recreate in homogeneous, custodial settings in which performance proficiency and response diversity are unnecessary. Successful educational outcomes in integrated settings, however, require that learners advance beyond the acquisition stage of learning. In the natural environment, parents, friends, teachers, and store clerks will not reinforce highly accurate, but agonizingly slow, responses. Skills must therefore be performed proficiently enough so that they are not only useful to the handicapped individual but gain reinforcement from community members adequate to ensure skill maintenance.

Generalization must occur across situations that may differ along a variety of stimulus dimensions, and response adaptations must be generated to cope with new situations (e.g., making a response with the left hand if the right hand is full in a situation in which the right hand has always been employed). Educators must become familiar with those instructional tactics that will move pupils through the hierarchy of learning stages and that offer, as well, the highest probability of success at each stage. Training in acquisition technology alone is no longer sufficient. For a discussion of instructional methods appropriate to specific stages of learning, see White and Haring (1980) and Haring and Bricker (1976).

Progress and Evaluation By and large, the procedures taught in personnel preparation programs for evaluating ongoing pupil performance have been consistent with the emphasis on instructional methods related to acquisition. That is, teachers of severely handicapped pupils have learned to use pupil progress data that measure behavior along the accuracy dimension of performance only (i.e., correct and error counts or percentage of correct statements). In addition, these data are frequently used in such a way that their only function is to tell the teacher when he or she should move the pupil to the next curricular step. Although it is certainly important to measure accuracy and to establish criteria for proceeding from step to step in the curriculum, teachers of severely handicapped pupils in integrated settings need additional information to make timely and effective instructional decisions.

Because performance proficiency is so essential in natural environments (Barrett, 1979), evaluation systems must measure both accuracy and fluency dimensions of behavior. In other words, the data collected should relate behavior to a time base. Time-based measures, including response rate, duration, and latency, provide greater sensitivity to performance change than do accuracy measures alone, and thereby increase the instructional decision-making capability of the teacher (Billingsley & Liberty, 1982; White & Haring, 1980). Time-based data may then be employed in conjunction with data-based decision rules such as those provided by Haring, Liberty, and White (1980) to determine when and what to change if the program is unsuccessful, when to continue the program unchanged, and when to move to the next step. A significant outcome of personnel preparation programs, therefore, should be that graduates are prepared to evaluate pupil performance along dimensions critical to functioning within natural environments and to determine, on the basis of evaluation data, when and what changes should be implemented to assure instructional success.

Parent Education

There is a desperate need to build or strengthen the relationship between home and school. The essential commitment to the right of all to live in a home setting, to interact with parents and siblings, and to share the joys of a natural environment has come to be accepted by all who work with severely handicapped individuals. The development of education programs for parents—based on this commitment—requires systematic examination of the emotional and physical demands placed on the family, and the dynamics of family life as they are affected by the presence of a family member with severe handicaps.

A competent educator of severely handicapped students is one who can facilitate parent-school interactions and assist parents in developing the skills necessary to effect change in their child's behavior. The partnership between home and school can be greatly enhanced by effective training in parent education.

Curriculum Development

Just as assessment practices must pinpoint areas of strength and weakness in the development of functional skills, curricula for severely handicapped students must be built around functional objectives. Commercially available curricula based upon the normal developmental sequence possess the same weakness as do assessment instruments based upon normal development; i.e., they may contribute to the implementation of instructional programs that have a negligible impact on the ability of the pupil to function within natural environments. Although educators of severely handicapped pupils have almost always found it necessary to adapt existing curricula to the needs of individual pupils, the development of curricula comprised of functional objectives requires a different approach. A new curriculum strategy must be applied, using ecological inventories (Brown et al., 1979) to determine work and work-related skills, recreational activities, and domestic and general community-functioning skills that have the most relevance to individual pupils. Individualized curriculum building is a task likely to be unfamiliar to most educators. As the curriculum provides the structure within which programming will occur, the development of ecologically valid curricula is an area that deserves close attention in personnel training programs.

The Scientific Orientation to Instruction

The investment of significant effort in the education of severely handicapped individuals is a relatively recent phenomenon. The provision of training in natural, integrated settings is even more recent. Educators, therefore, must be active consumers of research literature in order to keep informed on the best instructional methods, and should strive, as well, to incorporate relevant research findings into their programs. The effective use of research requires that educators be able to differentiate the valuable and believable from the trivial or suspect. This ability is often difficult and may be impossible without formal training in research methodology and interpretation. In addition, the natural environment is replete with variables that may facilitate or hinder our programming efforts. The educator must, therefore, conduct systematic observations and undertake precise analyses of those variables that may maintain, strengthen, or weaken behaviors. In effect each program becomes a mini-experiment, the results of which should conribute to the educator's fund of instructional knowledge. Better education of severely handicapped students is possible if our personnel preparation programs train graduates to interpret and utilize research findings accurately as well as to apply the scientific method to the instructional process.

CONCLUSIONS

This chapter has conceptualized professional preparation that trains professional educators working with severely handicapped students to employ systems-change strategies in a wide variety of communities, whether in sparsely populated rural areas or densely populated metropolitan areas. This training should enable educators to identify the primary community agencies and forces that can help to change the environment so it will accept, integrate, and involve severely handicapped individuals as productively as possible.

If educators are to train severely handicapped students to work and live, as much as possible, within the community, they must be able to identify and develop methods to teach behaviors necessary for success in integrated settings. They must also be able to provide their students with the information, skills, and experiences necessary to make the transition to the community, to use community services, and to live in alternate residential settings. Moreover, future professionals must learn to function as educational synthesizers by coordinating a comprehensive transdisciplinary team of professionals, paraprofessionals, and family members. Ultimately, educators must help to train the community-at-large to accept handicapped persons as individuals with an equal right to and stake in the benefits of the normal environment.

Preparation programs must give educators a broad conceptual base in related disciplines and field-based practica in settings that use the systems-change model. Only then can the systems-change model be fully implemented and severely handicapped individuals have the full opportunity for integration into the community.

REFERENCES

Adams, M.E. Foster care for mentally retarded children: How does child welfare meet this challenge? *Child Welfare,* 1970, *49,* 260–269.

Baer, D.M., Wolf, M.M., & Risley, T.R. Some current dimensions of applied behavior analysis. *Journal of Applied Behavior Analysis,* 1968, *1,* 91–97.

Baker, B.L., Seltzer, G., & Seltzer, M. *As close as possible.* Boston: Little, Brown and Co., 1977.

Barrett, B.H., Communitization and the measured message of normal behavior. In: R.L. York & E. Edgar (eds.), *Teaching the severely handicapped,* Vol. 4. Seattle: American Association for the Education of the Severely/Profoundly Handicapped, 1979.

Bell, N. IQ as a factor in community lifestyle of previously institutionalized retardates. *Mental Retardation,* 1976, *14* (3), 29–33.

Bellamy, T., Peterson, L., & Close, D. Habilitation of the severely and profoundly retarded: Illustration of competencies. *Education and Training of the Mentally Retarded,* 1975, *10,* 174–186.

Billingsley, F.F., & Liberty, K.A. The use of time-based data in instructional programs for the severely handicapped. *Journal of The Association for the Severely Handicapped,* 1982, *7*(1), 47–55.

Bricker, D.D. Educational synthesizer. In: M.A. Thomas (ed.), *Hey, don't forget about me! Education's investment in the severely and profoundly handicapped.* Reston, VA: The Council for Exceptional Children, 1976.

Bronfenbrenner, U. *Is early intervention effective?* Washington, D.C.: U.S. Department of Health, Education and Welfare, Office of Child Development, Publication (OHD) 74–25, 1974.

Brown, L., Branston-McClean, M.B., Baumgart, D., Vincent, L., Falvey, M., & Schroeder, J. Using the characteristics of current and subsequent least restrictive environments in the development of curricular content for severely handicapped students. *AAESPH Review,* 1979, *4,* 407–424.

Brown, L., Nietupski, J., & Hamre-Nietupski, S. Criterion of ultimate functioning. In: M.A. Thomas (ed.), *Hey, don't forget about me! Education's investment in the severely and profoundly handicapped.* Reston, VA: The Council for Exceptional Children, 1976.

Crowner, T.T. Developing and administering programs for severely and profoundly handicapped students in public school systems. In: R.L. York & E. Edgar (eds.), *Teaching the severely handicapped,* Vol. 4. Seattle: American Association for the Education of the Severely/Profoundly Handicapped, 1979.

Cuvo, A.J., Leaf, R.B., & Borakove, L.S. Teaching janitorial skills to the mentally retarded: Acquisition, generalization and maintenance. *Journal of Applied Behavior Analysis,* 1978, *11,* 345–355.

Gollay, E., Freedman, R., Wyngaarden, M., & Kurtz, N.R. *Coming back.* Cambridge, MA: Abt Books, 1978.

Haring, N.G. (ed.). *The experimental education training program.* Seattle: University of Washington, 1977.

Haring, N.G. Review and analysis of professional preparation for the severely handicapped. In: B. Wilcox & R. York (eds.). *Quality education for the severely handicapped: The federal investment.* Washington, D.C.: U.S. Department of Education, Office of Special Education, Division of Innovation and Development, 1980.

Haring, N.G., & Bricker, D. Overview of comprehensive services for the severely/profoundly handicapped. In: N.G. Haring & L.J. Brown (eds.), *Teaching the severely handicapped,* Vol. 1. New York: Grune & Stratton, 1976.

Haring, N.G., Liberty, K.A., & White, O.R. Rules for data-based strategy decisions in instructional programs: Current research and instructional implications. In: W. Sailor, B. Wilcox & L. Brown (eds.), *Methods of instruction for the severely handicapped.* Baltimore: Paul H. Brookes Publishing Co., 1980.

Haring, N.G., & Lynch, V. *State-wide systems change model for severely handicapped children and youth*. Division of Innovation and Development, Office of Special Education and Rehabilitation, U.S. Office of Education, Contract no. 300800753. 1981.

Haring, N.G., & Pious, C. Future directions in work with severely and profoundly handicapped persons: An overview. In: N.G. Haring & L.J. Brown (eds.), *Teaching the severely handicapped*, Vol. 1. New York: Grune & Stratton, 1976.

Hart, V. The use of many disciplines with the severely and profoundly handicapped. In: E. Sontag, J. Smith, & N. Certo (eds.), *Educational programming for the severely and profoundly handicapped*. Reston, VA: The Council for Exceptional Children, 1977.

Iacino, R., & Bricker, D. The generative teacher: A model for preparing personnel to work with the severely/profoundly handicapped. In: N.G. Haring & D.D. Bricker (eds.), *Teaching the severely handicapped*, Vol. 3. Seattle: American Association for the Education of the Severely/Profoundly Handicapped, 1978.

Kenowitz, L.A. Identifying services for the severely handicapped. In: R.L. York & E. Edgar (eds.), *Teaching the severely handicapped*, Vol. 4. Seattle: America Association for the Education of the Severely/Profoundly Handicapped, 1979.

Larsen, L.A. Community services necessary to program effectively for the severely/profoundly handicapped. In: E. Sontag (ed.), *Educational programming for the severely and profoundly handicapped*. Reston, VA: Division on Mental Retardation, The Council for Exceptional Children, 1977.

Lynch, V., McGuigan, C., & Shoemaker, S. An introduction to systematic instruction. In: N.G. Haring (ed.), *The experimental education training program*. Seattle: University of Washington, 1977.

President's Committee on Mental Retardation. *Mental retardation: Century of decision* (Report to the President). Washington, D.C.: U.S. Government Printing Office, 1976.

Public Law 94-142, *Education for All Handicapped Children Act*, 1975.

Reynolds, M.C., & Birch, J.W. *Teaching exceptional children in all America's schools*. Reston, VA: The Council for Exceptional Children, 1977.

Ruch, F.L. *Psychology and life* (7th ed.). Glenview, IL: Scott, Foresman and Co., 1967.

Scheerenberger, R.C. A model for deinstitutionalization. *Mental Retardation*, 1974, *12*, 3–7.

Scheerenberger, R.C. *Current trends and status of public residential services for the mentally retarded: 1974*. Madison, WI: National Association of Superintendents of Public Residential Facilities of the Mentally Retarded, Central Wisconsin Center for the Developmentally Disabled, 1975.

Scheerenberger, R.C. *Public residential services for the mentally retarded*. Madison, WI: National Association of Superintendents of Public Residential Facilities for the Mentally Retarded, Central Wisconsin Center for the Developmentally Disabled, 1976.

Scheerenberger, R.C. *Public residential services for the mentally retarded*. Madison, WI: National Association of Superintendents of Public Residential Facilities for the Mentally Retarded, Central Wisconsin Center for the Developmentally Disabled, 1978.

Schreibman, L., & Koegel, R.L. A guideline for planning behavior modification programs for autistic children. In: S.M. Turner, K.S. Calhoun, & M.E. Adams (eds.), *Handbook of clinical behavior therapy*. New York: John Wiley & Sons, 1975.

Schulman, E.D. *Focus on the retarded adult: Programs and services*. St. Louis: C.V. Mosby Co., 1980.

Smith, D.D., & Smith, J.O. Trends. In: M.E. Snell (ed.), *Systematic instruction of the moderately and severely handicapped*. Columbus, OH: Charles E. Merrill Publishing Co., 1978.

Sontag, E., Smith, J., & Certo, N. (eds.) *Educational programming for the severely and profoundly handicapped*. Reston, VA: Division of Mental Retardation, The Council for Exceptional Children, 1977.

Sowers, J., Thompson, L.E., & Connis, R.T. The food service vocational training program: A model for training and placement of the mentally retarded. In: G.T. Bellamy,

G. O'Connor, & O.C. Karan (eds.), *Vocational rehabilitation of severely handicapped persons*. Baltimore: University Park Press, 1979.

Stainback, S., Stainback, W., & Maurer, S. Training teachers for the severely and profoundly handicapped: A new frontier. *Exceptional Children*, 1976, *42*, 203–210.

Stedman, D.J., & Eichorn, D.H. A comparison of the growth and development of institutionalized and home-reared mongoloids during infancy and early childhood. *American Journal of Mental Deficiency*, 1964, *69*, 391–401.

Sternat, J., Messina, R., Nietupski, J., Lyon, S., & Brown, L. Occupational and physical therapy services for severely handicapped students: Toward a naturalized public school service delivery mode. In: E. Sontag, J.J. Smith & N. Certo (eds.), *Educational programming for the severely and profoundly handicapped*. Reston, VA: The Council for Exceptional Children, 1977.

Thorndike, E.L. The law of effect. *American Journal of Psychology*, 1927, *39*, 212–222.

White, O.R., & Haring, N.G. *Exceptional teaching* (2nd ed.). Columbus, OH: Charles E. Merrill Publishing Co., 1980.

Wilcox, B. A competency-based approach to preparing teachers of the severely and profoundly handicapped: Perspective I. In: E. Sontag (ed.), *Educational programming for the severely and profoundly handicapped*. Reston, VA: Division on Mental Retardation, The Council for Exceptional Children, 1977.

Wyngaarden, J., Freedman, R., & Gollay, E. *Descriptive data on the community experiences of deinstitutionalized mentally retarded persons. A study of the community adjustment of deinstitutionalized mentally retarded persons*, Vol. 4. U.S. Office of Education, Contract No. OEC-0-74-9183. Cambridge, MA: Abt Associates, Inc., 1976.

REFERENCE NOTE

1. Galloway, C. Hearing: Impact of continuum of services on people with disabilities. Testimony to the California Senate Subcommittee on Disabilities, Sacramento, October 29, 1979.

6

Preparing School Systems for Longitudinal Integration Efforts

Susan Hamre-Nietupski,
John Nietupski, William Stainback,
and Susan Stainback

Throughout the nation, parents, educators and others vitally concerned with the welfare of severely handicapped students are attempting to determine the least restrictive environment (LRE) for this population. Of the considerable debate that has surrounded the topic, much has centered on the issue of student placement. While several authors have voiced strong opposition to regular school placement (Burton & Hirschoren, 1979 a,b), others have argued forcefully in support of self-contained classes in regular schools (Brown, Branston, Hamre-Nietupski, Johnson, Wilcox, & Gruenewald, 1979; Sontag, Certo, & Button, 1979). As space does not allow an in-depth discussion of the debate, Table 1 summarizes the major arguments.

In discussing the fact that the debate over least restrictive environment has revolved around the narrow aspect of physical placement (i.e., where a student is placed), Kenowitz, Zweibel, and Edgar (1978) state, and the authors concur, that a careful examination of what constitutes a least restrictive environment must be conducted before the issue can be resolved.

Table 1. Arguments for and against regular school placement

Arguments against regular school placement		Counter-arguments in support of regular school placement
1. Ancillary services are more efficiently delivered in a segregated facility.	1a.	Use of integrated therapy model (Nietupski, Hamre-Nietupski, Schuetz, & Ockwood, 1980; Sternat, Nietupski, Lyon, Messina, & Brown, 1977) is as/more efficient.
	1b.	Longitudinal needs of severely handicapped students override administrative efficiency concerns.
2. Architectural barriers are eliminated in segregated facilities.	2a.	Segregated facilities are not necessarily barrier-free.
	2b.	Not all severely handicapped students require barrier-free environments.
	2c.	Law precludes exclusion of severely handicapped students from regular schools on the basis of handicap.
3. Social relationships among students of similar functioning levels are more easily developed. Teasing, abuse, and exploitation more likely in integrated settings.	3a.	The demands of the present and future "real world" require ability to interact with nonhandicapped population.
	3b.	Severely handicapped students cannot be prepared to meet real-world demands if school years do not provide such opportunities.
	3c.	The risk of teasing, etc., to severely handicapped students is no greater than for nonhandicapped students; all are exposed to risk.
	3d.	Tolerance/understanding of severely handicapped persons by the general population is extremely unlikely if segregation continues.
4. Nonhandicapped students suffer socio-emotional trauma.	4a.	Initial reactions toward severely handicapped students may be negative, due to lack of exposure and understanding. This can change with structured interaction.
	4b.	Research indicates no negative effects on behavior of nonhandicapped students (Guralnick, in press).

Utilizing a continuum of placement options (Figure 1), proponents of regular school placement have argued that options farther to the right on the continuum represent lesser degrees of restrictiveness. Proponents apparently recognize that

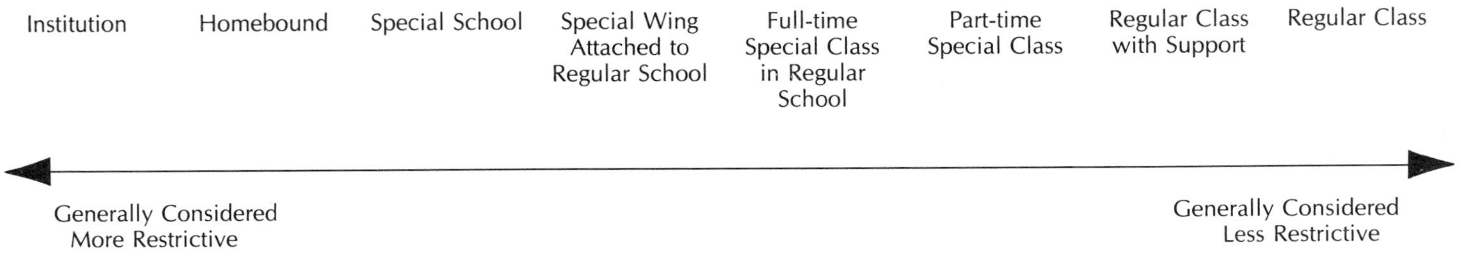

Institution   Homebound   Special School   Special Wing   Full-time   Part-time   Regular Class   Regular Class
                                              Attached to   Special Class Special Class with Support
                                              Regular School in Regular
                                                              School

Generally Considered   Generally Considered
More Restrictive   Less Restrictive

Figure 1. A continuum of placement options.

the divergent educational needs of severely handicapped students must be taken into account, as regular class placement has not been advocated. However, it is generally assumed that placements that involve close physical proximity with nonhandicappd peers are less restrictive than physically segregated options.

Unfortunately, the failure of some administrators and educators to consider factors other than placement option gives rise to, and potential support for, arguments against regular school placement. School districts cannot assume that in placing severely handicapped students in regular schools an LRE automatically is achieved. If regular school placement results in relegation to basement or remote classrooms, separate entrances and exits, differing arrival and departure hours, separate lunch hours or lunchrooms, separate playground areas, or extensive taunting, it might be argued that regular schools do not represent a least restrictive environment for severely handicapped students. From this perspective, a segregated facility in which students are not confined or ridiculed might be considered by some to be less restrictive.

However, the fact that isolation and occasional teasing might have occurred in some instances in regular school placement should not be viewed as justification for segregated facilities. In the authors' experience such negative occurrences are infrequent, although even nonhandicapped students occasionally are teased. Rather, such negative occurrences demonstrate the need for a broader concept of LRE. As Kenowitz et al. (1978) emphasize, least restrictiveness should involve not only placement in close physical proximity with nonhandicapped peers but also *ongoing, meaningful, positive interactions* between severely handicapped and nonhandicapped students. Thus, educators need to concern themselves not only with securing regular school placement for severely handicapped students, but also with promoting positive interaction experiences between nonhandicapped and handicapped students.

Severely handicapped students can function in regular school environments, particularly when systematic efforts to involve them in the regular school milieu are continually made. The success of reported integration efforts (Almond, Rodgers, & Krug, 1979; Donder & Nietupski, 1981; McHale & Simeonsson, 1980; Poorman, 1980; Rynders, Johnson, Johnson, & Schmidt, 1980; Voeltz, 1980, 1982) make clear that mutual benefits for severely handicapped and nonhandicapped students can accrue through close physical proximity combined with structured interaction opportunities.

This chapter describes factors to consider in the transition to regular schools; staff and student preparation for integration; and procedures for assessing the effectiveness of integration efforts.

FACTORS TO CONSIDER IN THE TRANSITION TO REGULAR SCHOOLS

School Selection Factors

Kenowitz et al. (1978) report that approximately 70% of programs for moderately and severely handicapped students are located in segregated facilities. This being the case, most districts adopting an integrative model will be required to select the school(s) appropriate to house severely handicapped students. Several factors should be considered in selecting regular school sites. The first is the *chronological age* (CA) of students. It is extremely difficult for example, for educators to promote normalized interactions if elementary schools house 16–21-year-old severely handicapped students. In school districts such as Madison and Milwaukee, Wisconsin, general age guidelines are employed (e.g., preschool–13 CA in elementary schools; 13–16 CA in middle/junior high; 17–21 CA in high school). Rural districts, which typically serve fewer students, may have only elementary/ high school placements. For example, Maquoketa, Iowa, (population: 5,700) plans to serve preschool–14-year-old severely handicapped students in an elementary school and 15–21-year-olds in the high school.

A second factor in school selection is *building accessibility*. School districts need not assume that placement in regular schools automatically necessitates expensive building modification. Some severely handicapped students may not require any modifications. Furthermore, it may not be necessary to make the entire school immediately accessible. Of major importance is that school entrances used by the nonhandicapped student population and primary use areas (e.g., lunchroom, gymnasium, library, home economics classes, workshop) be accessible. The fact that a high school houses its chemistry, foreign language, and mathematics units, for example, in an inaccessible area, need not preclude consideration of this school. However, inaccessibility to areas regularly used by nonhandicapped students, such as lunchrooms, might suggest consideration of building modifications or another site.

A third and extremely important factor is the *receptiveness of the school staff*, particularly the principal. In the authors' experience, sites with supportive principals are more conducive to integration. Special education administrators should work closely with regular education central office personnel to identify and communicate with principals who are interested in serving severely handicapped populations. This is not to say that schools with reluctant or hesitant principals should be avoided. As later discussed in this chapter, methods for actively involving principals in integration efforts can be employed. However, given a choice between a site with a supportive principal and one whose principal is indifferent or antagonistic, the former site should be given more serious consideration.

A fourth factor to consider is the *number of classes* at any one site. Problems with delivery of ancillary services (e.g., speech/language; occupational/physical therapy) and with teacher isolation are more serious if several one-class sites are employed. On the other hand, overloading a school with classes for severely handicapped students runs the risk of creating a segregated school within a school. If student numbers are sufficient, administrators should consider placing at least two, and at most three, classes in one site. In this manner, it might be possible to balance concerns over teacher isolation and ancillary service delivery with the problem of the percentage of severely handicapped students at any one site.

Obviously, rural districts may not have sufficient numbers to allow for several classes within one site. In this case, it may be beneficial to consider placement in sites that house a class for mildly handicapped students or low incidence populations such as deaf or visually impaired students. In this way, the teacher of severely handicapped students may not feel as isolated from special education peers.

A fifth factor, one that may be more appropriate in larger urban areas, is to consider the establishment of *geographical articulation units;* that is, one might divide a large city into two or three geographical districts and establish programs at elementary, middle/junior high and senior high school levels for severely handicapped students residing in those districts. Severely handicapped students might thus encounter some of the same nonhandicapped students throughout their school years. An additional advantage of this arrangement is a possible reduction in transportation costs and time.

The above five factors are not all-inclusive, but were selected merely as a starting point for districts contemplating the transition to regular schools.

Establishing Environmental Arrangements and Routines That Facilitate Interaction Opportunities

Prior to the move to regular public schools, it is important that administrative staffs (both regular and special education), representatives from the regular and special education teaching staffs, and, possibly, parent representatives jointly consider a variety of environmental arrangement factors that may affect the extent of integration. First, efforts should be made to *locate classrooms amidst classrooms for nonhandicapped students*. The location of classes for severely handicapped students in the regular school buildings can influence positively the number of daily interaction opportunities.

A second consideration is *separating individual classes for severely handicapped students* so that they are not all in one area of a hallway or building. Such arrangements may increase the probability that special educators will interact with teachers of nonhandicapped students, with the added result that the special education program is not perceived as separate from other programs in the building.

A third consideration is arranging for severely handicapped students to *share common building entrances and arrival/departure times with their nonhandicapped peers*. A frequent practice when programs for severely handicapped students are first placed in regular schools is to establish different entrances and/or arrival and departure hours. Often the rationale is to minimize potential ridicule and abuse of the handicapped students. Unfortunately, once such arrangements are made, they are difficult to modify (Nietupski, Hamre-Nietupski, Schuetz, & Ockwood, 1980), and are often maintained long after any need exists. It is thus important for school districts initially to establish normalized routines and attempt to prevent/solve potential problems through procedures discussed, for example, in the following section of this chapter, rather than to create unnecessary nonnormalized routines. Often, anticipated problems fail to materialize or can be remedied with minimal effort.

The *lunchroom routine* is a fourth consideration. It is common practice either to restrict severely handicapped students to their classrooms for lunch, or not have them use the lunch line and/or seat them at separate lunchroom tables (Donder, Hamre-Nietupski, Nietupski, & Fortschneider, Note 1). Since the lunchroom represents a major interaction opportunity, schools should consider arranging for severely handicapped students to use the lunchroom just as their nonhandicapped peers do, perhaps with the assistance of nonhandicapped student partners (Nietupski et al., 1980). If modified routines are considered essential, it is important to target an early date after which regular lunchroom use will be expected. The short time between the start of the school year and this targeted date might then be used to train students and/or make accommodations for more normalized lunchroom use. If a modified routine is employed, it is crucial that the date to begin regular lunchroom use be specified and adhered to. Failure to do so may result in a permanent, nonnormal, stigmatizing situation.

A fifth consideration is *providing for "specials"* such as art, music, adaptive physical education, library, home economics, and so on. Since most nonhandicapped students go to a music room, art room, gym, etc., for these activities, it is suggested that severely handicapped students do likewise, thus affording them a more normalized routine and the opportunity to interact with nonhandicapped students in the hallway.

A sixth consideration is arranging for severely handicapped students to *share the playground area with their nonhandicapped peers*. In one midwestern community, parents of nonhandicapped students advocated a fence separating their students from the moderately and severely handicapped school population. To the administrator's credit, she successfully resisted such attempts. While adapted playground equipment may be necessary, there is little reason to locate it in separate areas of the playground or to restrict its use to severely handicapped students.

A seventh consideration is arranging for severely handicapped students to *follow the daily routine experienced by the nonhandicapped school population*. This includes observing between-period break times, moving in the hallway between classes, attending school assemblies, and so forth. Following a normalized routine further helps to create a sense of unity between the program for handicapped students and the rest of the school and provides, as well, for additional interaction opportunities.

As in the previous section, the above seven considerations are not intended to be exhaustive. Given the potential effects of physical arrangements and routines on the number and types of interactions, both should be addressed prior to, as well as subsequent to, the transition to regular school sites.

STAFF AND STUDENT PREPARATION FOR INTEGRATION

In addition to considering factors of school selection and physical arrangement, regular school staff and students also must be prepared for the integration of severely handicapped students. With appropriate preparation of both staff and students, severely handicapped students can become integrally involved in regular public schools throughout a school district. Without appropriate preparation, the exact opposite could occur; severely handicapped students attending a regular school could have few, none, or predominantly negative interactions with other persons in those environments. "Preparation" involves employing a variety of procedures to promote positive interactions between severely handicapped students and their teachers with other students and staff members. Those staff members needing preparation include, at a minimum, administrators (e.g., principals), regular education teachers, special education teachers, paraprofessionals, support service personnel (e.g., physical and occupational therapists, program support teachers), and secretarial, custodial, and lunchroom personnel (the term "staff" in this chapter henceforth refers to any of these members). Those students needing peparation would include, at a minimum, nonhandicapped students, severely handicapped students, and other handicapped students.

The following two sections of this chapter suggest methods for preparing staff and students for integration. Recent research has documented the effectiveness of several of the procedures discussed (Donaldson, 1980; Stainback & Stainback, Note 2). All of the procedures described have been employed on a systemwide basis within the Milwaukee (Wisconsin) Public Schools to integrate approximately 80 students with moderate to profound levels of retardation into regular elementary, middle, and high schools from 1979 to 1981. The procedures are recommended on the basis of clinical evidence of their apparent effectiveness (e.g., positive comments from administrators and regular special education faculty; positive responses by nonhandicapped students in the form of comments and offers to participate in activities with severely handicapped students; and positive comments by parents and school board members).

As a general caution, experience gained through integration efforts, such as those carried out in Milwaukee, suggests that a *combination* of procedures must be employed on a *longitudinal* basis. In other words, a variety of procedures for integration must be adhered to continuously throughout the school year. It is also necessary to maintain these procedures from year to year, while possibly adding new procedures to accommodate new handicapped and nonhandicapped students as well as new staff. (For example, to hold one all-school student assembly program at the beginning of the school year to discuss having severely handicapped students in the building is insufficient.) It is highly probable that isolated, infrequent use of the procedures suggested here will have minimal positive impact on the integration of severely handicapped students.

Both the procedures outlined below for staff, as well as those that follow for students could be used for a) *advance* preparation prior to the transition of severely handicapped students into regular public schools; and for b) *continued* preparation, to be used subsequent to the transition of severely handicapped students into regular schools.

Staff Preparation and Involvement

A staff member and/or consultant whose major responsibility is the integration of severely handicapped students on a system-wide basis could be employed. This person or persons could be responsible for planning and implementing efforts to integrate severely handicapped students within the regular schools throughout the school system. Responsibilities might include planning with special and regular education classroom teachers and administrators, conducting information sessions with students and staff, and formally evaluating integration efforts. The authors' experience would suggest that a staff member within the school system may be able to organize and implement integration efforts on a day-to-day basis more effectively than a part-time consultant. While a part-time consultant could participate directly in integration efforts, his or her primary role might be to work with the school system on the long-term planning for, and formal evaluation of, integration efforts. If a full-time consultant cannot be hired to handle both integration activities and evaluation, a designated person within the school system should be given responsibility for the day-to-day integration activities and held accountable. However, this should be looked upon as a temporary solution, and a full-time person hired as soon as possible.

Information sessions to explain integrating efforts could be presented to all staff. Prior to school opening, information sessions could be provided on several occasions for all staff members who will be in contact with severely handicapped students. Included should be administrators, staff in direct teaching roles, support staff, as well as nonteaching staff (e.g., secretaries, custodians, lunchroom personnel). Special and regular education staff should meet jointly whenever possible. An initial information session could be presented prior to transferring severely handicapped students (e.g., in the spring and/or summer) and might include accurate information on specific handicapping conditions, the goals of integrating severely handicapped students, and federal and state legislation related to integration. At this initial session, staff members could generate their own ideas for possible integration procedures.

Subsequent information sessions could be provided after integration efforts are well underway. These sessions might include, for example, information on: 1) the success of developing interactions between severely handicapped students and their nonhandicapped peers in nonacademic and/or academic situations in the regular school; and 2) systematic attempts to prepare students and staff for integration and to alter staff attitudes toward having severely handicapped students in the school. The authors' experience suggests that these subsequent sessions are most effective when classroom teachers of the severely handicapped students serve as presenters. Remuneration in the form of inservice training salary or credit benefits could be provided staff members who serve as presenters or participants.

Special and regular school visits for staff members could be arranged. Prior to the school year in which integration is to occur, special education staff could visit the selected school building to observe various aspects of the school environment, including entrances, hallways, bathrooms, regular classrooms, and possible physical barriers. Visits when school is in session are useful for obtaining general information about, for example, the student population, the daily schedule, and age-appropriate behaviors that may help special education staff prepare severely handicapped students for the transition to the regular school environment. Visits to the special education school/classroom(s) should assist the regular education staff to understand the needs of severely handicapped students and to appreciate how relocation in regular public schools can meet these needs.

Advance planning for building usage and scheduling could be performed. As indicated earlier, meetings prior to the transfer of severely handicapped students can be held to discuss issues such as the location of the classroom; what entrance(s) will be used; and lunchroom procedures. As already stated, the authors found that many modifications in typical school routines (e.g., early lunchroom arrival or departure, entering school at a separate door, sitting at a separate lunch table), made ostensibly to minimize possible difficulties for severely handicapped students, either were unnecessary or soon became unnecessary. Thus, it is strongly suggested that care be taken in contemplating modifications and that they be minimized or avoided if possible.

If initial modifications are planned, it would be appropriate at these meetings to discuss procedures for terminating the arrangements as the school year progresses (e.g., severely handicapped students will arrive at lunch 5 minutes early initially, but eventually will be expected to arrive at the same time as their nonhandicapped peers). It is important that all staff view arrangements as *flexible* and adaptable to the changing behavior and needs of students. Failure to emphasize the temporary nature of initial arrangements may result in difficulty in changing those arrangements. It may be necessary to conduct similar meetings throughout the school year to alter the situations as necessary.

Meetings might also deal with issues such as the manner in which the severely handicapped students' physical education, art, music, occupational and physical therapy, and communication therapy needs can be met within the regular school building. Such a meeting would require transdisciplinary input from many persons, possibly including the building principal; regular and adaptive physical education, art, and music teachers; special education staff; regular education staff; occupational therapists; physical therapists; and communication therapists. If regular education teacher(s) are to include severely handicapped students in their programming, other specific issues may need to be addressed, including scheduling, entering skills, appropriate curriculum objectives, and the amount of support needed from the special education staff, for example.

Arrangements for maximum use of school facilities for severely handicapped students could be made. In order to maximize interaction opportunities between severely handicapped students and other students, it is important that, whenever possible, severely handicapped students use the same school facilities at the same times as nonhandicapped or other handicapped students. For example, the following interaction opportunities might be considered: beginning and ending the school day at the same time as the nonhandicapped school population; using the same transportation (school bus, city bus, walking, etc.) to and from school; using school entrances and exits that nonhandicapped students use; sharing the same recess times on the same parts of the playground; using the same bathrooms; having lunch at the same time and sharing the lunchroom and lunch tables; occupying the library at the same times; and attending the same school assemblies. Again, it should be emphasized that arrangements made prior to or at the beginning of the school year should be flexible and subject to change during the year as students acquire new skills.

A "drop-in" to discuss integration questions could be held. Both regular and special education staff members may have questions concerning the integration of severely handicapped students into the regular education building. Administrators, supervisors, program support persons, and/or other persons involved with the integration efforts could make themselves available in each integration site for an informal "drop-in" to answer questions. For example, in the spring, prior to the fall arrival of severely handicapped students, a "drop-in" could be held in the regular school staff lounge, at which personnel would be available for informal discussion. Refreshments could be provided as further inducement to attend. Staff members who may not feel comfortable asking questions or commenting about the integration of severely handicapped students in a staff meeting often will tend to discuss their concerns in a less formal gathering. The authors found that after refreshments and small talk, many teachers asked numerous questions and expressed interest in the program. Teachers also indicated that they were not as apprehensive at the prospects of having severely handicapped students in their school as a result of the get-together.

Additional support personnel initially could be provided at the integration sites. In order to help ensure a smooth transition of severely handicapped students into regular school buildings, supportive personnel, such as program support teachers, could be assigned to assist the program during the initial weeks of the semester. Assistance could be provided in potential problem areas, such as: getting on and off the bus; using correct entrances and exits; building orientation, including locating classrooms, bathrooms, and offices; using lockers and locks; following lunchroom procedures; and using recess time appropriately. This extra support can greatly assist special education teachers and severely handicapped students, and can serve to minimize "beginning of the school year hassles" for staff and building principals. Additional support gradually should be phased out as students acquire necessary skills.

An "open door" visitation policy for special education classroom(s) could be offered. When severely handicapped students first begin attending a regular public school, the staff and other students will likely display an increased interest in the special education classrooms. Special education teachers can make other staff members feel welcome in their classrooms by announcing a willingness to have visitors. Nonhandicapped students who express interest in observing in the special education classroom could, with permission (e.g., study hall passes, hall passes), spend time there. As appropriate, visitors could observe ongoing instruction, observe the room and its materials, and possibly interact with the handicapped students. This policy may serve to remove some of the "mystery" that often surrounds a special education classroom, and eventually could lead to having observers—other students or staff members—work with the severely handicapped students.

A contact person(s) to facilitate integration activities within each integrated school site could be identified. Many schools have a person (or persons) whose responsibilities include working with other faculty in planning school or department-wide activities. Such a person(s) often can assist the special education staff in organizing integration activities. Examples of such persons would include a school curriculum coordinator, a human relations or human services coordinator, a department or subject chairperson, or a head teacher. This person can be an extremely helpful resource for information on, for example, scheduling groups of staff and students, curriculum areas by grade level, and special upcoming events. In particular, this person may be able to easily contact, gain information from, or pass information to, both staff and students within a school. Since many preparation procedures require considerable planning and cooperation and time investment from many persons involved, the assistance of such a contact person can improve program efficiency.

A training course for teachers on sensitizing nonhandicapped students to their handicapped peers could be offered. Such a course might include information about methods of dealing with possible negative attitudes and fears of nonhandicapped students, arranging for positive interactions between nonhandicapped and handicapped students, and exposure to media that provide students with information about handicaps. As an incentive for teacher participation in such a course, inservice credit toward salary advancement might be offered. Should the school system not provide a course, it may be possible to attend a course at a local college or university. Staff members who participate in the course could be instrumental in leading/assisting their students as well as their professional peers in school integration activities.

Special education teachers could join with a "team" of teachers. Special education faculty members could join with a "team" of teachers, such as the "seventh grade team" or the "social studies department" to plan cooperative activities, exchange students as appropriate, share resources, and organize scheduling. In many school districts, this would necessitate working with the building administration.

Staff members could be made aware of media available for sensitizing nonhandicapped students to their handicapped peers. Both special and regular education staff members could be informed of relevant media by being involved in presentations of examples of books, filmstrips, and movies that might be age-appropriate for nonhandicapped students in the school. A brief media presentation might be given by the consultant (on integration) at a staff meeting, for example. Media reference lists might be provided to staff members and also made available in the school instructional materials center/library for staff members as well as students to check out. (For further information on media references for elementary/middle and middle/high school, the reader is referred to Nietupski et al., 1980.)

Special education staff members could be encouraged to spend time in the regular staff lounge. In most schools, the staff lounge provides a place for teachers to take a break from their daily instructional responsibilities. Congregating in the lounge provides special and regular education staff members a chance to get to know one another. The lounge also provides opportunities to discuss and compare objectives, methods, and new "units." If special education staff members typically use a separate lounge area, those staff members could spend at least a portion of their break time in the regular education staff lounge. Since it is probable that different lounges for special and regular education staff only serve to segregate them (and, in turn, their students) from each other, eliminating the separate lounge areas is recommended.

Information could be provided to special education teachers who may be sending additional handicapped students to the integrated site in the future. For severely handicapped students who are still in self-contained settings, important information concerning the type of behaviors/skills conducive to successful integration in the regular school can be provided their teachers. Such information should *not* be provided in order to exclude any student from being integrated into a regular school. Rather, it could be used to refine tasks and curriculum objectives in use in the self-contained setting to more accurately reflect skills functional in regular school settings. This information might include, for example, age-appropriate dress, use of lockers, and behaviors expected in hallways, bathrooms, cafeteria, assemblies, and free time. As an extension of this information-sharing process, teachers from the staff of the self-contained school might be provided the option of visiting regular education sites to observe integration activities and daily school routines.

Information regarding integration efforts could be provided through school-wide and/or system-wide newsletters. Many schools and school systems have newsletters that are circulated throughout the school or the school district. Information regarding systematic efforts being made to integrate severely handicapped students could be included in such newsletters. School wide newsletters may serve to increase the visibility of special education programs within that school and give recognition to special and regular education staff and students participating in integration efforts. System-wide newsletters may provide staff members in other schools, who are working with students of varying handicapping conditions, with information on integration efforts they could undertake. The newsletter articles might include brief overviews of formal sensitization sessions, ongoing informal integration activities, and useful printed or audiovisual media. A person, telephone number, and/or central location (see below) for further information could be included. The information could be updated during the year as new activities are implemented.

Copies of integration activity information could be provided in a system-wide central location for staff member use. Specific information such as staff and student information session outlines, sample lesson plans used for combining regular and special education classes, and reference lists of appropriate media might be accumulated in a central location such as a system-wide materials center. This could provide an excellent method for sharing information with other staff interested in implementing integration activities in other schools. Under such an arrangement, staff members might be able to check out and/or duplicate copies of the information.

Documentation of integration activities could be conducted to serve as a model for future integration efforts. Keeping records of integration activities at each school site can facilitate efforts to expand integration. By noting both successful and unsuccessful efforts, future integration attempts might be conducted more efficiently. Attitude change surveys, for both staff and students, might also be conducted as a means of social validation of the success of integration efforts. The reader is referred to the assessment section of this chapter for an in-depth discussion of documentation strategies.

Student Preparation and Involvement

There are a variety of procedures that can be extremely useful for preparing all students for the integration of severely handicapped students. Those students in need of preparation would include, at the least, severely handicapped students, other handicapped students, and nonhandicapped students. As previously indicated for staff preparation, it should be noted that the procedures described may be used for *advance* preparation prior to the transition of severely handicapped students into regular public schools; and for *continued* preparation procedures after the transition.

Information/sensitization sessions could be provided for students. Large group (more than 30 people) or small group information/sensitization sessions could be presented. Large group information/sensitization sessions might include the following general information: A statement of goals for the sessions; explanation of why new handicapped students have been assigned to this particular school; a discussion of inappropriate and appropriate words used to describe the new students; a discussion of some inaccurate (stereotypical) information students might have about handicapped people; presentation of important accurate information about handicaps (the reader is referred to Budoff, Siperstein, and Conant, 1979, for a discussion of nonhandicapped students' deficient knowledge of mental retardation, for example); viewing of a movie or filmstrip related to handicapped people; a question/answer period; and a discussion of integration activities that could take place during the school year. Since large group presentations alone may not result in significant attitude change (Forader, 1970), it is recommended that they *not* be used as the sole method of providing student information/sensitization. If used, large group sessions might best be considered a lead-in to subsequent small group sessions.

Small group sensitization sessions might be held in the nonhandicapped students' regular classrooms, or the nonhandicapped students could be invited to the special education classroom (the severely handicapped students may or may not be in the room at the time). When determining information to be presented in small group sessions, it might be possible to integrate information about handicaps into topics currently being covered in the regular class(es).

Small group presentations might include the following information: A statement of goals for the sessions; more in-depth accurate information about specific handicapping conditions; an instructor-guided group discussion of the similarities and differences between handicapped and nonhandicapped persons (studies by Siperstein, Bak, and Gottleib, 1977, and Donaldson, 1980, recommend that such group discussions be based on information rather than opinion or emotion and that differential reinforcement be provided by the instructor); a discussion of the pros and cons of integrating handicapped peers; simulation activities to experience what it might be like to have a disability; (Clore and Jeffrey, 1972, and Donaldson, 1980, suggest that the most effective simulations are those in which the role-player is perceived as truly disabled rather than play-acting and that enable the role-player to observe the reactions of nondisabled strangers); a live or videotaped presentation made by a successful disabled peer, college student, or adult (Donaldson, 1980, discusses the use of disabled persons as credible presentors); movie/ filmstrip relating to handicapped persons; an ''assignment'' to determine how the media deal with handicapped individuals; viewing slides of the severely handicapped students who will attend the school, portraying them in activities similar to, as well as different from, those in which the nonhandicapped students engage; a discussion of the differences between mental retardation and mental illness; an ''assigned'' written paragraph in which each student describes how he or she could make a severely handicapped student feel more a part of the school; and a discussion of possible follow-up projects in which nonhandicapped students might participate with severely handicapped students. (For more detailed information on possible information/sensitization session content, the reader is referred to Nietupski, et al., 1980.)

Large and small group sessions could be directed by a variety of persons. Classroom teachers, program support persons, supervisors, paraprofessionals, trained student leaders, and the integration consultant are possible group leaders. Sessions could be conducted individually or in teams (e.g., a classroom teacher with a program support person; a trained nonhandicapped student leader with a supervisor).

Although the sessions are designed for nonhandicapped students, any personnel in the school building, including regular and special education classroom teachers and paraprofessionals, therapists, psychologists, social workers, building principals, clerical staff, custodial staff, lunchroom staff, and handicapped students, might be invited to attend. Parents of students within the school and other interested community members (for example, school board members) also might be invited.

Nonhandicapped students could be trained to assist in conducting information/sensitization sessions as student leaders. It is the authors' experience that nonhandicapped students, particularly high school age, can be given information about handicapped students and then trained to serve as student leaders in presenting such information to their peers. Obviously, it is important that prospective student leaders receive accurate general information about severely handicapped students, specific information regarding the handicapped students attending their school, and that they display sensitivity to the needs of handicapped persons. Student leaders could then assist in planning sensitization sessions by offering views on activities they believe their peers might find interesting and informative. The could also assist adult leaders in conducting information/ sensitization sessions. Student leaders can be particularly effective in generating discussion stimulating to their peers. Student leaders could be solicited from classes/groups such as human services, human relations, psychology, student council, or future teachers' clubs.

Information/sensitization sessions could be integrated into the regular education curriculum.   Eventually, if severely handicapped students are to become and remain integral components of their regular school environments, sensitization to handicapped peers should become an established part of ongoing curricula for nonhandicapped students. For example, if, as discussed previously, information/sensitization sessions are presented to social studies classes in a middle school during an ongoing unit on cross-cultural similarities and differences, it would seem appropriate that special education staff members work with social studies teachers to make information on similarities and differences between handicapped and nonhandicapped people a permanent part of the social studies curriculum. As another example, if information/sensitization sessions are being presented to health classes during an ongoing unit on mental illness, special education staff could work with regular education health class teachers to permanently incorporate into the curriculum discussion of the differences between mental retardation and mental illness, and/or the causes and prevention of mental retardation.

Information/sensitization sessions relating to handicapped persons can be incorporated as ongoing units in several other subjects, such as: English, with a discussion, for example, of the treatment of a mentally retarded person in the book *Flowers for Algernon;* "careers" classes, with teachers of severely handicapped students discussing, for example, why they entered special education and the pros and cons of teaching handicapped persons as a profession; and human relations classes, with a discussion of how past and present treatment and rights of handicapped persons parallels society's treatment of minority groups, for example.

In order for sensitization information to become a permanent part of regular education curricula, cooperative planning between special and regular education staff, possibly involving supervisory personnel responsible for curriculum areas on a system-wide basis, is required. Although permanent incorporation of this information into curricula may take several years, building information/ sensitization on handicaps into different subjects in several schools can provide an excellent foundation for such a task.

Nonhandicapped students could serve as tutors or partners of severely handicapped students.   Almond et al. (1979) and Donder and Nietupski (1981) have suggested nonhandicapped students can be effective teachers of their handicapped peers. Beginning with the first day of school, there are many skills severely handicapped students will need to acquire in order to function more independently in the regular school environment. For example, severely handicapped students probably would need skills in becoming oriented to the building, using lockers with locks, eating lunch in a lunchroom filled with nonhandicapped peers, and spending free time on the playground in age-appropriate ways with nonhandicapped peers. Although special education staff members would spend time teaching these and other similar skills, other students may be just as effective in teaching the skills. Other students, particularly after they have received accurate information about their severely handicapped peers and how to work appropriately with them, could serve as partners for a variety of tasks. In one school in the authors' experience, for example, nonhandicapped students who had participated in information/sensitization sessions volunteered to serve as lunch partners. Their "duties" included meeting their handicapped partner at the beginning of the lunch period, sitting with him or her during lunch, modeling age-appropriate lunchroom behaviors, and talking with him or her after lunch. In another school, non-handicapped students volunteered to work in pairs or small groups to teach age-appropriate games and activities to nonhandicapped partners during recess. In still another school, nonhandicapped student volunteers taught playground game skills to severely handicapped students (Donder & Nietupski, 1981). Student partners can be a great resource for teaching a wide variety of skills to their handicapped peers.

Other students also can provide assistance to severely handicapped students and their teachers in special education classrooms. Peer tutors could teach topics designated by the classroom teacher, tutoring, for example, in self-care, communication, or functional academics. They also might tutor severely handicapped students in special classes such as physical education, home economics, music, or art. For example, in one high school setting in the authors' experience, tutors worked on functional word reading tasks in the special education classroom. As another example, tutors in a physical education class in a middle school taught roller skating to handicapped peers and later accompanied them on a trip to a community roller rink.

Nonhandicapped students could write articles for the school newspaper and/or yearbook regarding integration activities. Many schools use school newspapers and the yearbook as a means of informing all students about school events. Students might write articles on the integration of severely handicapped students and report on information/sensitization sessions and other integration activities. In one of the middle schools in the authors' experience, nonhandicapped students "interviewed" some handicapped students, who previously had attended a self-contained school, about the positive and negative aspects of their present integrated school. With teacher direction and parental and school approval, students might take photographs of their handicapped peers and write appropriate accompanying stories to produce their own localized material about handicaps (a take-off on commercial books about handicapped children).

Integration activities could be made a school "objective." In many school groups, certain "objectives" or "priorities" are decided upon by students. Helping to make severely handicapped students become and remain an integral part of the regular school environment could be established as an objective. Groups such as a "human relations task force" or student council frequently set such objectives. With information from staff members, students could determine several ways in which assistance on integration efforts could be provided and could then endeavor to accomplish the necessary steps toward the objective.

Severely handicapped students could be taught age-appropriate behaviors. The severely handicapped students may need to acquire a repertoire of behaviors considered more acceptable in their regular school building. This might be accomplished effectively through modeling, physical priming, and, with some students, discussing age-appropriate behaviors, role-playing, and evaluating and reinforcing those behaviors.

It may be beneficial for special education teachers to begin working with their severely handicapped students on age-appropriate behaviors prior to their transition to a regular school. Such teachers initially might determine behaviors on which to work by observing in regular school sites. Sample age-appropriate behaviors include greeting a peer or teacher (verbally and/or nonverbally), interacting with a peer(s) during free time such as recess, and asking an appropriate person for assistance when necessary. Role-playing sessions might be conducted to teach age-appropriate behaviors. Once in the regular school, these sessions might involve nonhandicapped as well as handicapped students with special and regular education staff members playing various roles. Such role-playing sessions may need to be conducted frequently and should involve both positive and negative situations that arise during the school day, for example, handling teasing and how to respond when greeted in a positive way by nonhandicapped peers. As part of the role-playing instructional activities, it would be important to assist and reinforce each student in recognizing a problem, implementing solutions to the problem, and evaluating whether his or her responding behavior was effective.

Severely handicapped students could be included in a variety of extra-curricular activities. Most schools have extra-curricular social activities, frequently after school or during the lunch period, in which students can participate. Examples of such activities include clubs, newspaper and yearbook staff, student council (usually elected positions), school dances, and sports events. It is very possible that severely handicapped students could acquire some of the skills necessary to participate to some degree in many of these activities. For example, a severely handicapped student might attend the library club meetings and subsequently help shelve books in the library. In one of the middle schools in the authors' experience, severely handicapped students participated on the production of the school newspaper by collating, stapling, and delivering the newspapers to each classroom. If at all possible, the special education classroom might elect a representative to attend student council meetings. Participation in any of these extra activities can provide severely handicapped and other students opportunities to work together in a positive manner.

Severely handicapped students could be taught to participate in school jobs. Most schools have a variety of relatively simple tasks such as delivering written messages; taking attendance slips to classrooms; stamping tardy passes; collating and stapling papers; stuffing envelopes in the office; and delivering the operating audiovisual (AV) equipment. Typically, these jobs are carried out by nonhandicapped students. It is quite likely, though, that severely handicapped students can acquire the skills necessary to participate at least partially in many of these school jobs. For example, in a middle school in the authors' experience, severely handicapped students were paired with nonhandicapped students to learn to deliver, operate, and later pick up AV equipment. Eventually, one of the severely handicapped students was taught by her nonhandicapped partner to operate some of the AV equipment independently. Thus, this student was provided an opportunity to be viewed as a competent service provider rather than an assistance seeker. Such opportunities are rarely afforded severely handicapped students. Participation in school jobs has an additional advantage of providing increased visibility in the school environment and increased interactions with other students and adults.

Special and regular education classes could be brought together for special lessons. Special and regular education teachers could hold joint classes for selected lesson activities. For example, in one school in the authors' experience, a special education teacher had been showing his students the environmental changes that occur in the spring. He was aware that one of the regular education science classes was working on a similar science unit, so he invited the regular education class into his room when a visitor brought in several baby animals. As a follow-up activity, the regular education class was invited to take "walks" with the special education class around the school neighborhood to observe changes in trees and plants. Teachers might bring classes together on a periodic basis when similar objectives are being worked on, or teachers might plan cooperatively to bring their classes together on a more regular basis (i.e., every Friday, once every two weeks) for specified activities.

Obviously, in order for such activities to occur, teachers must be aware of objectives/"units" covered in other classrooms. Discussion in the staff lounge may be one vehicle for obtaining such information—thus further underscoring the importance of getting acquainted with other staff members.

PROCEDURES FOR ASSESSING
THE EFFECTIVENESS OF INTEGRATION EFFORTS

Assessment is a critical component in developing and implementing plans for integrating severely handicapped students into regular school programs and activities. Data are needed regarding present integration practices, the attitudes of regular teachers and nonhandicapped students toward severely handicapped students, and the frequency and type of interactions that occur between severely handicapped and nonhandicapped students in integrated situations. These data can be collected through systematic assessment procedures.

Several assessment instruments may be used by educators to determine: 1) the degree of integration that is occurring in various settings within a regular school; 2) the attitudes of regular education teachers toward integration; 3) the perceptions of nonhandicapped students toward severely handicapped students; and 4) the frequency and type of interactions exhibited by nonhandicapped and severely handicapped students in integrated situations.

Assessing the Degree of Integration That Is Occurring

It has been noted earlier in this chapter and elsewhere that in addition to physically locating severely handicapped students in regular schools, every effort should be made to integrate them into as many regular school activities as possible (Nietupski et al., 1980; Stainback, Stainback, & Jaben, 1981). The following is a discussion of a Severely Handicapped Integration Checklist (SHIC), developed by Stainback and Stainback (1983), that was designed to estimate the degree to which severely handicapped students placed in regular schools are integrated into various regular school environments.

The SHIC contains 14 items, which were determined by analyzing and listing the various environments within a regular school setting in which both severely handicapped and nonhandicapped students generally can participate. Several principals and regular and special education teachers reviewed the list and suggested modifications. Based on the results of this procedure, 14 questions, one for each of the environments selected, were compiled into a checklist format. The checklist (Figure 2) addresses environments such as the playground, lunchroom, hallways, and selected regular class environments.

Response options to each statement or item included are on a 5-point Likert-type scale. The options are designed to reflect degrees of integration based on the number of severely handicapped students integrated in a designated school environment. The options range from "all," indicating that 100% of the severely handicapped students in the school are integrated in a particular environment, to "none," in which 0% of the severely handicapped are integrated. The SHIC is arranged so that each response option is given a point score that can be totaled to arrive at a score for a school's integration rating on the overall checklist.

The score for each item is a 4 if "all" (100%) is marked; 3 if "most" (>50% but <100%) is marked; 2 if "some" (≈50%) is marked; 1 if "few" (<50% but > 0%) is marked; and 0 if "none" (0%) is marked. The scores for the items can be added together to give a total score that could range from 0 to 56. While a score of 56 indicates the highest level of integration, the most appropriate score for any particular school should be determined in relation to the needs of the school's students. Generally speaking, however, the higher the score the stronger is the integration environment.

The SHIC could be used in any regular school setting in which severely handicapped students receive educational services. Administration of the instrument requires less than 10 minutes. An individual who is intimately familiar with the activities of the severely handicapped students in the school, such as the special education teacher or principal, should provide the data. The accuracy of the information obtained is a direct function of the knowledge of the individual providing the data; therefore, selection of an informed individual is important.

The SHIC could be used by a variety of individuals to obtain an objective measure of the degree to which severely handicapped students are integrated into the regular school milieu. For example, the teacher of the severely handicapped class could use the checklist to evaluate the degree to which his or her students are

Severely Handicapped Integration Checklist

Date _____ Name of School _____

_____

Directions: After reading each question, put an "X" under the category that best reflects how many severely handicapped students engage in the activity or environment.

Do severely handicapped students:	ALL (100%)	MOST (>50% but <100%)	SOME (approx. 50%)	FEW (<50% but >0%)	NONE (0%)
1. Ride the same school buses that nonhandicapped students ride?					
2. Have their classrooms located throughout a regular school building with the classrooms for nonhandicapped students?					
3. Attend some school assembly programs with nonhandicapped students?					
4. Eat lunch in the school cafeteria during the same time as nonhandicapped students?					
5. Eat lunch at the same table in the school cafeteria with nonhandicapped students?					
6. Share recess (or recreational times) with nonhandicapped students?					
7. Go on some school field trips with nonhandicapped students?					
8. Share special events such as Halloween and Thanksgiving parties or football homecoming celebrations with nonhandicapped students?					
9. Share homeroom with nonhandicapped students?					
10. Use the same bathroom as nonhandicapped students?					
11. Use the school hallways at the same time as nonhandicapped students?					
12. Share one or more classes such as art, music, and/or PE with nonhandicapped students?					

(continued)

Figure 2. Severely Handicapped Integration Checklist (SHIC). (From Stainback, S., and Stainback, W. A Severely Handicapped Integration Checklist, *Teaching Exceptional Children*, 1983; reprinted by permission.)

Severely Handicapped Integration Checklist
(continued)

Do severely handicapped students:	ALL (100%)	MOST (>50% but <100%)	SOME (approx. 50%)	FEW (<50% but >0%)	NONE (0%)
13. Have their school pictures interspersed with their nonhandicapped peers throughout school publications (e.g., yearbook, newsletters, or displays)?					
14. Share some of the same school jobs and responsibilities as nonhandicapped students (e.g., arranging the chairs in the gym for an upcoming assembly program)?					

Scoring procedures: Determine the score for each question (None = 0; Few = 1; Some = 2; Most = 3; All = 4). Add the scores for each of the questions together to obtain the total score.

TOTAL SCORE _____

Figure 2. *(continued)*

provided integrated activities in the school situation. Results of the checklist can provide the teacher with a clearer picture of relatively strong and weak areas of integration. The information subsequently could be used to guide the teacher in upgrading the integration level of his/her students.

Similarly, the instrument could be beneficial to other school officials and educators. A principal could use the checklist to evaluate an entire school's integration status. A consultant for a school district could use the SHIC to systematically evaluate the schools under his or her supervision to assist in guiding integration suggestions. State department personnel also could use the SHIC to determine state progress in integration activities. And outside evaluators and researchers could use it to obtain an objective measure of the degree to which a school is integrated. The relative ease, speed, objectivity, and simplicity of scoring the instrument provides a practical, viable means of collecting useful integration information.

Attitudes of Regular Education Teachers Toward Integration

It has been pointed out that regular education teachers should work cooperatively with special class teachers to help maximize the integration of severely handicapped students into regular schools (Stainback et al., 1981). Regular education teachers can facilitate integration of severely handicapped students with nonhandicapped students by, for example, accepting severely handicapped students into their classrooms during certain activities such as homeroom, art, music, recess, holiday and birthday parties, show and tell, and/or rest periods. Also they can encourage their nonhandicapped students to visit the special education classroom(s) to work as tutors and/or simply to spend a little time with a severely handicapped peer. In addition, regular education teachers can join with special education teachers in encouraging interactions between nonhandicapped and severely handicapped students in the school cafeteria, at assembly programs, in the hallways and/or at the bus loading and unloading zones. Nietupski et al. (1980) reported that regular class teachers who hold positive attitudes toward integration of severely handicapped students are more likely to be willing to do the types of integration activities listed above.

The following is a description of the Severely Handicapped Integration Attitude Survey (SHIAS), developed by the latter two authors, that could be used to determine regular education teachers' attitudes toward integration of severely handicapped students into regular school environments. The SHIAS (Figure 3) is simply a modification of the Severely Handicapped Integration Checklist presented in Figure 2.

The SHIAS was designed to assess the degree to which teachers believe severely handicapped students should be integrated within the regular school setting. It consists of 14 statements regarding integration options for severely handicapped students. Responses to the statements are on a 5-point Likert-type scale. Response options range from ''strongly agree'' to ''strongly disagree.'' Scoring is done by giving each option a point value, from 5 for ''strongly agree'' to 0 for ''strongly disagree.'' The possible acceptance score range is from 0 to 70. Teachers are requested to state their opinion regarding whether severely handicapped students should be integrated with nonhandicapped students into various regular school environments. Based on the teachers' responses, a score can be determined reflecting the degree each teacher believes that severely handicapped students should be integrated into these environments.

The environments included in the questionnaire were determined by analyzing various regular school environments (excluding academic) in which students are generally involved. Several principals and teachers were requested to review the list and to add or modify items as appropriate. Based on the results of this procedure, 14 items or statements, one for each of the environments selected, were compiled in a questionnaire form. The final form of the questionnaire was submitted to 27 professionals in special education consisting of teachers, consultants, and administrators, who unanimously agreed on the validity of the content areas included.

The instrument has been field-tested on a limited basis. It was first administered to 92 regular education teachers in the state of Iowa. All of the teachers had at least an awareness of the type of students referred to as ''severely handicapped.'' In addition, many of the teachers worked in schools in which severely handicapped students had been integrated, while others had a relative or acquaintance who was severely handicapped. A split-half reliability analysis was carried out on the responses of the 92 teachers. An odd item/even item split was utilized. Analysis of the reliability coefficient was done by computing an Equal Length Spearman-Brown. The reliability coefficient obtained was .89.

The SHIAS could be administered to all of the regular education teachers in a school building. Like the SHIC, it requires less than 10 minutes to complete. The person administering the instrument should be sure that the teachers know the

Severely Handicapped Integration Attitude Survey

Name _____ Position _____

Directions: Place an X in the appropriate box.

Assuming that severely handicapped students are located in regular neighborhood public schools, what is your professional opinion about the following situations? Severely handicapped students should:	Strongly Agree	Agree	Neutral	Disagree	Strongly Disagree
1. Be transported to school on the same school buses that nonhandicapped students ride.					
2. Have their classrooms mixed throughout a regular school building with the classrooms for nonhandicapped students.					
3. Attend some school assembly programs with nonhandicapped students.					
4. Eat lunch in the school cafeteria during the same time as nonhandicapped students.					
5. Eat lunch at the same table in the school cafeteria with nonhandicapped students.					
6. Have recess (or recreational times) with nonhandicapped students.					
7. Go on some school field trips with nonhandicapped students.					
8. Share some of the same school jobs and responsibilities as nonhandicapped students (e.g., arranging the chairs in the gym for an upcoming assembly program).					
9. Be placed in a regular homeroom with nonhandicapped students.					
10. Use the same bathroom as nonhandicapped students.					
11. Use the school hallways at the same time as nonhandicapped students.					
12. Have some classes such as art, music, and/or PE with nonhandicapped students.					

(continued)

Figure 3. Severely Handicapped Integration Attitude Survey (SHIAS).

| 13. | Have their pictures interspersed throughout the school yearbook. | | | | | |
| 14. | Share special events such as Halloween and Thanksgiving parties with nonhandicapped students. | | | | | |

Scoring procedures: Each option is given a point value, from 5 for "Strongly Agree" to 0 for "Strongly Disagree." Add the scores for each of the statements together to obtain the total score.

TOTAL SCORE _____

Figure 3. *(continued)*

population of students being referred to as "severely handicapped" and specifically what is being requested of them. The survey should not be given to teachers without an explanation and/or an opportunity to ask questions.

The data collected from administration of the survey could be used to determine which teachers in a school building are the most receptive to the integration of severely handicapped students into regular school activities. The teacher of severely handicapped students could contact those teachers who express the most accepting attitudes to see what arrangements could be made to integrate severely handicapped students in activities with nonhandicapped students. Data obtained from administration of the attitude survey also could be used to determine which teachers will need inservice training regarding the value of integration to nonhandicapped students as well as severely handicapped students. The data collected could also be used to determine which environments regular education teachers feel most comfortable about sharing with severely handicapped students. For example, regular education teachers might indicate a high degree of acceptance in regard to recess or recreational times but less favorable attitudes about severely handicapped students being placed in regular homerooms. To help ensure a smooth transition to integration, it might be worthwhile to initially introduce severely handicapped students into those settings in which integration is most widely and uniformly accepted. However, movement into other appropriate school environments should follow as soon as a smooth transition can be made.

Nonhandicapped Students' Perceptions of Severely Handicapped Students

For the first time in their lives, many nonhandicapped students are coming into direct contact with severely handicapped students. It may be helpful to know nonhandicapped students' perceptions of severely handicapped students, especially when planning training sessions for nonhandicapped students about severely handicapped students and/or organizing opportunities for interaction between the two groups of students.

The third instrument described in this section is the Severely Handicapped Perception Inventory (SHPI), developed by Stainback and Stainback (1982). The SHPI was designed primarily to examine several aspects of nonhandicapped students' perceptions of severely handicapped students. The inventory also assesses nonhandicapped students' perceived knowledge of, experiences with, and interest in severely handicapped students. The inventory consists of 106 questions that are orally presented. The students respond either "yes" or "no". The questions are divided into eight subsections, as follows:

1. *Knowledge of severely handicapped persons.* Section 1 includes questions that ask the students how much they know about severely handicapped students. The purpose is to assess nonhandicapped students' perceived knowledge of severely handicapped students.

2. *Experience with severely handicapped persons.* Section 2 includes questions about how much and what type of experience students have had with severely handicapped students.

3. *Characteristics of severely handicapped persons.* Section 3 includes 20 descriptive terms that can be used to describe individuals. Ten of the terms are positive human attributes and 10 are negative. The nonhandicapped students are asked to respond to each of the terms in regard to whether or not the term is an appropriate or accurate descriptor for most severely handicapped students.

4. *Characteristics of nonhandicapped persons.* Section 4 asks the students to respond to the same 20 descriptive terms included in Section 3. However, in Section 4 the terms are evaluated in regard to their applicability to most of the students' nonhandicapped peers. This section provides a *baseline or comparison* for the answers given in Section 3.

5. *Feelings toward severely handicapped persons.* Section 5 includes 16 terms that are descriptions of personal feelings toward others. Eight of the terms included are considered indicative of pleasant feelings and 8 of unpleasant feelings. The nonhandicapped students are asked to respond to each of the terms in regard to whether or not the term is an accurate descriptor of their feelings toward severely handicapped students.

6. *Feelings toward nonhandicapped persons.* Section 6 asks the students to respond to the same 16 descriptions of personal feelings included in Section 5. However, in Section 6 the students are asked to respond to the terms in regard to their feelings toward their nonhandicapped peers. Section 6 provides a *baseline or comparison* for the answers given in Section 5.

7. *Interest in severely handicapped persons.* Section 7 includes 11 questions that focus on the students' expressed desire to learn more about and interact with severely handicapped students.

8. *Reliability check.* Section 8 provides a measure of reliability. Ten questions from throughout the inventory are restated. The purpose is to determine the consistency of the students' responses.

Figure 4 contains an overview of SHPI. The number of questions included within each section of the inventory along with a sample question from each section are provided.

The inventory was developed for use with nonhandicapped students attending schools that provide educational services to severely handicapped students.

Severely Handicapped Perception Inventory
(overview)

Section number	Section title	Number of questions	Sample questions
1	Perceived Knowledge of Severely Handicapped Persons	5	Do you know the type of students who are called severely handicapped?
2	Experience with Severely Handicapped Persons	8	Do you have any friends who have severe handicaps?
3	Characteristics of Severely Handicapped Persons	20	Healthy? Sickly?
4	Characteristics of Nonhandicapped Persons	20	Healthy? Sickly?
5	Feelings Toward Severely Handicapped Persons	16	Attracted? Repelled?
6	Feelings Toward Severely Handicapped Persons	16	Attracted? Repelled?
7	Interest in Severely Handicapped Persons	11	Would you like to have more school activities with severely handicapped students?
8	Reliability Check	10	Do any of your friends have severe handicaps? (Restatement of question in Section 2.)

Figure 4. Overview of the Severely Handicapped Perception Inventory (SHPI). (A copy of the complete SHPI can be obtained by writing Drs. William and Susan Stainback, Department of Special Education, University of Northern Iowa, Cedar Falls, IA 50614.)

Although designed for upper elementary age students, it could be used with younger or older students with minor modifications in the administration procedures and/or adjustments in the vocabulary level.

The inventory was constructed so that any part of it may be administered depending on the information desired and the time available. Similarly, a score for each individual section can be determined. It may be useful to compare the scores for sections 3 and 4, for example, with those for Sections 5 and 6. Individual item answers may also be useful on a per-child or per-group basis. Approximately 45 minutes is required to administer the entire instrument, which can be given to individual students or groups of students.

The authors were conceptually guided in the construction of the inventory by reviewing several "acceptance scales" recently employed by researchers (McHale & Simeonsson, 1980; Voeltz, 1980) in investigations of nonhandicapped students' attitudes toward severely handicapped students. The specific questions included in the inventory were based on recommendations by principals, teachers, and other school personnel who have been involved in the integration of severely handicapped students. The selection and positivity and/or negativity determination of the terms included in Sections 3, 4, 5, and 6 were based on the results of polling several classes of upper elementary-age students regarding words they felt were descriptive of their feelings toward other students. The total score per section was designed to indicate the degree of positivities toward other students; consequently, scoring of sections with positive and negative items is done by giving a point for each positive item chosen and a point for each negative item not chosen. Independent evaluations of each section by 10 professional educators strengthened the instrument in the area of content validity. The final draft of the instrument included the recommendations of the evaluators and was approved by consensus.

The instrument has been field-tested on a limited basis. As previously noted, Section 8 was designed to provide an internal check on the reliability of the inventory. In this section, 10 items from throughout the inventory are reworded to help determine the consistency of the responses obtained. The internal reliability coefficient for the administration of the inventory to 31 fifth-grade students resulted in a composite or total reliability coefficient of .89, with the range on the items being from .77 to .97. The reliability coefficients were computed using the formula: agreements ÷ (agreements + disagreements).

In addition to the internal reliability check, a test-retest procedure was used. The subjects included 31 fifth-grade students who were administered the questionnaire 2 weeks following the first administration. The composite test-retest correlation coefficient was .93. The coefficients for the total, as well as each of the subsections, were found to be significant beyond the .001 level. The coefficients for each subsection were: knowledge, $r = .92$; experience, $r = .83$; characteristics of nonhandicapped persons, $r = .79$; feelings toward handicapped persons, $r = .84$; feelings toward nonhandicapped persons, $r = .67$; and interest in handicapped persons, $r = .78$.

The following are a few suggestions of how the SHPI might be utilized. First, it might be used to organize training for nonhandicapped students. Information from the inventory could suggest training sequences as well as content areas and activities for a training program of interest and relevance to nonhandicapped students. For instance, characteristics noted of severely handicapped students could be used as a discussion topic. If, for example, the nonhandicapped students should indicate that the severely handicapped are boring, then a discussion could be initiated around why they feel this way and how it influences their relationships with their severely handicapped peers. Also, information obtained from the inventory regarding student experiences could be capitalized upon by asking students who have had extensive experience with severely handicapped persons (e.g., living with a handicapped brother or sister) to share their experience in order to add a measure of realism to any training discussions or activities.

A second possible use of the SHPI could be for organizing training for severely handicapped students. In the area of curriculum planning, for example, the special education teacher might be provided some cues in regard to the behavior(s) of the severely handicapped students that need changing to make them more acceptable to their nonhandicapped peers. If, for example, the non-handicapped students perceive severely handicapped students as having a particularly distasteful social characteristic or behavior, then a part of the curriculum for severely handicapped students might include instruction focused on changing the distasteful behavior(s). For instance, if severely handicapped students are seen as being "dirty," the special education teacher should evaluate whether inclusion of additional instruction regarding cleanliness and grooming is needed.

A third possible use could be for planning integrated school activities. When planning opportunities for interaction between severely handicapped and non-handicapped students, it might be helpful for regular and special education teachers to know the perception the nonhandicapped students have of severely handicapped students. This is specially true when integration activities are first initiated, as this often constitutes the "testing ground" for subsequent activities. Information from the SHPI might facilitate successful planning and organization, by providing teachers with information about nonhandicapped students' prior experiences, desire to share activities with their severely handicapped peers, and the overall positivity or negativity of the nonhandicapped students' perception of severely handicapped students. Nonhandicapped students with more positive perceptions toward severely handicapped students could be involved in initial integration activities. Also, the information from the inventory could be used when nonhandicapped students with unfavorable feelings toward severely handicapped students are included in integrated activities. For example, teachers could endeavor to educate those nonhandicapped students with negative feelings before involving them in integrated activities. Also, teachers could place any nonhandicapped student with negative feelings in a group of nonhandicapped students with more positive feelings, thereby hoping to correct the negative feelings.

The SHPI could be used in a variety of additional ways—for example, for measuring changes in nonhandicapped students' perceptions of severely handicapped students as a result of participating with severely handicapped students in integrated activities.

Direct Observational Procedures

One of the advantages of integrating severely handicapped students into regular schools is the possibility for increased interaction between severely handicapped and nonhandicapped students. It has been found that both nonhandicapped and severely handicapped students can benefit from interacting in integrated situations (Stainback & Stainback, 1981). The following is a description of direct observation procedures that teachers could use to measure the frequency and type of interactions that occur between severely handicapped and nonhandicapped students in integrated situations.

School personnel can assess interactions by observing nonhandicapped and severely handicapped students during play or work situations and simply recording their interactions. In recent years, researchers have developed observational instruments for directly observing interactions between preschool and school-age peers in naturalistic settings (Guralnick, 1980; Strain & Kerr, in press). Many of these instruments could be adapted for use by school personnel to measure interactions between nonhandicapped and severely handicapped students.

An observation instrument employed by Strain and Timm (1974) and Strain, Kerr, and Ragland (1979) could be used to measure nonhandicapped-severely handicapped student interactions. The coding system for the instrument includes two general classes of interaction behaviors, motor-gestural and vocal-verbal, along with negative and positive topographical features. In addition, whether the interaction behavior is initiated or received is noted. Each coded item is operationally defined. (The operational definitions can be found in Strain and Timm, 1974, p. 584). As in most observational coding systems, behaviors are recorded on a coding sheet specifically designed to assist the observer in collecting the designated information. Behaviors are recorded in a continuous manner on one student at a time. The interaction behaviors that each nonhandicapped and severely handicapped student displays are coded according to the previously noted categories (e.g., positive/negative, initiated/responded). By using an observation coding system such as this, school personnel can determine how much and what type of interactions occur between nonhandicapped and severely handicapped students.

More comprehensive data can be collected using the observation coding system by simply modifying and/or expanding the behavior categories to be coded. For example, duration as determined by recording the beginning and ending time of a social behavior, and the specific type of activity the subject is engaged in (i.e., observer, isolate, parallel, game, cooperative, or fantasy) has been used in an observation coding system by Tremblay, Strain, Henderson, and Shores (1980). Another modification of the coding system used by Strain and Timm (1974) and Strain et al. (1979) was developed by Stainback and Stainback (Note 2). This instrument is specifically designed to measure the social behaviors of nonhandicapped and severely handicapped students in integrated school settings. The coding system uses a momentary time sampling rather than a continuous observation approach. The observer is cued (e.g., by a tape recorder) at 15-second intervals and the observer notes what the target subject is doing when cued. If an interaction is occurring at a given interval, the interaction is coded according to three characteristics (physical-verbal, positive-negative, initiated-responded) plus whether the interaction occurred on a group or individual basis, and the sex of the peer(s) the target subject was interacting with. As with the other coding systems, each behavior category is operationally defined, and a coding sheet is used by the observer. An example of a coding sheet is shown in Figure 5.

Thus, observation coding systems can involve complex to simplistic behaviors and can be geared to meet data collection needs for specific students in specific settings. Selection or development of an observation coding system should be an individual consideration of each teacher. Also, due to the nature of the data collected and the supervisory demands on the teacher, it is generally most appropriate to collect the data in an integrated (severely handicapped students and nonhandicapped students) free play or joint work activity period in which both

Interactions Observations Record

Date _____ Setting _____   School _____

Directions to observer: Each block of codes represents one minute of coding per target subject (four 15-second samples). At the end of each 15-second interval, mark the appropriate columns (moving horizontally across the line). Remember, do not record coding sections 2 through 6 if section 1 is coded "NI" (no interaction).

	1. Interaction		2. Type				3. Climate			4. Role		5. Sex			6. Size	
	I	NI	P	V	P/V	O	P	N		I	R	M	R	B	I	G

Student: _____
Time: _____

Student: _____
Time: _____

Student: _____
Time: _____

Key: 1. Interaction: I = interaction, NI = no interaction. 2. Type: P = physical, V = verbal, P/V = physical and verbal, O = other. 3. Climate: P = positive, N = negative. 4. Role: I = initiated, R = respond. 5. Sex: M = male, F = female, B = both males and females. 6. Size: I = individual, G = group.

Figure 5. An example of a coding sheet for recording interactions observations.

regular and special teachers are present (so one teacher can observe and the other supervise). The teachers' supervisor or another colleague may periodically do interrater reliability checks to monitor the reliability of the instrument throughout its use.

It should be noted that while direct observation of interaction behaviors in a school situation does not necessarily have to be difficult or complex, preparation time usually is necessary. Prior to using any observation coding system, whether it be a published or custom-made system, the individual(s) serving as the observer(s) should engage in practice sessions until he or she becomes proficient in the use of the system. Also prior to the actual use, interrater reliability of the coding system should be determined. In addition, as noted above, periodic interrater reliability checks should occur throughout the time the observational system is used. (The reader is referred to Cartwright and Cartwright (1974) for additional information on how to construct and use direct observation systems.)

As with the other data collection instruments discussed in this chapter, data collected with an observational coding system can be used in a variety of ways. For example, the specific types and frequency of severely handicapped student and nonhandicapped student interactions that occur in various school environments can be evaluated. This data could be analyzed to determine if there is a need for intervention to promote more frequent positive interactions. Observational data can also be used to determine the effectiveness of intervention programming throughout the intervention process.

Summary of the Assessment Instruments

The above section described four types of assessment instruments. The Severely Handicapped Integration Checklist was designed to estimate the degree to which severely handicapped students placed in regular schools are integrated into various regular school environments. As noted previously, it should be emphasized that the accuracy of the information obtained will be directly related to the knowledge of the individual providing the data on the activities of severely handicapped students; therefore, it is crucial that a knowledgeable individual be selected.

The Severely Handicapped Integration Attitude Survey was designed to assess the degree to which regular class teachers and/or other school personnel believe severely handicapped students should be integrated within a regular school setting. Again, administrators of the survey should be certain that those individuals asked to respond are knowledgeable about severely handicapped students and understand what is being asked of them.

The Severely Handicapped Perception Inventory was designed to assess nonhandicapped students' perceptions of severely handicapped students. The inventory also can be used to assess nonhandicapped students' perceived knowledge of, experiences with, and interest in severely handicapped students. As previously noted, Section 8 of the inventory can be administered to help determine the consistency of the nonhandicapped students' responses. In addition, the nonhandicapped students should be frequently asked throughout administration of the instrument if they understand the questions being asked. A follow-up interview with several randomly selected nonhandicapped students might also assist the teacher in determining if the students understood the questions.

Direct observational coding procedures, the fourth type of assessment instrument described, can be used to obtain an objective measure of the frequency and type of interactions that occur between severely handicapped and nonhandicapped students in integrated settings. It should be emphasized that prior to the actual use of any direct observational system, interrater reliability should be determined and periodic interrater reliability checks should be performed throughout the time the observational system is used.

It should be emphasized that the above methods are not the only types of evaluations that can be used to assess integration. Other methods include, for example, sociometric and interview techniques. Information gleaned from sociometrics could be useful in determining which nonhandicapped students accept severely handicapped students the most or least, as well as providing general information regarding the social acceptance of severely handicapped students by their peers. (The reader is referred to Caldwell, 1959; and Gronlund, 1969, for more detailed information about sociometrics.) In regard to interview techniques, nonhandicapped and severely handicapped students could be interviewed about their thoughts and feelings toward working and playing in integrated situations. Properly constructed interviews can often provide in-depth information that is difficult to obtain by other means (Gordon, 1980). (The reader is referred to Cormier and Cormier, 1979, for information about how to organize and conduct an interview.)

SUMMARY

Longitudinal integration of severely handicapped students includes considerably more than transfer to regular school buildings within a school district. Significant advance and continued preparation of all staff and students involved in the integration is essential. As described, a number of instruments for assessing the degree of integration, as well as teacher attitudes and other students' perceptions toward severely handicapped students, are available to help improve the quality of integration activities. It is the authors' firm conviction that with systematic integration efforts, severely handicapped students can become, and indeed are becoming, an integral part of their regular school environments. Benefits to both the nonhandicapped and the severely handicapped population can accrue if regular school placement is accompanied by vigorous efforts to promote positive interactions.

REFERENCES

Almond, P., Rodgers, S., & Krug, D. A model for including elementary students in the severely handicapped classroom. *Teaching Exceptional Children*, 1979, *11*, 135–139.

Brown, L., Branston, M.B., Hamre-Nietupski, S., Johnson, F., Wilcox, B., & Gruene-wald, L. A rationale for comprehensive longitudinal interactions between severely handicapped students and nonhandicapped students and other citizens. *AAESPH Review,* 1979, *4*(1), 3–14.

Budoff, M., Siperstein, G., & Conant, S. Children's knowledge of mental retardation. *Education and Training of the Mentally Retarded,* 1979, *14*(4), 277–281.

Burton, T.A., & Hirschoren, A. The education of severely and profoundly retarded children: Are we sacrificing the child to the concept? *Exceptional Children,* 1979, *45,* 598–602.(a)

Burton, T. A., & Hirschoren, A. Some further thoughts and clarifications on the education of severely and profoundly retarded children. *Exceptional Children,* 1979, *45,* 618–625.(b)

Caldwell, E. *Creating better social climate in the classroom through sociometric techniques.* San Francisco: Fearon Publishers, 1959.

Cartwright, C., & Cartwright, G. *Developing observational skills.* New York: McGraw-Hill Book Co., 1974.

Clore, G., & Jeffrey, K. Emotional role playing, attitude change and attraction toward a disabled person. *Journal of Personality and Social Psychology,* 1972, *23,* 105–111.

Cormier, W., & Cormier, L. *Interviewing strategies for helpers.* Monterey, CA: Brooks/Cole Publishing Co., 1979.

Donaldson, J. Changing attitudes toward handicapped persons: A review and analysis of research. *Exceptional Children,* *46*(7), 1980, 504–514.

Donder, D., & Nietupski, J. Nonhandicapped adolescents teaching playground skills to their mentaly retarded peers: Toward a less restrictive middle school environment. *Education and Training of the Mentally Retarded,* 1981, *16*(4), 270–276.

Forader, A.T. Modifying social attitudes toward the physically disabled through three different modes of instruction. *Dissertation Abstracts International,* 1970, *30*(9B), 4360.

Gordon, R. *Interviewing: Strategy, techniques, and tactics.* Homewood, IL: The Dorsey Press, 1980.

Gronlund, N. *Sociometrics in the classroom.* New York: Harper, 1969.

Guralnick, M. J. Social interactions among preschool children. *Exceptional Children,* 1980, *46,* 248–253.

Guralnick, M. J. The social behavior of preschool children at different developmental levels: Effects of group composition. *Journal of Experimental Child Psychology,* in press.

Kenowitz, L., Zweibel, S., & Edgar, E. Determining the least restrictive educational opportunity for the severely and profoundly handicapped. In: N.G. Haring & D. Bricker (eds.), *Teaching the severely handicapped,* Vol. 3. Seattle: American Association for the Education of the Severely/Profoundly Handicapped, 1978.

McHale, S., & Simeonsson, R. Effects of interactions on nonhandicapped children's attitudes toward autistic students. *American Journal of Mental Deficiency,* 1980, *85*(1), 18–24.

Nietupski, J., Hamre-Nietupski, S., Schuetz, G., & Ockwood, L. (eds.). *Severely handicapped students in regular schools.* Milwaukee, WI: Milwaukee Public Schools, 1980.

Poorman, S. Mainstreaming in reverse with a special friend. *Teaching Exceptional Children,* 1980, *12,* 136–142.

Rynders, J., Johnson, R., Johnson, D., & Schmidt, B. Producing positive interaction among Down's Syndrome and nonhandicapped teenagers through cooperative goal structuring. *American Journal of Mental Deficiency,* 1980, *85,* 268–273.

Siperstein, G., Bak, J., & Gottlieb, J. Effects of group discussion on children's attitudes toward handicapped peers. *Journal of Educational Research,* 1977, *70,* 131–134.

Sontag, E., Certo, N., & Button, J. On a distinction between the education of the severely and profoundly handicapped and a doctrine of limitations. *Exceptional Children,* 1979, *45,* 604–616.

Stainback, S., & Stainback, W. A Severely Handicapped Integration Checklist. *Teaching Exceptional Children,* 1983, *15,* 168–171.

Stainback, W., & Stainback, S. A review of research on interactions between severely handicapped and nonhandicapped students. *Journal of The Association for the Severely Handicapped,* 1981, *6,* 23–29.

Stainback, W., & Stainback, S. Nonhandicapped students' perception of severely handicapped students. *Education and Training of the Mentally Retarded,* 1982, *17,* 177–182.

Stainback, W., Stainback, S., & Jaben, T. Providing opportunities for interaction between severely handicapped and nonhandicapped students. *Teaching Exceptional Children,* 1981, *13,* 72–75.

Sternat, J., Nietupski, J., Lyon, S., Messina, R., & Brown, L. Occupational and physical therapy services for severely handicapped students: Toward a naturalized service delivery model. In: E. Sontag, J. Smith, & N. Certo (eds.), *Educational programming for the severely and profoundly handicapped.* Reston, VA: The Council for Exceptional Children, 1977.

Strain, P., & Kerr, M. Modifying children's social withdrawal: Issues in assessment and clinical intervention. In: M. Hersen, R. Eisler, & P. Miller (eds.), *Progress in behavior modification,* Vol. 2. New York: Academic Press, in press.

Strain, P., Kerr, M., & Ragland, E. Effects of peer-mediated social initiations and prompting/reinforcement procedures on social behavior of autistic children. *Journal of Autism and Developmental Disorders,* 1979, *9,* 41–54.

Strain, P., & Timm, M. An experimental analysis of social interaction between a behaviorally disordered preschool child and her classroom peers. *Journal of Applied Behavior Analysis,* 1974, *7,* 583–590.

Tremblay, A., Strain, P., Henderson, J., & Shores, R. The activity context of preschool children's social interactions: A comparison of high and low social interactors. *Psychology in the Schools,* 1980, *17,* 380–385.

Voeltz, L. Children's attitudes toward handicapped peers. *American Journal of Mental Deficiency,* 1980, *84,* 455–464.

Voeltz, L. Effects of structured interactions with severely handicapped peers on children's attitudes. *American Journal of Mental Deficiency,* 1982, *86*(4), 380–390.

REFERENCE NOTES

1. Donder, D., Hamre-Nietupski, S., Nietupski, J., & Fortschneider, J. Integrating moderately and severely handicapped students into regular schools: Problem solving and strategy development. In: R. York, W.K. Schofield, D. Donder, D. Ryndak, & B. Reguly (eds.), *Organizing and implementing services for students with severe and multiple handicaps: Proceedings of the 1981 Illinois Statewide Institute for Educators of the Severely and Profoundly Handicapped.* Springfield, IL: Department of Specialized Educational Services, Illinois State Board of Education, 1981.

2. Stainback, S., & Stainback, W. *A nonhandicapped/severely handicapped social interaction observational instrument.* Unpublished manuscript, University of Northern Iowa, Cedar Falls, 1981.

7

Facilitating
Integration
through
Personnel
Preparation

William Stainback
and Susan Stainback

The placement of severely handicapped individuals in natural community settings has many implications for the preparation of a variety of service providers, including special educators, regular educators, and other community members. This chapter discusses the changing focus of personnel preparation that has resulted from the integration of severely handicapped persons into community settings. The first section of the chapter describes how the preparation of special educators has been altered as a result of integration efforts; the second section offers a rationale for training regular classroom teachers in the techniques of integration and outlines what these training needs are; and the final section presents an overview of the training required by a variety of other community members, in both school and nonschool settings, to facilitate integration.

PREPARING SPECIAL EDUCATORS

Preparing special educators to deal with the educational needs of severely handicapped students has received considerable attention in the last decade. Articles in the professional literature have been devoted to content consideration (Stainback, Stainback, & Maurer, 1976), training program structure (Stainback, Stainback, Schmid, & Courtnage, 1977), rationales for rigor in teacher training (Sontag, Certo, & Button, 1979), and updating the state of the art (Thomas, 1980). There has been little or no discussion, however, related to necessary changes in personnel preparation resulting from the integration of severely handicapped students into regular neighborhood public schools and other natural community settings. This section examines some basic components that need to be incorporated into existing teacher training programs in order to adequately prepare special educators to work in integrated school and nonschool settings.

Integration

One component requiring attention in personnel preparation involves providing prospective and practicing special educators with a basic understanding of the philosophical and legal premises behind the integration movement and equipping them, as well, with a working knowledge of how integration can best be accomplished, i.e., of ways of promoting positive interactions between severely handicapped and nonhandicapped persons in integrated settings.

During preservice training, special educators should be given the opportunity for extensive field experience in integrated school and nonschool settings. Only through such experience can educators become familiar with the day-to-day obstacles that often occur in educating severely handicapped students in integrated settings, and experience the successes (and failures) involved in attempting to overcome these obstacles. Field experience also enables prospective special educators to determine if they have the ability and attitude necessary to work with a wide variety of school and community personnel in fostering the integration of severely handicapped persons into a normalized pattern of school and community life.

Appropriate Goal Selection and Evaluation

As a result of the integration movement, the major goal of educational programming for severely handicapped students has become that of enabling such students to live and function as effectively as possible in natural community environments. This aim represents a radical shift from the previous goal of preparing severely handicapped students to function in segregated settings.

Personnel preparation programs must therefore train special educators to develop and evaluate programming goals that facilitate integration. Such goals must incorporate qualities such as functionality, age-appropriateness, and social validity. For example, if a suggested goal for a nonambulatory severely handicapped female adult is to have her say "poop" whenever she feels the need to defecate, the special educator should have the expertise to consider such questions as: 1) Is this an appropriate verbal behavior to describe the need to defecate for individuals of her age group? And 2) Is the behavior likely to be considered socially acceptable by others in natural integrated settings? If special educators are not provided skills for appropriate goal evaluation and development, the successful integration and acceptance of severely handicapped persons into integrated community settings is less likely to occur.

Teaching Strategies and Materials

Special educators should also be prepared to develop and apply teaching strategies and materials in natural integrated settings. The best setting in which to teach a severely handicapped student to exhibit a specific behavior is the setting in which the student will be expected to perform that behavior. Trying to teach a severely handicapped student to function in a natural setting, when the teaching takes place outside of that setting, is like trying to teach someone to swim outside of water.

The false logic of placing severely handicapped students in segregated settings for the purpose of preparing them for integration is thus being recognized. Moreover, the fact that increasing numbers of severely handicapped students are being placed in natural settings from birth necessitates that special educators be competent in identifying, developing, and/or adapting instructional materials and strategies for use in integrated settings. For example, personnel preparation programs should train educators to implement instructional strategies, such as partial participation, that have relevance for teaching severely handicapped students in natural settings (Baumgart, Brown, Pumpian, Nisbet, Ford, Sweet, Messina, & Schroeder, 1982; Brown, Branston-McClean, Baumgart, Vincent, Falvey, & Schroeder, 1979). The principle of partial participation recognizes that we sometimes wrongly decide that an activity is too complex for a severely handicapped student. The real problem is that special educators (and others) have not been instructed in how to adapt the activity and/or physical/social environment so that the severely handicapped student can participate (at least partially) and/or in how to provide the assistance necessary for the student to participate. Unfortunately, severely handicapped students have been excluded or excused from numerous activities because it was thought by those in charge that they could not perform "adequately." Brown et al. (1979) and Baumgart et al. (1982) have outlined methods by which severely handicapped students can participate in activities in natural settings that may, at first glance, be considered too complex or difficult for them.

Advocacy

Special educators have frequently been called upon to act as advocates for the rights of severely handicapped persons. In the past, advocates have stressed the severely handicapped person's right to an education and to freedom from institutional incarceration. Owing to the large-scale success of these advocacy efforts, special educators of tomorrow will be faced with issues unheard of several decades ago. Personnel preparation programs should prepare special educators to confront these issues. For example, educators may have to serve as spokespersons for severely handicapped students in ensuring their right to: 1) ride the same school bus as their nonhandicapped peers, eat lunch in the school cafeteria, and play on the same playground as their nonhandicapped peers; 2) attend "regular" community churches and/or perform community jobs for which they are capable; and 3) live in normalized home placements.

Involvement of special educators in advocacy for severely handicapped persons could be a critical variable in the successful integration of severely handicapped students into normalized school and nonschool environments. In order to effectively serve as advocates, special educators should be prepared to provide information to school administrators, community voters, and policymakers regarding the needs of severely handicapped persons and how such persons can be integrated into the mainstream of community life. Broad support from a variety of people will be required if integration of severely handicapped students into a diversity of natural settings is to become a reality.

In summary, personnel preparation programs should prepare special educators to work in integrated settings. All aspects of such educators' coursework and field experiences should be relevant to meeting the educational needs of severely handicapped students for functioning as effectively as possible in natural community environments.

PREPARING REGULAR CLASSROOM TEACHERS

To date, little emphasis has been given to preparing regular class teachers for the integration of severely handicapped students into regular school programs and activities. Nevertheless, teacher trainers in special and regular education should join forces in personnel preparation programming to provide at least minimal training for regular classroom teachers. This could be accomplished through activities such as workshops, mainstreaming courses, and/or by incorporating information and experiences with severely handicapped students into existing regular education coursework and field experiences.

Rationale for Training

As integration progresses, many regular classroom teachers for the first time in their lives are coming into direct contact with severely handicapped students. Since many such teachers were themselves educated in segregated schools (i.e., devoid of severely handicapped students) and also did their student teaching in such schools, they often have little prior experience to guide their responses to severely handicapped students. Yet, the manner in which regular classroom teachers respond to severely handicapped students is critical to the success of the integration movement (Stainback, Stainback, Strathe, & Dedrick, in press), for a number of reasons. First, nonhandicapped students often model the behaviors of their teachers. Thus, it is important that regular classroom teachers be prepared to set a good example in their interactions with severely handicapped students. Otherwise, the probability that nonhandicapped students will react positively toward and accept their handicapped peers is reduced. Second, regular classroom teachers must work cooperatively with special education teachers to maximize the integration of severely handicapped students into regular schools. In fact, the integration of severely handicapped students into regular school programs and activities will be virtually impossible without the cooperation and support of regular class teachers (Stainback, Stainback, & Jaben, 1981).

In summary, teacher training programs need to provide regular classroom teachers with the knowledge and understanding of severely handicapped students that will enable them not only to model appropriate behavior toward such students but to work supportively with special education teachers in fostering integration.

Training Needs

From conversations with regular classroom teachers and observations and analyses of their duties in integrated (severely handicapped students and non-handicapped students) school settings, the authors have found that regular classroom teachers need answers to at least three basic questions: 1) Who are students with severe handicaps? 2) Why are they being integrated into regular schools? and 3) What is the regular teacher's role in educating severely handicapped students? Providing the answers to these questions constitutes the basis for the training needs discussed here.

Who are students with severe handicaps? What does a regular classroom teacher fundamentally need to know about who severely handicapped students are in order to interact with and provide appropriate guidance to them—for example, in the bus loading area, lunchroom, selected regular class activities, and/or on the playground? Because most regular classroom teachers' university courses are likely to devote minimal time to learning about severely handicapped students, any information provided about the nature and needs of such students should be concise and functional (Stainback & Stainback, in press).

Many teacher training programs define handicapped populations by traditional data such as incidence statistics, chromosomal structural abnormalities, and syndrome characteristics. However, technical medical information and terminology may be of little assistance to regular classroom teachers when faced with the need to provide overall guidance and supervision to severely handicapped students. Rather, information should be presented in preparation programs that emphasizes that severely handicapped youngsters are individuals, first, and students, second, who may have physical and intellectual difficulties that interfere with, yet do not necessarily preclude, their participation or at least partial participation in many regular school activities (Brown et al., 1979). For example, severely handicapped students can be defined through explanations of the types of things they learn in school and by emphasizing that they are students in need of educational training just as any other member of the student body. Such definitions, based on educationally related needs and functions, appear to be a more useful approach to understanding "who severely handicapped students are," since it is in regard to the educational aspects of a severely handicapped student's functioning that prospective teachers will be expected to have the strongest impact. In other words, for regular classroom teachers, severely handicapped students should be defined as integral members of the general school population who should be approached as individuals rather than as exotic syndromes to be pitied, ignored, or feared.

Why are severely handicapped students being integrated into regular schools? Preparation programs should include a brief review of the history of special education in order to assist regular classroom teachers to understand that the current integration movement is not just a minor pendulum swing or a temporary trend, and thus encourage them to lend their wholehearted support to it. As Reynolds and Birch (1977) stated: "The whole history of education for exceptional children can be told in terms of one steady trend that can be described as progressive inclusion" (p. 22).

Regular classroom teachers should be familiarized with the philosophical and conceptual bases (e.g., normalization principle) for integrating all handicapped students into or as close to the mainstream of society as possible. In addition, teachers should be made aware of the inherent legal rights of all students in regard to an education. Teachers should moreover, be informed of the results of research on integration (see Stainback & Stainback, 1981b). While the basic reasons for integrating severely handicapped students into regular schools are philosophical and legal in nature, research findings do support integration (Guralnick, in press; Rynders, Johnson, Johnson, & Schmidt, 1980; Voeltz, 1980, 1982). Regular classroom teachers who are apprised of the potential benefits of integration to both severely handicapped and nonhandicapped students may be more likely to make these benefits a reality in their school setting.

What is the regular classroom teacher's role in educating severely handicapped students? As stated earlier, one basic ingredient in the regular classroom teacher's role is the need to work cooperatively with special education teachers to achieve an optimal environment for integration. Once such a cooperative relationship has been established, the role of the regular classroom teacher in integration can begin to mature. First regular classroom teachers need to provide their nonhandicapped students with opportunities to interact with severely handicapped students. Teacher training programs can help teachers make knowledgeable professional decisions about integration activities. For example, regular classroom teachers should understand that their nonhandicapped students can be provided opportunities to interact with severely handicapped students in the school cafeteria, hallways, restrooms, at recess, and at the bus loading and unloading zones. Teachers should also investigate ways of bringing handicapped and nonhandicapped students together for special activities such as field trips, parties, and other events, as well as selected regular classroom activities. While joint class activities in certain academic or highly competitive tasks may not always be feasible, regular class teachers should be made aware of the numerous opportunities for interaction that do exist.

To promote optimal integration, research suggests that it is not enough for regular classroom teachers to simply provide opportunities for interaction of severely handicapped and nonhandicapped students (Guralnick, 1980; Porter, Ramsey, Tremblay, Iaccobo, & Crawley, 1978; Ray, Note 1). Severely handicapped/nonhandicapped students do not always spontaneously interact when opportunities are provided. Thus, regular class teachers may need to understand organizational arrangements and procedures in order to facilitate interactions as opportunities develop. Teacher preparation programs should endeavor to make teachers aware of how they can encourage interactions, for example by organizing small groups to work on cooperative goals (Rynders et al., 1980) and by encouraging and reinforcing interactions among nonhandicapped and severely handicapped students (Stainback, Stainback, Raschke, & Anderson, 1981).

The final role of the regular classroom teacher to be discussed here is that of training nonhandicapped students to promote severely handicapped and nonhandicapped student interactions. The regular classroom teacher should be aware of methods for teaching nonhandicapped students about severely handicapped students, particularly those methods recently proposed that go beyond (or replace) teaching nonhandicapped students about handicapping conditions and that focus on instilling in nonhandicapped students a respect for individual differences and an appreciation of the benefits that can be derived from interacting with persons of different abilities and backgrounds (Stainback & Stainback, 1981a). Thus, one of the regular classroom teacher's roles might be to foster positive interactions by teaching nonhandicapped students skills for responding appropriately to human differences.

In conclusion, regular classroom teachers should be prepared for their role in: 1) providing nonhandicapped students with opportunities to interact with severely handicapped students, 2) encouraging and reinforcing interactions between the two groups, and 3) training nonhandicapped students in regard to human differences.

TRAINING OTHER COMMUNITY MEMBERS

In general, personnel preparation has dealt primarily with the preservice and inservice training of teachers. While the training of teachers can be expected to have a significant impact on integration efforts, teachers alone cannot assume the total responsibility. There is a critical need to educate a number of other groups about integrating severely handicapped students into the community (Hamre-Nietupski & Nietupski, 1981).

In an ideally integrated society, numerous community members other than special and regular classroom teachers can be expected to interact daily with severely handicapped persons in various settings. Many community members, due to past practices of segregating severely handicapped persons from the mainstream of society, have not had the opportunity to interact with and/or recognize and understand the needs of severely handicapped individuals. As a result, some nonhandicapped persons in community settings may not always exhibit appropriate interaction behaviors. Thus, in order to achieve the successful integration of severely handicapped individuals into natural community settings, there is a need for professionals involved in personnel preparation to consider the training needs of a variety of community members.

The following discussion on the preparation of community members to facilitate integration describes, first, the training needs of professional service personnel in communities; second, the preparation needed by family members; and third, the preparation needed by the general public.

Professional Service Personnel

Among the most obvious professional service personnel requiring training are school administrators, school psychologists, occupational therapists, physical therapists, speech therapists, and social workers. These individuals require a knowledge base from which to provide services and make decisions. For example, it is school administrators who generally are responsible for determining the classroom location of severely handicapped students, as well as lunch and activity scheduling that can influence the daily interactional patterns of nonhandicapped and severely handicapped students during the school day.

Other community service professionals such as lawyers, nurses, physicians, and dentists can also influence the success of integration. For example, lawyers need to be able to recognize, understand, and administer to the legal needs and problems encountered by severely handicapped persons living in the community. Legal assistance is a particularly salient need of severely handicapped individuals, whose rights have been and may continue to be abused if legal advocacy and assistance is not provided. Similarly, community medical personnel such as nurses, physicians, and dentists will be called upon increasingly to deal with a multiplicity of health problems inherent among many members of the severely handicapped population, problems that such professionals may not have had to deal with in the past. With the assistance of special educators, preparation programs in a variety of disciplines need to critically evaluate the provision of preservice and/or inservice training components to assist graduates in meeting the needs of severely handicapped persons in integrated communities.

Family Members

The success of the family living unit is probably the single most critical factor influencing the success of community integration of severely handicapped individuals. After all, it is generally the parents and other family members (e.g., siblings) who will spend the greatest amount of time with severely handicapped individuals in integrated community settings. The family members involved may be the natural, foster, and/or group home parents and siblings.

The role of family members in meeting the needs of severely handicapped individuals is basically the same as with any family member. However, the responsibilities of carrying out the role may be considerably more complex and demanding, due to the multiplicity of difficulties that some severely handicapped individuals face daily. Training of family members may be needed not only to assist them in keeping abreast of the most recent developments in special education but to provide stress reduction techniques in coping with a handicapped child. Due to the sometimes demanding nature of caring for some severely handicapped individuals, both parents and siblings may furthermore require a knowledge of the community support systems available (e.g., respite care).

Without the aid of supportive and productive home living-environment, positive community integration of severely handicapped individuals will be difficult. Thus, professionals in personnel preparation programs should not overlook the training needs of family members. University personnel preparation specialists can work with community agencies (e.g., the Association for Retarded Citizens) to ensure that parents and siblings of severely handicapped persons receive appropriate information, assistance, and training when needed.

The General Public

The general public will be called upon to interact in numerous ways with severely handicapped individuals as fellow community members. On city buses, at recreational activities, in local stores and churches, and at other community functions, severely handicapped and nonhandicapped individuals will be in close proximity. Just as some severely handicapped individuals may require training to enable them to react appropriately to nonhandicapped individuals, some nonhandicapped individuals may require basic information to help them understand and effectively interact with severely handicapped individuals. Unfortunately, many nonhandicapped adults were not only educated in segregated schools but never otherwise had the opportunity to learn how to approach and interact with severely handicapped members of society.

It is not necessary that the public undergo formal, technical training regarding severely handicapped individuals. However, there is a need for a basic awareness and understanding of severely handicapped individuals on the part of the general community. Recognizing the needs and abilities of severely handicapped persons can assist nonhandicapped community members to feel more comfortable and secure in their company. Ignorance tends to breed fear and misunderstanding. This has been clearly indicated by some recent activities in which local community members have attempted to prevent group homes for severely handicapped individuals from being located in their neighborhoods.

Some efforts to acquaint the general public with severely handicapped individuals have been provided through the media. News stories on severely handicapped individuals and documentaries on pertinent issues such as "euthanasia" have done much to promote greater awareness and acceptance of severely handicapped individuals. Far greater efforts are needed, however, not only in the media but through face-to-face experiences with severely handicapped persons in the community in order for the general public to finally accept severely handicapped individuals as fellow community members.

Finally, it should be noted that as the integration movement progresses and becomes more of a reality throughout the nation, there will be increasing opportunities for all young, nonhandicapped persons to learn firsthand throughout their school years about severely handicapped individuals. As a result, the need for public education in regard to severely handicapped persons will become less of a burden in the future. As noted by Brown et al. (1979), when severely handicapped and nonhandicapped students attend the same schools from childhood onward, the chances of nonhandicapped persons learning tolerance, understanding, and acceptance of differences are enhanced substantially. In other words, in integrated school settings, many young nonhandicapped persons will be given opportunities daily to learn ways to interact naturally with and understand individuals who experience severe difficulties in physical, emotional, and/or learning characteristics. The benefits of such integration will ultimately be felt by the community-at-large, for it is the young nonhandicapped students of today who will be the parents, teachers, therapists, lawyers, and neighbors of the severely handicapped individuals of tomorrow.

CONCLUSION

Personnel preparation of severely handicapped individuals has expanded in breadth and complexity over the last decade as a result of the integration movement. We have moved from training a few special educators to work in staid, segregated settings to training special and regular educators and a broad range of community members to assist severely handicapped individuals to function as effectively as possible in natural settings. We are thus making considerable progress toward providing comprehensive quality education for students with severe handicaps. Although in many personnel preparation areas (i.e., education of community service workers and training of regular educators) service delivery approaches and training content verification are still in the beginning stages, attention and study in these areas are intensifying. Much remains to be learned and accomplished. However, with the assistance of dedicated professionals in personnel preparation programs across the nation, quality education for severely handicapped students within integrated community settings can continue to advance.

REFERENCES

Baumgart, D., Brown, L., Pumpian, I., Nisbet, J., Ford, A., Sweet, M., Messina, R., & Schroeder, J. Principle of partial participation and individualized adaptations in educational programs for severely handicapped students. *Journal of The Association for the Severely Handicapped*, 1982, *7*, 17–27.
Brown, L., Branston-McClean, M.B., Baumgart, D., Vincent, L., Falvey, M., & Schroeder, J. Using the characteristics of current and subsequent least restrictive environments in the development of curricular content for severely handicapped students. *AAESPH Review*, 1979, *4*, 407–424.
Guralnick, M. Social interactions among preschool children. *Exceptional Children*, 1980, *46*, 248–253.
Guralnick, M. Social behavior of preschool children at different developmental levels: Effects of group composition. *Journal of Experimental Child Psychology*, in press.
Hamre-Nietupski, S., & Nietupski, J. Integral involvement of severely handicapped students within regular public schools. *Journal of The Association for the Severely Handicapped*, 1981, *6*, 30–39.
Porter, R.H., Ramsey, B., Tremblay, A., Iaccobo, M., & Crawley, S. Social interactions in heterogeneous groups of retarded and normally developing children: An observational study. In: G.P. Sackett & H.C. Haywood (eds.), *Observing behavior, Vol. 1: Theory and applications in mental retardation*. Baltimore: University Park Press, 1978.

Reynolds, M., & Birch, J. *Teaching exceptional children in America's schools.* Reston, VA: The Council for Exceptional Children, 1977.

Rynders, J., Johnson, R., Johnson, D., & Schmidt, B. Producing positive interaction among Down Syndrome and nonhandicapped teenagers through cooperative goal structuring. *American Journal of Mental Deficiency*, 1980, *85*, 268–273.

Sontag, E., Certo, N., & Button, J. On a distinction between the education of the severely and profoundly handicapped and a doctrine of limitations. *Exceptional Children*, 1979, *45*, 604–617.

Stainback, S., & Stainback, W. Educating nonhandicapped students about severely handicapped students: A human differences training model. *Education Unlimited*, 1981, *3*, 17–19. (a)

Stainback, S., Stainback, W., & Maurer, S. Training teachers for the severely and profoundly handicapped: A new frontier. *Exceptional Children*, 1976, *42*, 203–210.

Stainback, S., Stainback, W., Schmid, R., & Courtnage, L. Training teachers for the severely handicapped: An accountability model. *Education and Training of the Mentally Retarded*, 1977, *12*(2), 170–174.

Stainback, W., & Stainback, S. A review of research on interactions between severely handicapped and nonhandicapped students. *Journal of The Association for the Severely Handicapped*, 1981, *6*, 23–29. (b)

Stainback, W., & Stainback, S. Preparing regular class teachers for the integration of severely handicapped students into regular schools. *Education and Training of the Mentally Retarded*, in press.

Stainback, W., Stainback, S., & Jaben, T. Providing opportunities for interaction between severely handicapped and nonhandicapped students. *Teaching Exceptional Children*, *13*(2), 1981, 72–75.

Stainback, W., Stainback, S., Raschke, D., & Anderson, R. Three methods for encouraging interactions between severely handicapped and nonhandicapped students. *Education and Training of the Mentally Retarded*, 1981, *16*, 188–192.

Stainback, W., Stainback, S., Strathe, M., & Dedrick, C. Preparing regular class teachers for integration: An experimental study. *Education and Training of the Mentally Retarded*, in press.

Thomas, A. Current trends in preparing teachers of the severely and profoundly retarded: A conversation with Susan and William Stainback. *Education and Training of the Mentally Retarded*, 1980, *15*, 43–49.

Voeltz, L. Children's attitudes toward handicapped peers. *American Journal of Mental Deficiency*, 1980, *84*, 455–464.

Voeltz, L. Effects of structured interactions with severely handicapped peers on children's attitudes. *American Journal of Mental Deficiency*, 1982, *86*, 380–390.

REFERENCE NOTE

1. Ray, J.S. *Ethological studies of behavior in delayed and nondelayed toddler.* Paper presented at the annual meeting of the American Association on Mental Deficiency, Toronto, May, 1974.

8

Program and Curriculum Innovations to Prepare Children for Integration

Luanna Meyer Voeltz

In all fairness, those who advocate segregated programs and specialized institutional living environments for severely handicapped persons are not necessarily motivated by negative intentions. Intolerant community attitudes may have influenced the decision to exclude handicapped persons from community environments, but this public policy of the recent past (and present, in many parts of the country) was instigated by professionals who believed at the time that segregated services were best suited to the needs of children whose abilities and behavior seemed irrevocably discrepant from those of other children. The performance demands of the regular education campus, the school and neighborhood play-

This work was completed while the author was affiliated with the University of Hawaii, and was supported in part by the CETA Special Friends Projects Program Grant No. 3006 and by Contract No. 300–80–0746 from Special Education Programs, Division of Innovation and Development, U.S. Department of Education, awarded to the University of Hawaii. The opinions expressed herein do not necessarily reflect the position or policy of the U.S. Department of Education, and no official endorsement should be inferred.

Special thanks are due to Jerry Brennan, Sue Brown, Royal Fruehling, Norma Jean Hemphill, Gloria Kishi, and Gail Levy for helpful input in many discussions of the issues included in this chapter.

ground, the public assembly, the shopping center, the competitive workplace, the typical community recreation program, open swim at the YMCA, the public bus system, and even the average home were considered beyond the abilities of children with severe handicaps. Moreover, such settings were presumed irrelevant to the children's needs and were variously described as: physically inaccessible ("There are no ramps . . . too many stairs"); unacceptably risky ("My students will catch cold in the drafts," "He'll fall down," "There are too many germs in public schools"); too difficult ("The first grade curriculum is too high-level," "The rules of the game are too complicated"); and psychologically damaging ("These children will be ridiculed, teased, hit, abused, ignored"). Thus, separate and segregated programs and clinical-educational environments to which severely handicapped children were sent to live and learn were either constructed ("We have a lovely, brand new facility for our severely handicapped students") or located in remodeled, existing facilities ("This used to be a tuberculosis hospital," "A wealthy local resident donated the mansion to us in his will").

Not surprisingly, these separate settings presented and are presenting serious problems of their own that are apparent even to their proponents: Facilities were indeed accessible to severely multiply handicapped individuals, but were so isolated and so specialized that they were frequented only by the residents, the students, and the professional staff. (Stein, 1977, comments sardonically, for example, on "trails for the blind" that are used and usable by no one.) The separate facilities were so safe and so healthy that we now have an increased incidence of hepatitis B carriers in such settings, a fact acknowledged by professionals and often used (paradoxically) by the press and by segregationists to resist efforts to transfer children into community school programs. The educational and adaptive performance demands were so easy that the skills learned were almost totally irrelevant to any other environment; even self-help skills were idiosyncratically adapted to the environment and not the child (How many homes have urinals? How many children take group showers? How many adults eat from plastic trays in a cafeteria for three meals a day?). And the settings were so psychologically healthy that—based on descriptive studies of children who lived in them—severely handicapped persons are characteristically described by not only severe developmental delay but also the presence of such extreme behavior problems as aggression, self-abuse, self-stimulation, and noncompliance.

Most professionals serving severely handicapped learners now agree that past practices were fundamentally flawed. An increasing awareness of the abuses, deficits, and basic inhumanity of institutions and other segregated programs isolated from public scrutiny no doubt stimulated the current movement to recognize the rights of all children to live in a home environment, attend a neighborhood school, and participate in community programs and services (see, for example, Blatt, 1970, and Biklen, 1977). Special educators in particular have become convinced that public school and community environments are not only more humane and physically healthy for severely handicapped children, but that they are also more conducive to children's optimal development. There are two major reasons why physical, programmatic, and attitudinal integration into community environments are essential to meet the educational needs of severely handicapped children:

1. Natural contexts are necessary for the development of functional and generalized skills and behaviors that will allow maximum individual adjustment and independence in both current and future environments. A major reason for placing severely handicapped children into integrated schools and other community environments is, of course, to provide them a normalized, natural learning context in which to develop the skills needed to function as independently as possible as adults in the community (Brown, Nietupski, & Hamre-Nietupski, 1976). It seems logical that such skills are best taught and practiced in criterion environments, not in artificial and segregated settings or in simulations of natural situations (Falvey, Brown, Lyon, Baumgart, & Schroeder, 1980). By establishing classrooms for severely handicapped students in the general education community, teachers, parents, and the handicapped students themselves are exposed to the natural cues, correction procedures, and contingencies likely to be available on a continuing basis in the "real world," as opposed to the various manipulations and simulations provided in highly artificial instructional environments. Highly structured, one-to-one discrete trial instruction in isolated classroom settings may indeed result in the acquisition of behaviors in the classroom. But it has become readily apparent that such skills are not functionally useful outside the instructional environment, are rapidly forgotten, and even when they do generalize and maintain over time are often maladaptive or inappropriate (e.g., age-inappropriate leisure skills taught in elementary school and still maintained at secondary school age). As a result, recommendations to teach functional responses in integrated, community environments represent today's "educational best practices" rather than minority professional opinion. Classroom instructional models and strategies reflecting normalized behaviors for natural environments have already been field-tested and are readily available (Ford, Brown, Pumpian, Baumgart, Nisbet, Schroeder, & Loomis, this volume; Holvoet, Guess, Mulligan, & Brown, 1980; Neel, 1981; Wilcox & Bellamy, 1982).

2. Integrated environments and interactions with nonhandicapped persons are necessary for the development of social competence by severely handicapped persons. An equally compelling reason to transfer services for severely handicapped learners to neighborhood public schools and other integrated community environments is a concern for social competence. Segregated environments serving only severely handicapped individuals generally provide only two possible social interaction opportunities: 1) the severely handicapped person can interact with another severely handicapped person; and 2) the severely handicapped person interacts with a large number of "helpers," including teachers, therapists, ward personnel, aides, work supervisors, psychologists, custodial staff, cafeteria workers, physicians, dentists, volunteers, university students, etc. Clearly, the only "peer-type" interaction possible is with other children whose developmental and behavioral characteristics may be similar, but who still cannot offer a variety of social interactions. Patterns of social interaction between severely handicapped peers can and should be facilitated and encouraged (see

Landesman-Dwyer, Berkson, & Romer, 1979, for a review, and Certo & Kohl, this volume, for a curriculum effort in this direction). But it also seems inappropriate that these be the *only* truly social opportunities available to a severely handicapped learner.

In almost all interactions (excepting those of a purely social, spontaneous nature) with caregivers and professionals, the severely handicapped person is the recipient. He or she is helped to do something by a more competent performer, who sets the rules and generally requires rather rigid adherence to established expectations. This limited range of social experiences cannot promote social competence nor does it allow for the development of rewarding social relationships. We have simply not acknowledged the restrictive nature of the caregiver-client and teacher-child interaction that currently dominates all planned and spontaneous social interactions experienced by severely handicapped children in special education settings isolated from their nonhandicapped peers.

We must ask ourselves: What would our lives be like if our experiences were restricted to interactions with authority figures and surreptitious peer interactions, in which we and our peers had limited mobility, possible sensory and motor impairments, few resources, and almost no opportunity to share activities and conversation? What varieties of social experiences, interactions, and relationships have been continuously available to nonhandicapped individuals, from birth to now? Can severely handicapped persons justifiably be denied similar social interaction experiences for any reason whatsoever?

This chapter describes innovative program activities and curriculum components developed in integrated public school settings over a 5-year period to prepare children—both severely handicapped students and their nonhandicapped peers—for day-to-day, mutually rewarding interactions in integrated community environments. The procedures and activities described are not simply ideas or ideals that have yet to meet the test of the classroom. They have been extensively field tested and are being continuously refined in more than a dozen public schools in Hawaii, and in a variety of community settings. Extensive evaluation data are and will be available to document the utility and validity of the program components. The context for the development of these curricula and program elements is described in some detail in the chapter by Kohl, Moses, and Stettner-Eaton. Briefly, however, a statewide administrative decision was made in Hawaii to locate classes (generally self-contained) for severely multiply handicapped, severely to profoundly retarded, and autistic children and youth in elementary and secondary schools serving primarily regular education peers, close to home. The first such classes were established in 1977, and we now estimate that 85% of Hawaii's severely handicapped learners are receiving an education in integrated public schools. The state-sponsored Special Friends Project followed by the Hawaii Integration Project have served throughout this period to facilitate interactions between the children and to prepare them—as well as administrators, teachers, parents, and other constituents—for this dramatic change from the segregated services of the past.

Three program components, all focusing on the needs of the children, are discussed in this chapter: 1) modifications to the existing regular education curriculum and program to incorporate integration concerns; 2) a social performance curriculum component to prepare severely handicapped children for integrated environments; and 3) the Special Friends Program, a systematic, structured, peer interaction program for severely handicapped and non-handicapped same-age dyads and groups of children. The first two innovative curriculum components have undergone 2 years of development and field testing in several Hawaii public schools, and the Special Friends Program has been conducted and evaluated in 12 elementary and secondary schools in the state over the past 4 years. A brief summary of evaluation concerns and available findings follows the description of the three components.

INTEGRATING GENERAL EDUCATION

Once severely handicapped pupils are attending school on general education campuses, interactions between them and their nonhandicapped peers are possible. Such interactions may be initially structured and facilitated by the kinds of programmatic efforts described throughout this volume, including the Special Friends Program discussed later in the chapter. But, eventually, these interactions should occur spontaneously—as natural social activities among children, as well as in the context of integrated group events that are scheduled into the school day. Nearly all severely handicapped children can be included within regular classrooms for various selected activities and programs, e.g., story time, art, and music in elementary grades, etc. For some severely handicapped pupils, mainstreaming in the regular classroom would even be appropriate, but it is doubtful that most severely handicapped children could be appropriately placed with non-handicapped peers for traditional academic instruction. Thus, for most of the academic instruction experienced by nonhandicapped students, severely handicapped peers will not be present. Nevertheless, there are numerous occasions and opportunities during this academic instruction when nonhandicapped students do now or could receive information about and develop attitudes toward their handicapped peers and handicapping conditions. This section outlines the strategies and materials developed by the Hawaii Integration Project to help provide information on and introduce positive attitudes toward severely handicapped students in existing, regular education instructional situations.

In a thought-provoking review of research on attitudes toward disabled persons, Donaldson (1980) noted that most work in this area has simply described existing attitudes of children and adults as if these attitudes were intrinsic to the human condition rather than being the *product* of past and current practices. According to Donaldson, such research neglects the possibility that negative attitudes and behaviors may be both created and maintained by social practices. One such current social practice includes a variety of "charitable" perspectives, services, and activities directed to handicapped persons, such as telethons that evoke sympathy for poster children, volunteerism that honors the magnanimity of the volunteers serving the "less fortunate," and a popular philosophy that whatever is provided to handicapped persons is *given* them because of their needy condition rather than because they have a right to receive the same services and opportunities as other children. Donaldson contends that such attitudes and practices not only contribute to a condescending and archaic philosophy about public services to handicapped persons that many of us would like to change, but that such practices may be responsible for negative attitudes and behavior toward this population. Donaldson also emphasizes that most existing information on attitudes toward handicapped persons is merely descriptive in nature, in other words, it investigates existing attitudes in teachers, administrators, children, etc., and that future work should be focused on validating interventions that are associated with positive *changes* in such attitudes.

Research findings on the social status of mildly handicapped students have often been cited as indicating that these children may be socially isolated from their nonhandicapped peers (Asher & Taylor, 1981; MacMillan, Jones, & Aloia, 1974), prompting some special educators to conclude that even greater rejection would be the fate of severely handicapped pupils (Burton & Hirshoren, 1979) in integrated school settings. Taking into account Donaldson's insights, however, past findings on mildly handicapped pupils should be regarded *not as a justification for continued segregation* but as evidence that something may be at work to create and maintain those negative attitudes and behaviors. Thus, our conclusion would be not that children are naturally cruel toward and/or socially exclude peers who have problems, but that current social practices do not adequately prepare children to interact positively with their peers and may, in fact, even teach negative behavior. As for how to alter this situation, there is considerable empirical evidence that the teacher's behavior in particular can significantly facilitate acceptance of mildly handicapped children by their nonhandicapped classmates in mainstream settings (see Gottlieb, 1978, for a review of such studies). It seems logical to suppose that the modeling of positive versus negative verbal and physical behavior by the numerous adults with influence over a child's life—not the least of whom is the regular classroom teacher who spends 6 hours each school day, 9 months of every year with the child!—would play an important role in determining what a child believes and how he or she behaves.

We currently have little information on how regular education teachers might model attitudes toward handicapped children on a day-to-day basis, and there does not appear to be any systematic effort underway to investigate this issue. One would have to observe systematically the behavior of regular classroom teachers over a long time period and measure student behavior as a function of teacher behavior—a prodigious investment of time and resources. But on the basis of those studies that do exist—which clearly show that when teachers *do* successfully model positive behaviors toward handicapped children, the nonhandicapped children follow suit—the Hawaii Integration Project has attempted to identify program and curriculum areas that exemplify one of two characteristics: 1) the program, printed materials and/or the instructional behavior of the classroom teacher may model negative practices and stereotyped attitudes toward handicapped children and handicapping conditions; or 2) an excellent opportunity to model positive practices and attitudes toward handicapped children and handicapping conditions is overlooked altogether.

Two major mechanisms exist to correct these conditions. First, many areas of the present regular education curriculum could potentially incorporate information and activities to facilitate positive attitudes. Identifying those areas requires a close examination of the purposes and content of a school district's curriculum. Second, many existing "extra" school programs and activities—such as assemblies or field trips that comprise part of the social life of the school, so to speak—can do more to integrate severely handicapped students, and, in the process, foster more positive attitudes. To bring about improvement in this area, knowledge of the individual school's specific routines is needed. The section following outlines our approach to each "need area" in the general education program, and provides sample activities and guidelines to facilitate integrative attitudes and behavior.

Adapting the Regular Education Curriculum

Close scrutiny of the regular education curriculum at each grade level and for each conceivably relevant instructional content area will reveal either areas in which negative portrayals of handicapped persons are presented *or* areas in which opportunities to present positive images and deal constructively with related issues are lost. For example, negative stereotypes of handicapped children throughout a basal reading series for nonhandicapped students may variously include portrayals of helpless children who must be cared for, suggest that handicapped persons belong in institutions or other "protective" (segregated) environments, and emphasize the disabilities and differences of handicapped children such that they are depicted as a group apart from others—a "them" rather than an "us." Many areas of existing curricula also deal with content that ought to logically include reference to handicapped persons. For example, a civil rights unit in social studies may refer to race, ethnicity, religion, sex, and even age as factors that may not be used as criteria to exclude persons from services and activities, but fail to mention handicaps. In our investigation of the regular education curriculum in the Hawaii public schools, we have found numerous *integration information opportunities* that require either correcting negative images and stereotypes or integrating more information and process activities into already existing curriculum units. Our strategy for changing these existing curriculum materials includes: establishing priorities for revisions based upon a school district's regular timetable for curriculum revisions; locating the key personnel throughout the system who both implement the revisions and are responsible for the revised product; and literally preparing suggested units and materials for inclusion into existing materials. In each case, the approach has been to build upon existing goals, objectives, activities, strategies, and materials, rather than adding isolated material or material without regard to the current policies and practices of the district and school.

Analyzing Regular Education Instructional Objectives The state of Hawaii has developed a core set of Foundation Program Objectives (FPOs) that are essentially goal statements for the regular education curriculum. Behaviorally defined Performance Expectations (PEs) provide a breakdown of each FPO; responsibility for each of the PEs is assigned throughout specific grade levels and subject matter within grade levels from kindergarten through grade 12. Ultimately, accountability for the content of the FPOs and their PEs will be measured by a competency test that Hawaii's students will soon be required to pass for high school graduation. The majority of U.S. school districts have likely prepared similar statements of goals and performance objectives for each grade level and content area in regular education (special educators are not the only systematic instructors!). Such goals and objectives can be analyzed in terms of intended and possible attitude changes for regular education children as a function of participation in integrated activities and the provision of information related to handicapping conditions. When suggestions for changes in content or activities are presented with reference to the stated educational goals for a regular education child, curriculum developers and other general educators are far more likely to incorporate such revisions into existing materials and activities.

For example, Hawaii's eight Foundation Program Objectives include three that we utilized as reference points for revisions: 1) develop positive self-concept; 2) develop decision-making and problem-solving skills; and 3) develop a continually growing philosophy that reflects responsibility to self as well as to others. Major responsibility for instructional activities supporting all three of these FPOs is assigned to social studies and guidance courses at various grade levels. Thus, by locating specific performance expectations at each grade level within the social studies and guidance curricula, we were able to identify opportunities to correct negative information and/or integrate positive information and activities. For example, one such PE in the elementary school social studies units for grades K–3 (under the FPO regarding positive self-concept) is that the student "describes and accepts ways in which people are alike and different"; therefore, we developed supplemental activity units to increase understanding and acceptance of handicapped students (Brown, Hemphill, & Voeltz, Note 1). The units emphasize discussion of similarities and differences among nonhandicapped students, discussion of parallel similarities and differences among handicapped students, and problem-solving sessions to help nonhandicapped students critically evaluate statements of fact and assumptions regarding handicapped peers and handicapping conditions. The units include interaction with severely handicapped students that focuses upon the different forms used by nonhandicapped and handicapped students (talking versus signing, walking versus using a wheelchair) to accomplish similar functions (communication, mobility), an approach advocated by White (1980).

In addition to the units surrounding the self-concept FPO, we suggested revisions relating to the FPO on developing decision-making and problem-solving skills (PE: learning and applying decision-making and problem-solving skills) and the FPO on developing a continually growing philosophy that reflects responsibility to self and to others (PEs: acquiring beliefs and values consistent with a democratic society; clarifying and affirming beliefs and values). The problem-solving FPO, in particular, offered a natural vehicle for the children themselves to generate integrative alternatives, as opposed to teachers telling them what to think and do. Ironically, many of us now planning integrated programs as professional educators and parents recognize that we generally grew up in "segregated" childhoods. Today's students, however, are not only best acquainted with the social life of their school and community, but also may not be constrained by traditional concepts and existing possibilities. Thus, while professionals may plan the initial structure of integration efforts, students may ultimately provide the expertise to design optimal programs. Accordingly, the section below outlines a strategy to solicit and facilitate input from students at the same time that integrative information is being presented.

Alternative Instructional Strategies   While the incorporation of positive information into the regular education curricula may be the most obvious strategy for revision, the "decision-making and problem-solving" objective provides a crucial instructional strategy as well. A problem-solving approach is integral to many current social studies curricula, for example, actively involving the children in the learning process. We incorporated a problem-solving approach into instructional activities generally as a supplement to the more traditional lecture and reading formats. For example, one of the social studies lessons in the PE relating to problem solving focuses upon alternative methods and multiple solutions to a problem (Brown, et al., Note 1). In the course of the lesson, we introduce the various "prostheses" that handicapped children use, viewing them not primarily as specialized (i.e., different) equipment but rather as tools, similar to the various tools that all of us use to perform tasks and to accomplish functions that would otherwise be impossible. The lesson is introduced by a discussion of how a child in an illustration (see Figure 1) might be able to reach an apple in a tree. The children's responses are organized into two strategy types: 1) extraordinary "human" effort (e.g., jumping, finding a tall person to reach the apple), and 2) using a tool (e.g., a ladder, stool, apple picker). The first strategy type emphasizes that differences exist among nonhandicapped persons that allow some persons to do things others cannot (e.g., height, strength). The second strategy type emphasizes that all of us regularly use tools to extend our "human" capabilities to obtain needs and wants. Children are asked to generate examples of tools and functions, such as a car or bus to get from home to school, airplane to get from one city to another, spaceship to get to the Moon, writing implements to aid memory, toothbrush to brush teeth, glasses to see more clearly, etc. Finally, the term "prosthesis" is introduced *as a tool* that enables persons to extend their capabilities and accomplish something regardless of a handicapping condition. The main point is that while a prosthesis initially appears to be something different, when viewed as a tool to help us solve a problem (obtain something we need and want) it is quite similar to things we all use. The lesson is presented in a nonlecture format. In over a dozen field tests of the activity at various age levels, the children as a group have never failed to generate the necessary information and insights themselves.

Other problem-solving instructional strategies are utilized in a secondary unit on alienation (Hemphill, Zukas, & Brown, Note 2), an elementary-age "Mystery Game" (Fruehling & Sunabe, Note 3), and a "Special Alternatives" game in which students generate solutions to a series of integration problems in the school

Special Friends Program

Figure 1. Illustration to accompany unit on use of tools and prostheses. Artwork by Sunny Aigner Pauole.

and other community settings (Fruehling, Hemphill, Brown, & Zukas, Note 4). Each of these, as well as other regular education curriculum units and activities, is indexed with the Foundation Program Objective and Performance Expectations that they are intended to support, and therefore are willingly being incorporated into curriculum revisions as they occur.

Integrative, Not Additive, Activities

As should be clear from the previous sections, the Hawaii Integration Project adheres to the principle of integrative—as opposed to additive—procedures to facilitate the integration of severely handicapped children into schools and activities (Hemphill, Note 5). *Additive procedures* are those that require an addition to events and programs already occurring within the school community. Most traditional teacher inservice training sessions are additive, e.g., a 2-hour inservice training session offered on a nonschool day on a voluntary basis. *Integrative procedures*, on the other hand, are those that expand upon and refine events already occurring within the school community, and require identification of existing programs and events as well as adaptations and expansions of those events. Thus, an existing unit on alienation in an eighth grade social studies curriculum could be expanded to include reference to the exclusion of handicaped persons from the "in" group as another example of alienation (see Hemphill et al., Note 2). The integrative principle has also been applied in the design of the instructional strategies incorporated into existing curricula. Thus, in the program modifications discussed in the previous section, a problem-solving approach that was integral to the existing social studies curricula is also utilized in the learning process of our integrative social studies units. Rather than presenting material in lecture format, for example, game format activities are available to support the various social studies and guidance objectives (e.g., Fruehling et al., Note 4).

An integrative approach to influencing the regular education curriculum, then, involves exploring options for adapting and expanding units and activities to include ideas and issues relevant to the disabled. Hemphill (Note 5) outlines several parameters that should be kept in mind when developing such curriculum options: 1) The purpose is not to rework the existing curriculum so that the major focus shifts to disabled persons; instead, ideas in the curriculum should be expanded to include reference to the disabled. 2) Personalized and process activities are preferable to information-oriented and static activities. Thus, whenever an adaptation can be made by arranging integrated and personalized inter-actions between regular education and nonhandicapped children and their con-stituents, this should be done rather than presenting nonhandicapped children with information about handicapped persons or simulating handicapping conditions. If, as part of the regular orientation program, nonhandicapped kindergarten children are to learn something about their severely handicapped peers in the room down the hall, an activity should be arranged in which the two groups of children interact, rather, for example, than giving talks to the nonhandicapped children on cerebral palsy or on how they should be nice to children with handicaps. Also, rather than providing nonhandicapped students with positive alternatives, solu-tions, and the proper perspective on the disabled, the nonhandicapped students should, whenever possible, be asked to generate such solutions and critiques themselves. Not only will they become more actively involved in the issues and their solutions, but, in our experience, children produce creative "answers" that often have not occurred to us! After all, children probably know the possibilities and constraints of the school social environment and of their own "world of the child" far better than project staff and teachers do.

Finally, in developing integrative strategies, general educational principles should be presented and analyzed with reference to real-life situations and people at the school, rather than in the abstract. Thus, an activity to support the general education Performance Expectation of "learning to understand and relate effec-tively to others" might include experience and skill development in actual interactions with severely handicapped peers who communicate using sign lan-guage and augmentative communication aids. The Special Alternatives game, mentioned above, is designed so that the children generate solutions to 11 different problem categories that imply exclusion of handicapped children, from physical, programmatic, and attitudinal access to events and places (Fruehling et al., Note 4). The game can provide an excellent way to begin to analyze a specific school in order to target integration activities within that school's schedule and routines. Even though severely handicapped children may attend school on a general education campus, they may nevertheless be effectively segregated from the general education community. The physical location of the classroom in relationship to same-age nonhandicapped peers; whether or not lunch and recess allow for interactions between the children; and various other arrangements of time, space, and events can isolate handicapped children. Parallel and segregated activities, such as separate orientations, teacher meetings, open houses, field trips, and assemblies, for handicapped versus nonhandicapped students and their parents and teachers, should be identified and replaced by integrated ones.

SOCIAL PERFORMANCE OBJECTIVES
FOR SEVERELY HANDICAPPED STUDENTS

An important reason for integrated educational services is to provide a positive and natural context for the development of social competence by severely handicapped students. Given the expectation that today's severely handicapped learners are being prepared to attend school, live, work, and play in integrated community settings, it is crucial that severely handicapped persons acquire the various social skills associated with these "normalized" patterns of behavior and interaction. Social skills allow individuals access to environments, situations, and relationships that, in turn, provide valuable primary and social reinforcement as well as the chance to acquire new skills. Nearly every task that we perform also requires mastery of certain social behaviors. Failure to follow certain social "rules" and the presence of maladaptive and disruptive social behaviors have been consistently related to lack of success in community placements for severely handicapped persons (Gaylord-Ross, 1980; Renzaglia & Bates, 1983). But perhaps even more important than overall social competence is that acquiring the social performance skills involved in interactions with other persons allows for the development of positive social relationships, i.e., friendships. Friendships are generally considered important in their own right, and are associated with benefits for the individual such as support in stressful situations, personal satisfaction and pleasure, and as the context for further development in other, nonsocial areas (such as language, leisure skills, vocational skills, motor skills, etc.).

Traditionally, social skills have been a neglected area in curricula for severely handicapped children and youth. Discussions of "social competence" typically outline a dichotomous set of isolated target behaviors, some of which are to be increased and others decreased (Renzaglia & Bates, 1983); furthermore, teaching strategies directed toward "good" (teach those) or "bad" (get rid of those) behaviors seem to be viewed as equally meritorious approaches to meeting the social needs of severely handicapped learners. As Renzaglia and Bates (1983) emphasize, special educators do not appear to adhere to any theory of social competence that might guide curriculum development and programs in this area. There does not now exist any systematic hierarchy or complex of social skills organized into what could be termed a "social performance curriculum" to guide goal selection and programming. This is in marked contrast to the numerous materials available in traditional curricular domains such as motor, language, self-help, etc., as well as those focused on community living skills, e.g., vocational, leisure, and domestic living curriculum components.

A Social Performance Curriculum Component

McFall (1982) presents a model of social skills in which he emphasizes that any behavior ("public or private; verbal, motoric or autonomic") can be analyzed in terms of its social implications. Persons who are judged socially competent by others in a particular situation (which may or may not involve interaction with another person) are apparently evaluated according to social rules that apply in that situation—even though persons cannot always articulate what those rules are. The social performance curriculum model utilized by the Hawaii Integration Project reflects McFall's perspective on social skills, and focuses upon the context and content of the social rules that govern expected behavior. Major features of this curriculum include: 1) a skill acquisition perspective, as opposed to the incorporation of a deviance reduction component; 2) a view of social skills that involves not only exhibiting appropriate behavior (or withholding certain behavior) but also making important discriminations among multiple cues that indicate which behaviors are appropriate; and 3) the interrelatedness of social skills with responses from other domains.

Our perspective on excess (problem) behavior is to view it as a source of information on the learner's current repertoire of functional strategies used to satisfy needs and to express preferences. Knowing how a child accomplishes certain functions in given situations provides the teacher with valuable information on what is important to that child, as well as the status of his or her existing behavioral skills. The eradication of problem behaviors, however, is not considered an appropriate social performance objective to incorporate into a child's individualized education program (IEP). Rather, the social skills that should be included in the educational plan should consist of positive, functional skills that would provide that learner with maximum use in multiple situations and across time. At most, the presence of an excess behavior—which the child uses to perform a certain function—may indicate that programming an alternative positive social behavior should be a priority over another social skill objective that might otherwise have been selected. But the approach here is to teach new, social performance skills to prepare the child to be maximally independent and able to function in current and future integrated community environments.

We have (arbitrarily) divided all social skill task performance contexts into eight major interactive situation types, as depicted in Figure 2. These are defined in Table 1 along with examples of each type. Note that not all of these "situation types" involve social interaction per se with another person, but that each situation

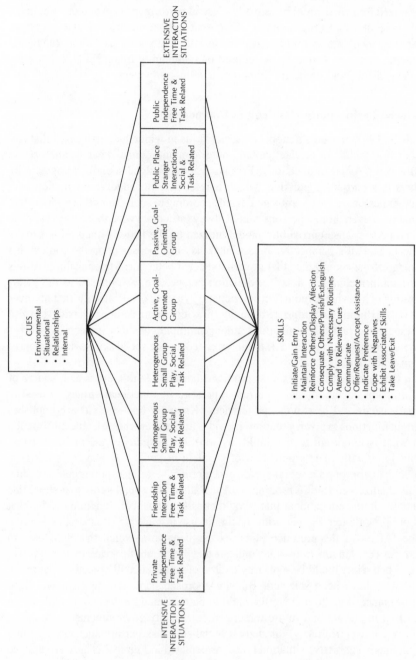

Figure 2. A model of social performance: cues, context, and skills. From Voeltz et al. (1983).

168

Table 1. Major social performance situations and examples

Situation type[a]	Examples of situation type
Private Independence: Free Time and Task Related	Playing Pac Man on a home video computer (no one else is at home); watching television alone; repairing a leak in the ceiling
Friendship Interaction: Free Time and Task Related	Playing Pac Man with a best friend; eating dinner with one's spouse; arguing with a close friend; going swimming with a lover
Homogeneous Small Group: Play, Social, Task Related	Attending a slumber party of four sixth-grade peers; three close friends looking together for an apartment to rent; discussing a problem with two close colleagues
Heterogeneous Small Group: Play, Social, Task Related	Mother with son and daughter going to the movies together; older sister, friend, and younger sister going to store together; children from different classes talking at recess
Active, Goal-Oriented Group	Playing soccer; playing baseball; working on road construction with a road crew; learning regrouping in third-grade math class lesson
Passive, Goal-Oriented Group	Watching a movie at the theater; attending a football game; attending a Broadway play or opera at the Met
Public Place Stranger Interactions: Social and Task Related	Helping a small child who has dropped a package on the bus; asking the grocery clerk where to find the milk; asking the bus driver for a transfer; ignoring loud shouting from a motorist on the street
Public Independence: Free Time and Task Related	Walking through the supermarket shopping for groceries; taking the bus to work; jogging along a jogger's path in the park; waiting for a plane at the airport

From Voeltz et al. (1983).

[a]The situation types listed here and in Figure 2 are arranged from intensive interactions (at the top of this table) to extensive interactions (at the bottom). Intensive suggests closer interactions or adherence to social rules over which the individual performer has a great deal of control regarding what is acceptable behavior and what is not. Extensive suggests more "distant" interactions where the individual performer follows a set of social rules that are usually more rigid and assumed to be less forgiving; these rules are almost identically applied to every person in that environment with some allowances for variables such as age (Examples: Nearly everyone will ask the bus driver for a transfer in exactly the same way—an extensive interaction. On the other hand, conversations between best friends—an intensive interaction—differ markedly from dyad to dyad).

does require adherence to a set of social rules that are somehow known to and followed by persons judged to be socially competent by others. Thus, walking along the sidewalk at a shopping mall requires the utilization of various social rules regarding the display of certain social responses, depending upon certain characteristics of the environment, the situation, and the other person(s) who may happen to be present. If one is walking with a best friend, this is a friendship interaction, and one can engage in familiar and friendly social responses with that person.

Note, however, that the social "rules" of a shoppping mall and those of interacting with a best friend are not mutually exclusive, since in the example given, the
"best friend" situation type is somewhat constrained by the "public independence" situation type. Thus, the full range of intimate behaviors ordinarily
permitted in a close friendship would not generally be permitted in the public arena
of the shopping center as they would in a more private context. Another set of
social rules also dictates expected behavior toward strangers who happen to be
walking along the mall, and a variation of those "stranger rules" applies to
interactions with a clerk in one of the stores. Each situation type involves the
application of similar responses, mediated in form by the rules of that situation.
One may hug a close friend upon meeting at the shopping mall after a long
absence, but one smiles politely and briefly, being careful not to maintain eye
contact for too long a period of-time, at a stranger on the mall, and then only if your
paths have somehow unavoidably crossed. Teaching a social skill such as "greeting," then, is far more complicated than teaching the verbal response *hi* when
another person says *hello*.

Table 2 presents the major feature categories or cues of each situation type.
Descriptions of the categories (and examples) are listed, each of which requires
that the social performer make certain discriminations. Table 3 lists the 12 major
skills that form the basic core of social responses needed in all the situation types.
With rare exceptions, each response is at times used in each situation, but the exact
nature of the response will differ based upon that situation—hence the importance
of discrimination training in addition to teaching the skills themselves. A general
definition and examples for each social skill are included in the table.

Peer Interactions and Social Skill Development

Interactions with nonhandicapped peers provide an ideal context for the development of the social skills described in Table 1. In particular, the Special Friends
Program is designed to facilitate such interactions during the initial stages of
integration. We have developed guidelines for teachers to follow in selecting
appropriate social skill goals to include on each severely handicapped child's IEP,
along with references to interactions with nonhandicapped peers as part of the IEP
instructional objectives and/or evaluation procedures (Voeltz, Hemphill, Brown,
Kishi, Klein, Fruehling, Collie, Levy, & Kube, 1983). The section following
describes the Special Friends Program in more detail, but the important point here
is that the peer interactions are not formal tutor-tutee situations in which the
nonhandicapped child *instructs* the handicapped child. Rather, the interactions are
designed as "generalization sessions" that provide an additional, more natural
opportunity for the handicapped child to practice, and the teacher to measure, the
acquisition of skills as outlined in the student's IEP. The social skills targeted for
emphasis in these peer interactions should be natural for that context. Though such
experiences clearly are learning situations for both children, it is crucial to
preserve their integrity as social and mutually enjoyable interchanges. The
rewards for participating in the interaction must be intrinsic to the social exchange

Table 2. Description of situation features and examples

Major features of situation	Description (examples)
Environmental Cues: Place/Setting	Physical surroundings in which the interaction occurs (swimming pool, park, kitchen)
Materials	Objects manipulated or in contact during the interaction (video game, card game, bus fare)
Situational Cues: Event	Occurrence or happening that may impact the interaction or provide the context in which responses are to occur (soccer game, dramatic play, argument)
Goal-Oriented Task	A complex of behavior leading to an end result; behavior of participants is expected to accomplish a specific purpose (taking the bus to intended destination, winning a basketball game, marriage proposal)
Time	Temporal elements/restrictions (weekends, lunch break, evening)
Relationship Cues: Stranger	Unfamiliar person, not an acquaintance (other shoppers at shopping center, riders on the bus, children in another grade at school)
Nonpersonal Significant	Person who is not an acquaintance but who occupies a role through which information/services may be acquired or sought; interactions with this person are part of the specific social context (police officer, cashier at supermarket, principal of school)
Personal Significant	Person known to individual, an acquaintance or intimate friend (family member, classmate, lover, best friend)
Internal Cues: Personal Interest	Whether or not the situation or activity reflects a personal preference or nonpreferred event/interaction, based upon previous experiences, etc. (a preference: person may enjoy a Broadway play but not a football game)
Physiological Need	Internal/intrinsic desire or impulse that may not be related to obvious external stimulus event (turning on the radio, stretching, yawning)

From Voeltz et al. (1983).

between the severely handicapped and nonhandicapped child. Anything that serves to interfere with or decrease these rewards, or that provides potentially competing and distracting rewards (e.g., social reinforcement from the teacher)

Table 3. Definitions and examples of major skill needs

Major skill need	Definition (examples)
Initiate/Gain Entry	Behavior that allows a person to gain access to interaction, either to initiate an interaction or to enter one that is already underway; to begin or start an event/exchange (joining a game of kickball, starting a conversation with a classmate, inquiring regarding the cost of a ticket to a movie)
Maintain Interaction	Behavior that allows the interaction, activities, and/or event to continue (tolerate noise at a school assembly, taking one's turn in a game)
Reinforce Others/Display Affection	Provide others with positive feedback that is rewarding to them (smiles, verbal/social reinforcement, hug)
Consequate Others/Punish/ Extinguish	Provide others with feedback that indicates that their response was inappropriate, unpleasant, etc., and that extinguishes such behavior (telling another to stop teasing, turning away from a group, ignoring obscene and aggressive remarks by passing motorist)
Comply with Necessary Routines	Adhere to minimal "rules" of a particular context, follow routines of given situation (passing ball to next person, standing in line at checkout counter in supermarket, waiting until it is one's turn in card game)
Attend to Relevant Cues	Behavior that enables person to discriminate/ delineate stimuli critical to that situation and thus respond in appropriate manner (orient to visual display of video game, localize sounds, watch when ball comes within reach)
Communicate	Verbal (vocal or nonvocal) and/or gestural behavior that makes needs known to others; sharing of information and feelings with others (looks toward desired toy, pounds on door to go out, talking on the telephone with a friend)
Offer/Request/Accept Assistance	Behavior that provides assistance or instruction to another person, asking for help when needed, accepting help from another person when needed (tolerate being physically guided through a response, asks Mom to tie shoelaces, picks up package for a child on the bus)
Indicate Preference	Behavior that allows person to make a choice/ decision from among alternatives available or presented by others (pointing to favorite ice cream flavor in store, select Space Invaders from video games)

(continued)

Table 3. (*continued*)

Major skill need	Definition (examples)
Cope with Negatives	When presented with a negative consequence for previous response or a difficulty in effecting needs or intent, can exhibit alternate strategy to continue an interaction or complete a task (find another toy if first choice is broken, go to another movie if first choice is sold out)
Exhibit Associated Skills (Nonsocial)	Engage in the nonsocial skills necessary to the interaction situation, i.e., those skills that may be exhibited in a social context but are considered to be in another domain such as motor, cognitive, language, etc. (move arm to push ball to peer, run to participate in relay race, keep score in pinball game)
Take Leave/Exit	Behavior to terminate or withdraw from an interaction situation, cease participation in an activity when appropriate, desired, etc. (wave good-bye, turn off toy, say good-bye and hang up the telephone, tell a peer that you must leave because you have an appointment)

From Voeltz et al. (1983).

jeopardizes the likelihood that the relationship will endure beyond that immediate situation or extend into the daily lives of both children now and in the future.

For this reason, leisure time activities that are intrinsically interesting to both the nonhandicapped and the severely handicapped child are an ideal context for the peer interaction. Wuerch and Voeltz (1982) describe selected leisure time activities that are interesting to most children (e.g., pinball, video games, Simon); and emphasize that the leisure curriculum component can be used as a starting point for interactions. Table 4 provides a sample leisure activity interaction and a list of accompanying social skills that were targeted for one of the elementary-age students in our program. According to procedures detailed in Wuerch and Voeltz (1982), a preferred leisure activity to meet this child's leisure time needs was identified. In this case, the teacher included the leisure skill objective on the IEP, and conducted leisure skill instruction as part of the child's educational program. Interactions with nonhandicapped peers provided the opportunity to expand a leisure objective originally designed for independent free-time use into a skill that could also be used in friendship and small-group situations. Thus, in addition to the leisure objectives that were targeted for direct teacher instruction, the teacher identified specific responses for the 12 major social skill categories that the student could develop and practice in interactions with nonhandicapped peers where the children play together with the Musical Flute. The nonhandicapped children do not actually instruct the severely handicapped child, but are attuned to the skills that the child is practicing and can naturally provide a model and physical assistance for individual responses, just as they would normally do in any peer interaction. The teacher, on the other hand, may well include teacher-instruction on each of these

Table 4. Sample social skill objectives for situation "Playing Musical Flute with Peers"

Category	Sample for situation
Situation	Heterogeneous Small Group: Play/Social
Major Features:	
Environment	"Musical Flute"
Situation	Start of activity; end of activity play period
Relationship	Classmates
Internal	Preferred activity for target child
Skill Needs:	
Initiate	Approaches others by moving wheelchair to group
Maintain	Presses keys to activate flute
Reinforce	Smiles, nods, eye contact with other children
Consequate	Ignores interruptions
Comply	Takes turns with other group members
Attend	Orients to flute and watches other children's play
Communicate	Signs "Want to play" and "My turn"
Accept Help	Tolerates physical assistance to reach toy
Indicate	
Preference	Points to flute when asked to make choice
Cope with	
Negatives	Makes other choice when game is not available
Associated	
Skills	Motor behavior to activate flute; language behavior to communicate with other children
Exit	Waves good-bye when other children leave

From Voeltz et al. (1983).

social skills in other contexts throughout the school day consistent with that child's educational goals. Thus far, the Hawaii Integration Project has incorporated over 100 such social skill development objectives into severely handicapped children's IEPs over a 2-year period, and included, in each IEP, reference to interactions with nonhandicapped peers as part of the objective and/or the evaluation procedures to measure mastery of the objective (Voeltz et al., 1983).

THE SPECIAL FRIENDS PROGRAM

Both The Association for the Severely Handicapped (TASH) and the National Society for Children and Adults with Autism, (NSAC) have adopted formal resolutions supporting community placement of severely handicapped persons to allow access to comprehensive, systematic, and chronological age-appropriate interactions with persons who do not have identifiable handicaps. Yet, serious concerns remain as to whether community services will be equipped to provide appropriate quality services for severely handicapped learners and whether the nonhandicapped community will accept this integration (Sullivan, 1981). The premise of the program components presented in this chapter is that all handicapped children—without exception—have the right to receive a quality education in a neighborhood public school that serves primarily nonhandicapped chronological age peers, according to the natural population proportions (Brown, Branston, Hamre-Nietupski, Johnson, Wilcox, & Gruenewald, 1979; Brown, Ford, Nisbet, Sweet, Donnellan, & Gruenewald, 1983; Sontag, Certo, & Button, 1979; Voeltz, 1980a). This dramatic change from past practices requires personal and professional adjustments by a variety of professionals, as well as attitudinal and behavioral adjustments by parents, children, and the community. The concerns expressed by those who oppose integration (see Sullivan, 1981, for a summary of these issues) emphasize the necessary adjustments. While concern over adjustments should *under no circumstances* be allowed to delay the provision of integrated services, there is much that can and needs to be done to ensure a comfortable transition period for all involved.

The Special Friends Program was designed to prepare both nonhandicapped and severely handicapped children in Hawaii for the transition to integrated public school services. The program has undergone extensive planning and development, and data regarding intended outcomes are provided later in the chapter. We view Special Friends as a temporary intervention for the initial years of integrated public school services—a model of "extra help" to allow children (and their constituents) to develop the attitudes and skills needed to engage in positive and mutually rewarding interactions with one another. These peer interactions have been designed to be as normalized as possible and can be expected to generalize to other nonschool environments and to maintain over time in a variety of educational and community settings and situations. Implementation of the program is appropriate only if the following basic conditions can be met:

1. Both severely handicapped and nonhandicapped chronological age peers attend the same neighborhood public school. This is not a program of "reverse mainstreaming" whereby nonhandicapped "volunteers" make periodic field trips from their general education campus to a segregated, special education school. We view this as an unacceptable compromise to integration.
2. The children who will interact with one another are within a similar age range. The program is not designed for nonhandicapped secondary students to interact with handicapped elementary age children, or vice versa.
3. The school setting is physically, programmatically, and attitudinally capable of supporting integrated activities. The classroom serving severely handicapped children must be located in reasonable proximity to classrooms serving nonhandicapped peers; recess and lunch times and places should be shared; and the educational staff—both regular and special education—must be willing to allow natural interactions and integrated activities to occur.

Given these minimal "conditions," the Special Friends Program can be initiated by any qualified person on the school staff (e.g., special education teacher, guidance counselor, vice principal, regular education teacher. The training manual outlines adaptations for various grade levels, based upon extensive field testing and feedback on previous versions of the manual (Voeltz et al., 1983).

Again, it should be emphasized that Special Friends is a transitional program. Once the program has been operating for 2 to 4 years, the educational staff, the children, their parents and constituents should be ready to progress to a more normalized and natural level of integration and interaction. Indeed, the true measure of the success of integration would be the demise of a need for such special programs or even the concept of and terms "special friend."

Philosophy and Purpose of Special Friends

The Special Friends Program has two major goals: 1) to develop positive, mutually rewarding personal relationships between severely handicapped and non-handicapped children that will generalize to nonschool environments and will maintain over time; and 2) to support the development of social competence by both severely handicapped and nonhandicapped children, in order that they can acquire the social performance skills to successfully function in integrated community environments. To accomplish these two goals, the Special Friends Program focuses upon *personalized interactions* between the children as the context for the development of *social interaction skills*.

Most intervention programs to date have been primarily of two types: 1) providing children with information about handicapping conditions (the difference between mental retardation and mental illness, definitions of autism and cerebral palsy, etc.); and 2) utilizing nonhandicapped children as tutors or helpers in programs for severely handicapped children (Donaldson, 1980). The Special Friends Program attempts to avoid both of these approaches. In contrast, it seems logical that nonhandicapped children are more likely to accept their severely handicapped peers if they: first, come to appreciate severely handicapped children *as peers*—i.e., as other persons more like themselves than different, and who thus deserve the same opportunities, considerations, and affections as do "normal" individuals (personalization); and, second, if they feel comfortable around their severely handicapped peers because they have acquired the social and communication skills to engage in a meaningful and enjoyable interchange (social skill development).

While definitions of disabilities are not particularly important to children (Special Friends does provide lists of typical questions children ask and answers that have worked well; see Voeltz et al., 1983), children do need to learn specific social interaction skills that are relevant to the individual severely handicapped peer's current repertoire. Both severely handicapped and nonhandicapped children will need assistance in learning how to interact with one another initially. For nonhandicapped children, the approach is not simply to offer reassurance so that fears and uncertainties can be alleviated, or provide a philosophical lecture on acceptance. Though the program allows for the expression and discussion of such concerns in group sessions (discussed briefly below), the major emphasis is peer interactions and the skill development needed for those interactions. Since the severely handicapped child's behavioral repertoire is probably quite unlike that of nonhandicapped children, regular education students, quite honestly, do not initially know how to play, communicate, and thus interact with handicapped peers. Just as each severely handicapped student is learning new social skills in the interaction, the nonhandicapped child must learn specific functional strategies if a meaningful exchange is to occur.

Special Friend interactions are intended to be primarily social. The nonhandicapped child is not viewed as a "helper" or "tutor" for the severely handicapped child, and subtle pressures to cast the relationship in these terms must be resisted. Based upon our experiences over several years—working with many adults who view the relationships as helping ones regardless of how the children see them—we have developed strategies to avoid common pitfalls and to help ensure the success of these interactions (Voeltz et al., 1983). For example, a mistake to avoid would be distributing end-of-the-year awards only to the nonhandicapped Special Friends—a practice sure to undo any pretense that the interaction was a friendship and not a service. If nonhandicapped children view themselves as dispensers of time and resources to help other children, how can they develop respect for the civil rights of their severely handicapped peers? In addition, all children—handicapped and nonhandicapped—who participate in the program should be referred to as "special friends," and interaction activities must be carefully selected so as to allow natural interactions in which both children can perform alternating responses that are mutually reinforcing. If, on the other hand, the special education teacher takes advantage of the presence of a nonhandicapped fourth grader to "run a program," "take Johnny to the therapy room," help set the snack table, or even feed a severely handicapped student, the helper-helpee line is irrevocably drawn. To thus utilize nonhandicapped children in this way would be inconsistent with their educational needs (after all, they too are in school to learn), and can even be dangerous to one or both children (e.g., a nonhandicapped child should *never* lift, carry, feed or toilet a severely handicapped child!).

Program Structure and Activities

The program includes three major activity areas: 1) a general school orientation that focuses on social interactions and friendships among severely handicapped and regular education children and that also serves as the "recruiting" mechanism for Special Friends; 2) a core of eight regular education group activity sessions for the nonhandicapped Special Friends; and 3) scheduled social interactions, primarily dyadic and small group, between severely handicapped and same-age nonhandicapped peers.

Orientation A Special Friends slide/sound show is developed for each school that will conduct the program. The project has produced three scripts and synchronized audio sound tracks for lower elementary, upper elementary, and secondary levels that we provide to the school as an introduction to the program. The package is professionally made, with an "upbeat" and fast-moving sound track and a script that discusses common feelings about severely handicapped children and the possibility of learning new friendships in the program. A scenario is also provided for the content of approximately 70 slides that are taken at the school to complete the production (a small number of introductory and ending slides are standard and are provided by the project). These slides are school scenes, primarily of the students themselves. A special effort is made to include attractive photographs of each severely handicapped child, and, whenever possible, the children are photographed in integrated contexts with nonhandicapped peers. Also, a general rule of thumb for the pictures is that severely handicapped children should not be portrayed in any manner that would be embarrassing to a non-handicapped peer (e.g., in diapers or not fully dressed). We obtain parental permission prior to taking the pictures, and offer those families a preview of the finished slide/sound production (and the right to remove any photo of their child that they do not like) before it is actually shown at the school.

The finished production (which is slightly over 5 minutes long) is scheduled for school-wide showing, but to no more than two classrooms at a time—to allow for more active student participation. After seeing the show, children are told that they will be given an opportunity to sign up for Special Friends in about a week. Large numbers of children (not all of whom are serious) will do so immediately; a more realistically interested group results from the week's waiting period. Even so, in our experience approximately 20%–30% of elementary age and 5% of secondary age youngsters typically begin the program.

The Regular Education Sessions   After sign-ups, a series of eight weekly group sessions is conducted for the regular education participants, led by the program trainer (who can be a teacher, counselor, etc.). Following are those "core" sessions that have been extensively piloted; not all of them are essential, however, and many others are available and could be substituted. The eight lessons are: 1) What Is a Disability? 2) How Do We Communicate? 3) What Is a Prosthesis? 4) How Can We Play Together? 5) How Does a Disabled Person Live? (this session is conducted by a disabled guest speaker, or can be one of a number of films) 6) How Do Nonhandicapped People View Handicapped People? 7) What Is a Friend? and 8) Why Integration? Each session requires approximately 15–30 minutes, and detailed lesson plans are provided for the trainer (Voeltz et al., 1983).

The Interactions   Each nonhandicapped child spends weekly recess and other free-time periods with a selected severely handicapped Special Friend. The nature of these one-to-one interactions is usually structured by each special education teacher, and may include a wide variety of activities that are all primarily social in nature. In the development of our Social Interaction Observation System (SIOS), which was designed to allow us to study these interactions, we found that at various age levels children were engaged in joint movement (e.g., pushing a wheelchair, riding a bike), toy play, music, grooming (e.g., styling another child's hair—something regular education children do among themselves and thus considered "normalized"), instructing (e.g., showing a child how to work a toy), watching (a movie, etc.), and general social play (e.g., one-two-three). Whenever possible, the interactions are coordinated with specific IEP objectives for the special education student so that they support social skill development (see earlier discussion in this chapter), but never to the extent that the interaction itself becomes an instructional situation rather than a peer exchange.

The actual length of the program has varied from a minimum of 8 weeks to an entire year. We generally recommend that the program take place within a semester's time—to allow the regular education children to participate again the following semester if they wish to do so, to allow for participation on an informal basis (our ultimate goal, after all!), and to allow nonhandicapped children to drop out gracefully without experiencing loss of status or self-doubts. The intention throughout the program structure is that the experience be a positive one, regardless of the degree of a child's involvement.

INTEGRATION AND PEER INTERACTION OUTCOMES

There is now considerable evidence that systematic interventions designed to promote positive social interactions between severely handicapped and nonhandicapped children result in significantly more positive behaviors and attitudes by both groups of children (Rynders, Johnson, Johnson, & Schmidt, 1980; Voeltz 1980a, 1980b, 1982; Voeltz & Brennan, in press). These positive changes occur simply as a function of exposure over time, so that placement of self-contained classes on a general education campus results in more positive attitudes toward children with handicaps by regular education children as compared to the attitudes expressed by the latter in settings without such classes (Voeltz, 1980a, 1982). However, structured and systematic interaction experiences between the children are most clearly associated with significant improvements on various social behavior measures (Rynders et al., 1980; Voeltz, 1982; Voeltz & Brennan, in press).

Friendships between Handicapped and Nonhandicapped Children

Aside from evidence that nonhandicapped children will develop positive attitudes and behavior toward their severely handicapped peers in integrated school settings, what other benefits might occur for regular education children as a consequence of integration? Rubin (1980) has emphasized that current patterns of friendship most likely to receive the approval of adults are unnecessarily restrictive and may inhibit children's social development. For example, cross-age friendships between a younger and an older child were once quite typical in children's lives but now are socially disapproved—probably as a result of our age-graded education system. Yet there are potentially many benefits to children from such heterogeneous friendships: older children may develop an increased self-concept, sense of responsibility, and personal satisfaction from a "big brother/big sister" relationship with a younger child. In addition, the younger child may learn more easily and feel more comfortable in the presence of an older child—only slightly more "skilled" in comparison to the younger child—rather than an adult. Many social and other skills are undoubtedly learned by children from other children rather than from adults (certainly, everything that nonhandicapped children learn is not directly taught by their regular education teachers or even by their parents). To some extent, an interaction between same-age severely handicapped and nonhandicapped children resembles the kind of cross-age interaction that Rubin discusses, and presumably similar benefits might occur.

Current social patterns among children and adults in our culture are most likely to be highly homogeneous, restricted to a small set of "best friends" who are very much like ourselves. These relationships reflect an "in group/out group" orientation, in which we extend social acceptance to those who are very much like ourselves and meet other exclusionary criteria. Surely it is possible to value and experience mutually rewarding, "heterogeneous" friendships—with people who are somehow quite different from our usual friends. Heterogeneous interactions among individuals and cultures most probably represent a higher stage in social development than do segregation, rejection, and isolation from one another. Provided that social interactions among severely handicapped children and children who are not handicapped are mutually beneficial—that is, they are not charitable-type, uni-directional relationships in which one child is seen as the giver and the other as the taker—they should result in increased skills in social interaction, not only for the handicapped child but also for the nonhandicapped peer. Which of us would reject outright an opportunity to improve our own social skills? Learning how to interact with severely handicapped persons not only implies the development of new social and communication skills, but also provides practice in adapting behavior to widely varying social demands. Regular education children do, in fact, describe their relationships with handicapped peers in such positive terms when asked for their own perceptions of the interactions (Voeltz, 1980b; Voeltz & Brennan, in press; Note 6).

We are monitoring several data sources in an effort to gain specific evidence regarding the effects of the three program components upon the children involved: 1) individual pupil progress on the social skill IEP objectives for each severely handicapped project participant is being measured (observational data are being collected in time-series format over a 2-year period); 2) attitudes of non-handicapped project participants—with appropriate control samples—toward handicapped peers are being measured (group-administered attitude measures are available, adapted for different age levels K–12); 3) commercially available assessment of self-concept and peer affiliation (both teacher- and self-ratings) are being collected on a preprogram and postprogram basis for a sample of program participants in comparison to nonparticipants; 4) narrative and interview self-reports regarding students' perceptions of the social interactions have been collected for a large sample of regular education children while participating in integration activities; and 5) systematic behavioral observation of the handicapped-nonhandicapped peer dyads over time and in comparison to teacher-child dyads are being collected for a sample of project children and youth. The Social Interaction Observation System (SIOS), noted earlier, was designed specifically for this last measure, and is available in computer scan scoring format. The SIOS monitors seven major categories of behavior for both the handicapped and nonhandicapped children involved in the interaction, including over 44 individual behaviors. Specific findings regarding the nature and quantity of these dyadic peer interactions are available in Voeltz and Brennan (in press). In addition to already published studies that have been referenced throughout the chapter, further evaluation data reports will be available as a result of both the Hawaii activities during 1981–1982 and replication efforts now underway in several Minnesota schools.

CONCLUSION

Ultimately, an accepting community that also has acquired the skills to communicate and interact with severely handicapped persons not only removes the last barriers to integration but also dramatically increases opportunities available to severely handicapped persons. Severely handicapped learners may not have sufficient time during their school years to learn everything they would need to know in order to function independently in all integrated community environments. If, however, those environments contain nonhandicapped persons who have gone to school with children with severe handicaps, who have learned to enjoy personal satisfactions from their interactions with severely handicapped persons, and who now respect their right to be at home, school, and work without restriction, then almost no activity would be inaccessible. Whenever an additional cue or even assistance of some kind might be needed by a handicapped person in a community setting, nonhandicapped persons—even strangers—would then be available, capable, and willing to provide such assistance as a nonextraordinary, everyday event. Integrated programs, far more than instilling a willingness to tolerate and even help handicapped peers, create the possibility that genuine, mutually rewarding friendships will also emerge from these interactions. Such friendships would represent a considerable growth in social development for everyone involved.

REFERENCES

Asher, S. R., & Taylor, A. R. The social outcomes of mainstreaming: Sociometric assessment and beyond. *Exceptional Education Quarterly,* 1981, *1,* 13–30.

Biklen, D. The politics of institutions. In: B. Blatt, D. Biklen, & R. Bogdan (eds.), *An alternative textbook in special education.* Denver: Love Publishing Co., 1977.

Blatt, B. *Exodus from pandemonium: Human abuse and reformation of public policy.* Boston: Allyn and Bacon, 1970.

Brown, L., Branston, M. B., Hamre-Nietupski, S., Johnson, F., Wilcox, B., & Gruenewald, L. A rationale for comprehensive longitudinal interactions between severely handicapped and nonhandicapped students and other citizens. *AAESPH Review,* 1979, *4,* 3–14.

Brown, L., Ford, A., Nisbet, J., Sweet, M., Donnellan, A., & Guenewald, L. Opportunities available when severely handicapped students attend chronological age appropriate regular schools. *Journal of The Association for the Severely Handicapped,* 1983, *8,* 16–24.

Brown, L., Nietupski, J., & Hamre-Nietupski, S. The criterion of ultimate functioning and public school services for the severely handicapped student. In:A. Thomas (ed.), *Hey, don't forget about me! Education's investment in the severely, profoundly and multiply handicapped.* Reston, VA: The Council for Exceptional Children, 1976.

Burton, T. A., & Hirshoren, A. Some further thoughts and clarification on the education of severely and profoundly retarded children. *Exceptional Children,* 1979, *45,* 618–625.

Donaldson, J. Changing attitudes toward handicapped persons: A review and analysis of research. *Exceptional Children,* 1980, *46,* 504–514.

Falvey, M., Brown, L., Lyon, S., Baumgart, D., & Schroeder, J. Strategies for using cues and correction procedures. In:W. Sailor, B. Wilcox, & L. Brown (eds.), *Methods of instruction for severely handicapped students.* Baltimore: Paul H. Brookes Publishing Co., 1980.

Gaylord-Ross, R. A decision model for the treatment of aberrant behavior in applied settings. In:W. Sailor, B. Wilcox, & L. Brown (eds.), *Methods of instruction for severely handicapped students.* Baltimore: Paul H. Brookes Publishing Co., 1980.

Gottlieb, J. Observing social adaptation in schools. In:G. P. Sackett (ed.), *Observing behavior, Vol. 2: Data collection and analysis methods.* Baltimore: University Park Press, 1978.

Holvoet, J., Guess, D., Mulligan, M., & Brown, F. The Individualized Curriculum Sequencing Model (II): A teaching strategy for severely handicapped students. *Journal of The Association for the Severely Handicapped,* 1980, *5,* 337–351.

Landesman-Dwyer, S., Berkson, G., & Romer, D. Affiliation and friendship of mentally retarded residents in group homes. *American Journal of Mental Deficiency,* 1979, *83,* 571–580.

McFall, R. M. A review and reformulation of the concept of social skills. *Behavioral Assessment,* 1982, *4,* 1–33.

MacMillan, D. L., Jones, R. L., & Aloia, G. F. The mentally retarded label: A theoretical analysis and review of research. *American Journal of Mental Deficiency,* 1974, *79,* 241–261.

Neel, R. S. *Teaching autistic children: A functional curriculum approach.* Seattle: University of Washington College of Education, 1981.

Renzaglia, A., & Bates, P. Teaching socially appropriate behavior: In search of social competence. In:M. E. Snell (ed.), *Systematic instruction of the moderately and severely handicapped* (2nd ed.). Columbus, OH: Charles E. Merrill Publishing Co., 1983.

Rubin, Z. *Children's friendships.* Cambridge: Harvard University Press, 1980.

Rynders, J., Johnson, R., Johnson, D., & Schmidt, B. Producing positive interaction among Down syndrome and nonhandicapped teenagers through cooperative goal structuring. *American Journal of Mental Deficiency,* 1980, *85,* 268–283.

Sontag, E., Certo, N., & Button, J. E. On a distinction between the education of the severely and profoundly handicapped and a doctrine of limitations. *Exceptional Children,* 1979, *45,* 604–616.

Stein, J. U. Physical education, recreation and sports for special populations. *Education and Training of the Mentally Retarded,* 1977, *12,* 4–13.

Sullivan, R. C. What does deinstitutionalization mean for our children? *Journal of Autism and Developmental Disorders,* 1981, *11,* 347–356.

Voeltz, L. M. Children's attitudes toward handicapped peers. *American Journal of Mental Deficiency,* 1980, *84,* 455–464. (a)

Voeltz, L. M. Special Friends in Hawaii. *Education Unlimited,* 1980, *2,* 10–11. (b)

Voeltz, L. M. Effects of structured interactions with severely handicapped peers on children's attitudes. *American Journal of Mental Deficiency,* 1982, *86,* 180–190.

Voeltz, L. M., & Brennan, J. Analysis of interactions between nonhandicapped and severely handicapped peers using multiple measures. In: J. M. Berg (ed.), *Perspectives and progress in mental retardation, Vol. I: Social, psychological, and educational aspects.* Baltimore: University Park Press, in press.

Voeltz, L. M., Hemphill, N. J., Brown, S., Kishi, G., Klein, R., Fruehling, R., Collie, J., Levy, G., & Kube, C. *The Special Friends Program: A trainer's manual for integrated school settings* (rev. ed.). Honolulu: University of Hawaii Department of Special Education, 1983.

White, O. R. Adaptive performance objectives: Form versus function. In: W. Sailor, B. Wilcox, & L. Brown (eds.), *Methods of instruction for severely handicapped students.* Baltimore: Paul H. Brookes Publishing Co., 1980.

Wilcox, B., & Bellamy, G.T. *Design of high school programs for severely handicapped students.* Baltimore: Paul H. Brookes Publishing Co., 1982.

Wuerch, B. B., & Voeltz, L. M. *Longitudinal leisure skills for severely handicapped learners: The Ho'onanea curriculum component.* Baltimore: Paul H. Brookes Publishing Co., 1982.

REFERENCE NOTES

1. Brown, S., Hemphill, N. J., & Voeltz, L. M. *Supplemental activities for social studies: Lower elementary (similarities and differences).* Honolulu: University of Hawaii Department of Special Education, 1982.

2. Hemphill, N. J., Zukas, D., & Brown, S. *Social studies, 8th grade level. Proposal of Unit on Alienation.* Honolulu: University of Hawaii Department of Special Education, 1982.

3. Fruehling, R., & Sunabe, S. *The Mystery Game.* Honolulu: University of Hawaii Department of Special Education, 1982.

4. Fruehling, R., Hemphill, N. J., Brown, S., & Zukas, D. *Special Alternatives: A learning system for generating unique solutions to problems of special education in integrated settings.* Honolulu: University of Hawaii Department of Special Education, 1981.

5. Hemphill, N. J. Application of an integrative inservice model to promote social interactions between severely handicapped and regular education students in public school settings. Paper presented at the 8th annual convention of The Association for the Severely Handicapped, New York, October, 1981.

6. Voeltz, L. M., & Brennan, J. Children's descriptions of their relationship with severely handicapped peers: A comparison to best friend and Mom. Paper presented at the 8th annual convention of The Association for the Severely Handicapped, New York, October, 1981.

9

A Systematic Training Program for Teaching Nonhandicapped Students To Be Instructional Trainers of Severely Handicapped Schoolmates

Frances L. Kohl, Lucy G. Moses, and Barbara A. Stettner-Eaton

This chapter was supported in part by grant #G00–80–01719 to the University of Maryland-College Park from the U.S. Department of Education, Special Education Programs, Division of Innovation and Development, Handicapped Children's Model Programs, Washington, D.C. and grant #G00–81–01732 to the University of Maryland-College Park from the U.S. Department of Education, Special Education Programs, Division of Personnel Preparation, Washington, D.C.

With the advent of federal legislation mandating that all handicapped children are entitled to a public education in the least restrictive environment, severely handicapped students are being educated in public schools with their non-handicapped peers. While opportunities for interactions between handicapped and nonhandicapped students are plentiful and exist, for example, while students are walking in the halls, eating lunch in the cafeteria, attending assemblies, and participating in extracurricular activities, interactions may not occur spontaneously (Guralnick, 1980; Stainback & Stainback, 1981). Several approaches for promoting meaningful interactions between these two groups of students have been developed. One approach has focused on teaching social skills to severely handicapped students (Stainback & Stainback, 1982; Stainback, Stainback, Raschke, & Anderson, 1981). However, social skills training, although necessary, may not in itself be sufficient to initiate and maintain interactions (Stainback, Stainback, & Jaben, 1981). Specific strategies for engaging nonhandicapped students in structured activities with handicapped schoolmates must therefore be implemented concurrently.

An example of a structured activity involving nonhandicapped and handicapped students is a buddy system (Almond, Rodgers, & Krug, 1979). In such a system, a nonhandicapped student is paired with a specific severely handicapped student and is responsible for such duties as walking with the handicapped student to and from the bus, sitting with him or her at assemblies, etc. Another approach to facilitating interactions involves establishing chronologically age-appropriate cooperative goals for nonhandicapped and handicapped students (Rynders, Johnson, Johnson, & Schmidt, 1980; Stainback, Stainback, & Jaben, 1981), in which students work together to achieve a common goal, such as planting and harvesting a garden or collecting newspapers for recycling.

A third approach, and one that is the subject of this chapter, involves systematically training nonhandicapped students to serve as instructional trainers of handicapped schoolmates (Almond et al., 1979; Donder & Nietupski, 1981; Stainback & Stainback, 1982). As instructional agents, nonhandicapped students can assume a variety of teaching responsibilities ranging from modeling appropriate behavior (e.g., hands at side while waiting in line) to providing instruction on a multifaceted task (e.g., preparing breakfast). Training involves the dissemination of information, instruction in delivering cues and consequences, and opportunities for interpersonal interactions. This approach thus appears to offer the greatest potential for positive gains, not only in terms of the level of skills acquired by handicapped students, but in the opportunities for handicapped and non-handicapped students to communicate with each other.

This chapter describes a systematic training program for teaching non-handicapped fifth- and sixth-grade students to instruct severely handicapped students in appropriate and necessary cafeteria skills. Included are detailed procedures for instituting the training, as well as insights into the advantages and possible adjustments required in using students as trainers. It should be pointed out that the training program described here could be adapted to other age levels and skill areas.

IMPLEMENTATION

Trainers, Students, and Setting

Seven students attending a large (approximately 700-student) suburban elementary school volunteered to participate as trainers in the training program. Six trainers, one male and five females, were in the same fifth-grade class and the seventh, a female, was a sixth grader. The trainers, along with the rest of the nonhandicapped school population, had attended a presentation on handicapping conditions at the beginning of the school year and, prior to initiation of the program, had been eating lunch at the same tables as the handicapped students.

Eight severely handicapped students, six males and two females, participated as partners. These students were selected from eleven students, dispersed between two severely handicapped classrooms, because they were ambulatory and did not present feeding problems requiring professional assistance. The students ranged from 5 to 10 years of age ($\overline{X}$ = 7 years, 9 months). All students scored below 40 on either the Slosson or Stanford-Binet intelligence tests. A variety of communication systems were used by the students, including speech, manual signs, Blissymbols, and picture books. Prior to this academic year, the students had attended a self-contained special education center. This was the first year that severely handicapped students had been placed in a regular elementary school.

The training program was implemented in the school cafeteria during a lunch period when approximately 240 fifth and sixth graders also ate lunch. The program was instituted 4 days per week, since scheduling necessitated that the handicapped students eat during an earlier lunch period on the fifth day.

Instructional Sequence

Since eating in a school cafeteria encompasses many different tasks, the activity was divided into three sequential instructional phases: Food Service Line, Eating Lunch, and Cleanup. The first phase, Food Service Line, included skills such as waiting and advancing in line, obtaining milk, selecting utensils, taking a food tray, and giving a lunch ticket to the cafeteria worker. Eating Lunch included opening a milk carton, using a straw or drinking from a cup, using utensils, eating food, using a napkin, and interacting socially. The third phase, Cleanup, included checking one's place for disposable items, locating a trash basket, discarding paper items and excess food, depositing tray and utensils, and returning to the table. Several versions of the instructional sequence were used to accommodate student differences (e.g., use of only one hand, use of a cup instead of a straw). (Copies of the instructional sequences are available from the authors upon request.)

Lunch in the cafeteria was selected as the training activity for several reasons: 1) It was a regularly occurring activity for both groups of students and required only minimal schedule changes for implementation. 2) The trainers were familiar with the procedures involved in the task. 3) The activity took place in a naturally integrated setting (i.e., handicapped and nonhandicapped students of different ages were present). 4) The activity encompassed a variety of skills and lasted for an extended time period. 5) Nonhandicapped students could provide the extra lunch time supervision of handicapped students that was needed because some members of the teaching staff took breaks while others were engaged in feeding the physically handicapped students. 6) Social interactions were a natural and expected part of lunch.

Systematic Training Components

Training for the nonhandicapped students consisted of three components: Formal Information Sessions, *"In Vivo"* Instruction, and Feedback Sessions. Two University of Maryland project staff members, referred to in this chapter as "instructors," directed the activities in each component.

Formal Information Sessions Three formal information sessions were conducted prior to implementing the program in the cafeteria. Each session lasted approximately 45 minutes and was held in a vacant classroom during the trainers' lunch period. A lecture format was used in the first session, with information presented on the responsibilities and roles of an instructional trainer; characteristics of the handicapped students; alternative methods of communication; cues, corrections, and reinforcement procedures; effective use of voice and body; data collection procedures; and the cafeteria instructional sequence. The second session included participatory activities in which the trainers observed and commented on videotape sequences and engaged in role-playing exercises. In the third session, key points from the preceding sessions were reviewed and questions answered. The activities and information presented in the three sessions are delineated below.

Responsibilities and Roles of an Instructional Trainer Trainers' responsibilities were explained as follows: 1) knowing specific information about their handicapped partners (e.g., type of communication system, food allergies); 2) knowing what their partners were expected to do during lunch (e.g., keeping head up while eating, biting instead of stuffing food, holding flatware with an adult grasp); 3) monitoring their partners from the time they arrived in the cafeteria until they left; 4) notifying a university instructor as well as their partner if they had to leave the table for any reason; 5) completing data cards daily; 6) being punctual or notifying an instructor if they might be late or would miss lunch; and 7) keeping up with their school work. It was emphasized that the trainers' roles included model, friend, and helper, not teacher or parent.

Characteristics of the Handicapped Students Information was presented on the implications of students' physical impairments (e.g., a hemiplegic student who needs assistance to carry lunch tray), food allergies, behavior problems, and current level of performance for specific tasks. Handouts describing these characteristics were distributed to the trainers for future reference.

Methods of Communication and Conversational Topics Since only one handicapped student in the program was verbal, information was provided trainers on alternative communication systems, with discussion focusing on the use of manual signs, pictures, and Blissymbols. Trainers were shown examples of the handicapped students' communication books, were taught manual signs, and were given a sign dictionary containing 50 signs. The signs taught and included in the dictionary were selected because they related directly to lunch (e.g., labels for specific lunch items, actions, utensils) or could serve as the basis for conversational exchanges. Suggestions were provided for conversation topics (e.g., asking questions about lunch menu preferences, school and home activities, specific school events) and for encouraging the handicapped students to use their communication systems (e.g., asking questions that required more than a yes or no response). Trainers were instructed to obtain their partner's attention, usually in the form of eye contact, before initiating any interaction.

Cues and Correction Procedures A four-step method for instructing the handicapped students when they did not perform a required response, performed an incorrect response, or displayed an inappropriate behavior was presented and rehearsed with the trainers. The sequence included:

1. Secure your partner's attention (by calling his or her name; tapping the shoulder) and make certain he or she looks at you.
2. Give clear and specific directions; pair the directions with a gesture or model if necessary.
3. If your partner does not respond or responds incorrectly, repeat the specific instruction and provide hand-over-hand guidance.
4. If your partner still does not respond correctly, call an instructor for assistance.

The sequence was established because it reflected basic competencies identified in the literature as current practice for teaching severely handicapped students (Almond et al., 1979; Falvey, Brown, Lyon, Baumgart, & Schroeder, 1980; Fredericks, Anderson, & Baldwin, 1979; McCormick, Cooper, & Goldman, 1979), and it was easy for the trainers to remember. By combining the verbal cue and gesture into a single step and adding the step of calling the instructor, the sequence also minimized the number of errors a handicapped student could make. Trainers were instructed to use this four-step method for correcting all errors unless otherwise specified for a particular student.

When rehearsing the method with the trainers, emphasis was placed on trainers providing specific directions and hand-over-hand guidance. Specific directions were defined for the trainer as short instructions that tell the partner exactly what to do rather than what he or she needs to stop doing. In providing hand-over-hand guidance, it was stressed to trainers that they should refrain from doing any part of the task for their partner; instead, they were told to place their hands on top of their partners' hand, and guide them through the task. Trainers were also instructed to give as little help as necessary during hand-over-hand guidance, in order to ensure that their partners performed the response.

Reinforcement Another competency assumed necessary for effective teaching of severely handicapped students is the delivery of reinforcing consequences (Almond et al., 1979; Falvey et al., 1980; Fredericks et al., 1979; McCormick et al., 1979). Both verbal and nonverbal reinforcement were discussed with the trainers. Trainers were instructed to give praise when their partners correctly performed responses specified on their data cards and/or performed tasks they had previously done incorrectly. As with directions, giving specific praise was emphasized so that the handicapped students would know exactly what they were doing correctly.

Effective Use of Voice and Body Observations of the trainers' interactions with the handicapped students prior to training revealed that some of the fifth and sixth graders spoke in loud, shrill, authoritative voices, or sat at a distance from the handicapped students; others spoke very softly or allowed the handicapped students to lean on them physically. While some of these behaviors might be justified in certain contexts, they reflected general tendencies of individual trainers and were not varied across situations. As a result, a brief discussion on how to use one's voice and body effectively was conducted. The general rule presented for voice control was to speak in a calm, audible voice and to sound enthusiastic when praising. The trainers were instructed to speak naturally, varying their tone as they would with their friends, and to avoid sounding nervous, too authoritative, or, on the other hand, too timid. The discussion on how to use one's body effectively was less specific; trainers were encouraged to sit within an easy reach of their partners (for assistance purposes), not to allow partners to lean on them, and to use smiles, pats, and nods.

Data Cards Through the use of data cards, trainers recorded information about their partner's daily performance. Figure 1 depicts a sample data card for a handicapped student. As illustrated, the back of the data card contained information about the handicapped student, such as type of communication system, physical impairments, food allergies, material needs, and task expectations. While this information was included on the student information handouts, it was also recorded on the data card so that the trainers would have easy access to it each day. The front of the data card listed five to six performance behaviors that varied across students. Trainers were instructed to record a (+) or (−) for each of these behaviors, depending upon their partner's performance. Since the handicapped students had multiple opportunities to perform targeted behaviors within a single lunch period (e.g., uses spoon instead of fingers), a student had to demonstrate independent performance on the behavior consistently throughout the lunch period in order to be scored correct. Although the procedure was later modified (see below, ''Administrative Factors''), the initial plan was that a correct response was not scored until the end of lunch, while incorrect responses were scored as soon as an error occurred.

Videotape Sequence Four short videotape segments were shown of the trainers working with the handicapped students prior to the formal information sessions. The sequences were selected because they illustrated many of the procedures discussed in the first session (e.g., use of verbal reinforcers, hand-over-hand guidance). Examples of both correct and incorrect instruction were highlighted through stop-action and then discussed. The trainers had the opportunity to comment on their own performance, relate what they would do differ-

FRONT OF DATA CARD

Student:_____ Trainer:_____

(+) independent
(−) assistance needed
(N) no opportunity

	Date:				
1. Gives lunch ticket to cafeteria worker.					
2. Brings food to mouth.					
3. Pours milk into cup without spilling.					
4. Spears food with fork.					
5. Uses napkin to wipe mouth.					

Comments (by date): _____
_____
_____

BACK OF DATA CARD

Reminders:
1. Uses Blissymbols book.
2. Takes prepackaged flatware.
3. Uses cup for milk.
4. Has difficulty using left arm.
5. Allergic to bananas and nuts.
6. Needs reminders to keep head up.

Figure 1. Example of student Data Card. Card is laminated with clear contact paper on both sides. Felt-tipped pens are used and responses erased with alcohol.

ently, and practice generating specific directions and praise that would have been appropriate in the situations.

Role-Playing Role-playing exercises followed the videotape sequences. Several typical lunch situations were staged, with one of the instructors playing a handicapped student, the trainers playing themselves, and the other instructor supervising. Each role-playing exercise lasted only a few minutes. The trainers who were not actively participating in the situation observed and recorded information on a data card. The participating trainer also scored a data card. At the end of each exercise, the trainers discussed what had taken place, compared their data cards, and resolved any discrepancies.

"In Vivo" Instruction Following the three information sessions, *"in vivo"* instruction was conducted in the cafeteria on a daily basis and consisted of four conditions: 1) At the beginning of each lunch period the instructors reminded the trainers individually to reinforce their partners whenever they correctly

performed behaviors listed on the data card or exhibited novel appropriate behaviors (reinforcement reminders). 2) Throughout the lunch period, the instructors monitored the trainers' delivery of cues and corrections, and when necessary, gave the trainers specific verbal instructions and/or modeled the desired behavior (instruction monitoring). 3) The instructors reinforced the trainers on an intermittent basis when they were demonstrating appropriate instructional procedures or were interacting well with their partners (contingent feedback). 4) Finally, the instructors distributed and collected each trainer's data card and monitored appropriate data collection procedures (data monitoring).

Feedback Sessions Informal feedback sessions were conducted on a daily basis several minutes before and after each lunch period. Formal sessions, lasting 30 minutes each, were held every 2 weeks. During the scheduled sessions, trainers discussed lunch situations, rehearsed training procedures, and practiced signs from their dictionaries. Specific questions from the trainers also were answered.

Administrative Factors

In addition to the preparation and implementation of the three systematic training components, several administrative factors had to be addressed by the two instructors, classroom personnel, and lunchroom monitors. While most of these factors had been anticipated, others became apparent as the program progressed.

Scheduling Scheduling presented minimal problems, since both the trainers and the handicapped students ate during the same lunch period. In order to ensure that the program ran efficiently, trainers were provided an early release from their last morning class. Similarly, when lunch extended beyond the regular time because of late starts and slow lines, the trainers missed part of their next activity, which was recess. Occasional disruptions occurred in the schedule when special activities (such as chorus rehearsal) preempted lunch and recess for some of the student trainers. On those days, the handicapped students without partners were paired with trainers whose partners may have been absent, or the handicapped student simply ate without a trainer.

Designating Responsibilities The responsibilities of university project and classroom staff were clearly outlined prior to implementing the program. As stated, two university project staff coordinated the program and served as the instructors and monitors of both handicapped students and the trainers. Two additional members of the university project served as data collectors throughout the program. Their sole responsibility was to collect data on the trainers; they did not intervene in the activity unless one of the instructors or teaching staff was unavailable and intervention was imperative. Responsibilities of the classroom teaching staff present during lunch included supervising the handicapped students en route to and from the cafeteria, working with handicapped students not participating in the program, sharing in the management of specific behavior programs, and assisting the project instructors in the supervision of the trainers.

Trainer/Partner Assignments Student pairings were established on a 2-week rotating basis to provide enough time for the trainers and partners to become familiar with each other. Pairings were based upon general observations of the trainers and specific characteristics of the handicapped students. Initially, certain trainers were assigned partners from different classrooms so that the trainers would be seated apart and prevented from interacting only with each other. This proved necessary only at the start of the program. Typically, pairings were selected that would give the trainers an opportunity to develop skills in different areas across time. For instance, to help a trainer improve his or her general interaction skills, the trainer would be paired with one of the more outgoing, communicative handicapped students. Similarly, a trainer who was not attending well to a given partner (perhaps because the partner was proficient in eating), would be paired subsequently with a partner who required more assistance. Attention was also given to the degree of effort required to teach certain handicapped students as well as to the handicapped students' reinforcing characteristics. Some students are more difficult to teach than others because of skill level, physical conditions, behavior problems, etc., while some students are less reinforcing to be with (e.g., messy eaters, uncommunicative, withdrawn) as compared to others. In order to be fair and to maintain interest on the part of the trainers, pairings were rotated so that a given trainer would not have all difficult or all reinforcing partners. Finally, student pairings were affected by the fact that there were more handicapped students than trainers. Because one of the handicapped students required a great deal of adult supervision and frequently did not eat her lunch, she was not assigned a partner on a regular basis. However, if another handicapped student was absent on a particular day, that student's trainer worked with the extra student. This gave the extra student opportunities to interact with nonhandicapped schoolmates and gave the trainers uninterrupted practice in teaching severely handicapped students.

Modifying Procedures   It is common practice in any educational program to modify instructional procedures or task expectations based upon student performance. In the training program described here, data cards were updated for the handicapped students as they acquired the specified skills. Recording procedures for the trainers were also altered: Instead of the original plan of scoring incorrect responses when the error occurred and correct responses at the end of lunch, all behaviors were marked at the end of the lunch period. This change was instituted in response to the trainers' repeated tendency to literally stop everything and score their cards when an error occurred, even before correcting the behavior.

EVALUATION

The fifth- and sixth-grade trainers were taught to use effective instructional techniques with the severely handicapped students. Periodic data probes of the handicapped students' performance on the cafeteria instructional sequence indicated that all students acquired some skills independently and improved on others. Data recorded by the trainers on the data cards reflected similar findings. (For specific results refer to Kohl, Moses, and Stettner-Eaton, 1983.)

Self-evaluations and written feedback obtained from the trainers at the end of the academic year were positive. The trainers felt that they had learned a great deal from participating in the program, including how to communicate with the handicapped students and specific methods for teaching them new skills. Trainers' comments also indicated that they had learned things about handicapped individuals and themselves that extended beyond the lunch activity. One trainer felt she was now "more comfortable around handicapped people" and another noted that he had learned "how to finish [his] school work to get certain privileges." These and other indicators of personal growth (e.g., increase in self-concept and maturity) were noticed not only by the trainers themselves but by their teachers and parents.

As the year progressed, the training program became just one of many integration activities occurring in the school. Several trainers began spending their free time with the handicapped students in other activities and brought their friends to meet and work with the handicapped students. It was encouraging to see the trainers generalize their instructional skills to other activities and teach their friends to interact with their severely handicapped schoolmates. More informal interactions also began to occur, in the hallways when students passed, in the gym, and in the library. A level of friendship developed between two of the students that extended beyond school into the afternoons and weekends. The impact of the program, coupled with the concurrent efforts of the handicapped students' teachers to integrate their classes in other activities throughout the year, created a school environment that was highly supportive of integration. The fact that regular education teachers and students volunteered to help develop more opportunities for interactions and to participate in additional activities with the handicapped students the following school year demonstrated that a commitment to integration had developed.

A systematic program involving handicapped and nonhandicapped individuals has both immediate and long-range benefits. These benefits are not mutually exclusive in nature, nor do they apply only to the two groups of students discussed. One of the most obvious benefits for teachers of handicapped students who are willing to invest the time in such a training program is the availability of additional trained assistants. Trainers can provide one-to-one instruction for the handicapped students not only in the classroom but throughout the school and community as well. Similarly, small-group instruction can be orchestrated by the classroom teacher if several nonhandicapped trainers are available to assist.

Another benefit of such a training program is that it becomes a vehicle for educating nonhandicapped students about handicapped individuals, providing an ongoing forum for questions and discussions about handicapping conditions. As new information is provided, myths and stereotypes about handicapped individuals can be dispelled. Participants in the program will undoubtedly share what they learn with their schoolmates, teachers, parents, and siblings, as they did during the training program. This dissemination of information and regular contact with severely handicapped individuals can lead to positive attitude changes and a greater acceptance of individual differences in many people, not only those participating in the program.

REFERENCES

Almond, P., Rodgers, S., & Krug, D. Mainstreaming: A model for including elementary students in the severely handicapped classroom. *Teaching Exceptional Children*, 1979, *11*, 135–139.

Donder, D., & Nietupski, J. Nonhandicapped adolescents teaching playground skills to their mentally retarded peers: Toward a less restrictive middle school environment. *Education and Training of the Mentally Retarded*, 1981, *16*, 270–276.

Falvey, M., Brown, L., Lyon, S., Baumgart, D., & Schroeder, J. Strategies for using cues and correction procedures. In: W. Sailor, B. Wilcox, & L. Brown (eds.), *Methods of instruction for severely handicapped students*. Baltimore: Paul H. Brookes Publishing Co., 1980.

Fredericks, H.D.B., Anderson, R., & Baldwin, V. Identifying competency indicators of teachers of the severely handicapped. *AAESPH Review*, 1979, *4*, 81–95.

Guralnick, M. Social interactions among preschool children. *Exceptional Children*, 1980, *46*, 248–253.

Kohl, F.L., Moses, L.G., & Stettner-Eaton, B.A. The results of teaching fifth and sixth graders to be instructional trainers with severely handicapped students. *Journal of The Association of the Severely Handicapped*, 1983, *8*.

McCormick, L., Cooper, M., & Goldman, R. Training teachers to maximize instructional time provided to severely and profoundly handicapped children. *AAESPH Review*, 1979, *4*, 301–310.

Rynders, J.E., Johnson, T.T., Johnson, D.W., & Schmidt, B. Producing positive interaction among Down syndrome and nonhandicapped teenagers through cooperative goal structuring. *American Journal of Mental Deficiency*, 1980, *85*, 268–273.

Stainback, W., & Stainback, S. A review of research on interactions between severely handicapped and nonhandicapped students. *Journal of The Association for the Severely Handicapped*, 1981, *6*, 23–29.

Stainback, W., & Stainback, S. The need for research on training nonhandicapped students to interact with severely handicapped students. *Education and Training of the Mentally Retarded*, 1982, *17*, 12–16.

Stainback, W., Stainback, S., & Jaben, T. Providing opportunities for interaction between severely handicapped and nonhandicapped students. *Teaching Exceptional Children*, 1981, *13*, 72–75.

Stainback, W., Stainback, S., Raschke, D., & Anderson, R.J. Three methods for encouraging interactions between severely retarded and nonhandicapped students. *Education and Training of the Mentally Retarded*, 1981, *16*, 188–192.

10

Social Behavior Development in Integrated Secondary Autistic Programs

*Robert J. Gaylord-Ross
and Valerie Pitts-Conway*

RECENT APPROACHES IN TREATING AUTISM

Background

Since the identification of the disorder of autism four decades ago (Kanner, 1943), a burgeoning field for its professional study and treatment has emerged. Much of the research has defined autism as a medical problem, a psychiatric disorder whose causes are traceable to familial psychopathology. The most notable challenge to this psychiatric approach has been the growth of operant research and clinical findings, which conceptualized autism as a deficiency in learning style and behavioral repertoires (Lovaas, 1977) rather than as a product of a deep-seated emotional disturbance. The operant work has undertaken to build skill repertoires in the domains of communication, self-care, and behavior reduction (Lovaas & Newsom, 1976). The context for most of this research, however, has been clinical, with substantive behavior changes claimed on the basis of research variables that had theoretical import, but which lacked ecological validity (Gaylord-Ross, 1979) with respect to the types of home, school, and community settings to which autistic

197

persons must adapt. Certainly the findings of O.I. Lovaas, R.L. Koegel, A. Rincover, L. Schreibman, E.G. Carr, C.D. Newsom, and others have direct *implications* for educational practice. Yet, a gap still exists between research and implementation for such notions as overselective attention (Lovaas & Schreibman, 1971), stimulus control (Rincover & Koegel, 1975), and motivation (Koegel & Egel, 1979). Nevertheless, encouraging results have been demonstrated in work on group behavior (Koegel & Rincover, 1974), and in the recent emphasis given to practical issues related to instructional design (Koegel, Dunlap & Dyer, 1980).

This chapter focuses on the implementations of school programs for autistic persons. In contrast to the past clinical orientation of psychiatric and operant efforts, emphasis is given here to actual school settings and, in particular, to the development of social behavior within integrated school situations. In our view, social behavior is the instructional domain that will be most critical in determining whether autistic individuals succeed in less restrictive, more normalized settings. Therefore, considerable attention is given in the chapter to the types of contexts that promote the development of social skills and contact with nonhandicapped peers. In addition, the model we describe provides for the social integration of autistic students at the high school level. The majority of integration efforts with severely handicapped students have occurred at the preschool level (Guralnick, 1978). Of late, however, an increasing number of school systems have integrated severely handicapped students beyond preschool—for example, Madison, Wisconsin, Dekalb, Illinois, Charlottesville, Virginia, and many others cited in this text. Yet, integrating autistic students in regular high schools poses three potential problems:

1. A large developmental-intellectual disparity exists between severely handicapped students and their nonhandicapped, secondary peers. This is in contrast to preschool programs, where such cumulative, cognitive differences have not yet accrued. This cumulative difference holds for severely handicapped students, in general, and autistic students, in particular.
2. Secondary-level autistic students could be the target of ridicule, exclusion, and abuse by nonhandicapped students because of their visible and bizarre behavior patterns (e.g., hand self-stimulation).
3. Conversely, there is the presumed threat of disorderly behavior by the autistic student. The reality of behaviorally disordered teenagers with histories of aggression and who now have adult-sized physiques can cause understandable alarm among community members.

The program we describe asserts that these obstacles can be overcome, provided systematic efforts are made to promote social interaction. While every school setting is different, it is hoped that readers will be able to apply key aspects of our findings and beliefs to their own school situations.

OPERANT RESEARCH AND IMPLICATIONS FOR SOCIAL DEVELOPMENT

A number of authors have dealt comprehensively with operant research findings on autism (Koegel, Egel, & Dunlap, 1980; Lovaas & Newsom, 1976). One of the main thrusts of this research has been to investigate the learning characteristics of autistic persons—in other words, an operant model has been applied to analyze the manner in which antecedent and consequent events control behavior. Thus, such research has centered on the *process* by which autistic persons learn and perform. Relatively little emphasis has been placed on the content or curriculum of what is learned (an exception would be the language training program developed by Lovaas and colleagues, Lovaas, 1977). Rather, content, like social responses or fine motor responses, has served as a means to examine the way that antecedent and consequent events influence the expression of behavior. The main findings of this line of research can be summarized accordingly:

1. The presentation of contingent, positive reinforcing events can increase the rate of a variety of target behaviors (Ferster, 1961).
2. The delivery of contingent aversive events (punishment) is needed to suppress high rate, aberrant behaviors (Lovaas & Simmons, 1969); and in these cases is a prerequisite to substantive advances in learning (Koegel & Covert, 1972).
3. Nonverbal and echolalic autistic persons can acquire vocal language through a sequential, operant training package (Lovaas, 1977).
4. Autistic persons tend to perceive only one component of a stimulus array (overselective attention—Lovaas & Schreibman, 1971). Stimulus over-selectivity may be seen under certain experimental conditions (Schreibman & Lovaas, 1973) and it may be "trained out" so that the individual can process all of the critical components of a stimulus array (Schreibman, Koegel, & Craig, 1977). Overselectivity may deter generalization in certain autistic individuals (Rincover & Koegel, 1975).
5. A number of events related to instructional design, for example, intertrial interval (Koegel et al., 1980) and error rate (Koegel & Egel, 1979), can affect autistic persons' motivation to perform. This recent line of work seems to have promising implications for classroom work with autistic students.

Group Performance

It can be correctly argued that all behavior involving exchanges between two or more persons is social. In a typical experimental or educational setting an adult is continually influencing the behavior of an autistic person. The main objective of the exchange is the demonstration of some learning effect. The situation also is a social one because an exchange of behaviors occurs between the individuals over time. Although almost all instructional encounters can be viewed as social, studies that explicitly investigate social behavior tend to examine how group membership influences behavior. Some studies with autistic persons have had direct implications for both educational practice and social skill development.

Koegel and Rincover (1974) taught autistic children a variety of educational tasks in 1:1 (one trainer to one student), 1:2, 1:4, and 1:8 instructional settings. The first part of their study clearly demonstrated that learning performance deteriorated as group size increased—leading one to speculate that the presence of additional students served as perceptual distractions. In the second part of the study, however, a student began with 1:1 instruction, but as he or she reached criterion on a task, another student was "faded" into the learning situation so that a 1:2 ratio then existed. When criterion was reached with 1:2, two students were introduced so that a 1:4 ratio was obtained. The procedure was repeated to reach a terminal ratio of 1:8. Remarkably, the fading procedure resulted in the students performing in a small group with no concomitant decrease in performance. This study has critical implications for the instructional programming of severely handicapped students. Too many classes use a 1:1 training format exclusively. The Koegel and Rincover study demonstrated that severely handicapped and behaviorally disordered pupils can learn to function effectively in more normalized group contexts.

Another study, by Egel, Richman, and Koegel (1981), made an important contribution to the social learning literature by demonstrating that autistic students can imitate and learn from their nonhandicapped peers. In the study, four autistic children were taught discrimination tasks such as *on/under, yes/no*, etc. In a baseline condition in which correct responses were positively reinforced and errors physically prompted, the students failed to learn any of the tasks. In a modeling condition, however, the students observed a nonhandicapped peer make the correct response. The exposure to a peer model brought all of the autistic students to learning criterion on the tasks. Furthermore, criterion performance was maintained during a follow-up phase when the peer models were no longer present.

A fundamental study relating to social integration, conducted by Russo and Koegel (1977), should also be mentioned here. In the study, a primary-age autistic child successfully was mainstreamed into an elementary class. The student displayed a number of prerequisite social and academic behaviors that recommended an integrated placement. A training package was implemented so that an aide accompanied the child to the class to offer instructional and behavioral assistance. Over time, the aide was gradually "faded out" to the point that the autistic student was functioning adequately in the regular class. The Russo and Koegel study was particularly revealing because it was conducted in a real educational setting and used an effective operant training package that produced successful social integration.

Integrated Programs for Severely Handicapped Pupils

A number of integrated school programs for severely handicapped pupils have been developed over the past 20 years. The pioneering program was at George Peabody College for Teachers (Nashville, Tennessee) under the direction of William Bricker. The model classroom for preschoolers consisted of about 50% nonhandicapped students and 50% developmentally delayed students. The program was a landmark because it demonstrated that integrated programs were not only feasible to operate, but could provide clear benefits to both handicapped and nonhandicapped students. In the succeeding 15 years since the original Bricker program the majority of integrated school programs for students with severe handicaps (see Guralnick, 1978, for a review of these programs) have been at the preschool level. There are a number of reasons for the emphasis on preschools:

1. The cognitive-developmental differences between handicapped and non-handicapped persons are at a minimum during the preschool years.
2. It is operationally much easier to assemble a class of preschoolers, (at a university setting, for example) that is administratively autonomous from a public school bureaucracy.
3. Integration is simpler when all students are assembled in one classroom versus mainstreaming students for part of the day (a procedure that entails moving students from one class to another at different times of the day).

The integrated preschool movement has produced substantial advances in social integration. Nevertheless, the findings have limited application because of the specialized settings in which they were often conducted—that is, university laboratory settings that could not expose the students to the variety of school contexts present in regular school settings and that, moreover, were highly financed demonstration classes with resources not ordinarily found in local communities. In spite of these drawbacks, preschool classes have provided not only a rich data base for the types of behavior changes that can occur in integrated settings; but also an inspiration for developments at the primary and secondary levels. Fortunately, several state and local school districts have taken the lead in developing integrated school programs for severely handicapped students across preschool, primary, and secondary levels. The state of Hawaii is unique in making a statewide commitment to an integrated service delivery plan (see chapter in this volume by Voeltz).

Training Packages

Several effective training packages that promote social interaction between non-handicapped and handicapped students have been developed in these preschool programs. The training has primarily followed an operant format. The simplest means to promote social interaction is found in training based on a study by Hart, Reynolds, Baer, Brawley, and Harris (1968). In that study, students played freely in an unstructured setting. The training consisted of the teacher delivering a positive consequence to a student who initiated a social interaction with a peer. Training proved effective, as the rate of social interaction increased for all students in the free-play setting. This kind of training is the most straightforward, because only consequent (reinforcement) events are manipulated. In more complex training packages, not only is reinforcement delivered contingently, but a variety of prompting (stimulus) events are introduced to induce social interaction. Stimulus events that can prompt social interactions in such training are:

1. Verbal statements that describe the kinds of social behaviors that need to be made
2. Modeling actions in which a teacher shows the student how to interact
3. Physical primes in which a teacher puts the student(s) through the interaction with manual guidance
4. Materials such as games or toys placed in locations so that students will use them and produce social interactions

A variety of instructional formats, for example, trial-by-trial, can be used to prompt and reinforce social interactions (cf. Strain, Shores, & Timm, 1977). The procedures are straightforward, effective, and easy to implement. Their ease of implementation is reflected in an innovative procedure called peer imitation training (PIT) that was developed by Cooke, Cooke, and Apolloni (1978). In PIT a nonhandicapped, preschool peer serves as the instructor of a handicapped preschooler. The peer delivers prompts and reinforcers in a consistent fashion just as an adult teacher would. The procedure has been proven successful not only in teaching the targeted skills, but in increasing the amount of peer imitation by handicapped learners toward their peers. In terms of social development, this latter effect cannot be underestimated. Bogdon and Taylor (1976) have described how handicapped persons are almost exclusively influenced and controlled by adults. Thus, adults become discriminative stimuli (significant others) and peers evolve as unimportant persons in the lives of handicapped persons. PIT training reverses this trend by forcing the student to attend to a peer in order to receive reinforcement.

Social Response Measures

Before reviewing the outcomes of social interaction studies, it would be useful to delineate the types of social behaviors that can occur in integrative contexts. A number of interactional scales have been developed for this purpose (cf. Greenwood, Todd, Walker, & Hops, 1978). One of these scales, the Frisco Interaction Scale for the Handicapped (FISH) (Gaylord-Ross, Piuma, Murray, Halvorson, & Sailor, 1981) compiles 24 social responses that can sensitively measure exchanges (see Figure 1). FISH classifies responses into five categories: physical orientation to person, relation to objects, type of exchange, quality of interaction, and social-emotional. The 24 items are not mutually exclusive, so that more than one item can be scored in a given interval. One, two or more persons can be scored at a time. Because of the sizable number of items (particularly when combined with several persons to be scored), acceptable reliability is better achieved by videotaping an interaction. The tape can be replayed, with successive intervals (e.g., 20 seconds) scored. An important aspect of FISH is that it features a broad range of types of exchanges, including higher levels of social interactions such as symbolic play, altruism, and games—thus breaking Parten's (1932) cooperative play category into more differentiated categories—and negative behaviors and rudimentary responses like "proximity" and "touch."

Research Outcomes

A growing and consistent body of research has emerged on the types of interactions that occur between severely handicapped and nonhandicapped children in integrated settings. The research has included students who were autistic and moderately, severely, and profoundly retarded. Much of this research has been conducted in preschool, free-play settings (Guralnick, 1978). A study by Gomes (1981), for example, used a simultaneous treatment design (Hersen & Barlow, 1976) to contrast the social play behavior of two severely handicapped, primary-level children in integrated and segregated settings. The study found:

Physical Orientation to Person

1. Body orientation frontal
2. Proximity (0–5 ft.)
3. Visually attend person

Relation to Objects

4. Visually attend object
5. Appropriate object use
6. Inappropriate object use (also no function)

Type of Exchange

7. Body contact
8. Give object
9. Receive object
10. Communication (verbal, sign, signal)
11. Initiate interaction

Quality of Interaction

12. Imitative
13. Parallel play
14. Reciprocal/take turn
15. Symbolic/role play/ritual
16. Altruism (helping, sharing, prompt)
17. Teasing (verbal, gestures), taunt
18. Game (hide-and-seek)

Social-Emotional

19. Positive affect (smile, laugh)
20. Negative affect (frown, scowl, cry)
21. Physical aggression toward person (hit, kick, push)
22. Disruptive/tantrum
23. Self-stimulation
24. Self-injury

Figure 1. The Frisco Interaction Scale for the Handicapped (FISH).

1. Zero amounts of social play occurred between severely handicapped pupils in segregated settings.
2. Low but higher rates of play occurred between severely handicapped pupils when they had been moved to a regular public school and interacted with nonhandicapped pupils at other times of the day.
3. Substantial and higher rates of play occurred when severely handicapped pupils were involved in play settings with nonhandicapped pupils. By ''higher'' social play it is meant that the severely handicapped students were *initiating* social interactions.

From this study and others, then, it appears that when stimulated by actions from nonhandicapped peers, severely handicapped pupils not only reciprocate the actions but initiate actions at other times. This result offers an encouraging outlook for the responsivity of students with severe handicaps when exposed to integrated social settings.

A group of research studies has compared the difference between the amount of interaction displayed by students with severe handicaps and that displayed by nonhandicapped pupils. The studies, by Fredericks, Baldwin, Grove, Moore, Riggs, and Lyons (1978) and Peterson and Garalnick (1977) produced some consistent findings. The studies showed that:

1. Nonhandicapped students interacted at a rate noticeably higher than the students with severe handicaps. The latter group did not display zero rates of social behavior, though.
2. Nonhandicapped students manifested qualitatively higher types of social behavior (i.e., cooperative and associative play). Students with severe handicaps showed a greater proportion of lower level types of play (i.e., isolate play).

The Fredericks et al. (1978) study further developed an operant training procedure that successfully elevated the rates of appearance of social behaviors among the handicapped students.

The results of the above studies have positive implications for teaching social behaviors to students with severe handicaps in integrated settings. Since the students did not display zero rates of social behavior, there is a better prognosis for improving their rate and type of social responses. From an operant viewpoint, when a response exists in a person's repertoire, it should be fairly simple to increase the rate of that behavior through contingent positive reinforcement. When a behavior is not found in a person's repertoire, i.e., zero response rate, one is faced with the more formidable problem of first endeavoring to teach the behavior. Furthermore, if the person has physical disabilities that have in the past limited his or her basic social-motor responses like ambulation, reaching, touching and exchanging materials, the teacher must use exacting prompting and shaping techniques in order to induce rudimentary social behaviors. In spite of these difficulties and challenges, teachers and researchers have made substantive advances in promoting the social skill development of students with severe handicaps (cf. Peterson, 1978).

Thus, there appears to have emerged an effective technology to increase rates of social interaction in integrated, free-play settings. Handicapped persons socialize in a wide variety of settings that include classrooms, leisure, community, and domestic environments. It is important to identify the types of interactional contexts (sub-environments) where handicapped persons socialize. The types of behaviors that are needed to succeed in these settings must also be identified. Training strategies can then be delineated to remediate the discrepancies that exist in individual pupils. To date, little research has been conducted that demonstrates this approach with students with severe handicaps across a variety of social contexts (cf. Voeltz, Apffel, & Wuerch, 1981). Brown, Branston-McClean, Baumgart, Vincent, Falvey, and Schroeder (1979) have clearly described an ecological inventory strategy that would allow this approach to be accomplished. The following section of the chapter delineates the types of social contexts that are manifested in a secondary, severely handicapped school program and the kinds of social exchanges that can be promoted through instructional programming.

AN INTEGRATED SECONDARY AUTISTIC PROGRAM

Program Characteristics

The secondary-level class for autistic students described here is a public school program at San Rafael High School, administered by the Marin County (California) Office of Education. San Rafael is a suburban community with a sizable downtown area, located 15 miles north of San Francisco. The high school is attended primarily by middle- or upper-class students, although about 25% of the students are from working-class and/or Third World backgrounds. The campus is large and sprawling, with one main building and a number of auxiliary buildings. In addition to the class for autistic students, there are three other classes for handicapped students in a school of about 2,000 pupils.

Chapter author Pitts-Conway teaches the class, with the help of an instructional aide. There are seven students, five males and two females, ranging in age from 15–21. The students have been diagnosed as autistic and display a number of behaviors ordinarily associated with this disorder, e.g., self-stimulation, social withdrawal, limited language repertoires, and moderate to severe levels of inellectual functioning (retardation). The students attend daily classes (8:30 A.M.–2:30 P.M.) and reside with either their natural parents or in group homes for developmentally delayed persons.

The program has a number of core components. An operant instructional methodology is used (cf. Donnellan-Walsh, Gossage, LaVigna, Schuler, & Traphagen, 1976). Instructional sessions containing one to seven students structure the content of learning into a discriminative stimulus-response-reinforcement paradigm. For students under poor stimulus control, a continuous reinforcement schedule using primary reinforcers (e.g., edibles) is used. As students display more regulated behavior, they are moved to a token reinforcement system with more natural, leisure activities (e.g., listening to records, playing table games) used as back-up reinforcers. With further progress only natural cues and consequences (e.g., verbal praise) are used to structure learning activities. A functional learning curriculum is taught from a variety of educational domains, for example, personal management, cognitive, communication, social, leisure, vocational, community, and domestic. Ecological inventories (Brown et al., 1979) are generated with parental input to determine the skills that will be taught in the school and in the home.

Instruction occurs in multiple settings. A self-contained classroom with regular education classes serves as the base for about 35% of instruction. Other formal and informal instructional settings are listed below.

1. The gymnasium/pool are used for physical education with mildly mentally retarded students. Nonhandicapped students serve as peer tutors during these activities. The autistic students must change and dress in the locker room with minimal supervision and in proximity to 50 nonhandicapped students going to gym.
2. Students are mainstreamed into regular education classes on a person-by-

person basis. Selected students have attended art appreciation and home economic classes.

3. Attendance at school functions such as assemblies, rallies, and field trips is facilitated.
4. Students eat lunch and snacks at the high school cafeteria.
5. Students spend leisure time (between formal instructional settings) in a courtyard frequented by many nonhandicapped students.
6. Students participate in community training with teachers or nonhandicapped peers in stores and restaurants in the nearby shopping area.
7. On- and off-campus vocational training are conducted.
8. Vacations are taken to places as far away, for example, as Jamaica. Trips are arranged primarily with the group home where three of the students live. On vacation, the students have to complete their own self-care, share in chores, and interact with nonhandicapped individuals they meet.

Social Interaction Programs

The key social objctive of the Marin autistic program is to promote numerous and varied social interactions so that students may develop functional social skills. Before describing a continuum of *types* of social contexts and behaviors that can be developed in secondary, integrated settings, it is important to enumerate the teacher and administrative arrangements that need to be made to ensure that social activities are properly coordinated and attain maximum effectiveness.

Any effective social interaction program originates with the special education teacher, who is, in effect, a salesperson for the program. If a variety of social contacts are to accrue across peers, the teacher must display a number of social-administrative skills in order to facilitate the integration process. These skills include:

1. The special education teacher must view herself or himself as an integral part of the school faculty. Care must be taken to avoid isolation from the regular education faculty or administration. The teacher should socialize with the faculty, attend pertinent meetings, and participate in as many general school functions as is deemed appropriate (e.g., dances, sporting events, Parent-Teacher Association (PTA) meetings).
2. The special education teacher must promote the program to staff and students. Information about autistic persons and the types of program activities conducted should be disseminated. Students and staff should be encouraged to socialize and participate in the special education program as much as possible.
3. The teacher must become active in the community in order to increase awareness of the presence of his or her program and pupils. This means developing relationships with shopkeepers, bus drivers and police officers who will come into contact with students during community training. Also, relationships with potential employers must be cultivated in order to develop and maintain contacts for vocational training and employment.
4. Active relationships with parents must be engendered in order to gain their

support for the array of social interactions that may sometimes be risky, and to make sure that acquired social skills are generalized to domestic settings.

5. At school, the special education teacher must approach teachers who may have classes that could mainstream autistic students. By mainstreaming, it is meant that the student ultimately will be left alone in a regular education class without the presence of a special education staff person. The latter is a key person in facilitating successful mainstreaming. Regular education teachers must be:

a. Approached or solicited in a friendly manner.

b. Provided information about the student and instructional procedures.

c. Given staff support (e.g., an aide initially accompanies the student to the class) that is gradually faded out in a manner similar to that in the Russo and Koegel (1977) study.

d. Provided continued support and communication from the special education teacher. Verbally reinforcing the regular education teacher by stating your appreciation of his or her efforts is of key importance.

When the above context for social integration has been created, there is a good chance that social interaction programs will be successful.

Training Contexts for Social Interaction

Social interactions may occur in numerous contexts or settings. A comprehensive special eduation program seeks to improve social skills in most or all of these contexts. We have delineated four main contexts on a continuum according to the degree of "structure" inherent in the situation (see Figure 2). By "structure," it is meant that a fixed sequence for interacting is followed in every exchange. For example, peer tutoring can require a nonhandicapped peer to deliver 10 learning trials per session to a severely handicapped peer. At the other extreme, student-centered interactions entail no input or structure from staff with regard to how severely handicapped students and nonhandicapped peers should interact. Between these extremes are transient and leisure exchanges, which require initial structuring from staff but in which adult instruction is faded over time and the interaction pattern becomes less rigid. The following sections describe these contexts, with examples of instructional activities that can be used to promote social skill development.

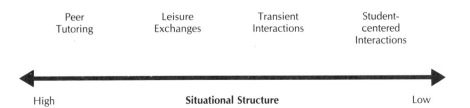

Figure 2. Contexts for social interactions.

Peer Tutoring   Peer tutoring, an instructional procedure that has been utilized with a variety of pupils (Allen, 1976), permits a pupil to serve as an instructor to one or more other pupils. Usually the tutor is older, developmentally more advanced, or in possession of specialized skills in relation to the tutee. Peer tutoring offers a number of benefits both to the school program and to the participants involved. Some of these benefits are:

1. It enriches the ratio of instructors to students in the class.
2. It permits the handicapped student to be exposed to peers in a structured learning situation.
3. It increases the chances that the handicapped student will generalize learned responses to a variety of peers (Peck, Apolloni, Cooke, & Rover, 1978), thus breaking the tendency for handicapped persons to attend only to particular adults (parents and teachers). The student learns that peers are important too.
4. The nonhandicapped peer increases his or her contact with handicapped persons and develops positive attitudes toward them (Voeltz, 1980).
5. For some nonhandicapped students who have had few successful experiences in school, it permits them to play a competent role as a knowledgeable resource (Allen, 1976).

In the autistic program at San Rafael High School, peer tutors, selected from grades 10–12, take a work experience course at the school that includes a minimum of one semester's involvement with the autistic program. The students come to the autistic class once a day under the supervision of chapter author Pitts-Conway. Approximately 12 students take the course per semester, interacting with the autistic students in a variety of social contexts.

In terms of teaching format, peer tutors are taught the rudiments of systematic instruction. They deliver cues and consequences in a trial-by-trial format; collect data on pupil performance; and follow the task-analyzed program for the objective on the student's individualized educational program (IEP). A variety of curricular activities are taught, including: money management, grooming, laundry, meal preparation, leisure, street crossing, communication, vending machine use, and vocational skills.

The program at San Rafael has been viewed as a success by both staff and participants. The structured setting gives security to the nonhandicapped students, who are often unfamiliar with the autistic students and the systematic learning format increases the likelihood that the nonhandicapped students will succeed at teaching specific skills to the autistic students. The structured setting also delineates the behaviors that tutors need to display. With time, tutors gain more confidence and familiarity with the students so that more informal and relaxed exchanges develop and friendships ensue. In addition, the nonhandicapped students' communicate their positive experience to other peers as well as staff, which helps to promote positive attitudes toward the autistic students and the program in general (cf. Voeltz, 1980).

In summary, peer tutoring has much to recommend for teachers of severely handicapped students working in integrated settings. It is easy to implement because it extends the existing instructional model (i.e., discrete trial teaching) to nonhandicapped peers, thus permitting peer tutors to be effective instructors and allowing the teacher to supervise them with little difficulty. Instructional time or impact is also increased by the addition of "teachers," so that more pupil gains should result (cf. Fredericks et al. 1978). Finally, out of this structured context more informal relationships and interactions seem to develop among the secondary students.

Student-Centered Contexts   At the other end of the "structure" continuum are student-centered contexts. Student-centered interactions do not involve directives from staff. Two or more students convene and interact according to their own proclivities. No adult training is provided by staff to designate the correct response or sequence of responses.

In the Marin County program severely handicapped students and non-handicapped students interact in a number of student-centered situations. In "special friend" exchanges a nonhandicapped student arrives at the autistic class at a given time. He or she and the autistic special friend are then told to go off and "hang out" (see below) together. On the first visit, the nonhandicapped student is often confused as to what he or she should do. After several 15–45 minute, student-centered episodes, however, the special friends become more at ease with each other and at choosing what they will do.

The activities in which the special friends engage are representative of what normal adolescents do with their free time at school. They:

1. Walk around the high school campus in a care-free manner.
2. Walk to the cafeteria for snacks.
3. Go to their lockers.
4. "Hang out" on a bench, against a car, etc., and pass the time of day. (The act of "hanging out" is central to American teenage culture and is discussed in more detail later in the chapter.)
5. Walk off campus and frequent stores and shops. (At San Rafael High School, students can leave the campus when assigned classes are not in session. To permit secondary autistic students to leave campus unescorted by an adult certainly involves a risk, and at some schools it would not be permitted. In our program, with parental support and permission, special friend off-campus trips are identified as a community training objective on the student's IEP. There have been no difficulties, and many benefits have resulted from the off-campus excursions.)

These are some of the settings in which student-centered interactions occur. Obviously, at a regular public school site there are many other times and settings when student-centered interactions occur—for example, in the 5-minute passing periods between classes, at lunchtime, when arriving at and leaving school, and during assemblies. In fact, we feel that these unprogrammed interactions offer one of the major social benefits for integrated school placements. As discussed in the next section, social behavior sequences can be trained through operant methods. Yet, a much easier way, and the way that normal persons acquire social behaviors, is through observational learning. If a severely handicapped child is imitative, we feel that the greater portion of social behaviors will be obtained through incidental observational learning. While this point needs research verification, it is a *modus operandi* for social skill learning in the Marin County program. For this reason, the autistic student is exposed to myriad social situations in which programmed and incidental social learning can transpire.

Transient Interactions　　Between the extremes of peer tutoring and student-centered interactions are transient interactions and leisure exchanges. The latter two contexts involve moderate amounts of structure because they initially require rigorous training; ultimately, however, they call for the student to make the social response(s) in a natural, unprogrammed setting.

Transient interactions involve brief exchanges, the main such exchanges being greetings and farewells. Other types of transient social interactions include asking directions, exchanges with merchants, etc. Greetings are of great functional importance because they establish minimal social contact with others. We have found that autistic persons who are both socially withdrawn and linguistically limited can be taught the minimal social responses of greetings and farewells. Saying or signing *hi* can effectively change a handicapped person from being an isolate to being perceived as a sociable individual. As severely handicapped persons and nonhandicapped persons become more acquainted, a greeting response tends to reaffirm that relationship on a day-to-day basis. From an operant perspective, if the severely handicapped student fails to give a greeting or any other social response, the nonhandicapped person is on an extinction schedule of reinforcement. It has been our observation that nonhandicapped students on such an extinction schedule tend to decrease or cease altogether their interactions with severely handicapped students. Conversely, when severely handicapped students provide some type of transient social reinforcement to the nonhandicapped student, their rate of interaction over days and weeks tends to be maintained at a substantial level. These observations are anecdotal and there is certainly a need for research to confirm the frequency of nonhandicapped/severely handicapped interactions as a function of severely handicapped transient responses.

Although transient social responses are often simple (e.g., *hi, good-bye*), they still need to be intensively trained through systematic procedures. One of the first considerations is what communication mode the response should be delivered in. Sailor, Guess, Goetz, Schuler, Utley, and Baldwin (1980) have delineated ways for professionals to decide which communication modality should be selected for training (i.e., vocal, sign, communication board). In training for transient social responses it is a good strategy to use the same communication system that is being used in other areas of the student's communication training. A special consideration for transient responses, though, is that the communicated response must be clear to the recipient. Transient responses are given to both familiar and unfamiliar persons in many natural situations. The response must, therefore, be clear to strangers if it is to have any functional effect.

Transient responses can be initially learned in structured situations by having pairs of persons (staff–severely handicapped, severely handicapped–severely handicapped, or severely handicapped–nonhandicapped) role-play the inter-action. A task-analyzed sequence could be:

1. Severely handicapped student ambulates toward nonhandicapped student.
2. Severely handicapped and nonhandicapped students orient their bodies toward each other in a frontal manner (frontal shoulder orientation is a useful minimal criterion since it tends to align the rest of the body).
3. Severely handicapped student communicates 'hi' response to non-handicapped student.
4. Nonhandicapped student reciprocates 'hi' response vocally and uses a gesture similar to that used by the severely handicapped student (e.g., sign).
    (Steps 3 and 4 can be reversed.)

The sequence is initially taught concurrently (Gaylord-Ross, 1980) or with "total task presentations" (Bellamy, Horner, & Inman, 1979) (the latter meaning that students are put through the sequence with no delays between response steps). A prompt-reinforcer strategy is applied according to the learning style of the students. For example, a prompt strategy could be used so that if either student fails to respond correctly within 5 seconds the trainer intervenes with a physical prompt so that the student is guided through the behavior. A reinforcement strategy could be used so that both students are verbally praised at the completion of the sequence. The prompt-reinforcer strategy must be individualized for each dyad. With successful acquisition of the sequence, though, both prompt and reinforcing events should be faded and thinned to the point that they are never used. If acquisition is slow or unsuccessful (see Haring, Liberty, & White, 1980, for making decision rules related to pupil progress and treatment selection), a serial (Gaylord-Ross, 1980) or isolated task presentation (Bellamy et al., 1979) may be used. In the isolated task presentation, a single step in the social sequence is taught in isolation. For example, the severely handicapped student might be taught to sign 'hi' in an isolated, massed trial format. Once the social sequence has been acquired, the next, and most critical, step is to train the sequence to occur in multiple, natural settings. The technology of discrimination and generalization training (see Stokes & Baer, 1977) is needed to achieve successful responses.

In the Marin County program, we first work on generalizing the response to multiple people and settings through use of a simultaneous training procedure. Here, the student is taken to at least three settings to practice the greeting response. In each setting at least three nondisabled persons are approached with a greeting. During generalization training a time delay (Touchette, 1971) procedure could be used to progressively fade out the trainer. For example, in the school courtyard the student is expected to make a greeting response within 10 seconds. If no response occurs, the trainer intervenes and verbally prompts the student to do so. After the greeting (and further social) exchange is completed, the trainer will wait 20 seconds before prompting the next greeting response to another student. If the response occurs before the 20 seconds have elapsed, no prompt is delivered. The time delay is then progressively increased to 30, 40, 50, and 60 seconds. Thus, about six trials can be run within 5 minutes in order to promote generalized responding. The same procedure can be repeated in a number of settings until the student is initiating greeting responses at a high rate and in a generalized fashion. Time delay is a useful procedure that can be used to promote generalized responding in a number of task domains—for example, identifying items in stores, and crossing at stoplights.

The next step is to teach discrimination of the transient response. The practical meaning of discrimination in the case of greetings is that the student does not offer greetings to every passerby. For instance, it may be proper to greet a friend at the beginning of lunch, but it would be inappropriate to repeatedly greet the person every time you pass him during lunch. More importantly, the context in which one meets strangers determines whether a greeting is delivered. For example, in a crowded city street or in a public bathroom it would be unwise to train autistic adolescents to make greeting responses. In contrast, at a party or in a small, familiar store it could be appropriate to initiate greetings. The number of contexts where it might be appropriate or inappropriate to initiate greetings are myriad. Further demonstration and research work is needed to delineate social discrimination patterns among this group of students.

Leisure Exchanges Although we have chosen to describe leisure exchanges last, they are possibly the most important social skills among the four mentioned. Leisure exchanges are equivalent to transient interactions in structural characteristics; they entail initial intensive training, but ultimately the student must perform the social act without staff intervention. Leisure exchanges are protracted interactions that do not cease after one or two responses; rather, leisure exchanges expand upon transient interactions. Figure 3 presents a schematic of a leisure exchange. First, a transient greeting is given by each member of the dyad. Second, a *pivotal* response is made by one of the persons to communicate *Let's play_____*. (e.g., *Let's play Frisbee*). The pivot phrase serves to expand the interaction beyond the transient phase. If no pivot phrase is given, the interaction may end with a farewell response. It has been our observation that most interactions involving severely handicapped persons terminate at the greeting phase. Considerable effort has been given to teaching greeting responses to severely handicapped persons (e.g., Stokes, Baer, & Jackson, 1974). Relatively little work has been completed in research or school settings, however, in extending the duration of a social sequence (Wehman, 1977).

After the pivot response, the other person must communicate an agreement response (e.g., *OK*, a nod, or grunt) so that the *play* phase can begin. The play phase entails an exchange of responses that takes the form of a game. Table 1 presents a list of games that are appropriate for students with severe handicaps. The ''reciprocity'' (Piaget, 1951) or exchange of responses continues in the play phase until the game has run its course or until the participants have decided to terminate the interaction with a farewell response.

Several considerations must be taken into account when attempting to train two or more persons to participate in a leisure exchange. First, there is the fact that the leisure exchange involves an extended chain of behavior. Many severely handicapped persons are able only to make single responses (e.g., *Throw ball*).

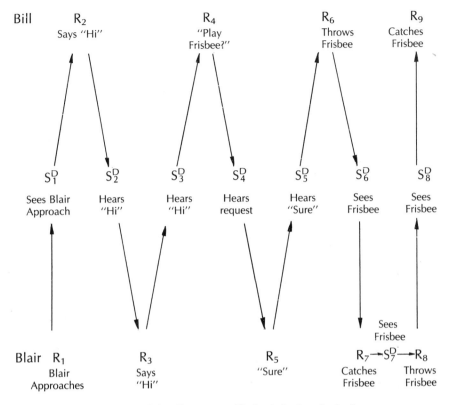

Figure 3. Social interaction chain. (R, response; S^D, discriminative stimulus.)

The technology of teaching students to make longer response chains must therefore be applied. Bellamy et al. (1979) have delineated a stimulus-response model for the acquisition of vocational response chains. Figure 3 presents a similar scheme for social chains. What is critical to remember in social chains is that the response of one person serves as a stimulus event for the other person. Thus, in Figure 3 Bill's response (R_6) is throwing the Frisbee. This response creates the stimulus (S_6) for Blair of seeing a Frisbee flying toward her. Blair, in turn, responds by catching the Frisbee (R_7). R_7 creates the stimulus of Blair viewing the Frisbee in her hand (S_7), which leads to the response (R_8) of throwing the Frisbee

Table 1. Leisure exchanges for students with severe handicaps

Dodgeball	Remote control cars	Pinball
Frisbee	Darts	Wheelchair races
Dancing	Card games (e.g., War)	Basketball
Four Square	Checkers	Swimming
Legos	Wrestling	Diving
Video games	Tag	Hide-and-Seek
Shoots and Ladders	Puzzles	Baseball
Kickball		

to Bill. This cycle of viewing-object throwing-perceiving-catching can be repeated an indefinite number of times. The point is that this chain of responses must be taught to the student. Other types of leisure skills that frequently occur in high schools and should be considered for instruction are hand-held video games, listening to portable radios, and playing handball. The same kinds of prompting and reinforcing techniques used to teach transient responses can be used. It is important to fade prompts and thin reinforcing events as rapidly as possible. If the leisure task selected is one of high interest to the student(s), it is likely that, with mastery, the intrinsic reinforcement properties of the task will preclude the need for continued external and artificial reinforcement.

Another potential problem with teaching leisure chains is that they are often linguistic as well as social. Severely handicapped students have limited language repertoires. It is unreasonable to expect students with limited language ability to communicate in extended verbal chains. Unfortunately, however, much social leisure behavior for the nondisabled population is conversational (e.g., parties, "coffee klatch"). Table 1, therefore, purposely lists selected leisure activities that are high in nonverbal content and low in verbal demands.

The Teenage Culture

We have noted that the preponderance of severely handicapped integration efforts have been at the preschool level. Practical aspects relating to the ease of implementation of early childhood programs, as well as the closer developmental levels between preschool severely handicapped children and nonhandicapped peers were mentioned earlier as some of the reasons for the emphasis on preschools. There are additional considerations, however, related to the type of cultural patterns into which the student with severe handicaps will be integrated in preschool versus high school. The preschool world is generally adult controlled and influenced. The American (Western) teenage subculture, however, is quite separate and unique from American mainstream culture (Friedenburg, 1959). When discussing the integration of secondary students with severe handicaps, it is therefore important not only to examine the types of interventions that will facilitate socialization, but also the characteristics of the subculture in which integration will occur. The Western teenage subculture seems to have both redeeming qualities that will nurture the development of severely handicapped adolescents, as well as negative characteristics that could be deleterious to these students. At San Rafael High School the nonhandicapped students have been extremely responsive in their dealings with severely handicapped students. Episodes of ridicule or abuse are rare or nonexistent. A number of students actively initiate interactions with severely handicapped students or are responsive to their initiations. In general, the peer culture is quite tolerant and open to behavioral encounters with special education students. At present, the Socialization Research Project (funded by the U.S. Department of Education) is trying to examine what types of nonhandicapped students engage, avoid, or are indifferent in their social dealings with severely handicapped students. The project (directed by chapter author Gaylord-Ross and

T. Haring) is examining the attitudes, behavioral interactions, and friendship patterns that develop in secondary, integrated settings. Some of the concerns the project is exploring are discussed below.

Concerns The possibility of physical or psychological abuse is probably the major concern among parents and professionals related to the integration of secondary students with severe handicaps. Physical abuse can take the form of assaultive acts or sexual offenses against the handicapped youth. Another concern is that psychological abuse, such as teasing and public ridicule, may occur. These concerns have a basis in reality, given the condition of many contemporary high schools. Particularly in urban areas, violence, illicit sex, and drug abuse can exist on the campus grounds. Schools where violence or other criminal activity is common are probably not good settings for the integration of students with severe handicaps, although they should not be automatically ruled out. At the secondary level, successful efforts have also occurred in large cities like Milwaukee and Honolulu. In selecting a school for the integration of students with severe handicaps the following conditions should be considered:

1. The school should have a relatively low rate of assaults and other forms of violence on the campus.
2. The school should have a good record of working with other handicapped students (e.g., visually handicapped students, mildly retarded students). A positive working climate among students and staff should facilitate social integration. The more that handicapped students can be included in the school's institutions and activities (e.g., student council, clubs, assemblies, yearbook pictures, sports activities), the better the likelihood of successful social integration.
3. Supportive parent and community groups interfacing with the school can be critical vehicles to enhance social integration.
4. An active inservice training program that includes both special educators and regular educators and that disseminates accurate information and demonstrates how handicapped persons can be contributing members of a high school, is important. Inservice programs should be afforded to students, staff, parents, and community members as a way of enlisting their help in the integration process.

When the above conditions exist, there is a good chance that successful integration may result in even the more difficult high schools of the nation.

Identity, Hipness, and Hanging Out While the secondary school environment may offer some potential threats to social integration, high schools and their students also bring many attributes to integration efforts. Teenagers are in a vibrant state of flux as they grapple with the transitional stage between childhood and adulthood. Although American adolescents often have been depicted negatively by the media, their energy is directed in many constructive ways as they cope with the problems of vocation and sexuality. Erikson (1968) has characterized these developmental years as devoted to the adolescent's search for identity. The formation of a positive and coherent identity seems to be the major developmental milestone during this period. Since adolescents are ascribed the status of quasi-adults in Western societies, they tend to create and rely on their own peer culture to formulate their own identity. Adults are given limited access to this peer culture (Friedenburg, 1959).

Because handicapped persons are embraced so totally by the adults around them, however, they have little contact with their nonhandicapped peers. The effect of such restricted contact on the development of severely handicapped adolescents' identities is unknown, as the development of self-concept and identity among this population has been studied little. Some investigators, such as Brown et al. 1979, have called for the development of age-appropriate curricula for these students. It is likely that age-appropriate instructional efforts will contribute to the appearance of more socially acceptable behaviors for these students. Yet, we feel further efforts in the socialization of severely handicapped adolescents are needed. A key step would be to expose the student with severe handicaps to the adolescent peer culture. By observing and interacting with nondisabled teenagers in more informal contexts, the severely handicapped youth may learn invaluable social skills and behavioral styles. Our emphasis on student-centered interactions reflects this need for informal teenage encounters. We have anecdotally observed autistic teenagers whose rates of bizarre behaviors were reduced when they were "hanging out" with nondisabled peers. In fact, the "hanging out" setting seems particularly suited for casual social interaction. In our analysis of what normal teenagers do, it appears that hanging out—or idly sitting/standing around, talking, etc.—is a key social event in a teenager's world. Hanging out seems to serve the useful function of breaking away from the pressures of school, while allowing the teenager to display his or her identity through talking about common interests (e.g., school, sports, friends). Much of the hanging out time of individual teenagers, though, is spent quietly, listening to another person speak. It is thus a useful context in which severely handicapped teenagers—many of whom do not have strong verbal skills—may interact with their peers. Few demands are placed on them, and they have the opportunity to observe appropriate modes of conduct, much of which is nonverbal posturing. We have observed some autistic teenagers imitating these appropriate hanging out behaviors. We feel that these encounters have helped to better socialize these students in ways that more formal, adult-oriented social skill programs could never accomplish. The benefits of integrated public schools are clearly demonstrated in the opportunities for incidental encounters among nonhandicapped and severely handicapped students that could never be obtained in segregated schools.

SUMMARY

This chapter synthesized some of the diverse information concerning the social integration of students with severe handicaps. Research on autistic persons and outcomes of integration studies have revealed that effective instructional procedures have been developed that can promote social interactions between severely handicapped students and nonhandicapped students. Recent efforts have attempted to extend these procedures beyond the preschool setting to primary and secondary schools. The program characteristics of an actual, integrated, secondary class for autistic students was described, and the types of social contexts that can promote social skill development were delineated. The contexts for social interactions were classified into four types: peer tutoring, transient interactions, leisure exchanges, and student-centered encounters. Finally, there was a brief discussion of the characteristics of the American teenage culture into which severely handicapped students will be integrated. There is an obvious need for further research and demonstration efforts to clarify the types of interventions and social contexts that will best promote the social behavior development of severely handicapped students. Although we have mentioned factors that may inhibit this process, our experiences overall lead us to be optimistic about the possibilities for effective social skill development and social integration of severely handicapped adolescents and nonhandicapped peers at the secondary level.

REFERENCES

Allen, V.L. (ed.). *Children as teachers: Theory and research on tutoring.* New York: Academic Press, 1976.

Bellamy, G.T., Horner, R.H., & Inman, D.P. *Vocational habilitation of severely retarded adults: A direct service technology.* Baltimore: University Park Press, 1979.

Bogdon, R., & Taylor, S. The judged, not the judges: An insider's view of mental retardation. *American Psychologist,* 1976, *31,* 47–52.

Brown, L., Branston-McClean, M.B., Baumgart, D., Vincent, L., Falvey, M., & Schroeder, J. Using the characteristics of current and subsequent least restrictive environments in the development of curricular content for severely handicapped students. *AAESPH Review,* 1979, *4,* 407–424.

Cooke, S.A., Cooke, T.P., & Apolloni, T. Developing nonretarded toddlers and verbal models for retarded classmates. *Child Study Journal,* 1978, *8,* 1–8.

Donnellan-Walsh, A., Gossage, L.D., LaVigna, G.W., Schuler, A.L., & Traphagen, J.D. *Teaching makes a difference.* Santa Barbara, CA: Santa Barbara County Schools, 1976.

Egel, A.L., Richman, G., & Koegel, R.L. Normal peer models and autistic children's learning. *Journal of Applied Behavior Analysis,* 1981, *14,* 3–12.

Erikson, E.H. *Identity: Youth and crisis.* New York: W.W. Norton & Co., 1968.

Ferster, C.B. Positive reinforcement and behavioral deficits of autistic children. *Child Development,* 1961, *32,* 437–456.

Fredericks, H.D.B., Baldwin, V., Grove, D., Moore, W., Riggs, C., & Lyons, B. Integrating the moderately and severely handicapped preschool child into a normal day care setting. In: M.J. Guralnick (ed.), *Early intervention and the integration of handicapped and nonhandicapped children.* Baltimore: University Park Press, 1978.

Friedenburg, E.Z *The vanishing adolescent.* New York: Beacon Press, 1959.

Gaylord-Ross, R.J. Mental retardation: Research, ecological validity, and the delivery of longitudinal educational programs. *Journal of Special Education,* 1979, *13,* 69–80.

Gaylord-Ross, R.J. *Task analysis and the severely handicapped.* San Francisco: Special Education Department, San Francisco State University, 1980.

Gaylord-Ross, R.J., Piuma, M.F., Murray, M.C., Halvorsen, A.T., & Sailor, W.S. *The Frisco Interaction Scale for the Handicapped (FISH).* San Francisco: Special Education Department, San Francisco State University, 1981.

Gomes, M. *Social interaction between severely handicapped and nonhandicapped students in segregated and integrated settings.* San Francisco: Special Education Department, San Francisco State University, 1981.

Greenwood, C.R., Todd, N.M., Walker, H.M., & Hops, H. *Social assessment manual for preschool level (SAMPLE)*. Eugene, OR: Center at Oregon for Reseach in the Behavioral Education of the Handicapped, University of Oregon, 1978.

Guralnick, M. (ed.). *Early intervention and the integration of handicapped and non-handicapped children*. Baltimore: University Park Press, 1978.

Haring, N.G., Liberty, K.A., & White, O.R. Rules for data-based strategy decisions in instructional programs. In: W. Sailor, B. Wilcox, & L. Brown (eds.), *Methods of instruction for severely handicapped students*. Baltimore: Paul H. Brookes Publishing Co., 1980.

Hart, B.M., Reynolds, N.J., Baer, D.M., Brawley, F.R., & Harris, F.R. Effect of contingent and non-contingent social reinforcement on the cooperative play of a preschool child. *Journal of Applied Behavior Analysis*, 1968, *1*, 73–76.

Hersen, M., & Barlow, D.H. *Single case experimental designs*. London: Pergamon Press, 1976.

Kanner, L. Autistic disturbances of affective content. *The Nervous Child*, 1943, *3*, 217–250.

Koegel, R.L., & Covert, A. The relationship of self-stimulation to learning in autistic children. *Journal of Applied Behavior Analysis*, 1972, *5*, 381–387.

Koegel, R.L., Dunlap, G., & Dyer, K. Intertrial interval duration and learning in autistic children. *Journal of Applied Behavior Analysis*, 1980, *13*, 91-99.

Koegel, R.L., & Egel, A.L. Motivating autistic children. *Journ l of Abnormal Psychology*, 1979, *88*, 418–426.

Koegel, R.L., Egel, A.L., & Dunlap, G. Learning characteristics of autistic children. In: W. Sailor, B. Wilcox, & L. Brown (eds.), *Methods of instruction for severely handicapped students*. Baltimore: Paul H. Brookes Publishing Co., 1980.

Koegel, R.L., Glahn, T.J., & Nieminen, G.S. Generalization of parent training results. *Journal of Applied Behavior Analysis*, 1978, *11*, 95–109.

Koegel, R.L., & Rincover, A. Treatment of psychotic children in a classroom environment. *Journal of Applied Behavior Analysis*, 1974, *7*, 45–59.

Lovaas, O.I. *The autistic child*. New York: Irvington Publishers, Inc., 1977.

Lovaas, O.I., & Newsom, C.D. Behavior modification with psychotic children. In: H. Leitenberg (ed.), *Handbook of behavior modification and behavior therapy*. Englewood Cliffs, NJ: Prentice-Hall, 1976.

Lovaas, O.I., & Schreibman, L. Stimulus overselectivity of autistic children in a two-stimulus situation. *Behavior Research and Therapy*, 1971, *9*, 305–310.

Lovaas, O.I., & Simmons, J.Q. Manipulation of self-destruction in three retarded children. *Journal of Applied Behavior Analysis*, 1969, *2*, 143–157.

Parten, M. Social participation among preschool children. *Journal of Abnormal Social Psychology*, 1932, *27*, 243–269.

Peck, C.A., Apolloni, T., Cooke, T.P., & Rover, S.A. Teaching retarded preschoolers to imitate the free-play behavior of nonretarded classmates: Trained and generalized effects. *Journal of Special Education*, 1978, *12*, 195–207.

Peterson, N.L. *The social ecology of intervention strategies for young handicapped children: Peer interactions*. Lawrence, KS: Kansas Research Institute for the Early Childhood Education of the Handicapped, 1978.

Peterson, N.L., & Garalnick, J.G. Integration of handicapped and nonhandicapped preschoolers: An analysis of play behavior and social interaction. *Education and Training of the Mentally Retarded*, 1977, *12*, 235–245.

Piaget, J. *Play, dreams and imitation in childhood*. New York: W.W. Norton & Co., 1951.

Rincover, A., & Koegel, R.L. Setting generality and stimulus control in autistic children. *Journal of Applied Behavior Analysis*, 1975, *8*, 235–246.

Russo, D.C., & Koegel, R.L. A method for integrating an autistic child into a normal public school classroom. *Journal of Applied Behavior Analysis*, 1977, *10*, 579–590.

Sailor, W., Guess, D., Goetz, L., Schuler, A., Utley, B., & Baldwin, M. Language and severely handicapped persons. In: W. Sailor, B. Wilcox, & L. Brown (eds.), *Methods of instruction for severely handicapped students*. Baltimore: Paul H. Brookes Publishing Co., 1980.

Schreibman, L., Koegel, R.L., & Craig, M.S. Reducing stimulus overselectivity in autistic children. *Journal of Abnormal Child Psychology*, 1977, *5*, 435–436.

Schreibman, L., & Lovaas, O.I. Overselective response to social stimuli by autistic children. *Journal of Abnormal Child Psychology*, 1973, *1*, 152–168.

Stokes, T.F., & Baer, D.M. An implicit technology of generalization. *Journal of Applied Behavior Analysis*, 1977, *10*, 344–367.

Stokes, T.F., Baer, D.M., & Jackson, R.L. Programming the generalization of a greeting response in four retarded children. *Journal of Applied Behavior Analysis*, 1974, *7*, 599–610.

Strain, P., Shores, R., & Timm, M. Effects of peer social initiations on the behavior of withdrawn preschool children. *Journal of Applied Behavior Analysis*, 1977, *10*, 289–298.

Touchette, P.E. Transfer of stimulus control: Measuring the moment of transfer. *Journal of Experimental Analysis of Behavior*, 1971, *15*, 347–364.

Wehman, P. *Helping the mentally retarded acquire play skills*. Springfield, IL: Charles C Thomas, 1977.

Voeltz, L.M. Children's attitudes toward handicapped peers. *American Journal of Mental Deficiency*, 1980, *84*, 455–464.

Voeltz, L.M., Apffel, J.A., & Wuerch, B.B. *Leisure activities training for severely handicapped students: Instructional and evaluation strategies*. Honolulu: University of Hawaii, 1981.

11

A Strategy for Developing Interpersonal Interaction Instructional Content for Severely Handicapped Students

Nick Certo
and Frances L. Kohl

An increasing number of public school systems throughout the country have either initiated or completed the transition from isolated, self-contained placements to integrated, age-appropriate placements for severely handicapped students. Although physical proximity with nonhandicapped peers is one of the first steps toward integration, there is an urgent need to go beyond placement decisions. Severely handicapped students must be taught to interact with their non-handicapped peers; conversely, nonhandicapped individuals must be encouraged

This manuscript was supported in part by Grant No. GOO-80-01719 to the University of Maryland–College Park from the U.S. Department of Education, Special Education Programs, Division of Innovation and Development, Handicapped Children's Model Programs, Washington, D.C., and by Grant No. GOO-81-01732 to the University of Maryland—College Park from the U.S. Department of Education, Special Education Programs, Division of Personnel Preparation, Washington, D.C.

and, in some cases, taught to interact with severely handicapped students. In addition, integration efforts must extend beyond school settings to home and community environments where severely handicapped individuals are currently functioning and will be expected to function in the future (Brown, Branston-McClean, Baumgart, Vincent, Falvey, & Schroeder, 1979; Brown, Nietupski, & Hamre-Nietupski, 1976; Vincent, Salisbury, Walter, Brown, Gruenewald, & Powers, 1980).

If integration of severely handicapped students into age-appropriate school and nonschool settings is to be successful, strategies must be developed for expanding the number and types of interactions between severely handicapped students and nonhandicapped individuals. Research into empirically validated methods that promote interactions and improve integration efforts is increasing (Stainback & Stainback, 1981). Some of this research has involved preschool populations (Guralnick, 1978, 1980), while other studies have focused on attitudinal changes (Donaldson, 1981; McHale & Simeonsson, 1980; Voeltz, 1980) and the development of social behaviors beyond preschool (Strain, Shores, & Timm, 1977). However, this research base must be broadened to address the growing number of problems confronted by educators engaged in integration.

This chapter discusses some of the current obstacles both to the integration of severely handicapped students and to the development of interpersonal interactions with other individuals, and delineates a strategy for teaching interactions to severely handicapped students in school, home, and community settings. The strategy described is now being developed and tested by the authors and their colleagues in the Prince George's County (Maryland) Public School System.

OBSTACLES TO THE
DEVELOPMENT OF INTERPERSONAL INTERACTIONS

A paucity of instructional information exists regarding the types of interactions that could be taught severely handicapped students. It is tempting to conclude, therefore, that the reason so little information is available is because few severely handicapped students interact with other individuals. Based on knowledge that is available, however, we believe that such a conclusion is totally unwarranted. Rather, other factors, which go beyond the ultimate capabilities of severely handicapped students, will soon be seen as contributing to the overall lack of instructional content in the interpersonal interactions area.

Perhaps most important, the placement of severely handicapped students in segregated facilities, whether institutions, public schools, or sheltered workshops, has been and continues to be a major obstacle to the development of interaction instructional content. Few severely handicapped students initiate and, in particular, maintain interactions with each other. The communication skills of most severely handicapped students are frequently so limited that the typical medium for an interaction is restricted. If, in addition to possessing a limited repertoire of social and communicative skills, a severely handicapped student is motorically impaired, the chance of initiating interactions through standard means (e.g., walking toward a peer or waving to get someone's attention) is negligible. As a result, the placement of severely handicapped students in segregated facilities reduces the opportunities for instructional personnel to examine interactional patterns, to gain insights into the nature of interactions, and to teach new interpersonal interaction skills between severely handicapped students and their peers.

The problem of placing students in self-contained facilities has been further compounded by the standard practice of grouping students in classrooms on the basis of *homogeneous student characteristics* (Brown et al., 1976). Such groupings often result in classes composed of all nonambulatory nonverbal students, all severe behavior problem students, all Down syndrome students, and so on. Homogeneous classroom groupings reduce the chances of peer interactions, and render group instruction difficult to implement. As a result, many severely handicapped students in homogeneous classes spend considerable time waiting in isolation (typically performing self-stimulatory behaviors) until a teacher or other instructional personnel is available to work with them directly.

A third factor that contributes to the scanty interaction instructional information is the narrow interpretation of an *interpersonal interaction*. The terms suggest a two-way exchange between people. Such exchanges are typically considered to be social in nature and often become narrowly defined as spontaneous verbal discussion focusing on any range of possible topics, including personal gossip. It is safe to say that making conversation, in general, and gossiping, in particular, are not skills easily acquired by severely handicapped students. It is this presumed requirement that an interaction involve a formal conversational exchange that limits our ability to recognize the many interaction possibilities for severely handicapped students. By recognizing that interactions do not have to be verbal, that they can involve nonverbal exchange as well, a range of interactions can be observed in the current repertoires of many severely handicapped students. For example, if a severely handicapped student touches a teacher's hand and the teacher responds by looking at the student, an interaction has occurred. In this case, a formal system of communication such as speech, American Sign Language (ASL), picture boards, or Blissymbols was not used. This example should not be construed, however, as minimizing th' importance of teaching formal communication skills to severely handicapped students. Whenever possible, interactions that require the use of a formal communication system and the expansion of the communicative content must be taught. However, informal interactions that occur between severely handicapped students and others need to be encouraged as well.

Interpersonal interaction in its broad sense, therefore, may be defined as "an overt motor response that occurs between two or more individuals in which there is an exchange of information, feedback, or assistance." However, the occurrence of an interpersonal interaction does not in itself necessarily satisfy instructional aims. The interaction must be linked to a functional purpose in school, home, and community contexts. It is our position that the interactional performance of severely handicapped students *can* be significantly improved, provided certain steps are followed, including: first, placing severely handicapped students in integrated heterogeneous settings; second, analyzing the interpersonal interactions that currently occur or could occur in a severely handicapped student's home, community, and social environments; third, determining the responses or adapted responses that will allow the student to engage at least partially in those interactions; fourth, teaching those interactions; and fifth, systematically expanding the number and types of interactions across environments according to predetermined criteria.

The following two sections of this chapter analyze the components of an interpersonal interaction and offer guidelines for determining the types of interpersonal interactions that are required or at least considered functional in relation to various environments. The combined use of the component analysis and the suggested guidelines on interactional content should facilitate the implementation of an overall strategy for teaching interactions to severely handicapped students and encouraging the systematic expansion of interactions over time. (Such a strategy comprises the last section of this chapter.)

COMPONENTS OF AN INTERPERSONAL INTERACTION

A seven-component diagram used to analyze interpersonal interactions is presented in Figure 1. Each of the components—*initiation, nature, purpose, communication system, communication mode, quality,* and *outcome*—relates to the behavior of the individuals involved in the interaction and provides a means to quantify interaction patterns. It should be noted that the student is the reference point when interactions are analyzed.

Initiation of the Interaction

The initiation component of an interaction concerns which party, the severely handicapped student or another individual, begins the interaction. Interaction initiation addresses an area of critical need, for rarely do severely handicapped students spontaneously initiate contact with other persons. The problem, however, does not always emanate from the student. Rarely do instructors arrange the environment or organize their teaching so that severely handicapped students are required or inspired to initiate interactions with other individuals. Repeatedly, the instructional pattern encourages students to wait patiently until the instructor begins an interaction. For example, it is easier and less time-consuming for the teacher to bring materials to a severely handicapped student while he or she is seated at a table than to have the student initiate the activity by going to a cabinet, retrieving the materials, and giving them to the teacher. Even in cases where interactions might begin by being teacher-initiated, however, teachers have the potential, through the fading of antecedent cues, of teaching severely handicapped students to initiate the interpersonal interactions.

Another factor that contributes to the lack of student-initiated interactions is the abundance of ''dead time'' in severely handicapped student classrooms. (Dead

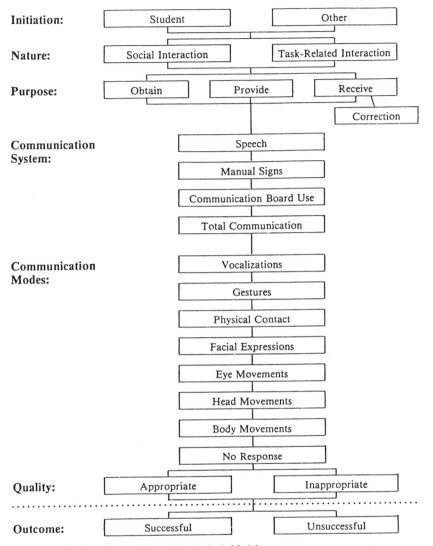

Figure 1. The Interpersonal Interaction Analysis Model.

time refers to the time a student spends in a nonstructured waiting period between instructional sessions.) Dead time can be minimized in heterogeneous classes that control for the overinclusion of any one student problem, characteristic, or disability; the range of skills among the students is sufficiently diverse to enable the teacher to pair a more capable student with one less capable. The establishment of heterogeneous class groupings would provide the base teachers need to organize instruction to encourage more student-initiated interactions. However, until such changes are implemented, we need to begin the transition by carefully scrutinizing instructional tasks and noninstructional situations to determine when and how students could initiate interactions in at least a small percentage of the total number of naturally occurring daily opportunities. This component of an interpersonal interaction must be analyzed critically to encourage the gradual expansion of the number of student-initiated interactions over time.

Nature of the Interaction

Repeated observations have revealed that interpersonal interactions can be categorized as either social- or task-related. The terms *interpersonal interaction* were selected as opposed to the more traditional *social interaction* to underscore the fact that the majority of severely handicapped students' daily interactions tend to be task-related. It is important not to ignore task-related situations as a possible source for analyzing and targeting new interactions. Since severely handicapped students engage in so few interactions in general, no current or potential source of interactions should be overlooked.

Social Interactions A social interaction is an event between two or more individuals consisting of an exchange of information, feedback, or assistance engaged in solely for the purpose of fraternization. For example, two severely handicapped students are sitting on a trampoline and one touches the other in a friendly gesture; or a teacher compliments a student's appearance and the student smiles in response. Social interactions are typically considered appropriate for certain situations or events—such as discussions in the hallway, birthday parties, class picnics, field-trips, or discussions around the dinner table—all of which occur either too infrequently or are difficult for a teacher to use to structure changes in a student's performance. However, if social interactions are permitted to occur in nontypical contexts, then opportunities for social exchanges involving severely handicapped students emerge throughout the school day. For example, the fact that one student touches another when they are on a trampoline is, in our opinion, significant. The question is, do we as educators recognize it as significant, encourage it, and subsequently plan for its reoccurrence? A severely handicapped student is on a trampoline to learn to use and enjoy that piece of equipment and/or to provide practice with various equilibrium and righting reactions. It is therefore highly likely that the action of a student touching another would be considered an inappropriate behavior, since it interferes with the instructional goals. However, touching and looking at someone are two rudimentary forms of social exchange, and are often spontaneously initiated by severely handicapped students; yet, they are probably discouraged more often than encouraged. We need to analyze those situations where severely handicapped students are closely grouped to determine suitable forms of social interaction and to ensure that such interactions are encouraged.

Another hindrance to social interactions involves the instructional content of the communication program commonly taught severely handicapped students. Often in the course of implementing project-related activities, during the 1980–81 school year, we and our colleagues found ourselves standing next to severely handicapped students in cafeteria lines, sitting next to them in restaurants, assisting students in wheelchairs on the orthopedically adapted buses, or traveling with them on city buses or subways to libraries, supermarkets, shopping malls, or public parks. When we happened to be paired with a severely handicapped student who had been taught to use a communication system such as a picture board or ASL, we therefore attempted to capitalize on this natural occurrence for a social interaction. However, it quickly became apparent that the specific pictures or signs (i.e., the instructional content) these students had acquired did not provide them the content needed for a social interaction. It is therefore critical to select and teach socially relevant instructional content to capitalize on social opportunities. Some suggestions that may be relevant include: 1) a yes/no response, 2) greetings and salutations, 3) activities that occur at home during the evenings and weekends (e.g., leisure activities, family outings, hobbies), 4) weather conditions, 5) health comments (e.g., *I feel fine [sick, great, terrible]*), 6) common conversational exchanges (e.g., *How are you?*, *What's happening?*, *¿Que pasa?*, *See you later*) and 7) social amenities (e.g., *please, thank you, you're welcome*).

We also noticed that students who had supposedly learned to perform manual signs or to touch pictures on a communication board still needed antecedent cues such as a model or verbal prompt to initiate or respond to social interactions. This led us to examine the execution of those communicative responses within school. After observing and recording students' performance of communication responses over several weeks, it became clear that on the majority of occasions in which communication responses were requested from students, models or other cues to signal the students' responses were provided. In essence, students were inadvertently being taught to imitate communicative responses. The problem was not that modeling was inappropriate, but that it had become the *de facto* norm at the school. We were not systematically adjusting our criteria to meet the standards of a more normalized social interaction.

Another problem in facilitating social interactions between severely handicapped students and other handicapped or nonhandicapped peers is that little time is spent developing or improving peer observing responses. Instead, considerable time is spent encouraging severely handicapped students to observe a variety of adults in their environment. There is no reason for such situations to continue, when instructional personnel can easily capitalize on many naturally occurring times in the home, school, or community in which simply restructuring the activity can facilitate the acquisition and maintenance of peer observing responses. For example, rarely do we structure lunch for severely handicapped students who have self-feeding skills in such a way that they are required to pass food to each other. Similarly, it is common practice in classes with nonambulatory students to position two students on bolsters or wedges that are facing the teacher. The teacher alternates giving attention to the students in succession, thus accomplishing a modified form of group instruction. Such instruction is organized on the basis of teacher convenience; that is, the students are positioned in reference to the teacher's needs and not necessarily their own needs. In the situation just described, the severely handicapped student who is not receiving the teacher's attention may remain passive between turns. However, it would take little effort to reposition the two students so they could see each other between instructional trials. Such a change would require the teacher not only to alternate attention, but also to shift his or her position between trials. The problem is not that teachers refuse to be inconvenienced during instruction, but that teachers do not recognize the need for restructuring the environment. The restructuring of everyday situations can lead to the discovery of more appropriate social interaction objectives for severely handicapped students.

A final impediment to programming for social interaction is the high rate of inappropriate behaviors in the repertoires of many severely handicapped students. Although socially inappropriate behaviors are not associated with any particular chronological age, they are most problematic when they have not been eliminated by the time of adolescence. Combinations of students' size and strength, frequency of occurrence, non-normalized appearance, and inappropriate behaviors with long histories of reinforcement (such as grabbing or kissing other people) do little to enhance the possibility of social interactions with nonhandicapped or other handicapped individuals. Although we acknowledge that the solution to the elimination of inappropriate behaviors is the consistent implementation of an individualized behavior management program, the prevalance of inappropriate behaviors generally is so high in self-contained schools that consistency is impossible to maintain.

For instance, consider a lunch shift involving five classes of severely handicapped students in a self-contained school. It is not unlikely that the following sequence of events could occur: One student runs out of the cafeteria screaming; another student is sitting at a table eating lasagna with his hands at five times the average rate; a third student accidently drops his tray and begins eating the food on the floor; a new class enters, and one student runs up and tries to kiss another student; and interspersed throughout are students who are producing random stereotypical verbalizations. Such a situation creates a unique climate for intervention. Those problem behaviors that actively infringe on others cannot be ignored and must be eliminated. Those behaviors that do not actively affect others, however, such as stereotypical verbalizations and accelerated rates of eating, can more easily be tolerated or overlooked in a problem-ridden context. It is the sheer number and frequency of socially inappropriate behaviors that contribute to the inconsistent implementation of behavior management techniques, which in turn contributes to the long-term maintenance of inappropriate behaviors.

On the other hand, consider a lunch shift in a cafeteria at a regular middle school, with one class of severely handicapped adolescents and four classes of nonhandicapped seventh graders. One of the severely handicapped students attempts to grab food from the tray of a nonhandicapped peer. The nonhandicapped peer would probably intervene immediately, providing a naturally occurring error correction (Falvey, Brown, Lyon, Baumgart, & Schroeder, 1980). Furthermore, since most nonhandicapped students do not grab food from each others' trays, food grabbing behavior clearly sets the severely handicapped student apart from the majority of students in the lunchroom. Such a discrepancy can provide the extra incentive needed to consistently monitor those situations where the problem behavior usually occurs. In addition, the small number of severely handicapped students makes such monitoring possible.

Due to the homogeneous grouping of the problem students, the service delivery system of self-contained schools can inadvertently support, rather than eliminate, socially inappropriate behaviors. If such an analysis is accurate, it is easy to see one reason why severely handicapped students are still displaying inappropriate behaviors. To compound the problem, the occurrence of inappropriate behaviors of 16-, 17-, and 18-year-olds discourages a teacher from venturing beyond the tolerant environment of the self-contained school for more functional skill training sites in community restaurants, supermarkets, or shopping malls, for example. Focusing on the longitudinal development of interaction skills within a heterogeneously organized and integrated service delivery system will tend to encourage consistent behavior management, the elimination of inappropriate behaviors, and the acquisition of appropriate interpersonal interactions.

Task-Related Interactions A task-related interaction is any event between two or more people consisting of an exchange of information, feedback, or assistance that is directly related to skills or materials needed to participate in a given activity. For example, a severely handicapped student needing assistance to remove her coat activates a buzzer to secure help; or a student fills a teapot with water when requested to do so by another student during a food preparation task. In general, individuals engage in more task-related interactions—ranging from asking a bank teller to cash a check, to ordering food at a restaurant, giving instructions to fellow workers, or answering a teacher's questions—than social interactions.

As mentioned previously, most interpersonal interactions, whether social or task-related, are less frequently initiated by severely handicapped individuals. Task-related interactions have an additional characteristic of requiring the performance of a series of reciprocal responses with another person. Williams, Hamre-Nietupski, Pumpian, Marks, and Wheeler (1978) refer to this characteristic as the need to *sustain* an interaction. In addition to initiating fewer new interactions, many severely handicapped students do not consistently sustain interactions. An example would be a situation where an ambulatory severely handicapped student has been asked to push a nonambulatory student's wheelchair at a shopping mall. As long as the teacher is present, the student continues to push the wheelchair. As soon as the teacher walks away, the student stops pushing. This on again–off again behavior continues until the teacher becomes frustrated and takes over the pushing responsibilities. In viewing this situation, one gets the impression that as soon as the teacher leaves, an electrical short circuit is created that immobilizes the severely handicapped student. A deficit in delayed imitation is a suitable explanation for this behavior; however, other factors emanating from the organization of task-related interactions throughout the school day may contribute to the occurrence of such "short-circuit" behaviors.

For instance, a commonly employed instructional arrangement involves grouping several severely handicapped students at a table, yet never requiring them to interact with each other. Generally, severely handicapped students are taught to wait until an adult initiates contact before performing any task-related response; students are taught to perform in response to cues intermittently delivered by an adult and to complete the task-related responses without engaging in a sustained exchange with a peer. Consider a finger-painting activity for five young severely handicapped students. The students are seated at a table, and between them on chairs around the table are positioned the teacher, an instructional aide, and a student teacher. Each student is given his or her own piece of paper, and a can of paint is placed near each adult. The teacher asks the students to start painting. Since most of the students do not begin the activity following this cue, the cue is repeated (or other form of assistance provided) by the closest adult. When a student stops painting, the nearest available adult cues the student to begin again. If a student is painting in the same area over and over again, an adult cues the student to paint in another area. These types of interactions continue until the activity is terminated by the teacher.

In analyzing this example, it is possible to speculate about the problems some severely handicapped students have in sustaining task-related interactions, especially when the exchange involves a peer or other noninstructional personnel. First of all, an obstructive "zone-press" method of instructional personnel deployment is used. Instructional personnel strategically place themselves between severely handicapped students so that task-related peer interactions are effectively blocked. Second, students are told when to start, what to perform, and when they are finished. As a result, the student does not have to learn to sustain activities independently, much less engage in a sustained task-related interaction with a peer. As soon as the activity stops, someone other than the student starts the activity again. Such an exchange is a task-related interaction; however, its continued practice is not necessarily useful. At the very least, such instructional arrangements may unwittingly be teaching severely handicapped students to wait for teacher cues prior to the initiation and continued performance of a task.

By their design, such instructional arrangements may also discourage severely handicapped students from initiating and continuing task-related exchanges with each other. Certainly, a simple task such as finger painting provides a prepotent situation for severely handicapped students to learn how to sustain a task-related interaction. By grouping two students together and giving them one sheet of paper and one container of paint, physical contact and peer observation may accrue as a natural outgrowth of finger-painting experiences. While making the transition to such an instructional arrangement, the students may still need some teacher assistance; however, a logical context is established that could eventually result in at least some severely handicapped students attending to the natural cues provided by their peers to sustain a task-related interaction.

The cues provided by a peer in a task-related interaction can be considered a form of peer modeling; however, few instances of peer modeling are seen in self-contained schools, due to the limited response repertoires of many severely handicapped students. In integrated elementary or secondary schools the possibility of having nonhandicapped peers model task-related responses is significantly enhanced. In such situations, the teacher's role as facilitator, as depicted in the "short-circuit" example, needs an additional word of caution. One project activity we were involved in during the 1980–81 school year featured planned integrated activities between one class of 6-year-old severely handicapped students and one class of first graders at a regular elementary school. At first, very few task-related or social interactions occurred. After a few visits, some simple task-related interactions began to occur, consisting primarily of nonhandicapped peers helping severely handicapped students get food from the cafeteria line or put their trays away after lunch. Often when a nonhandicapped peer attempted to interact with a severely handicapped student, however, a special educator stepped in to "facilitate" the interaction, with the usual result that the interaction was momentarily or completely disrupted. In analyzing our behaviors, we realized that we were automatically intervening when intervention was already being provided by the nonhandicapped peer. Thereafter, we controlled ourselves and refrained from such indiscriminate "facilitation" efforts. Although additional teacher intervention continued to be needed in various situations, the potential effectiveness of peer modeling was clearly noticed over time. Each week, the severely handicapped students appeared to improve in imitating the responses of their nonhandicapped peers when lining up for lunch, securing their lunch in the cafeteria, clearing their trays, and exiting the cafeteria. Improvement was most obvious during the last activity of the school year, a joint class picnic. With minimal prompting, nearly all of the severely handicapped students followed their peers through the lunch line, obtained their lunches, and sat next to other nonhandicapped students on chairs or on the grass. Although of course this explanation of improved severely handicapped student performance in terms of peer modeling is, at present, speculative, this and other experiences during the school year have led us to question the role that instructional personnel should take in facilitating task-related interactions. As a result, in future project activities we plan to explore the effect of the degree or amount of teacher intervention on task-related interactions, in the hope of discovering better methods to assist severely handicapped students in sustaining task-related interactions.

Purpose of an Interaction

Since most severely handicapped students are nonverbal, frequently the intent, or purpose, of an interaction must be inferred from the observable actions of the student. As conceptualized by our model, interpersonal interactions are classified in four ways: 1) to obtain assistance, information, or feedback, 2) to provide assistance, information, or feedback, 3) to receive assistance, information, or feedback, or 4) to be corrected (a special case of receiving assistance). The intent of a social interaction engaged in by a severely handicapped student could be classified into any one of these four categories; the same holds true for a task-related interaction. These classifications can be used to reference observed interpersonal interactions, or they can be used as guidelines for the selection of interpersonal interactions instructional content. It is in reference to the latter activity, instructional content development, that these classifications are most useful, since they can be used in longitudinal planning to achieve a gradual expansion of the number and types of interpersonal interactions engaged in by severely handicapped students.

To Obtain Assistance, Information, or Feedback   An interpersonal interaction is classified in this category when the primary purpose of the exchange is for
the student to request information, assistance, or feedback—such as asking for a
toy, tapping another student on the shoulder to request a napkin, or giving a waiter
a picture menu card indicating a preferred food item. In our experience, severely
handicapped students rarely attempt to obtain information, assistance, or feedback. Many of the issues that relate to this problem have been discussed in earlier
sections and will only be highlighted here.

The major obstacle to increasing any type of interpersonal interaction involves student-initiated responses. In order to secure an object, thought, or action
from another person, the interaction must be initiated by the student. Since
severely handicapped students initiate responses, initiations therefore need to be
taught. In teaching students to initiate interactions, particularly requests, common
reoccurring responses initiated by the students should be scrutinized. Some of
these responses are attempts to obtain information, assistance, or feedback that
may appear to be unimportant or trivial. However, the need for a starting point, in
our opinion, is most critical with this population.

Examples of how a teacher could increase his or her sensitivity to commonly
reoccurring responses that could be shaped into "obtain interactions" are as
follows: A group of young, severely handicapped students are seated at a table for
a snack. The teacher goes around to each student and asks if he or she wants a piece
of apple. Each student is required to communicate his or her intent by performing
the sign for apple. However, one student raises his hand and waves at the teacher
before his turn. The teacher reinforces the natural gesture as the initiation of an
"obtain" interaction by going over to the student and giving him a turn out of
sequence. The teacher, in this example, obviously inferred the purpose of the
student's raising his hand. The student may have raised his hand for an entirely
different reason; however, the teacher chose to reinforce this response in a
contextually appropriate way that could lead to student-initiated interactions.

Another example might be a student who, while being helped by a teacher to
hang up her coat, points to another person. In such a situation, the tendency would
be to redirect the student to the coat-hanging task. However, interpreting the
natural pointing gesture as an attempt by the student to obtain the teacher's
attention could facilitate an increase in the use of that response in other contexts.
Similarly, a severely handicapped student who is capable of movement hands her
lunchbox to a teacher. Rather than redirecting the student, the teacher puts the
lunchbox away and points out the response to the student; a student-initiated
interaction could result. Certainly, a decision needs to be made whether a student
is waving or pointing too often, or indiscriminately handing objects to the teacher.
However, when few "obtain" interactions are initiated by a severely handicapped
student, such responses may be easily facilitated and act as starting points toward
more formal exchanges.

Capitalizing on the naturally occurring context cues provided by physical
obstacles in the environment may also increase the frequency of a student's
requests to obtain information or assistance. Instead of organizing the instructional

environment prior to a task and minimizing physical obstacles for severely handicapped students, students should be taught to obtain the assistance of another in solving the problem with which they are confronted. For example, a parent was observed interacting with her severely handicapped daughter at home while preparing supper. In order to minimize any behavior problems and subsequent interruptions of meal preparation, the parent would have her 7-year-old daughter "assist" by washing dishes in the kitchen sink. The parent put a stopper in the drain and provided a stool for the daughter to stand on to reach a few dirty dishes in the sink. However, the parent did not proceed to model or prompt the child through the response. The parent simply left the child alone to confront the problem. Within seconds the daughter gestured and vocalized in the direction of the liquid detergent that was out of reach. This, of course, brought the parent back to give the bottle to the child. Next the child gestured toward the faucets that also were out of reach and received assistance from the parent. By taking advantage of the logical problems presented by the physical context, this parent was not only successful in teaching this child functional interactions, but had taught the daughter to use another person as a medium to solve a problem. By recognizing the natural contingencies present in the physical arrangement of the environment, the parent was able to make appropriate use of a functional situation.

To Provide Assistance, Information, or Feedback Interpersonal interactions classified in this category involve those exchanges in which the principal purpose is for the student to provide or give information, assistance, or feedback—such as informing the teacher that buses have arrived, grimacing when positioned to indicate discomfort, or on request handing a classmate the salt and pepper shakers at lunch. In our experience, severely handicapped students engage in more "provide" interactions than "obtain" exchanges, possibly because most, though not all, "provide" exchanges are initiated by another and involve very structured and direct cues.

One way to select instructional objectives to increase "provide" interactions would be to reverse those situations in which typically severely handicapped students are "allowed" to wait passively while being assisted; rather, students should be permitted to assist the teacher. For example, students' lunch trays are often routinely put away for them, yet many students are capable of bringing their own trays to the dishwashing area of a cafeteria. As another example, if several students are on a trampoline and one severely handicapped student is asked to hold a peer who is motorically impaired, a "provide" exchange has been created that also enables the teacher to work with another student. Or, when the group goes to a park, instead of the instructors pushing severely handicapped students on merry-go-rounds or swings why not ask students to provide assistance by taking turns pushing each other, as on the school playground? By examining activities that occur in school and nonschool settings, many opportunities for "provide" interactions for severely handicapped students emerge. Adding one such interaction to every major activity during the school day could result in a significant increase in the functional interaction repertoires of many severely handicapped students.

However, there are some occasions where it may not be appropriate over the long term for a severely handicapped student to provide assistance. As an example, during the 1980–81 school year several severely handicapped students were taught to assist the teacher by going to the cafeteria and bringing a cart with the students' lunches back to the classroom. Even though these students were providing assistance, an interaction had been selected and taught that was operative only in lunch programs in segregated schools. That is, because of a lack of space, or owing to disabilities that were presumed to interfere with eating in a more normalized setting, students ate their lunches in their classrooms and not in the cafeteria. Since most lunch situations, such as a cafeteria in a regular elementary or secondary school or a public cafeteria at a place of employment, do not segregate students, an interaction had been selected that was functional only in self-contained schools.

Another potentially problematic situation involves requesting help from severely handicapped students, when the longitudinal goal would be to have them independently help themselves (i.e., when an exchange probably should not occur). For instance, two severely handicapped students have just completed a game of darts. The teacher comes over with a box used to store the darts, and, on request, the students put the darts in the box. Although the students have provided assistance, and such assistance is preferable to providing no help, it probably is unnecessary. For the students in the example, dart instruction should not be considered complete until the students initiate and complete the entire task under the same expectations that would be operative for their nonhandicapped peers.

There are other considerations to be aware of when attempting to teach severely handicapped students to provide information, assistance, or feedback. If a severely handicapped student with motoric impairment, for example, tracks a moving object that a teacher moves in front of the student's face, the student has provided some feedback to the teacher that she saw the object. Because of the student's motor problems, the activity is conducted with the student in a supine position on a wedge placed on the floor. There is a problem, though, if the student is to functionally use this nonverbal response. In other situations where she could or should provide feedback to others in her environment, she probably will need to be in an upright position. The reason she is in a supported supine position is that for this particular student the position is best suited to inhibit interfering motor responses. Considerable experimentation would be needed to facilitate the occurrence of this response in an upright position. However, if we remain satisfied with simply applying the principle without regard to context, functional use may never be achieved.

Another problem in teaching severely handicapped students to provide feedback is that often language concepts are involved that many students have not yet learned. For example, current thinking in special education would dictate that if a severely handicapped student has not learned to identify the colors *red* and *yellow* in isolation, it would be senseless to teach that student to select either red or yellow paint prior to a finger-painting activity. The student may not consistently discriminate objects, much less an object based on the color attribute. However, this same student may cry when her diaper is wet (i.e., provide information), turn her head and refuse to open her mouth for certain foods (i.e., provide feedback), look up when someone approaches her (i.e., provide feedback), and spontaneously show the teacher a picture of a favorite activity, such as going for a walk. From a traditional developmental viewpoint, the student definitely is "not ready" to choose finger paint on the basis of color. Nevertheless, if this student can provide information or feedback in so many frequently occurring situations, there can be no harm in attempting to extend this skill by having the student grasp one jar of paint over another on request. Regardless of whether she wants that particular color, we just might be successful not only in teaching another interaction, but in getting her to look at a specific object.

There can be problems, though, in having students provide feedback in "choice" situations when they have not learned the components of the choice. Usually these difficulties stem from the task arrangement. Often in order to simplify the response requirements of a particular task for a certain severely handicapped student, we create choice situations in the absence of a choice. For example, a picture of crackers is held up to a severely handicapped student. The student is asked what she would like to eat. The student obliges by touching the only picture present. In response, the student receives a cracker. Chances are that the student in the example (or any student who experiences such a training paradigm) would touch any picture that was held up in front of her. Errorless learning (Touchette, 1971) is an extremely useful training technique. But it was designed to systematically build choice, not eliminate the need for choice. The transition to providing choice needs to occur, in addition to determining what the student might do when a choice exists.

To Receive Information, Assistance, or Feedback   The major purpose of interpersonal interactions classified in this category is for the student to receive or be given information, assistance, or feedback in an exchange initiated and maintained by another—such as being led by another person across the street or being handed a food tray by the teacher during lunch. Special cases in regard to interactions classified in the "receive" category involve when the student receives assistance after making an error or not making an expected response (i.e., is given an error correction)—such as being physically guided to touch a picture of a toilet to indicate the need to use the bathroom when the student has failed to do so independently, or when given a verbal model such as *Say help, please* to request assistance following an error in getting on a bus. Since error correction procedures are used frequently with severely handicapped students, they warrant emphasis here. An additional point in reference to "receive" interactions is that the severely handicapped student neither initiates nor sustains the interactions; rather, they are begun and completed by another person, and the student passively cooperates. The majority of interactions engaged in by severely handicapped students fall into the "receive" category. The primary issue becomes distinguishing between situations in which a severely handicapped student should or should not receive assistance.

For example, few people would question the appropriateness of a teacher positioning a severely motorically impaired student on a prone board; it would be impossible for the student to position himself. Likewise, there are very few situations where one would consider it inappropriate for a severely handicapped student to receive feedback on the correctness of her work. Lifting a severely handicapped student so that she can put money in the coin slot of a subway fare card vending machine or manipulating the switches on a videogame also would be considered acceptable examples of students' receiving assistance. However, as alluded to in previous sections, often assistance is provided to severely handicapped students when they are completely capable of independent performance.

An example would be pinning a note on the back of a 16-year-old severely handicapped student's jacket when that student should be learning independently to fold that note and put it in a pocket or purse. Mastery of this skill could lead to a self-initiated interaction where the student takes the note out of her pocket or purse and gives it to her parents. As another example, instead of bringing a wet washcloth over and washing every motorically involved student's face after feeding, it might be possible to teach a few students to communicate the need for the washcloth prior to receiving assistance. Sometimes ambulatory students are helped on and off buses, up and down steps, or on and off escalators so often that they automatically freeze in front of buses, steps, and escalators and hold out their hands. Luckily, there is usually an adult nearby to grasp the upheld hand. Frequently when severely handicapped students passively receive assistance in situations where they are capable of performing the responses, they never seem to learn the skill. In observing students who were being assisted in situations such as hanging up their coats, getting their lunches in the cafeteria, or locating the children's reading room at the local public library, one characteristic seemed common: the students rarely paid attention to the responses they were being physically guided to perform. By examining reoccurring situations in which severely handicapped students receive assistance, information, or feedback, certain situations will likely emerge as prime candidates for transition to "obtain" or "provide" interactions, thereby producing a reduction in unnecessary "receive" exchanges.

Just as severely handicapped students frequently receive automatic assistance unnecessarily, we also tend to inadvertently organize instruction so that receiving correction is inevitable. Certainly, if severely handicapped students are to learn new skills, incorrect responses must be corrected. However, sometimes, by applying a principle or technique without closely scrutinizing the instructional content, errors result. For example, on occasion severely handicapped students perform highly adapted responses that are misinterpreted to be errors. Consider a situation where a severely handicapped student is learning to put a glass, utensils, napkin, and a plate on a tray in preparation for eating in a cafeteria. The teacher asks the student to put a glass on the tray, followed by the utensils and a napkin. The teacher then asks the student to put the last item, the plate, on the tray. Following this request, the student grabs another napkin and puts it on the tray. The student then receives assistance as the teacher corrects the error. However, while physically assisting the student in putting the plate on the tray, the teacher realizes that there is little room for it on the tray. In short, the plate should have been put on first since it was the largest object, providing a concrete reference for the remaining items. Had the placement sequence been reversed, the need to correct the error may have been eliminated or substantially reduced.

Communication Systems

Formal communication systems that are typically used by severely handicapped students are delineated in Figure 1, namely, speech, manual signs, communication board use, and total communication. (For a detailed discussion of each system, the reader is referred to Kohl & Moses, Note 1; Kohl, Moses, & Hicks, Note 2.) Even though the acquisition of formal communication skills significantly improves the ease of teaching interpersonal interactions to severely handicapped students, formal communication skills are not necessary for interactions to occur. In addition, it is our position that a strict focus on the acquisition of formal communication skills may result in a reduction in the total number of interactions acquired over time. What is needed is a simultaneous focus on both the acquisition of a formal communication system and the acquisition of interpersonal interactions, so that one does not lag behind at the expense of the other.

Communication Modes

Communication modes are informal behavior responses that can be used in conjunction with a communication system either singularly (e.g., smile) or in combination (e.g., head turn and arm wave) by severely handicapped students to engage in interpersonal interactions with others. We advocate the teaching of interpersonal interactions that require formal and informal communication modes. As a result, the interaction skills selected for instruction are not tied to any one combination of mode and system. By determining the types of response modes a severely handicapped student is capable of performing, and determining the interpersonal interactions that need to be taught across school, home, and community environments over time, a student's repertoire of communication modes could be substantially increased. Such an expansion could result in the performance of many more interactions in functional environments than would be possible through the use of one mode and system alone, as examples in the previous sections illustrate.

Quality of the Interaction

In analyzing the appropriateness of each student's interaction(s), evaluation is based upon the context of the situation: the antecedent events, the student's behavior and expected performance level, and the consequences of the behavior. However, from a curriculum planning perspective this component is used to determine if an interaction should be taught (i.e., should the student be independent of or interact with another to perform a particular activity).

Outcome of the Interaction

The outcome of an interaction is judged to be either successful or unsuccessful depending upon whether the purpose of the interaction is achieved. When the purpose of the interaction is obvious, and the receiver reacts in a way that corresponds with and follows through on the purpose, the interaction is considered completed and therefore successful. If the purpose is not clear, or the receiver does not address or promote the resolution of the purpose, then the interaction is considered unsuccessful.

CONDITIONS FOR INTERPERSONAL INTERACTION INSTRUCTION

Based upon repeated observations, analyses of interpersonal interactions, and insights obtained from the use of the Interpersonal Interaction Analysis Model (Figure 1), four conditions should be met for interpersonal interaction instruction to occur. When adhered to, these four conditions maximize the acquisition of interpersonal interactions by facilitating interactions between severely handicapped individuals and a cadre of other individuals in different environments across a host of different activities.

The first condition is that *severely handicapped individuals should be taught to interact in integrated, normalized environments* that include: their homes and neighborhoods; public elementary, middle, and secondary schools; community stores and services establishments; public transit and transportation systems; recreational facilities; vocational sites; etc. It stands to reason that the probability of an interaction or a sequence of interactions occurring between severely handicapped individuals and others is greatly increased when severely handicapped individuals are provided the opportunity to be in integrated environments. Therefore, it is the responsibility of the classroom instructional personnel (in cooperation and coordination with school administrators) to plan and provide the opportunities for severely handicapped individuals to interact in integrated, normalized environments.

The second condition, which goes hand-in-hand with the first, is that *severely handicapped individuals should be taught to interact in the context of functional, age-appropriate activities.* The activities the individual is being taught must have some naturally built-in purpose for performance and must be appropriate for the student's chronological age (i.e., referenced to the activities of nonhandicapped peers).

The third condition is that *severely handicapped individuals should be taught to interact with the significant individual(s) associated with the functional activity.* That is, those individuals who naturally belong in the environment, who are responsible for the initiation and/or maintenance of the activity, are the individuals with whom severely handicapped students should be interacting in social or task-related exchanges. For instance, while making purchases in a supermarket, severely handicapped students should interact with or be taught to interact with other shoppers, the person in charge of the produce department, the salesperson at the delicatessen counter, the check-out cashier, and perhaps the store manager. Moreover, these significant individuals in the supermarket should be correcting errors (e.g., a cashier informing a student that she does not have enough money), providing directions (e.g., the manager showing a student where the deli is located), and giving prompts (e.g., a shopper gesturing a student to move ahead in the check-out line) as opposed to instructional personnel intervening at the necessary times. Instructional personnel need to step back and systematically delay intervention procedures (e.g., error correction procedures such as verbal or physical prompts) so that individuals who are in the environment will intervene at natural times.

The fourth condition is that *severely handicapped individuals should be taught to obtain (initiate) and provide information, assistance, or feedback in each activity in which they participate.* This particular condition derives from the all too obvious and frequently demonstrated fact that severely handicapped individuals rarely, if ever, attempt to obtain and provide information, assistance, or feedback. Over the 1980–81 school year our findings showed (through the use of the Interpersonal Interaction Analysis Model) that the vast majority of the interactions in which severely handicapped individuals were engaged consisted of interactions in which they received passive assistance, redundant information, or correctional feedback. If severely handicapped students are to increase the frequency of their interpersonal interactions, at least three instructional tactics must be instituted. First, each severely handicapped student should be taught an immediate and rudimentary means to obtain assistance or information. Depending upon the current skills of the individual, this may consist of teaching the student to sign, *Help, please,* to ask for help, or to point to a word or symbol on a communication board that represents *Help, please.* Second, given that each student has or is being taught a formal system of communication such as speech, manual signs, communication board use, or any combination of the three, the student must be taught or required to use the system in each activity in which he or she participates. And finally, in connection with the second point, vocabulary items (i.e., specific signs, words, pictures, symbols) should be selected and taught that are appropriate and relevant to the activities and enable the student to obtain and provide information, assistance, and feedback.

INTERPERSONAL INTERACTION INSTRUCTIONAL STRATEGY

Teaching severely handicapped individuals to interact with other individuals in functional activities is, needless to say, a difficult task that requires preparation, energy, and time on the part of all instructional personnel. To minimize these variables, we propose a six-step instructional strategy that assists in identifying appropriate instructional content and relevant interpersonal interactions and in adhering to the four conditions stated previously for interpersonal interaction instruction.

1. *Select appropriate, functional activities.* In order to address the longitudinal needs of each severely handicapped student, activities needed for normalized performance in home, neighborhood, school, community, and vocational settings must be identified; those activities that are appropriate to the student's chronological age and future needs should be targeted for instruction. An ecological inventory strategy, that is, a method of observing activities in natural settings, developed by Brown, Branston, Hamre-Nietupski, Pumpian, Certo, and

Gruenewald (1979), and expanded by Ford, Brown, Pumpian, Baumgart, Nisbet, Schroeder, and Loomis in this volume, should be used to maximize independence across environments.

2. *Observe the activity as it naturally occurs in the integrated environment.* To facilitate student acquisition, it is necessary to observe the activity in the natural setting and record relevant information that will be the basis of the educational program. It should be emphasized that the site of the activity, such as a shopping mall, supermarket, movie theater, fast food restaurant, or neighborhood park, should be the site that the student is most likely to use (i.e., a location close to the student's home). The following information should be gathered, but not necessarily limited to: 1) the skills, delineated in a sequential format, that are necessary to participate in the activity; 2) the duration of the activity from start to completion and, if relevant, a breakdown of the durations of subactivities; 3) the latency between naturally occurring cues and responses; 4) the naturally occurring rate and accuracy measures needed to establish a realistic criterion performance level; 5) persons participating in the activity; 6) a floor plan of the site including restroom facilities; 7) materials, equipment, and/or accessories needed for the activity; and 8) if relevant, the availability of transportation or the means by which one will get to and return from the site. In some cases, repeated observations may be necessary.

3. *Develop or modify a comprehensive and longitudinal task analysis.* Based upon the observation of the activity and the information collected, it is necessary to search for and review available curricula that relate to the activity or activities selected. This task should be followed up by making necessary adaptations or changes to the existing curriculum based upon the unique needs of the student and the characteristics of the site (i.e., incorporating response requirements that are indigenous to the site). If curricula do not exist, than a comprehensive educational program must be developed that includes a terminal objective, a sequence of skills needed to partake in and complete the activity, and a description of adaptations to materials to enable the student to perform the activity as independently as possible.

4. *Determine the interactions that occur in the activity based upon the Interpersonal Interaction Hierarchy.* Once the task analysis has been written and modified to meet the needs of the student, the next step is to generate all the possible interactions, both social and task-related, that must or could occur in the activity. In order to determine appropriate interpersonal interaction instructional content, one should analyze and then categorize each interaction generated based upon the Interpersonal Interaction Hierarchy, which is as follows:

> *Mandatory task-related interaction:* an interpersonal interaction that must occur to continue or complete an activity.
> *Contextual social interaction:* an interpersonal interaction that occurs in conjunction with a task-related interaction.
> *Optional task-related interaction:* an interpersonal interaction that is not essential to continue or complete an activity.
> *Optional social interaction:* an interpersonal interaction that occurs apart from any task-related interactions.

Table 1 presents several examples of the four types of interactions that occur in the community, home, and school activities of supermarket shopping, eating dinner, and using a school cafeteria, respectively. It should be noted that these examples are incomplete and, particularly in regard to the optional task-related and social interaction categories, could be expanded further.

5. *Identify specific interpersonal interactions to teach based upon the individual needs and characteristics of the student.* Once the interactions that must or could occur in the activity have been delineated, the next step is to identify which interactions to teach the student. It should be obvious that all students, regardless of any presumed limitations, must be taught the mandatory task-related interactions; if these interactions are not taught the activity cannot be continued or completed. Therefore, all mandatory task-related interactions must be selected for instructional content.

As for the other types of the interactions, selection depends upon the context of the interaction, the frequency of the interaction, the characteristics of the student, and the priority goals for the student. It is recommended that a finite number of interactions be selected and slated for continual, systematic instruction; the other interactions that may take place during the activity should be taught as they occur spontaneously within the context of the activity.

6. *Assess which skills/interactions the student can perform, and teach the skills/interactions that the student cannot perform.* After a decision has been reached on the specific skills and interactions that are to be taught to the student, the next step is to assess the student's present level of performance within the environment in which the activity naturally occurs. In so doing, the selection of a measurement procedure must be given careful consideration, for the same measurement procedure must be used to determine skill acquisition once instruction has begun. Quite possibly, different types of data will need to be collected. For instance, event recording procedures may be used to gather data on the number of instances a student independently initiates a task-related mandatory interaction; a duration measure may be used to gather information on the time it takes for a student to initiate and complete the activity; or an accuracy measure may be used to determine the number of steps in the task analysis that the student completes without assistance.

Once a stable baseline has been reached on each measure, instruction on the skills and interactions performed inadequately by the student should be started. Intervention procedures (e.g., reinforcers, error correction procedures) must be provided systematically, and student progress monitored as frequently as possible to determine if modifications in the task analysis or instructional procedures are necessary.

SUMMARY

Determining appropriate interpersonal interactions and teaching those interactions to severely handicapped students is an arduous task. This chapter reviewed instructional techniques and practices that may impede exchanges, and offered a

Table 1. Examples of interactions within Interpersonal Interaction Hierarchy in community, home, and school

Environment	Activity	Mandatory task-related interaction	Contextual social interaction	Optional task-related interaction	Optional social interaction
Community	Supermarket shopping	1. Gives money to cashier (provide) 2. Takes change from cashier (receive)	1. Says "hello" to cashier before item check-out (obtain) 2. Says "thank you" to cashier before leaving checkout (provide)	1. Asks someone for help to find an item (obtain) 2. Orders an item from clerk at the deli counter (obtain)	1. Nods and smiles to other shoppers (obtain) 2. Converses with other shoppers while waiting in line (obtain and/or provide)
Home	Eating dinner	1. Takes plate or dish of food from a family member when passed around the table (receive)	1. Smiles when passing food (provide) 2. Says "thank you" when food is passed on request (provide)	1. Passes food when requested by a family member (provide) 2. Requests a food item from a family member (obtain) 3. Asks for assistance cutting food from a family member (obtain)	1. Responds to social questions (e.g., How was your day?) (provide) 2. Communicates that food tastes good (provide)
School	Using the cafeteria	1. Receives food from cafeteria worker (receive) 2. Gives cafeteria worker lunch ticket (provide)	1. Says "hello" to cafeteria worker before receiving food (obtain) 2. Says "you're welcome" and "good-bye" to cafeteria worker (obtain)	1. Requests condiments from cafeteria worker (obtain) 2. Requests assistance when tray is spilled (obtain) 3. Requests spoon/fork when container is empty (obtain)	1. Smiles at cafeteria worker while going through the line (provide) 2. Responds to social questions and/or comments (provide)

concrete strategy for increasing the interpersonal interaction skills of severely handicapped students. It is our belief that the implementation of this strategy will aid in decreasing the passive dependence of many severely handicapped students by increasing their ability to actively engage in interpersonal interactions across different people in a variety of environments.

REFERENCES

Brown, L., Branston-McClean, M.B., Baumgart, D., Vincent, L., Falvey, M., & Schroeder, J. Using the characteristics of current and subsequent least restrictive environments in the development of curricular content for severely handicapped students. *AAESPH Review*, 1979, *4* 4078–424.

Brown, L., Branston, M., Hamre-Nietupski, S., Pumpian, I., Certo, N., & Gruenewald, L. A strategy for developing chronological age appropriate and functional curriculum content for severely handicapped adolescents and young adults. *Journal of Special Education*, 1979, *13*, 81–90.

Brown, L., Nietupski, J., & Hamre-Nietupski, S. The criterion of ultimate functioning and public school services for severely handicapped students. In: M.A. Thomas (ed.), *Hey, don't forget about me! Education's investment in the severely and profoundly handicapped*. Reston, VA: The Council for Exceptional Children, 1976.

Donaldson, J. Changing attitudes towards handicapped persons. A review and analysis of research. *Exceptional Children, 46*, 1981, 504–574.

Falvey, M., Brown, L., Lyon, S., Baumgart, D., & Schroeder, J. Strategies for using cues and correctional procedures. In: W. Sailor, B. Wilcox, & L. Brown (eds.), *Methods of instruction for severely handicapped students*. Baltimore: Paul H. Brookes Publishing Co., 1980.

Guralnick, M.J. (ed.). *Early intervention and the integration of handicapped and nonhandicapped children*. Baltimore: University Park Press, 1978.

Guralnick, M.J. Social interactions among preschool children. *Exceptional Children*, 1980, *46*, 248–253.

McHale, S., & Simeonsson, R. Effects of interactions on nonhandicapped children's attitudes towards autistic students. *American Journal of Mental Deficiency*, 1980, *85*, 18–24.

Stainback, W., & Stainback, S. A review of research on interactions between severely handicapped and nonhandicapped students. *Journal of The Association for the Severely Handicapped*, 1981, *6*, 23–29.

Strain, P., Shores, R., & Timm, M. Effects of peer social initiations on the behavior of withdrawn preschool children. *Journal of Applied Behavior Analysis*, 1977, *10*, 289–298.

Touchette, P.E. Transfer of stimulus control: Measuring the moment of transfer. *Journal of the Experimental Analysis of Behavior*, 1971, *15*, 347–354.

Vincent, L.G., Salisbury, C., Walter, G., Brown, P., Gruenewald, L.V., & Powers, M. Program evaluation and curriculum development in early childhood/special education: Criteria of the next environment. In: W. Sailor, B. Wilcox, & L. Brown (eds.), *Methods of instruction for severely handicapped students*. Baltimore: Paul H. Brookes Publishing Co., 1980.

Voeltz, L. Children's attitudes toward handicapped peers. *American Journal of Mental Deficiency*, 1980, *84*, 455–464.

Williams, W., Hamre-Nietupski, S., Pumpian, I., Marks, J.M., & Wheeler, J. Teaching social skills. In: M.W. Snell (ed.), *Systematic instruction of the moderately and severely handicapped*. Columbus, OH: Charles E. Merrill Publishing Co., 1978.

REFERENCE NOTES

1. Kohl, F.L., & Moses, L.G. Teaching interpersonal interactions to severely handi-
    capped students. A picture and Blissymbol communication program and specific
    instructional considerations. Department of Special Education, University of Mary-
    land, 1982.
2. Kohl, F.L., Moses, L.G. & Hicks, A. Teaching interpersonal interactions to severely
    handicapped students: A manual sign communication instructional program and
    specific educational considerations. Department of Special Education, University of
    Maryland, 1982.

12

Strategies for Developing Individualized Recreation and Leisure Programs for Severely Handicapped Students

*Alison Ford,
Lou Brown, Ian Pumpian,
Diane Baumgart, Jan Nisbet,
Jack Schroeder, and Ruth Loomis*

This paper was supported in part by Grant No. G007801740 to the University of Wisconsin-Madison from the U.S. Department of Education, Office of Special Education, Division for Personnel Preparation, Washington, D.C.; and in part by Contract No. 300-78-0345 to the University of Wisconsin-Madison and the Madison Metropolitan School District from the U.S. Department of Education, Office of Special Education, Division for Innovation and Development, Washington, D.C.

The authors wish to acknowledge the contributions of Beth Haskett, Pauline Hintz, Kathy Zanella, John Van Walleghem, Janet Garkey, Lynn Hobbie, Nancy Dodd, Pat VanDeventer, and many parents of severely handicapped students for making substantial contributions to the development of this chapter.

A substantially more detailed version of this chapter appears in Brown, L., Falvey, M., Pumpian, I., Baumgart, D., Nisbet, J., Ford, A., Schroeder, J., & Loomis, R. (eds.), *Curricular strategies for teaching severely handicapped students functional skills in school and nonschool environments,* Vol. X. Madison, WI: Madison Metropolitan School District, 1980.

Severely handicapped persons are becoming increasingly visible in neighborhoods, communities, and chronological age-appropriate regular schools. As severely handicapped persons continue to participate in a growing number of heterogeneous school and community environments, the need for a variety of constructive leisure skills they can perform in those environments also increases. Thus, in contrast to the segregation era, the focus of recreation and leisure curricula must now be to prepare severely handicapped students to function in the widest possible variety of heterogeneous community environments. Just as the leisure needs of severely handicapped students have changed, so must many past curricular orientations and practices involving the provision of recreation and leisure services. Several of these past orientations are reviewed below.

PAST ORIENTATIONS TOWARD LEISURE CURRICULA

A prevailing view in special education has been that leisure activities should occur primarily after school, on weekends, during vacations, etc., and that valuable school time should be devoted only indirectly or peripherally to such pursuits. This view has resulted in at least two major outcomes. First, the amounts of time and instructional energy allotted direct leisure instruction during school hours were minimal in comparison to other curricular areas. Second, it was commonly believed that nonschool personnel—such as local Associations for Retarded Citizens, departments of recreation, and Girl Scout troups—were primarily responsible for leisure activities.

Even when recreation and leisure activities were incorporated into public school programs, specialized personnel such as recreation therapists, adaptive physical education teachers, and adaptive art teachers were still held predominantly responsible. While the need remains for specially trained personnel, it is unrealistic to expect that such specialists will be present in numbers sufficient to "staff" numerous heterogeneous recreation and leisure environments (e.g., homes, public buses, and the waiting rooms of medical offices). Obviously, large numbers of nonhandicapped persons *without specialized training* must be allowed and encouraged to interact with severely handicapped students. In addition, it has become increasingly apparent that classroom teachers must take a direct teaching role to ensure that leisure skills are developed as part of individualized education programs (IEPs) and that these skills are performed in meaningful and functional ways in many environments both during and after school.

Furthermore, when examining past curricular orientations one cannot ignore the segregated nature of recreation and leisure programming. For several years the authors and their colleagues have been involved in evaluating the life spaces of severely handicapped graduates of the Madison [Wisconsin] Metropolitan School District from 1971 through 1978. While this follow-up evaluation is reported in detail elsewhere (VanDeventer, Yelinek, Brown, Schroeder, Loomis, & Gruenewald, 1981), it is important to share one of the most consistent and important findings: segregated school experiences lead to segregated adult experiences.

Graduates whose school programs consisted of large-group and handicapped-only leisure experiences now have adult leisure life spaces that are confined to segregated or handicapped-only environments. This progression from segregated school to segregated adult services can be interrupted, as evidenced by the less restrictive leisure life spaces of more recent graduates who seemed to have benefited from individualized leisure programs (ILPs) from which they learned to function appropriately in heterogeneous school and nonschool environments with nonhandicapped individuals.

Finally, educators have not always made conscientious attempts to secure and incorporate information from parents into instructional programs. Therefore, parental expressions of displeasure over the inability of their children to use free time constructively may not have been heeded by instructional personnel. In addition, in those situations where teachers attempted leisure skill instruction, the skills selected were typically skills that were convenient to be performed at school, in a classroom, or a gym, but did not necessarily reflect the leisure materials or leisure time patterns at home. At present, many attempts are being made to correct these home-school communication deficiencies. In accordance with Public Law 94-142, which requires that educators secure parental participation in the design and implementation of the IEPs offered handicapped children, parents/guardians, teachers, and school officials—many for the first time—are meeting in cooperative and constructive information-sharing arrangements regarding the current and longitudinal needs of large numbers of severely handicapped students.

In summary, no IEP should be considered even minimally acceptable unless it contains an ILP component that addresses both immediate and longitudinal, comprehensive recreation and leisure needs in representative proportions. Hence, this chapter describes a systematic decision-making process that can result in the development of individualized leisure skills for use in school and nonschool environments and that facilitates normalized interactions with nonhandicapped individuals.

CURRICULUM DEVELOPMENT
STRATEGY FOR USE IN DEVELOPMENT OF ILPs

Brown, Branston, Hamre-Nietupski, Pumpian, Certo, and Gruenewald (1979) have delineated a six-phase curriculum development strategy and suggest that it be used when attempting to develop curricular content for adolescent and young adult severely handicapped students. The curriculum development strategy presented in Figure 1 represents an expanded version of that strategy that can be used in the development of an ILP.

Phase I: Conducting Leisure Activities Inventories

Classroom teachers and other persons responsible for reviewing and contributing to the ILP of a particular student must contend with the question, ''Will this ILP significantly add to this student's leisure repertoire at this particular time?'' The

PHASE I: CONDUCTING LEISURE ACTIVITIES INVENTORIES
STUDENT
PARENT/GUARDIAN
ECOLOGICAL

PHASE II: SUMMARIZING LEISURE PROGRAM INFORMATION

PHASE III: ESTABLISHING LEISURE PROGRAM PRIORITIES

PHASE IV: CONDUCTING A DISCREPANCY ANALYSIS
A NONHANDICAPPED PERSON INVENTORY
A SEVERELY HANDICAPPED STUDENT
INVENTORY
A DISCREPANCY ANALYSIS

**PHASE V: USING PARTIAL PARTICIPATION
AND PROPOSING INDIVIDUALIZED
ADAPTATIONS**

**PHASE VI: DETERMINING INDIVIDUALIZED
INSTRUCTIONAL OBJECTIVES**

**PHASE VII: DESIGNING AN INSTRUCTIONAL
PROGRAM**
WHAT
WHERE
WHY
CRITERIA
MATERIALS
HOW
MEASUREMENT

Figure 1. A leisure curriculum development strategy.

responses to such an inquiry will undergo continuous revision, based upon information concerning the nature and effectiveness of past and present leisure and recreational services and the perceptions of future needs.

In Phase I, inventory strategies are used to secure and evaluate information pertaining to a student's past, current, and future leisure activities needs. These inventory strategies have been given labels that represent three primary sources of relevant information: *student inventories, parent/guardian inventories,* and *ecological inventories.*

Part 1: Conducting Student Inventories   In order to determine whether the goals of the ILP should be consistent with those of the past, or expanded or modified, both a student's past and current performance in school and nonschool environments must be examined. This leisure activities information can be obtained by examining school records, interviewing personnel who provide related and community services, and making direct observations of a student across a variety of recreation- and leisure-related places, persons, activities, and materials.

Part 2: Conducting Parent/Guardian Inventories   There is little doubt that parents or guardians can have a tremendous influence on the leisure environments in which their children are allowed and encouraged to function. In many cases, parents are in the best position to provide information about the past and current leisure activities performance of their children. Thus, various strategies should be used to gather parent input, including parent conferences, telephone conversations, written correspondence (informal notes sent back and forth or more formal letters and forms), and group meetings.

Intensive and sustained home–school communication is necessary to:

1. Determine the variety of nonschool leisure environments and activities in which the student functions
2. Determine the extent to which leisure skills taught during school hours have been performed in nonschool environments
3. Collect information about community resources utilized by the family for leisure needs
4. Secure information regarding plans parents may have made with respect to the future domestic environments and the associated leisure needs
5. Secure parent preferences for current and subsequent leisure activities
6. Secure information pertaining to the nonschool weekly routines during both summer and school-year months in order to determine the amount of leisure time available, the environments and activities in which the student functions, the persons with whom he or she interacts, etc.

A parent questionnaire can be designed that might facilitate a summation of critical nonschool information. Figure 2 illustrates one strategy for obtaining specific information about nonschool environments. Aside from the obvious immediate value, the information may also assist the teacher to select time intervals for direct observations during nonschool hours. Furthermore, the forms can serve as a basis for developing more specific information-gathering strategies for use in later parent conferences. Examples of questions one might consider asking a parent during such conferences are presented in Figure 3.

Part 3: Conducting Ecological Inventories   An ecological inventory is intended to help delineate the numerous recreation and leisure environments, subenvironments, and activities in which a student might participate. It is used to help ensure that all reasonable options have been explored and shared among the persons responsible for developing an ILP. A general ecological inventory strategy is presented below. In Phase IV a second type of ecological inventory is

---

After School Activity Form

Date: _____

Dear Ms. Johnson:

I am attempting to gather information about Sue's recreation and leisure needs. It is important to look at the manner in which her after-school hours are occupied. Please fill out this form at the end of each day. Briefly list *where* she is during the specified time periods, *what* she is doing, and *with whom* she is interacting.

Signature of parent/guardian
_____

Time	Day: _____
3:00 PM	Where _____ What _____ With Whom _____
4:00 PM	Where _____ What _____ With Whom _____
5:00 PM	Where _____ What _____ With Whom _____
6:00 PM	Where _____ What _____ With Whom _____
7:00 PM	Where _____ What _____ With Whom _____
8:00 PM	Where _____ What _____ With Whom _____

Note: Please make an additional list of recreational and leisure activities in which your child engages routinely that are not represented on the forms.

Figure 2. An after-school activity form for parents/guardians.

---

presented that involves a specific breakdown of leisure *skills* currently performed by a severely handicapped student, and how those same skills are performed by nonhandicapped individuals, so that an analysis of performance discrepancies can be conducted.

Identifying Leisure Environments In conducting the ecological inventory, the teacher must first identify the widest possible variety of leisure environments in which a student currently functions or could now function, as well as those in

Parent/Guardian Leisure Inventory Guide

Student _____ Age _____

Parent/Guardian Participants _____

Date _____

Possible discussion items* for ILP sessions include:

1. Are you satisfied with the extent to which your child:
   a. Occupies his or her free time in a constructive manner?
   b. Engages in a reasonable *variety* of activities while at home?
   c. Engages in a variety of nonschool leisure environments and activities, e.g., YMCA, public library, roller rink?
   d. Actively makes choices as to how he or she would like to spend his or her free time?
   e. Interacts with other than family members?
   f. Engages in activities without direct supervision?
   g. Engages in activities similar to those of nonhandicapped persons of the same chronological age or older?

2. Please identify the activities in which your son/daughter currently engages that seem to provide him or her with the most pleasure. For what length of time will he or she engage in each of these activities? How much supervision is required?

Most Pleasurable Activities	Amount of Time	Who Supervises

3. Please identify the five most important environments, activities, and persons that you think should be a part of your child's current leisure life space. What assistance do you think will be necessary in order for your child to participate in these places and activities with the individuals you have identified—e.g., transportation needs and a person to supervise throughout the activity?

Places	Activities	Persons	Kind of Assistance

4. How could your child's school program better meet his or her leisure needs in non-school environments?

5. When your child reaches age 21, where do you want him or her to live?

6. Do you feel that your child is prepared to occupy his or her free time in a constructive manner in a future home situation? What are some of your concerns? How do you think he or she will spend his or her free time in a future home?

7. Are there community agencies that have helped to meet the leisure needs of your child? If so:
   a. What are the names of these agencies?
   b. What services are provided?
   c. How long do you think that the agency will be actively involved with your child?
   d. Will another agency take over?

---

*The daily routines presented in Figure 2 might be used to stimulate this discussion.

Figure 3. A parent/guardian leisure inventory guide.

which he or she might function in the future. Strategies to collect this information include: 1) examining printed materials (e.g., newspapers, the yellow pages of telephone books, local entertainment guides, publications of special interest groups, and professional leisure publications and related literature); 2) visiting agencies and groups that sponsor leisure activities; 3) touring the community in search of additional ideas; and 4) interviewing parents, colleagues, friends.

Once current and subsequent leisure environments have been identified, it is usually necessary that they be organized into more manageable categories or groupings in order to functionally relate to instructional planning. While there are many systems that can be used to organize large numbers of leisure environments, a strategy is presented below with examples of environments listed under five nonmutually exclusive headings:

> *Domestic Environments Requiring Leisure Skills*
> > Home of parent/guardian
> > Home of advocate
> > Home of neighbor
> > Home of friend
> > Group home training site
> > Respite care facility
> > Supervised apartment
>
> *School and School-Related Environments Requiring Leisure Skills*
> > Elementary School
> > Middle school
> > High school
> > High school athletic field
>
> *Vocational Environments Requiring Leisure Skills*
> > Hospital
> > Restaurant
> > Civic center
>
> *General Community Environments Requiring Leisure Skills*
> > Airport
> > Public beach
> > Public bus
> > Clothing store
> > Drug store
> > Discotheque
> > Parks
> > Roller skating rink
> > Shopping malls
> > YMCA
> > YWCA
>
> *Community Environments in Which Specialized Leisure Services Are Provided*
> > Church
> > Youth Association for Retarded Citizens facilities
> > Municipal Parks and Recreation Department facilities
> > Girl Scouts of America facilities
> > Music school

Identifying Leisure Subenvironments Assume that a teacher decided that the public library is an appropriate leisure environment for a specific severely handicapped student. In order to gain a better understanding of the library for instructional purposes, the teacher might visit the environment and record information that he or she might divide into subenvironments, such as the parking lot; the entrance; the restrooms; the periodical and newspaper section; the large-print book section; the art, film and music sections; and the check-out desk.

Delineating Leisure Activities The task here is to delineate the many leisure activities appropriate for each subenvironment in which a student currently functions and/or will subsequently function. For example, the activity "playing pinball" is one of the many activities that are age appropriate for the lobby of a bowling alley. Other activities might include "ordering, paying for, and eating a meal at the lunch center" or "socializing with a friend." Specific skills, such as "hanging up outdoor apparel on the coat rack" or "purchasing soda from a vending machine," may also be identified for instruction.

For many subenvironments, it may be necessary to organize the numerous leisure activities associated with them into functional instructional groups. For example, consider a domestic environment and the subenvironment, "back yard." A list of the possible leisure activities appropriate for a "back yard" could be quite lengthy. A teacher may want to organize the list according to categories such as *Yard Games:*"throwing a Frisbee," "playing darts," "playing croquet"; *Sports Related Games:* "playing softball," "playing baseball," "playing volleyball"; and *Exercises:* "jumping rope," "swimming."

Phase II: Summarizing Leisure Program Information

It is critical that persons most responsible for the leisure programs of a severely handicapped student carefully examine environments, activities, materials, and so forth, that are longitudinal in nature. That is, if a student engages in an activity at age 8, will it remain an appropriate activity until he or she reaches 15? Consider the following: It is appropriate to play with dolls at age 6, but not at age 15. And, it is appropriate to listen to *Sesame Street* records at age 6, but not at age 15. On the other hand, it is appropriate to play Frisbee at age 6 and at age 15, to play cards at age 6 and at age 15, to ride a bike at age 6 and at age 15, etc. Summarizing IEP performance information on a regular basis should enable a ready analysis of the longitudinal nature of a leisure program. In addition, this summation should facilitate smooth transitions as students move from one environment, activity, and/or teacher to another.

One strategy for summarizing leisure information involves the delineation of: 1) environments that have been utilized for leisure purposes on a regular basis; 2) the primary leisure activities the student engaged in within each environment; 3) relevant performance information; and 4) the source from which the information was obtained. This strategy is illustrated for domestic environments in Figure 4.

Phase III: Establishing Leisure Program Priorities

It is relatively easy to delineate a list of environments and activities in which particular clusters of skills are appropriate. It is substantially more difficult,

Leisure Information Summary

Student: Sue Smith   Age: 15
Date: 9-8-83
Summary Based on Information From: 9/80 to present

Leisure environments	Activities	Performance information	Sources and comments
DOMESTIC ENVIRONMENTS Sue's house; Neighbor's house	*Indoor Activities:* Putting puzzles together	3 to 10 puzzle pieces completed independently. Sue will repeat this activity for a duration of about 30 minutes.	Direct observation; parent information. Comments: Puzzles were not chronological age-appropriate. Sue regularly initiates the selection of this puzzle-making activity
	Playing with a deck of cards	Does not demonstrate ability to play any specific card game; when left alone, she will shuffle and rearrange cards; plays a matching game with her siblings.	Direct observation; parent information
	Cutting pictures from a magazine	Can manipulate scissors but does not cut out pictures with purpose; for example, she will cut through the objects on the page so that the final product is not a recognizable picture.	IEP 1981-82; parent information

Figure 4. A form for summarizing sample leisure information.

however, to decide upon the actual environments and activities that will receive direct instructional attention each day in the educational life of an individual student. This decision-making process of establishing priorities among environments and activities can be facilitated by the following three-step strategy:

First, define a series of dimensions that must be considered *before* a particular environment and activity is included on an ILP;

Second, consider each dimension carefully as it relates to the *advantages* and *disadvantages* of selecting a particular environment and activity; and

Third, select a particular environment and activity and then record the precise *reasons why* it was selected.

It is important to reemphasize that the rationale for determining priorities among leisure environments stems from the extremely large number of environments in which leisure skills are required. It is unreasonable to ask a teacher to actually visit every possible environment and delineate the subenvironments, activities, and skills appropriate for each; yet caution must be exercised to prevent the unnecessary exclusion of environments on the basis of insufficient information. It is assumed that most teachers have a basic understanding of the activities that occur within a large number of leisure environments. However, if there is no clear understanding of the activities that occur within a given environment, an ecological inventory should first be performed.

Critical to the process of implementing the three-step strategy outlined above is the answer to the question, "What dimensions should a teacher consider when selecting the specific environments and activities that will comprise an ILP?" Nineteen dimensions are offered below to assist a teacher in establishing priorities for the leisure program and in determining the extent to which the ILP has been individualized to prepare a severely handicapped student to enjoy a variety of leisure and recreation activities in a range of environments.

1. Homogeneous/Heterogeneous Dimension Unfortunately, many assume that if a student is severely handicapped, the student should have leisure experiences that are specifically designed for him or her and should be confined to environments and activities common only to other severely handicapped students. Thus, throughout the nation we have "swimming for the retarded," the "Special Olympics," "handicamps," etc. Certainly, it may be necessary and appropriate to arrange for some portion of an individual's leisure life space to be confined to environments and activities that contain only other severely handicapped students. However, to restrict a severely handicapped student to only those environments and activities is unduly confining and antihabilitative. Thus, if humanly possible, all severely handicapped persons should be allowed the opportunity to participate in a wide variety of heterogeneous leisure environments and activities that contain a diversity of both handicapped and nonhandicapped persons.

2. Chronological Age Appropriateness Dimension Obviously, a severely handicapped student is incapable of learning to perform all the skills typically contained in the repertoires of nonhandicapped students of the same chronological age range. However, providing educational curricula for a severely handicapped student that are appropriate merely to a chronologically younger nonhandicapped student is unjustified. Instead, educational curricula should be designed to minimize the performance differences between a severely handicapped student and his or her nonhandicapped chronological age peers in as many leisure environments and activities as possible. One of the authors observed a 15-year-old severely handicapped student playing with a Busy Box, a commercially available item for preschoolers. Upon questioning the age appropriateness of this leisure activity, the response given was, "But that is the only activity in which Jim will engage independently. I have tried to replace this activity with an electronic game like Simon but he doesn't seem to like it." Here one must consider the fact that Jim has been playing with a Busy Box for almost 15 years. The pertinent question is, "If it took 15 years for Jim to acquire such an attachment to the Busy Box, how long will it take to attain a similar level of attachment to more age-appropriate activities and materials?" Conscientious and systematic attempts must be made to reject leisure environments and activities that foster the view that a severely handicapped student is comparable to a substantially chronologically younger nonhandicapped student, and to replace them with environments and activities that offer severely handicapped students opportunities to function in chronological age-appropriate ways with peers and older persons.

3. Social Interactions Dimension The social interactions dimension refers to the opportunities present in a given leisure environment for chronological age-appropriate interactions with nonhandicapped persons. The questions that need to be answered are: Is the leisure environment under consideration one in which nonhandicapped chronological age peers frequent, or is it one typically used by much younger or much older individuals? Is it an environment typically used by only severely handicapped persons? For example, an analysis of community leisure environments may yield the information that junior high school-age nonhandicapped students spend many weekend evenings at roller skating rinks, but rarely spend them at the "Y" swimming. Clearly it is important that leisure environments be frequented as much as possible when nonhandicapped chronological age peers are present.

4. Number of Persons Involved Dimension Most people have skill repertoires that allow them to function in a wide variety of leisure environments and activities involving varying numbers of persons. More specifically, most people have the necessary skills to: 1) engage in one-person leisure activities, such as listening to music, painting pictures, walking, and needlecraft; 2) engage in two- or three-person leisure activities, such as jogging with a friend, playing cards, going to a movie with a friend, playing tennis, and bowling; 3) engage in team leisure activities, such as playing softball and volleyball in which continuous physical participation may not be necessary, but that require obeying group rules, turn-taking skills, a variety of communication skills, etc.; and 4) enjoy some kind of spectator leisure activities in which participation is essentially vicarious, e.g., watching television, watching football games, and bird-watching.

Perhaps the most prevalent arrangement in which severely handicapped persons function is large group in nature. It is not uncommon to see large groups of severely handicapped persons going to the fair in a big green bus, playing organized dodgeball and organized softball, and attending monthly dances for the handicapped. A longitudinal and comprehensive ILP should contain components designed to teach a severely handicapped student to engage in leisure activities that involve differing arrangements such as one person, two persons, three or more persons, and large groups.

5. Number of Environments Dimension Most people develop leisure skills that can be performed in a wide variety of leisure environments; i.e., the skills necessary to play card games can be utilized during work breaks, while waiting in the doctor's office, sitting in an airplane, and during indoor recess at school. When the number of leisure environments in which severely handicapped students function is considered, it seems that 1) most students are limited to or allowed to function in fewer leisure environments than nonhandicapped persons; and 2) too often, the leisure activities a severely handicapped student engages in in one environment are not engaged in in any other leisure environments; i.e., using materials in an arts and crafts session at school that are unavailable at home, at church, or at the home of a neighbor. An ILP should be designed to ensure that a severely handicapped student will be prepared to function in a wide variety of leisure environments and to engage in activities that are appropriate to more than one environment.

6. Specialized Nature of Supervision and Facilities Dimension   As discussed previously, the orientation toward the consistent use of specially trained leisure personnel often has deleterious effects. Because of a heavy reliance on specially trained personnel, severely handicapped persons have been excluded from many leisure environments and activities that contain nonhandicapped age peers and other nonhandicapped persons. In addition, this "specialized" orientation has encouraged the development of select architecturally barrier-free leisure environments. It is not uncommon for severely handicapped persons to travel from all over a city just to get to one swimming pool where there is a ramp and a lifeguard who has taken one 3-week course on "saving" severely handicapped persons. Because it is assumed that a particular student needs intensive supervision, activities that take students away from intensively supervised environments, e.g., segregated classrooms and group homes that contain only severely handicapped persons, are generally avoided. Thus, severely handicapped students have access to leisure environments only when an adult in authority decides that the group in which that student is a member should go to that environment. This, of course, has an inhibitory effect on individualization. In order to minimize this negative effect and promote individualization, instructional personnel should consider the following statements;

1.   Although many severely handicapped students do, in fact, need personnel with highly qualified training, the overwhelming majority can be served quite well with minimal adaptations in the personal repertoires of generally trained leisure personnel.
2.   As much as possible, each student should be taught to function with the kinds and amounts of supervision approximating that offered nonhandicapped persons.
3.   The kinds and degrees of supervision afforded should be based on the individual needs of a particular student.
4.   It is better to adapt existing facilities utilized by nonhandicapped persons than it is to create a cadre of highly specialized environments.

7. Minimal Inference Dimension   Minimal inference refers to the premise that the more intellectually handicapped a student, the less confidence educators can have in his or her ability to generalize, to transfer, to perform skills across environments, persons, materials, language cues, etc. The assumption that skills acquired in one setting will be applied in other settings may be warranted when programming for nonhandicapped students. For example, consider a non-handicapped student who has demonstrated acceptable performance of the skills necessary to engage in the activity of dancing as a part of his physical education class. Generally, with minimal difficulty, this student is also able to demonstrate acceptable performance of these skills at a community dance held at a local club. Unfortunately, many persons responsible for leisure programming assume that the same degree of skill transference will be manifested by severely handicapped students. For example, a teacher might discover that a severely handicapped student who demonstrated appropriate dance skills in a physical education class, danced wildly to both fast and slow songs, alone, in the middle of the dance floor at a local club. Rarely, if ever, can it be inferred that a severely handicapped student who has demonstrated acceptable performance in one environment will be able to demonstrate that same level of acceptable performance in another environment without instructional interventions in that new environment. Thus, concerted and systematic efforts must be made to ensure that, when appropriate, the skills taught in one leisure environment are adapted for use and actually performed or taught in other environments.

8. Incomplete/Complete Performance of the Skill Sequence Dimension The incomplete/complete performance of the skill sequence dimension refers to the need for organizing or conceptualizing a particular leisure environment and/or activity to include the skills needed to engage in activities that both lead to and follow that activity. For example, consider the leisure activity of bowling. When nonhandicapped adolescents announce that they intend to go bowling, often their parents can assume that they will dress appropriately, make appropriate travel arrangements, secure necessary funds, make necessary social arrangements, act appropriately when bowling, return home safely, etc.

Unfortunately, when a severely handicapped adolescent goes bowling, the sequence may be quite different. More specifically, parents often decide what he or she will wear; money is usually exchanged between parents and service personnel rather than between the severely handicapped person and service personnel; the timing of the activity both in terms of when the severely handicapped person will start and finish is usually decided by other persons, etc. Stated another way, bowling for a severely handicapped student usually means the "responsibility" merely of rolling a ball down an alley, whereas bowling for a nonhandicapped student usually refers to the performance of a wide range of independence-related and complete skill sequences. Severely handicapped students should be given direct instruction as well as numerous opportunities to at least partially participate in the initiation and termination components of the leisure skill sequences in which nonhandicapped students and other persons typically engage.

9. Transportation Dimension This leisure dimension relates to: the amount of time required to reach an environment; the distance that must be traveled in order to get to and from a particular environment; the kind of transportation that will be used; and the convenience factors involved in transporting a severely handicapped student. While time, distance, kind, and convenience factors should be considered, they should not be allowed to unreasonably restrict the leisure environments in which a severely handicapped student functions.

10. Longitudinal Nature of the Curriculum Dimension The ILP offered must be systematically and directly related to preparing a student to function in a variety of least restrictive current environments, and in the extended range of his or her future environments. The ILP should include activities and materials that would remain appropriate as a student's chronological age increases. This is not to say that activities that are acceptable mainly at one but not another chronological age range should not be considered. It would be unreasonable to exclude young children from the activities appropriate to their chronological age group even though these same activities may not be appropriate for performance later in life. However, such activities should be systematically replaced, just as they are with nonhandicapped students.

11. Minimal/Maximal Participation Dimension One way of relating to the dimension of minimal/maximal participation is to address the concept of "dead time." "Dead time" refers to the amount of time available to a person during which few if any actions are required and during which a person engages in maladaptive, inappropriate, or counterproductive actions. Most nonhandicapped students can be allowed extended periods of time during which specific actions are not required. Fortunately, the actions they choose to perform during this time are usually considered adaptive or at least not counterproductive. Severely handicapped students, on the other hand, when given large amounts of time in which specific actions are not required, often engage in inappropriate chatter, body rocking, finger looking, and other self-stimulatory or socially obnoxious actions. Clearly, it would be impossible to completely eliminate the amount of "dead time" available to severely handicapped persons, as all instructors experience unexpected delays. Rather, the goal is to reduce inordinate amounts of "dead time" and to teach the student to act in socially acceptable ways when confronted with unavoidable "free time."

Another facet of the minimal/maximal participation dimension relates to the factor of intensity. It is relatively rare to see adolescent and/or young adult severely handicapped students engaging in a leisure activity intensively. How often, for example, does one see a severely handicapped student run to first base as fast as he or she is capable, sweat while participating in calisthenics, strain really hard when lifting weights, or consistently try to perform better than he or she performed the day before? Unfortunately, more often than not, severely handicapped students manifest an extremely casual orientation toward participation in leisure activities, such that their involvement is almost always low-intensity. This can have a negative effect on both severely handicapped students and the nonhandicapped persons with whom they interact. On the other hand, if a volunteer, a recreation specialist, or any other handicapped person senses that a severely handicapped student is really doing his or her best, there is a tendency to interact more with that student and to involve him or her in other leisure activities. In addition, the nonhandicapped person tends to feel good about contributing to the handicapped student's enjoyment of the activity. An ILP should be implemented that allows, as much as possible, a severely handicapped student to experience as close to the same degrees and kinds of participation as those experienced by nonhandicapped persons.

12. *Student Preference Dimension*   While a reasonable proportion of adult leisure environments and activities should be determined by nonhandicapped persons in authority, these determinations should always be scrutinized carefully and balanced against the potentially damaging effects of not allowing students to at least contribute to decisions regarding what leisure activities to engage in, where, and with whom. Thus the general rule offered here is that each student should participate *to the maximum extent possible* in the selection of the persons, places, activities, etc., to be included in his or her ILP. In view of this position, several factors should be considered.

First, a severely handicapped student might prefer to play with a particular object. Initially, this might seem a reasonably acceptable action. However, that student may choose to play with that object throughout his or her waking state—in other words, he or she might use the object in a repetitious manner or to self-stimulate. Obviously, this cannot be considered an appropriate leisure activity.

Second, many severely handicapped students manifest difficulty initiating leisure activities even when it is appropriate to do so. Thus, it is critical that severely handicapped persons be taught the skills necessary to initiate appropriate leisure activities in appropriate environments at appropriate times.

Third, a severely handicapped person often does not participate in selecting the person(s) with whom he or she will interact during a leisure activity. It is important, therefore, that a severely handicapped person be taught the social interaction skills necessary to develop and maintain friendships.

Fourth, many severely handicapped persons manifest difficulties remembering, recalling, or thinking of leisure activities in which they might engage. In fact, many persons have offered: "I would like them to perform, but if I leave them on their own they will sit there and do nothing." Essentially, our response is that it is necessary to teach strategies that can be used to review or recall leisure repertoires at critical times, and to teach the skills necessary to initiate those strategies appropriately. Referring to leisure activity picture booklets at appropriate times is but one example.

13. *Physical Benefits Dimension*   This dimension refers to the need to consider how a leisure environment or activity might contribute to the enhancement and maintenance of general physical health. It is assumed that if reasonable physical health is developed and maintained, other aspects of a person's life space will be improved accordingly. As a severely handicapped student becomes more physically active, negative social stigmatization might be minimized, the chances of becoming physically ill because of obesity, poor fluid circulation, poor muscle tone, etc., might be minimized, and overall performance across a variety of settings might improve.

14. Parent/Guardian Preferences and Determinations Dimension
Much of the success of school services can be evaluated in relation to the ability of a student to perform critical school-taught skills during nonschool hours and in nonschool environments. Since parents or guardians are the persons most likely to arrange for and monitor the performance of school-taught skills in nonschool environments, making educational decisions without their systematic input will often drastically diminish the overall value of the educational curriculum.

Prior to Public Law 94-142, parent participation was often limited to conferences during which teachers communicated: "This is what your child is learning," and/or "This is how your child is progressing." Such an approach might be characterized as "closed-ended," in that curricular content was predetermined, and parents were expected to accept progress-related information about the performance of their children in educational programs in which they had no input.

Although the IEP procedure required under PL 94-142 does provide a mechanism for increased parent participation, interpretations of this process can easily and unwittingly encourage many parents to maintain the relatively passive roles they held in the past. For example, consider an IEP meeting held at the start of a school year in which a teacher says to the parents, "This document contains what I think are extremely important educational objectives," and then asks, "Are there any questions?" Certainly, the parents have the opportunity to respond, but their responses will probably be attenuated by the relatively closed posture assumed by the teacher.

If a teacher, on the other hand, asks parents to offer their contributions *before* a program is designed, an "open-ended" approach to determining curricular content is in force. Open-ended approaches are more likely to result in increased parent participation, and thus may influence educational priorities in critical ways, as illustrated in the following example:

> John, age 16, had the same teacher design and implement his IEP for the 1978, 1979, and 1980 school years. At the 1978 and 1979 IEP meetings, the teacher presented predetermined long-term objectives and corresponding daily schedules to his parents for feedback.
>
> During the 1980 meeting, the teacher adopted an open-ended approach. That is, the parents were asked at the start of the meeting to identify areas that they felt needed to be addressed in order to enhance John's general level of functioning. The parents indicated that they had reached a point where they were seriously considering placing John in an institution because of the fact that he was unable to occupy 30 minutes of leisure time in constructive ways. The parents, both of whom worked, had employed a "baby-sitter" for 3 years to watch John from 3:30PM to 4:00PM on school days until John's sister arrived home from school. John's parents viewed his inability to occupy this 30-minute leisure period as an indication of unduly cumbersome lifelong dependency, which, in turn, led them to consider institutional placement. While the 1978 and 1979 IEPs did not contain objectives related to the constructive use of leisure time in nonschool environments, the 1980 IEP certainly did.

In order to avert such potentially tragic communication difficulties, critical information pertaining to nonschool life space of the student must be secured in an open-ended manner from parents, and such information must be given reasonable representation in the design and implementation of IEPs.

15. Related Services Dimension   The related services dimension refers to establishing priorities for leisure curricula content in concert with the judgments and preferences of ancillary staff members—e.g., occupational, physical, speech and language therapists; psychologists; social workers; art instructors; adaptive and physical education teachers; music teachers; and physicians. As special educators move toward more integrated service delivery and curriculum development and implementation models, it will be necessary to establish priorities for leisure environments jointly with related services personnel. For example, it is absurd to think that if 1 hour of the day is spent in a highly structured art class, the leisure needs of a student are met. One of the authors observed an art class in which severely handicapped students were to make designs using hot crayons. The students came to class; the materials were already arranged; the students were given very precise directions; they were physically guided through most of the required movements, etc. The result was that not one student was able to make designs from hot crayons in any other environment. Certainly, students should be exposed to environments other than those in which they can perform independently. However, it is extremely important that the special education teacher work with other personnel in a variety of leisure environments—in this case, the art teacher in the art room—to ensure that performance across environments is enhanced. Similarly, occupational, physical, speech, and language therapy, and other related services can, and actually should, be delivered in a wide variety of leisure environments.

16. Cost Dimension   Cost refers to the amount of money required to function in a particular leisure environment or activity. Obviously, in most cases, cost should be considered carefully *before* particular leisure environments and activities are selected for utilization. Costly leisure activities should be balanced with free or extremely low-cost activities. While funds available to school systems are increasingly uncertain, the goal should be that each student should have access to fair and reasonable financial resources so that he or she can function in an individually appropriate number and kind of leisure environments and activities.

17. Principle of Partial Participation Dimension   Unfortunately, severely handicapped students are excluded from a wide range of leisure environments and activities because it is assumed that they cannot perform complete sequences of skills independently. There is no doubt that some severely handicapped students may never be able to perform a particular leisure activity at a proficiency level anywhere near that of nonhandicapped persons. While a severely handicapped student may not be able to carry out the complete skill sequence needed for independent performance, accommodations can be made and enjoyment can be maximized if the activity is arranged so that the student can at least *partially participate*.

18. Individualized Adaptations Dimension   There may be many skills that a severely handicapped person can, in fact, perform in ways roughly equivalent to the performance of nonhandicapped persons. Browsing in a shopping center, watching airplanes take off and land, wading in a lake, taking a sun bath, and watching television are but a few examples. However, for many severely handicapped persons to function in leisure environments and activities in ways similar to nonhandicapped persons, *individualized adaptations must be designed and implemented*. (For example, softball rules can be changed so that one player hits balls off a batting tee, while others hit balls thrown by a pitcher.)

Both obvious and ingenious individualized adaptations to activities in the form of changes in rules, attitudes, and values; in the creation and utilization of materials; in offers of physical assistance, etc., if used properly, can allow many severely handicapped persons to at least partially participate in a substantially improved variety of leisure environments and activities than they are now allowed.

19. Seasonal Factors Dimension   This dimension refers to the relationship between leisure environments and activities and the seasons of the year. An acceptable ILP must prepare a student to function in environments appropriate for all seasons, accommodate to the local climate conditions, and take advantage of seasonal benefits. School officials and others responsible for the educational program of a severely handicapped student must recognize that there are many skills that can be most effectively acquired and practiced during a particular season, due to climate conditions (e.g., swimming at the beach, gardening, choosing apparel for warm weather), and the increased frequency in which activities are engaged in (e.g., attending outdoor carnivals, participating in softball leagues, riding a bicycle).

A review of these dimensions and the information secured in the conduct of Phases I and II should provide a framework from which more specific decision-making strategies can evolve. During initial ILP sessions, leisure environments and activities can be delineated and priorities set using the format offered in Figure 5.

Phase IV: Conducting a Discrepancy Analysis

There are thousands of skills that a severly handicapped student must acquire in order to at least partially participate in a reasonable number of leisure environments and activities. For example, the activity "purchasing soda from a vending machine" requires many specific skills such as the skills necessary to locate the vending machine, stand in line when appropriate, visually scan the array of selections, select the desired soda, determine price, etc. The three-component discrepancy analysis presented below is but one strategy that might be used to determine individually significant skills for instructional purposes.

Part 1:   Conducting a Nonhandicapped Person Inventory   Essentially, a nonhandicapped person inventory is a sequential record of the skills utilized by a nonhandicapped person as he or she engages in a particular activity. For example, a sequential listing of the skills necessary for a nonhandicapped person to engage in the activity "swimming at the YMCA" would include the skills required from the point of initiation ("indicates a desire to go swimming") through the point of termination ("once at home, hangs up the wet towel and swim suit").

Participants:	A. Johnson, parent	Student: Sue Smith Age: 15
	Q. Brown, teacher	Date: 9-12-83
	L. Ryan, speech and	
	language therapist	

Leisure environments	Activities	Rationale
DOMESTIC Sue's house; a neighbor's house; a friend's house; a group home	*Indoor Activities:*	*Minimal inference; parental preferences; longitudinally important*
	Playing the card game "Uno"	Social interactions: popular among CA peers
	Performing a daily exercise routine to music	Physical benefits
	Playing records and practicing dancing	Parent plans to purchase a record player; student preference
	Expanding the number of snacks that she can pre-pare for a friend, e.g., raw vegetables and dip, and fruit and cheese	Social interactions; many environments in which food preparation is appropriate
	Maintaining and increasing puzzle-making skills with the use of more sophisti-cated and chronological age-appropriate materials	CA appropriate; an activity that requires limited supervision
	Engaging in doodle art	Student preference; CA appropriate
	Playing the piano	Parent preference; music teacher can teach rudi-mentary piano skills

Figure 5. A form for recording leisure environments, activities, and related information to aid in establishing priorities.

Studying the skills performed by a nonhandicapped person engaging in a specific activity serves at least three major purposes:

1. To reduce the degree of inference made when determining the skills actually needed to function in a given environment
2. To provide an understanding of the skills a severely handicapped student has to display in the environment in order to function with reasonable efficiency
3. To provide a basis from which to compare the actual skills demonstrated by the severely handicapped person and the nonhandicapped persons inventoried

For the purpose of providing a visual representation of the information that might be collected when conducting a nonhandicapped person inventory, a partial listing of skills for "swimming at the YMCA" is presented in Figure 6.

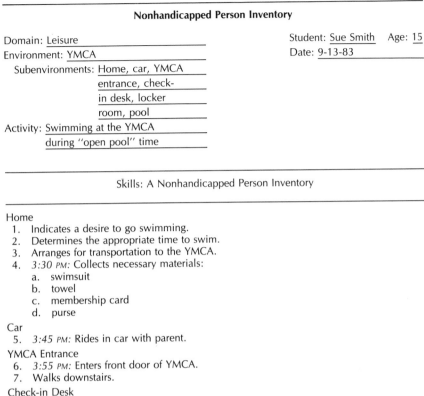

Nonhandicapped Person Inventory

Domain: Leisure

Environment: YMCA

Subenvironments: Home, car, YMCA entrance, check-in desk, locker room, pool

Activity: Swimming at the YMCA during "open pool" time

Student: Sue Smith   Age: 15

Date: 9-13-83

Skills: A Nonhandicapped Person Inventory

Home
1. Indicates a desire to go swimming.
2. Determines the appropriate time to swim.
3. Arranges for transportation to the YMCA.
4. *3:30 PM:* Collects necessary materials:
   a. swimsuit
   b. towel
   c. membership card
   d. purse

Car
5. *3:45 PM:* Rides in car with parent.

YMCA Entrance
6. *3:55 PM:* Enters front door of YMCA.
7. Walks downstairs.

Check-in Desk
8. Locates the desk.
9. Gives clerk her membership card.

Women's Locker Room
10. *4:00 PM:* Enters locker room.
11. Locates empty locker.
12. Removes clothing.
13. Places clothing in locker.

Figure 6.   A nonhandicapped person skills inventory (partial).

Part 2: Conducting a Severely Handicapped Student Inventory   In Part 1 above, strategies were described that rely upon ecological inventory techniques for determining the skill repertoires of nonhandicapped persons as they engage in a specific leisure activity in a specific environment. The same strategies should be used when observing a severely handicapped student so as to determine his or her skill repertoire. Part 2 is designed to bring meaning and purpose to Part 1 by comparing the two skill sequences. This process, referred to as *a discrepancy analysis,* is intended to result in an identification and analysis of the skills that are performed unacceptably or that are missing from the repertoire of the severely handicapped student.

The discrepancy analysis should lead to specific decisions related to the question: "What specific skills should be taught?" However, it is extremely

important to note that the purpose of referencing the skills of a severely handicapped person against those demonstrated by nonhandicapped persons is *not* to
dictate the exact skill sequence or the precise nature of the skills to be taught a
severely handicapped student. For example, if part of the skill sequence "going
swimming at the YMCA" manifested by a nonhandicapped person is the skill
"verbally indicates to a parent a desire to go swimming," this, obviously, does not
mean verbal indication skills must be taught to the severely handicapped student.
Even with systematic instruction, a severely handicapped student may not be able
to perform such verbal skills. Hence, it is important to utilize or create adaptations
of materials, skill sequences, rules, physical environments, devices, etc., that
might enhance or allow at least partial participation.

Figure 7 contains an example of one strategy that can be used to display the
skills in the repertoire of a severely handicapped student in relation to the skills
demonstrated by a nonhandicapped person.

Phase V: Using Partial Participation and Proposing Individualized Adaptations

When determining the skills required to engage in a particular leisure activity, a
teacher must carefully analyze the actual skills the student is unable to perform
acceptably. It is then critical to consider existing adaptations or create new
adaptations that might allow at least partial participation in the activity in question.
Such adaptations might include providing selective personal assistance; adapting
devices and materials; changing skill sequences, rules, and attitudes; and adapting
physical environments. (For a more detailed discussion of individualized adaptations see Baumgart, Brown, Pumpian, Nisbet, Ford, Sweet, Ranieri, Hansen, &
Schroeder, 1980.)

In Figure 8, a listing of the skills performed unacceptably by a severely
handicapped student in the initial stages of the activity "going swimming at the
YMCA" is presented with corresponding adaptation hypotheses.

Phase VI: Determining Individualized Instructional Objectives

Phase VI is designed to assist in the synthesization of much of the information
obtained through the use of strategies delineated in Phases I through V. It is hoped
that the actions associated with Phases I through V will lead to a truly *individualized* determination of skills and skill priorities to enable maximal functioning in leisure environments and activities. In Phase VI, such activities and skills
are translated into long- and short-term objectives that can serve as the foundation
for systematic instruction.

Figure 9 contains a form that can be used to organize and present information
on leisure activities according to at least three of the major IEP components
required by PL 94-142. Specifically, the form contains: 1) a statement of annual
leisure goals, including short-term leisure instructional objectives (these are based
upon information obtained through the use of a nonhandicapped person inventory,
a discrepancy analysis and individualized adaptation hypotheses); 2) the projected

Discrepancy Analysis

Domain: Leisure _____

Environment: YMCA _____

    Subenvironments: Home, car, YMCA ____

                      entrance, check- _____

                      in desk, locker _____

                      room, pool _____

Activity: Swimming at the YMCA _____

          during "open pool" time _____

Student: Sue Smith Age: 15

Date: 9-15-83 _____

Skills: A Nonhandicapped Person Inventory	Skills: Sue Smith (+ = acceptable performance)
Home	
1. Indicates a desire to go swimming.	Does not indicate a desire.
2. Determines the appropriate time to swim.	Does not read schedule for "open pool" times
3. Arranges for transportation to the YMCA.	Parent makes arrangements.
4. 3:30 PM: Collects necessary materials:	
a. swimsuit	+
b. towel	+
c. membership card	Does not look for membership card.
d. purse	+ (Takes knapsack.)
Car	
5. 3:45 PM: Rides in car with parent.	+
YMCA Entrance	
6. 3:55 PM: Enters front door of YMCA.	+
7. Walks downstairs.	+
Check-in Desk	
8. Locates the desk.	Does not stop at desk.
9. Gives clerk her membership card.	Does not hand clerk her card.
Women's Locker Room	
10. 4:00 PM: Enters locker room.	+
11. Locates empty locker.	+
12. Removes clothing.	+

Figure 7. A discrepancy analysis.

dates for initiation of specific leisure services and the anticipated duration of those services; and 3) performance criteria, evaluation procedures, and schedules for determining, at least on an annual basis, whether the short-term instructional objectives are being realized.

Phase VII: Designing an Instructional Program

In Phase VII, information secured through the utilization of the strategies delineated in Phases I through VI should be reviewed. In Part I, below, components of an instructional program are presented. Part 2, below, addresses administrative factors that may influence the implementation of instructional programs.

Discrepancy Analysis with Adaptation Hypotheses

Domain: Leisure

Environment: YMCA

    Subenvironments: Home, car, YMCA

                   entrance, check-

                   in desk, locker

                   room, pool

Activity: Swimming at the YMCA

          during "open pool" time

Student: Sue Smith Age: 15

Date: 9-15-83

Skills: A Nonhandicapped Person Inventory	Skills: Sue Smith (+ = acceptable performance)	Possible adaptations and comments
Home		
1. Indicates a desire to go swimming.	Does not indicate a desire.	Include an appropriate picture in her leisure communication book.
2. Determines the appropriate time to swim.	Does not read schedule for "open pool" times.	May need to predetermine times, days, etc. for her.
3. Arranges for transportation to the YMCA.	Parent makes arrangements.	Request could be made in sign language (the sign for driving is the motion of driving).
4. *3:30 PM:* Collects necessary materials:	+	
a. swimsuit	+	Could be placed in communication book next to the YMCA picture.
b. towel		
c. membership card	Does not look for membership card.	
d. purse	+ (Takes knapsack)	
Car		
5. *3:45 PM:* Rides in car with parent	+	
YMCA Entrance		
6. *3:55 PM:* Enters front door of YMCA	+	
7. Walks downstairs	+	

Figure 8. A discrepancy analysis with corresponding adaptation hypotheses.

Part 1: Components of an Instructional Program The phrase "instructional program" refers to at least the following components (Falvey, Brown, Lyon, Baumgart, & Schroeder, 1980):

    Component 1: *What* skills will be taught?

    Component 2: *Where* will the skills be taught?

    Component 3: *Why* will the skills be taught?

    Component 4: What *performance criteria* will be sought?

ILP Components

Student: <u>Sue Smith</u> Age: <u>15</u>
Date: <u>9-15-83</u>

Domain: <u>Leisure</u>
Environment in which systematic instruction occurs: <u>YMCA</u>
Activity: <u>Sue will perform acceptably the sequence of skills</u>
<u>required to swim at the YMCA during an "open pool"</u>
<u>time</u>
Assessment Procedures and Performance Criteria:
<u>Direct and continuous measures will be taken on each weekly trip to the YMCA. The</u>
<u>performance criterion will be three consecutive correct trials. A correct trial entails the</u>
<u>performance of the sequence of skills required to swim at the YMCA as delineated in the</u>
<u>nonhandicapped person inventory with adaptations. Sue will be expected to perform this</u>
<u>adapted skill sequence on three consecutive occasions without assistance from personnel who</u>
<u>are not naturally present in the environment. Her performance will be assessed at least once</u>
<u>during nonschool hours.</u>

Starting date	Short-term objectives	Progress information and dates
9-13-83	Discrepancy Analysis of: 9-15-83	
	Required Skills (the skills missing from Sue's repertoire):	
	1. Locates membership card.	
	2. Goes to the desk and gives clerk membership card.	
	3. In the locker room:	
	a. Places coat and other clothing articles in locker.	
	b. Positions swim suit (sits down, places suit on floor with tag facing up and at feet, places one foot in suit, etc.).	
	4. Takes towel and hangs it on hook outside of shower.	
	5. Tests water temperature	
	6. Rinses body completely before entering pool area.	

Figure 9. A form for presenting components of an ILP.

Component 5: What *instructional materials* will be used?
Component 6: *How* will the skills be taught?
Component 7: What *measurement strategies* will be utilized?

The task in Part 1 is to integrate the information obtained in Phases I through VI into the above components of an instructional program, and then to determine which components have not been addressed sufficiently. While Components 1 through 5 have been addressed directly in Phases I through VI of this chapter, Component 6 (*How* will the skills be taught?) and Component 7 (What *measurement strategies* will be utilized?) have not been dealt with extensively.

How a student will be taught to perform a skill sequence involves many complex decisions related to factors such as instructional arrangements, the use of instructional and natural cues and correction procedures, the degree to which a given skill will be emphasized within a sequence, and the use of behavior management practices. More specifically, questions similar to these should be asked:

1. Are the cues and correction procedures employed directly related to the instructional objectives?
2. Is the instructional arrangement appropriate for the intervention that is to occur?
3. Is there enough time for the hierarchy of cues and correction procedures decided upon to be employed?
4. Are individualized instructional cues and correction procedures utilized?
5. Are naturally occurring cues and correction procedures utilized?
6. Are meaningful contexts provided even when simulation is used?
7. Are the teaching strategies chronologically age-appropriate? Do they encourage social interactions and appropriately reinforce individual performance?
8. Are appropriate contingencies arranged and adhered to?

Regarding measurement strategies designed to empirically verify and analyze performance, one such strategy, presented in Phase IV, analyzed the discrepancies between the performance of nonhandicapped persons and a severely handicapped student. Although this discrepancy analysis strategy provides a basis from which important instructional decisions can be made, other types of measurement strategies must also be considered. More specifically, questions similar to the following should be posed in determining measurement strategies:

1. Is the measurement tool designed in such a way as to minimize instructional inference?
2. Are objectives presented in an empirically verifiable manner?
3. Are the measurement strategies directly related to the actions specified in the objectives?
4. Are data sheets organized so as to allow for efficient recording and the subsequent use of the information recorded?
5. Are data utilized for the purpose of determining the most appropriate subsequent intervention?
6. Are the measurement tools utilized as efficient, as unobtrusive, and as natural as possible?

Part 2: Administrative Factors   Often the stumbling blocks to implementing an appropriate ILP relate to scheduling, staff-to-student ratios, logistics, and other administrative factors. Certainly, logistical constraints may force teachers to make less than desirable educational concessions. However, a point worthy of reemphasis is that these concessions should not be made until after individual needs are determined. Once individual needs are determined, sincere efforts should be made to work cooperatively with administrators and others to achieve the best accommodations possible in relation to such factors as nonschool instruction, transportation, related service allocations, and financial resources.

Strategies designed to assist in the development of leisure environment and activity schedules that reflect information secured through the procedures described in Phase I through Phase VII, Part I, are presented below. These strategies are designed to delineate intervals of time for leisure instruction in both school and nonschool environments. Examples of scheduling forms are provided in Figures 10, 11, and 12.

Personnel Availability Schedule

Class: Homeroom 10, Roosevelt Middle School   Date: August 29, 1983

Times	Monday	Tuesday	Wednesday	Thursday	Friday
8:00– 8:30 AM	CT	CT	CT	CT	CT
8:30– 9:00					
9:00– 9:30	CT/CA	CT/VT/CA	CT/CA	CT/CA/VT	CT/CA/V
9:30–10:00		CA			
10:00–10:30					
10:30–11:00					
11:00–11:30	LM/OT/PT/V ──────────────────────────────→				
11:30–12:00					
12:00–12:30 PM	SLT	SLT			CT/CA
12:30– 1:00					
1:00– 1:30	CT/CA	CT/VT	CT/CA	CT/CA	
1:30– 2:00		CA			
2:00– 2:30	A	A	PT	A	
2:30– 3:00					
3:00– 3:30	CT	CT	CT	CT	CT
3:30– 4:00					

Codes: CA = Classroom Aide; CT = Classroom Teacher; PT = Physical Therapist; LM = Lunch Monitor; OT = Occupational Therapist; A = Art, Music, or Adaptive Physical Education Teachers; SLT = Speech and Language Therapist; V = Volunteer; VT = Vocational Teacher.

Figure 10.   A weekly personnel availability schedule.

Instruction Chart

Teacher: Q. Brown

Date: <u>September 30, 1981</u>

Student	Direct instruc- tional hours per week	School/ nonschool	Domains:					
			Domestic	Community	Vocational	Leisure	Other	Total
Lynn	25	School	7	3	0	3	0	13
		Nonschool	3	3	3	3	0	12
Ian	25	School	5	2	0	1½	0	8½
		Nonschool	1½	4½	6	4½	0	16½
Diane	25	School	5	1½	0	1½	0	8
		Nonschool	3	4½	6	3½	0	17
Jan	25	School	3	2	2	2	0	9
		Nonschool	4	4½	3	4½	0	16

Figure 11. A school and nonschool instruction chart.

Instruction Schedule within Domains

Time	Monday	Tuesday	Wednesday	Thursday	Friday
	Domain	Domain	Domain	Domain	Domain
8:00– 8:30 AM					
8:30– 9:00	Community (S)	Community (NS)	Community (NS)	Community (NS)	Community (NS)
9:00– 9:30		Vocational (NS)		Vocational (NS)	Domestic (NS)
9:30–10:00					
10:00–10:30					
10:30–11:00					
11:00–11:30	Domestic (S)				
11:30–12:00					
12:00–12:30 PM	Leisure (S) & (NS)				
12:30– 1:00		Domestic (NS)	Domestic (S)	Domestic (NS)	Leisure (NS)
1:00– 1:30					
1:30– 2:00		Leisure (S) & (NS)	Leisure (S)	Leisure (S) & (NS)	
2:00– 2:30					
2:30– 3:00					
3:00– 3:30					

Figure 12. Weekly instruction schedule within each domain. (S, school; NS, nonschool.)

The following strategies may be helpful when organizing leisure information.

1. Construct a grid, a chart, or other aid that can be used to delineate blocks of time in which all personnel available for direct instruction are listed (Figure 10).

2. Construct a grid, a chart, or other aid that can be used to delineate the anticipated amount of time required for each student, each week in each domain, in school, and nonschool environments, and the times during which direct instruction will be offered (Figures 11 and 12). This scheduling format should assist a teacher to record at least the following information for each student in the class:

    a. The total number of *direct instructional hours* per week
    b. The estimated number of *school* instructional hours in each domain
    c. The estimated number of *nonschool* instructional hours per week in each domain
    d. The days and time intervals in which each unit of instruction will occur

SUMMARY

It is intended that the curriculum development strategies described in Phases I through VII will challenge special educators to continue to expand and actualize the most creative and significant meanings of such terms as "appropriate," "individualized," and "least restrictive." The ILP component of an IEP must not be viewed as a document that is written and filed in the cumulative folder once each school year. Rather, it must be viewed as a continuous process of asking and answering questions; selecting, analyzing, and determining objectives and measurement strategies; and implementing teaching strategies that are designed to meet the constantly changing recreation and leisure needs of an evolving and unique person.

REFERENCES

Baumgart, D., Brown, L., Pumpian, I., Nisbet, J., Ford, A., Sweet, M., Ranieri, L., Hansen, L., & Schroeder, J. The principle of partial participation and individualized adaptations in educational programs for severely handicapped students. In: L. Brown, M. Falvey, I. Pumpian, D. Baumgart, J. Nisbet, A. Ford, J. Schroeder, & R. Loomis (eds.), *Curricular strategies for teaching severely handicapped students functional skills in school and nonschool environments*, Vol. 10. Madison, WI: Madison Metropolitan School District, 1980.

Brown, L., Branston, M.B., Hamre-Nietupski, S., Pumpian, I., Certo, N., & Gruenewald, L. A strategy for developing chronological age appropriate and functional curricular content for severely handicapped adolescents and young adults. *Journal of Special Education*, 1979, *13*(1), 81–90.

Falvey, M., Brown, L., Lyon, S., Baumgart, D., & Schroeder, J. Strategies for using cues and correction procedures. In: W. Sailor, B. Wilcox, & L. Brown (eds.), *Methods of instruction for severely handicapped students*. Baltimore: Paul H. Brookes Publishing Co., 1980.

Public Law 94-142, Education for All Handicapped Children Act of 1975, 20 U.S. Code, 1401 et seq.

VanDeventer, P., Yelinek, N., Brown, L., Schroeder, J., Loomis, R., & Gruenewald, L. A follow-up examination of severely handicapped graduates of the Madison Metropolitan School District from 1971–1978. In: L. Brown, D. Baumgart, I. Pumpian, J. Nisbet, A. Ford, R. Loomis, & J. Schroeder (eds.), *Educational programs for severely handicapped students,* Vol. 11. Madison, WI: Madison Metropolitan School District, 1981.

13

Statewide Integration of Severely Handicapped Students
Issues and Alternatives for States

Judy A. Schrag

It has been largely within the past 10 years that the states have given systematic attention to educating severely handicapped children. Prior to 1970, educational programs for severely handicapped youngsters were the exception rather than the rule, with the majority of such children remaining at home or residing in private residential or public institutional facilities. Although many states have now initiated efforts on their own, the federal government has provided notable direction and encouragement for the education of severely handicapped children since 1966. The section following contains a brief review of major federal initiatives that have served to support and stimulate state efforts to educate those children.

FEDERAL LEADERSHIP

Thompson, Wilcox, and York (Note 1) have discussed federal efforts to support and promote the development of state educational and training programs for severely handicapped children. The Bureau of Education for the Handicapped (now Special Education Programs) initiated an advocacy role for this population in 1966. In 1973, the Bureau adopted a 5-year plan to support this priority. A task force formed at that time to assist in implementing the plan observed that in 1973, 5 states (Maryland, Missouri, Montana, North Carolina, and Tennessee) had mandated services to severely handicapped children; 23 additional states had adopted legislation that implied support for such services; 13 states had legislation that implied lack of support; 6 states (Alabama, Connecticut, Delaware, Florida, New Jersey, and New York) did not allow for state funding of such education programs; and 3 states (Louisiana, Mississippi, and Pennsylvania) had no mandatory special education laws. The task force estimated that, at that time, less than one-third of the severely handicapped children were being served in the states.

The task force's work at the federal level included the development of a working definition of severely handicapped children, as well as the funding of various program support activities between 1974 and 1978 to stimulate state demonstration activities for specific types of severely handicapped children. In 1974, [then] U. S. Commissioner T. E. Bell issued a memorandum to chief state school officers that emphasized a priority to initiate, expand, and improve training and educational services for severely handicapped youngsters. Also in that year, representatives from 29 states attended a conference in Salt Lake City, Utah, sponsored by the Rocky Mountain Regional Resource Center, to discuss state issues in program development for this population. Subsequently, the National Association of State Directors of Special Education (NASDSE) sponsored a strategy-planning session focusing on issues identified in the Salt Lake City conference (Thompson, et al., Note 1).

In 1974, as well, a Special Services Branch was established in the Division of Assistance to States (within the then Bureau of Education for the Handicapped) to oversee programs supported by Public Law (PL) 89-313 and the Education of the Handicapped Act of 1974, Part B. This Branch was moved to the Special Needs Section in the Division of Innovation and Development in fiscal year 1978 to more clearly support innovative long-range planning as well as efficient programs for severely handicapped students. The Bureau also increased its funding for Centers and Service Programs for Deaf-Blind Children from $1 million to $16 million from 1969 to 1979 (Thompson et al., Note 1).

In the late 1970s, the federal government took several steps to initiate interagency collaboration, with the aim of better coordinating federal support of service delivery efforts in the states for handicapped children (including severely handicapped youngsters) (Crossen et al., 1979). Several written agreements were developed and signed between Vocational Education, Vocational Rehabilitation and Special Education; between the Office of Special Education and the Office of Civil Rights; and between Special Education and Maternal and Child Health Services. Other federal special education interagency agreements included those with Crippled Children's Services; Supplementary Security Income; Disabled Children's Program; Developmental Disabilities; Early and Periodic Screening, Diagnosis and Treatment; Head Start Programs; and Social Services Act of 1935 Title XX.

STATE INITIATIVES

Paralleling, but also independent of federal leadership and support, has been a growing concern for and commitment to severely handicapped children on the part of the states. With the passage in 1975 of PL 94-142 (Education for All Handicapped Children Act), all handicapped children were guaranteed a free and appropriate education and related services. This law gave priority to providing an education to those handicapped children, first, who are not currently receiving an education and, second, to those who have severe handicaps and are receiving an inadequate education. PL 94-142 further stated that handicapped children should be educated with nonhandicapped children to the maximum extent possible. In the early 1970s states had already begun to initiate long-term planning efforts and to expand program options for severely handicapped students; passage of PL 94-142 served to spur their efforts.

A review by Education Turnkey Systems, Inc. (Blaschke, Note 2) of state laws prior to PL 94-142 indicated that 14 states had specific laws regarding due process, and 13 states had administrative policies regarding due process implementation. In 1974, the National Education Association also reported that 22 of the states had state laws or regulations requiring handicapped children to be placed in regular classrooms on at least a part-time basis. During the brief time since passage of state laws and PL 94-142, a number of significant changes have occurred for severely handicapped students. In 1981, The Association for the Severely Handicapped estimated that as many as 95% to 98% of the nation's severely handicapped students are currently served in public schools, and 15% of served students are taught in self-contained classrooms in regular education buildings. (This latter percentage is increasing each year as the success of self-contained educational placement becomes better known and understood.)

Numerous challenges and educational issues have accompanied increased educational programs and services for severely handicapped children within the states. Discussion of issues in this chapter is based on the author's extensive review of articles and research on present and future planning/service efforts, as well as survey information obtained from 33 states regarding state efforts to support the integration of severely handicapped children into public schools, various problems and solutions encountered in program development, and future challenges and problems. In addition to discussing integration issues in the states, this chapter emphasizes statewide training, demonstration, and support efforts, as well as future challenges. Note that the chapter deals with the general integration of severely handicapped children in the public schools, without focusing on the advantages or disadvantages of specific educational placements (i.e., special schools, self-contained classes in neighborhood schools, and so forth).

DEFINITION OF SEVERELY HANDICAPPED CHILDREN

This chapter recognizes the federal definition of severely handicapped children, which refers to those who because of the intensity of their physical, mental or emotional problems or a combination of such physical, mental, or emotional problems need educational, social, psychological and medical services behond those which are traditionally offered by regular and special education programs to maximize their full potential for useful and meaningful participation in society and for self-fulfillment (Thompson et al., Note 1)

Definitions of severely handicapped children, however, vary by state. As late as 1979, 20 states reported that they did not have a current definition that included severely and profoundly handicapped children. Table 1 provides a profile of various state definitions in place during 1979 (NASDSE, Note 3).

IDENTIFICATION/EVALUATION

The first step in providing a free, appropriate public education for severely handicapped children is identifying and evaluating such children. All states report Child Find programs in place for the purpose of locating severely handicapped children needing services. Finding such children is sometimes difficult, however. Many parents, especially in rural areas, keep their retarded or physically handicapped child hidden (Kurtz & Lamb, Note 4). David and Greene (Note 5) found that local education agencies' (LEAs') Child Find activities are heavily influenced by the kinds of programs the LEA provides directly, the services the LEA obtains from other agencies, and the number of "slots" open in specific programs. Because appropriate programs for severely handicapped students have been available less often, Child Find efforts have been less aggressive for this population. Nevertheless, states have explored and implemented a variety of Child Find efforts to locate severely handicapped children, and there has been a great deal of sharing of appropriate identification strategies in the past 5 to 7 years.

Existing identification and evaluation methods for handicapped children are not readily adapted to multihandicapped, infant, or multicultural severely handicapped children. States have thus utilized their state Title VI-B discretionary funds to support identification, screening, and evaluation activities for such children. Vermont, for example, has developed a statewide interdisciplinary team to provide diagnostic and consultation services for school districts. Other states (Arizona, Florida, Idaho, Washington) provide backup diagnostic services through their state institutions and/or colleges and universities.

INTERAGENCY PLANNING/COORDINATION

Following the lead of the federal government and the mandates of PL 94-142, many states have initiated written interagency agreements. In the majority of states, the state education agency (SEA) does not have legal authority over all other social and human agencies. However, under PL 94-142, SEAs are given the sole responsibility for insuring that all appropriate service and special education are provided to severely handicapped children, regardless of the agency providing the services. So far, only two states, New Jersey and Indiana, have passed legislation (in 1978) placing all state agencies serving handicapped individuals under the statutes and regulations of the state education agency. A recent finding

Table 1. Categories included in the definition of severely and profoundly handicapped individuals[a]

State Territory	Categories							
	1	2	3	4	5	6	7	8
Alabama		X						
Alaska	X	X	X	X	X		X	
American Samoa	X	X						
Arizona	X	X	X	X	X		X	
Arkansas	X	X	X		X	X	X	
California	X	X						
Colorado								
Connecticut	X							
Delaware								
District of Columbia	X	X	X	X	X	X	X	
Florida	X							
Georgia	X							
Hawaii	X	X	X	X	X		X	
Illinois								
Indiana								
Iowa	X	X						
Kansas	X	X	X	X	X	X	X	
Kentucky	X	X	X	X	X	X	X	X
Louisiana	X							
Maine	X	X				X	X	X
Maryland								X
Massachusetts								X
Michigan	X	X	X					
Minnesota	X	X	X	X	X		X	X
Mississippi	X	X						
Missouri	X	X	X				X	
Montana	X	X		X	X		X	
Nebraska	X	X		X	X			
Nevada	X							
New York	X	X	X	X	X		X	
North Carolina	X	X	X					
North Dakota								
Ohio		X						X
Oklahoma	X	X	X	X	X		X	
Oregon	X	X	X				X	X

(continued)

Table 1. (*continued*)

State Territory	Categories							
	1	2	3	4	5	6	7	8
Pennsylvania	X	X	X	X	X	X	X	X
Puerto Rico		X						
South Carolina	X							
South Dakota	X	X				X	X	
Texas	X	X	X	X	X	X	X	X
Vermont		X						
Virgin Islands								
Virginia		X						X
Washington	X	X	X	X	X			
West Virginia	X	X						
Wisconsin								
Wyoming								

*Taken from *Special Education Program for Severely and Profoundly Handicapped Individuals, A Directory of State Education Agency Services,* August, 1979.

Key: 1 = mentally retarded; 2 = multi-handicapped; 3 = physically handicapped; 4 = blind; 5 = deaf; 6 = learning disabled; 7 = emotionally disturbed; 8 = other.

(Blaschke, Note 2) indicates that the SEA supervision requirement has had the largest impact in the states of any feature in PL 94-142. The provision not only conflicts with many state laws/constitutions, but also represents a serious deviation from traditional SEA roles, forcing state and local education agencies to renegotiate their boundaries with other social service agencies. Other agencies, however, do not necessarily give priority to providing services to severely handicapped children enrolled in the schools, nor do their regulations necessarily allow them to provide services without cost. Lacking a charge similar to that given the SEAs, such agencies are not always willing to collaborate and make first-dollar commitments. In addition, state and local education agencies have no leverage to require other agencies to honor SEA priorities, submit to SEA supervision, or provide ample free services.

Interagency collaboration has been extensively explored by states over the past several years, and has improved increasingly in recent years as the national economy has been tightened. Reduced resources and concern for maintenance and enhancement of needed programs and services for severely handicapped students will continue to challenge the states to identify strategies to more effectively improve communication and collaboration between agencies, so that optimum services can be provided with limited resources.

SECURING QUALIFIED PERSONNEL

Before the 1950s, teacher preparation programs for personnel serving severely handicapped students numbered a half-dozen or less. Starting in the late 1960s and continuing in the 1970s, there was a rapid growth in professional preparation as special education services expanded across the country. The University of Wisconsin initiated the first nationally recognized program for preparation of personnel for severely handicapped students in 1969. Ten years later, in 1979, the NASDSE (Note 3) surveyed 43 states and found that 22 reported colleges and universities preparing teaching personnel of severely handicapped students at the bachelor of arts level; 27 reported colleges and university preparation programs at the master's level; and 14 states reported preparing personnel in the area of severely handicapped students at the doctoral level. Today, virtually all states have preservice training programs for teachers of severely handicapped students. Preservice training programs for other needed personnel serving severely handicapped students, such as communication disorders specialists, occupational therapists, physical therapists, nurses, and social workers, also are increasing.

In addition to preservice training programs, state certification requirements for teachers of severely handicapped students have increased dramatically. The above-mentioned survey (NASDSE, Note 3) also found in 1979 that 11 states had instituted specific procedures for certification in the severely handicapped area; 31 states indicated there were no specific procedures established for certification in this area, and of these states, 9 reported certification at the bachelor of arts level and 6 at the master of arts level. A number of states are currently reviewing the need for certification standards for personnel serving severely handicapped individuals.

Improved methods of recruiting and retaining special education and related services staff have also been identified as a national need—particularly in rural and sparsely populated areas. Studies conducted by the National Rural Project Center for Innovation and Development (Helge & Marrs, Note 6) have reported annual teacher turnover rates of 30%–50% and complete turnover every 3 years in rural areas. Studies in Idaho (Schrag, Note 7) have found similar results. A pilot study conducted at the University of Kansas (Meyen, Note 8) indicated that special education teachers have a higher rate of attrition than regular education teachers, because of professional "burn out" due to stressful conditions they encounter on the job. Two National Rural Project studies (Helge & Marrs, Note 6) determined that 94% of all states and 64% of all local districts experience problems recruiting and retaining personnel. Social and cultural isolation of service delivery in rural areas and low salaries were factors cited by the National Rural Project and Idaho studies as primarily responsible for the high annual turnover; additional factors included stresses of implementing new roles and responsibilities, problems of working with parents of handicapped students, increased staff time and paperwork requirements, and lack of appropriate or modified curricula. Personnel changes cost money, and also take their toll in time and efficiency. Many rural districts reported thay they were compelled to hire young and inexperienced special education staff members, a practice that has serious ramifications for personnel development and program stability. Constant turnover makes it almost impossible to develop and implement long-range plans for staff improvement. In order to circumvent these problems, many states have implemented effective strategies aimed at retaining personnel serving severely handicapped children. These activities include allowing for cross-filed exchange of information, providing release time for professional development opportunities, implementing incentives for participation in development activities, reducing paperwork requirements, and allowing teachers of severely handicapped students the opportunity to transfer to a regular classroom assignment for a year or two.

While recruiting certificated personnel for work with severely handicapped students still remains a problem for public schools in some parts of the country, adequate numbers of teachers *are* being trained. More aggressive recruitment procedures, direct and active SEA and LEA linkages with university teacher-training programs, and more effective use of the above-mentioned incentives should help to alleviate existing recruitment problems.

PROVISION OF AN "APPROPRIATE EDUCATION"

Many educational controversies in the states have stemmed from efforts to define an "appropriate education" for severely handicapped children, required under PL 94-142. One issue that has been the subject of several state lawsuits is whether or not school districts must provide severely handicapped children a free, publicly funded education beyond the typical 180-day school year. PL 94-142 focuses on the need for appropriate education for handicapped children as defined by an individualized education plan (IEP). The courts have not defined "appropriate." In *Mills* v. *Board of Education of District of Columbia*, 348 F. Supp. 866 (D.D.C. 1972) the court ordered that a handicapped child's education be "suited" to his needs; and in the *Pennsylvania Association for Retarded Citizens* v. *Commonwealth of Pennsylvania*, 343 F. Supp. 279 (E.D.Pa. 1972) the court required that education be "appropriate to his learning capacities." It was the opinion of the expert witnesses in the *Armstrong* case that a significant loss of skills occurs during substantial interruptions in educational programs (3 months). A recent study of teachers of severely handicapped children (Fredericks, Baldwin, Moore, Templeman, Moore, Alrick, & Wadlow, 1979) found that the minutes of instruction provided each day and the percentage of task-analyzed programs used were the major teaching factors responsible for the difference between students who made high gains and those who made low gains. With such findings and current curriculum and instructional methodologies for severely handicapped children in mind, some individuals have concluded that continuous, year-round programming is needed. However, parents of nonhandicapped children have expressed concern that such programming is an unfair allocation of resources at the expense of nonhandicapped children (Makuch, 1981). In addition, the National School Boards Association (Larsen, 1981) has argued against year-round programming for handicapped students from the perspective of cost. The provision of year-round programs for severely handicapped students will continue to be a controversial issue due to current economic conditions. Certainly public schools have an obligation to use tax dollars responsibly and equitably. However, a free appropriate public education has been mandated by PL 94-142, and year-round programming has been upheld as appropriate by the courts in the few test cases that have occurred. Therefore, we should be careful not to let cost be used to deny the hard-earned rights of severely handicapped students.

Related Services

Public Law 94-142 requires the provision of related services if such services are necessary for a child to benefit from special education. This "need to profit from" criterion is vague. Many states have argued that the intent of PL 94-142 was not to expand the role of the public school to that of provider of all social and human services.

Ross (Note 9) has indicated that third-party payments for related services has been an emerging policy issue as states and local school districts have reviewed and explored various funding options for financial support of program mandates. Cost sharing and the elimination of duplication in program development and service delivery are and have been a crucial concern by virtue of the fact that related services are costly. Education agencies sometimes lack experience and capability to ensure the availability and delivery of related services (traditionally delivered by health and welfare agencies), and private insurance companies have disclaimed liability for related services provided by or through the school system. Other public agencies have also often reduced their previous commitments to providing such related services. However, expression of concern on the part of school-board members, general educators, and parents of nonhandicapped students regarding the responsibility of public schools to provide services such as speech therapy, physical therapy, and occupational therapy is not unexpected, since prior to PL 94-142 the definition of public educational services had been allowed to develop without regard for the needs of severely handicapped students. It is to be hoped that the continued placement of severely handicapped students in visible, integrated, public school settings will assist elected officials, general educators, and parents of nonhandicapped students to understand that developing a program—in consultation with a physical therapist—to teach a physically involved, severely handicapped student to go through a cafeteria line, for example, is not only important, but qualitatively the same as consulting the school nurse when a nonhandicapped student is injured in gym class, or supplementing an elementary education teacher's skills with the related services of music, art, and physical education teachers in order to address the full needs of nonhandicapped students.

The majority of problems of educating severely handicapped students may be attitudinal, rather than technical in nature. Whereas all states have implemented pilot projects that have demonstrated effective technology and curriculum approaches for severely handicapped students, and each state also has identified "experts" and backup technical resources to rely upon, attitudinal barriers must still be surmounted, in legislatures, communities, and schools. Opposition may emerge, for example, when severely handicapped students are placed in regular public schools along with their nonhandicapped peers. Often, parents of nonhandicapped children are wary of their child being educated with physically handicapped, mentally retarded, or other severely handicapped children, with the result that parents transfer their fears, superstitions, and prejudices to their nonhandicapped children. Parents of severely handicapped children likewise become concerned about the loss of specialized services when their child is placed in the public school setting, as well as the stigma their child is confronted with in an integrated setting. Such parents are anxious both about the treatment their child will receive from other children and about the services their child will receive— such as physical therapy, occupational therapy, adaptive physical education, etc. Parents and children, themselves, may have become comfortable in a segregated environment and may not be prepared for the name-calling, the staring, or other inappropriate responses to severely handicapped children that can occur in a regular public school.

However, educators and others must work to instill upon the public the understanding that the only way to break down such attitudinal barriers is to allow severely handicapped and nonhandicapped students to have regular contact with each other as they grow up in the same elementary, middle, and high schools. In support of this view, it is encouraging to note that recent research shows that severely handicapped students can be successfully integrated into public schools; that interactions can be taught or facilitated with nonhandicapped peers; and that significant positive shifts in the attitudes of nonhandicapped students and their teachers occur following the planned integration of severely handicapped students in the same school setting.

Architectural concern is another barrier in the planning of public school programs for severely handicapped students. Although many public school buildings built within the last 25 years are accessible to physically handicapped students, some buildings still in use are inaccessible to them. Recent trends to consolidate schools in various systems throughout the country, because of dwindling enrollments, may result in some additional natural attrition of inaccessible building. Requirements of Section 504 of the Rehabilitation Act of 1973 have also encouraged adjustments such as lifts, elevators, special toileting facilities, ramps, and wider doors; unfortunately, however, limited federal and state funds have been available for such changes.

SERVICE DELIVERY IN RURAL AREAS

Problems in recruitment and retention of special education personnel in rural areas have been discussed earlier in the chapter. Other rural service delivery problems have been discussed by Schrag, Farago, and Walker (Note 10). One of the first challenges of special education in a rural area is determining how to deliver services to small numbers of severely handicapped children scattered over a large geographic area. Attempting to group severely handicapped children on any kind of homogeneous basis is virtually impossible and educationally questionable (Brown, Nietupski, & Hamre-Nietupski, 1976). Various types of regional services have been developed within the states (e.g., Delaware, Idaho, Massachusetts, New York, North Carolina, Oklahoma, Texas, Vermont, Washington) to provide coordinated services between and within school districts, public and private agencies, colleges and universities, and so forth. Such regional services provide effective ways for rural areas to share personnel and materials, disseminate information, engage in diagnostic and prescriptive planning, and provide parent support. With such backup support, itinerant personnel can also train parents to be effective change agents.

Transportation is an additional and particularly difficult problem in rural areas. The fuel expense of extra traveling time; bus aides needed; additional driving time to take advantage of related and specialized services; and need for lifts, ramps, door-to-door loading, and loading zones that are adjacent to classrooms and away from traffic patterns must all be considered and the additional costs computed. Transportation in rural areas is also a factor in curriculum development, in that itinerant personnel spend a great deal of time in transit and have less time for pupil contact.

Low incidence of severely handicapped children in rural areas presents an additional service dilemma. A sparsely populated, rural school district with two or three deaf, blind, or severely retarded children may have difficulty justifying employing a skilled teacher to serve so few students. The University of New Mexico Release Time Consultant Model provides one example of how backup services may be provided rural school districts with low incidence of handicapped children to service. As another example, Vermont's Consulting Teacher model was originally developed for mildly handicapped children programs, but is now being extended to low-incidence severely handicapped programs.

States have also investigated the effective use of technology to meet the challenges of serving severely handicapped students in low population areas. For example, teacher consultants are effectively transmitted via television programs presented by teacher consultations and ''resource hot lines.'' Telecommunications offers emerging communication and service-delivery alternatives.

SERVICES FOR DEAF-BLIND CHILDREN

It is estimated that 6,117 deaf-blind children are being served nationwide. The percentages of deaf-blind children who have severe and multiple impairments has been recently reported to range from 30% in some states to 96% in others. Half of the states indicated that 50% of deaf-blind children have the range of conditions associated with children exposed to rubella during the 1960s epidemic. Federal categorical funds for deaf-blind children were initiated in response to that epidemic. Project FORUM surveyed 11 states (California, Colorado, Georgia, Massachusetts, Minnesota, Mississippi, Nebraska, New Jersey, North Carolina, Ohio, and South Carolina) to determine past and present state efforts to serve the 1960s ''rubella population.'' The survey found that a decade ago only limited educational and diagnostic services were provided mentally retarded, deaf, or blind children, and in settings that included public and private institutions, residential and hospital facilities, and only occasionally day programs. The services provided were medical and custodial in nature. Today these 11 states report that services have improved owing to several factors, including: federal and state laws requiring the education of handicapped children (including severely handicapped youngsters) in the least restrictive environment; increases in local, state, and federal funds; the targeting of Part B funds for severely handicapped students; and the use of Title VI-C funds for development, demonstration, and dissemination activities. The same states also now report a greater diversity of settings to meet the specific needs of multiply handicapped children, rather than serving such children in distinct programs for deaf-blind individuals. Services now include diagnostic services, infant stimulation, prevocational training, parent training, and occupational/physical therapy. The Project FORUM survey found that during the last 3 to 8 years, deaf-blind children have been moving into less restrictive settings that provide educational opportunities structured to meet their specific combination of handicapping conditions. As a result of the emphasis of teacher training on the more generic population of severely handicapped students and the availability of curricula for severely handicapped students that are readily adaptable to deaf-blind children, separate programs for deaf-blind children have come to be unnecessary and unjustified (Lewis, Note 11).

SPECIFIC STATE INITIATIVES

As this chapter has discussed, in the last decade, states have been engaged in many exemplary efforts to support the integration of severely handicapped children into the public schools as well as to address emerging issues. Among specific actions taken by state education agencies are: first, the gradual adding of consultants specifically responsible for severely handicapped individuals. In 1979, the National Association of State Directors of Special Education (Note 3) reported that 32 state education agencies had such consultants, while 11 did not. Second, legislative and policy changes have occurred. For example, funding incentives have been initiated within state special education finance systems that recognize the added costs of educating severely handicapped students. Federal funds have been used specifically to alleviate priority service needs of severely handicapped students. The 20% discretionary set-aside Title VI-B funds have been critical to the significant strides made by the states in integrating severely handicapped children in the public schools and communities. Within the last 5 years, SEAs have implemented statewide training, development, and demonstration projects to develop state and local structures and mechanism to provide quality services. The author's survey and a study recently completed by Education Turnkey Systems, Inc. (Blaschke, Note 2) have identified such efforts.

Third, many states have developed cooperative statewide training programs with their colleges and universities, for personnel working with severely handi-capped children. For example, since 1977, the state of Washington has contracted with the University of Washington to provide training and technical assistance to professional and paraprofessional service providers working with severely handi-capped students in public and nonpublic school settings. The techniques and procedures utilized by this project were developed by the Center for the Severely Handicapped, a project funded by the then Bureau of Education for the Handicapped from July, 1974 to June, 1980. Two procedures developed at the Center for the Severely Handicapped—the systematic instructional process and the comprehensive educational team approach to service delivery—are the crux of the outreach model. These procedures have proven both effective and adaptable to a variety of settings. The training and technical assistance program has included two summer workshops, during which personnel received intensive training in program procedures; a series of one-day workshops presented around the state on the comprehensive educational team process; and follow-up assistance to selected districts during which project staff provided ongoing training and assistance to school staff in the home sites.

Summaries and descriptions of individual state-implemented programs and services for severely handicapped can be found in sources such as the document "Innovative Projects Serving Severely Handicapped and Deaf-Blind Children and Youth" funded by Title VI-C (OSE, printed December, 1980).

FUTURE CONCERNS AND CHALLENGES

In every state in the nation, educational service delivery models have been and are being developed to educate severely handicapped students in the least restrictive environment. Longitudinal curriculum sequences are being attempted, and instructional programs are being implemented, including needed related services. In recent surveys conducted by the author and others, states have identified future issues and challenges for public school programs for severely handicapped students. Following is a listing of these future concerns:

Funding Concerns

1. Without continued federal support, many LEAs cannot maintain programs.
2. State funding is a critical problem in two-thirds of the states.
3. Funding needs of other social and health agencies compound the present and possible service delivery needs of severely handicapped students.
4. Creative and effective interagency coordination must be implemented.
5. Tightened fiscal resources may result in greater resistance by regular education personnel and the general public to educate severely handicapped children.
6. Funding cutbacks may affect agencies' ability to obtain needed, qualified personnel.
7. Transportation costs will continue to be a concern (e.g., transporting over long distances necessitating additional runs, specialized equipment, bus aides, etc.).

Service Delivery Concerns

1. Given the current economic and political climate, less emphasis may be placed on development of innovative programs, which are essential to the growing body of knowledge regarding effective service delivery to the severely handicapped population.

2. There will be a continued need for competent and qualified personnel.
3. More parent training and support programs will be needed.
4. Problems of rural service delivery will remain a challenge.
5. There is a continuous need for public awareness activities concerning the needs of the severely handicapped population.
6. There will be continued discussion regarding "What is an appropriate education?", "What is treatment versus education?", and "What is the role of the public school?"
7. A strong need exists for alternative living arrangements for severely handicapped adults, as well as for continuous services into adulthood.
8. Issues such as extended school year and related services must be resolved.
9. Adult and continuing education for handicapped individuals must become a priority.
10. Issues surrounding placement of severely handicapped children in the least restrictive environment need resolution.
11. More assessment tools need to be developed.
12. More emphasis must be placed on early childhood intervention and prevention.
13. Staff development is needed.
14. There exists a need for greater use of individualized tutors/interpretors assigned to severely handicapped children.
15. Parent resistance to integration of their severely handicapped child in the public schools remains a concern.
16. Staff burnout is a continuing problem.

States included in the Project FORUM survey discussed earlier in this chapter were also asked to identify problem areas they face and future directions. Preparing students for and assisting in the transition from school to work and alternative living arrangements were reported to be the most critical challenges because of the severely handicapped individuals' extensive need for continuous support. The states also indicated that progress achieved during childhood through provided services will not necessarily continue into adulthood because such services are limited. One state reported that although most deaf-blind students do not reside in institutions, 80% will have to be institutionalized in adulthood because services for older deaf-blind individuals are not available. Specific problems reported included the "lack of demonstrated approaches to providing pre-vocational and vocational training, the reluctance of state vocational rehabilitation agencies to accept deaf-blind youth as clients, and the lack of alternative living arrangements."

Another concern noted was that attempts to develop and provide diverse service options must avoid "dilution in an attempt to accommodate too diverse a range of children within a single setting." States studied indicated that federal support needs to shift from categorical assistance to support that focuses on the severely handicapped population, a shift that is consistent with the change in state delivery systems. Two goals for the future, as identified by the states, include working to ensure continuation of needed state and federal funding for programs and services for severely handicapped individuals, and joining with other social service providers to develop comprehensive and continuous services for this population.

CONCLUSION

Many efforts have been occurring throughout the nation in the federal government, state educational agencies, colleges and universities, local educational agencies, other agencies state, legislatures and in the courts to improve the education of severely handicapped children. The most significant result of these efforts is the number of severely handicapped students who no longer are in state and private institutions receiving only custodial care, but who are integrated into their home communities and schools. The requirements of PL 94-142 and state laws have aided these changes and have drawn attention to related concerns in implementing needed programs and services. This chapter has identified some past and present state initiatives to integrate severely handicapped students in local educational programs, has discussed various state problems, and outlined future programming challenges. The future of quality education for severely handicapped students may be uncertain in light of limited state and federal funds, the unsure future of PL 94-142, and changeable federal and state policies. However, a clear sense of mission and commitment for this population has developed throughout the country as a result of the experiences and successes of the last decade—a dedication that will inevitably prove a source of strength in tackling the goals ahead.

REFERENCES

Brown, L., Nietupski, J. & Hamre-Nietupski, S. The criteria of ultimate functioning and public school services for severely handicapped students. In: A. Thomas (ed.), *Hey, don't forget about me! Education's investment in the severely, profoundly and multiply handicapped.* Reston, VA: The Council for Exceptional Children, 1976.

Crossen, J., et al. Interagency collaboration on full services for handicapped children and youth. Regional Resource Center Task Force on Inter-Agency Collaboration, August, 1979.

Fredericks, B., Baldwin, V., Moore, W., Templeman, Moore, W., Alrick, B., & Wadlow, M. *A data-based classroom for the moderately and severely handicapped* (3rd ed.). Monmouth, OR: Instructional Development Corporation, 1979.

Larsen, L. Issues in the implementation of extended school year programs for handicapped students. *Exceptional Children,* 1981, *47*(4), 256–263.

Makuch, J. Year-round special education and related services: A state director's perspective. *Exceptional Children.* 1981, *47*(4), 272–276.

Mills v. *Board of Education of District of Columbia,* 348 F. Supp. 866 (D.D.C. 1972).

Pennsylvania Association for Retarded Citizens v. *Commonwealth of Pennsylvania,* 343 F. Supp. 279 (E.D.Pa. 1972).

REFERENCE NOTES

1. Thompson, R.P., Wilcox, B. & York, R. The federal program for the severely handicapped: Historical perspective, analysis and overview. In: R. P. Thompson, B. Wilcox, & R. York (eds.), *Overview in quality education for the severely handi-*

capped. The federal investment. Washington, DC: U.S. Department of Education, 1980.

2. Blaschke, D. PL 94-142: *A study of the implementation and impact at the state level.* Washington, DC: Educational Turnkey Systems, 1981.

3. *Special education programs for severely and profoundly handicapped individuals.* Washington, DC: National Association of State Directors of Special Education, 1979.

4. Kurtz, P.D., & Lamb, K. *Finding and screening children in rural areas: Finding a needle in a haystack.* Paper presented to the annual meeting of the Council for Exceptional Children, New York, April, 1977.

5. David, J.L., & Greene, D. *Organizational barriers to full implementation of PL 94-142.* Unpublished manuscript, Stanford University, Stanford, CA, 1980.

6. Helge, D., & Marrs, L. W. *Recruitment and retention in rural america.* In: D. Helge & L. W. Marrs (eds.), *A national problem: Recruitment and retention of specialized personnel in rural areas.* Murray, KY: Murray State University, 1981.

7. Schrag, J.A. *A study of special education manpower.* Unpublished paper. Idaho State Department of Education, 1979.

8. Meyen, E. *Comments on the three R's: Recruitment and retention in rural areas.* In: D. Helge & L. W. Marrs (eds.), *A national problem: Recruitment and retention of specialized personnel in rural areas.* Murray, KY: Murray State University, 1981.

9. Ross, J.W. *Third party payments for related services: Policy issues and implications for handicapped students.* Reston, VA: The Council for Exceptional Children, 1980.

10. Schrag, J.A., Farago, L., & Walker, L. *Education of handicapped children in rural areas.* Unpublished paper. Idaho State Department of Education, 1979.

11. Lewis, L.M. Selected issues in service delivery to deaf/blind children. *Forum.* National Association of State Directors of Special Education, Washington, DC, July, 1981.

14

Implementing the
Integration
Principle of
PL 94-142

Dave Rostetter,
Ron Kowalski, and Dawn Hunter

In an era of declining enrollments, financial austerity, eroding confidence in public schools, and rapid technological changes in our society, educational institutions and organizations are being challenged as never before to adjust and adapt. The message is clear: If public schools fail to adapt to the social, economic, and educational demands of the communities, consumers, and clients they serve, a drastic restructuring of public education could result. At all levels, initiatives to cut social programs and to support increased voluntary participation in nonpublic schools with public funds are growing. These initiatives, if one believes the arguments presented by public educators and their constituent support groups, will threaten the basic foundation of public education, which has until recently prospered over its 150-year history. Clearly, today's public education, including education for handicapped students, cannot continue to prosper if it is based solely upon parochial interests.

Among the multiple factors that will influence the future growth and health of

---

Opinions expressed in this volume do not necessarily reflect the positions or policies of the U.S. Department of Education or the University of Maryland, Department of Special Education, and no official endorsement by those departments should be inferred.

public education, undoubtedly a major determinant will be how well education prepares all learners—handicapped and nonhandicapped—to gain entry, grow, and thrive in our rapidly changing social, economic, and political environments. Who, if anyone, is responsible for public education? The specific constitutional responsibility for education rests first with the states. However, in a democracy such as ours, there is a legitimate and critical need for a federal role—a legitimacy that is framed in the U.S. Constitution and validated by the courts, and a necessity based on the difficulty of otherwise achieving qualitatively significant equal education.

This chapter describes the issues associated with educating severely handicapped students with their nonhandicapped peers. The chapter is organized into four sections: 1) background issues, 2) problems encountered, 3) analysis of the integration principle, and 4) synthesis. The background section briefly summarizes the legal and educational underpinnings of the integration imperative (Gilhool & Stuttman, 1978) that was established in Public Law (PL) 94-142 as the mandated response to educating handicapped children. The problems section examines difficulties resulting from the perceptions, events, and circumstances of those involved (legislators, administrators, teachers, parents, students, etc.) in implementing the integration imperative through the least restrictive environment (LRE) clause of PL 94-142. The analysis section describes a logical framework for LRE as a basis for identifying and describing problems encountered by relevant participants in the educational process, their roles and responsibilities, and their interrelationships. The synthesis section discusses the particular perspective each participant group brings to the LRE issue and uses the logical framework introduced in the analysis section to integrate all participant information across LRE-related characteristics.

BACKGROUND ISSUES

The Supreme Court of the United States in *Brown* v. *Board of Education* (1954) decreed that all children were to be guaranteed equal educational opportunity. At the core of equal education opportunity is the belief that individuals in our society have a right to opportunities that result in successful participation within the fabric of society and that lead to economic independence.

The history of segregating handicapped children and of denying them opportunities to obtain an education has resulted in litigation affirming the rights of handicapped children to an education on equal terms with nonhandicapped children. The foundation for the development of a right to education for handicapped children is based on the *Brown* decision as directly extended by two federal court cases argued on behalf of handicapped children—*PARC* v. *Commonwealth of Pennsylvania*, 1972, and *Mills* v. *Board of Education of District of Columbia*, 1972.

Although this litigation, and subsequent federal legislation, including PL 94-142 and Section 504 of the Rehabilitation Act of 1973, ensured education for all handicapped children, the result for severely handicapped students generally

has been education in segregated settings. Only in two recent court cases—
Campbell v. *Talladega Board of Education*, 1981, and *Fialkowski* v. *Shapp*,
1975—has integrated education, that is, education of severely handicapped
students in the same buildings as nonhandicapped students, specifically been
ordered.

PL 94-142 mandates that each state adopt a policy that makes a free
appropriate public education available to all handicapped children in the least
restrictive environment. An important consideration in designing an appropriate
education for any severely handicapped child is the provision of specially designed
instructional content and related services (i.e., those services that are determined
to be necessary in order for a child to benefit from special education). Another
significant criterion of an appropriate educational placement is that these services
be provided, to the maximum extent possible, in settings shared with nonhandicapped students (i.e., to fulfill the integration imperative). The dual considerations of educational content and integration logically should lead to new
service options for severely handicapped students. Yet it is tempting to conclude
from the current pattern of segregation of severely handicapped students in most
public schools that placements are made on the basis of where appropriate services
(i.e., content) currently exist, without regard for the equally important criterion of
integration.

The overall problem, needs, educational goals for, and the basis for action in
regard to educating handicapped individuals were addressed in PL 94-142 and
Section 504 of the Rehabilitation Act of 1973, and may be summarized as follows:

PROBLEM   Isolation of handicapped children and adults in institutions and
    other types of segregated facilities solely designed to separate these
    individuals from society; the unavailabilitay of medical, social, and
    educational services; the existence of architectural barriers in most
    community settings that deny access to buildings and programs avail-
    able to the general population

NEED   Services for several million handicapped children who previously
    had been excluded from participation in school and who had not been
    receiving the services needed to successfully participate in integrated
    community schools with their nonhandicapped peers

GOALS   To recognize and support the right of handicapped children to
    equal educational opportunities (educational opportunities being the
    means for the individual to successfully live and work in normalized
    settings as a productive member of an integrated society)

BASIS FOR ACTION   An awakening of public interest in millions of
    handicapped children and youth who had been isolated and forgotten;
    incorporation of the major principles of the right to education litigation,
    including the requirement that states establish procedures to ensure that
    handicapped children, to the maximum extent appropriate, are educated
    in an integrated setting with their nonhandicapped peers; recognition by
    Congress that the government's policy could no longer be that of merely

establishing an unenforceable goal, and that henceforth the government had to take positive steps to ensure that the rights of handicapped children and their families were protected

Simply stated, central to PL 94-142 and Section 504 was the recognition that if handicapped children were to be successful participants in society, including the opportunity to be economically independent, then the opportunity for education would have to include integration with nonhandicapped peers in educational and community activities.

PROBLEMS ENCOUNTERED

Current economic realities have forced a review and restructuring of the federal role in education. "Reaganomics," in addition to the current administration's plans to dismantle the U.S. Department of Education and to establish educational blockgrants to states, the cutting of social programs in general, and the existence of large deficits, all these factors contribute to a new national awareness of the needs of handicapped children and the limited services available to meet those needs in ways consistent with the integration imperative. The cooperative partnerships developed between federal, state, and local education officials have in the past several years significantly improved educational opportunities for handicapped children and their families. However, disparities still exist between the number of children eligible for service and those actually receiving a free appropriate public education (General Accounting Office, 1981).

Number of Handicapped Children Served

Nationally, the number of children enrolled in public schools is declining and is expected to continue declining for the next several years. However, the number of handicapped children who receive special education services has increased 4% over the past year and 13% over the past 5 years (U.S. Department of Education, 1982). In 1976, 3,708,588 handicapped children were reported served by the states participating in Public Law 94-142. By 1981 the number had increased by almost 500,000 more students to 4,189,478 children (see Table 1). This number still falls short of the 8,000,000 handicapped children Congress believed were living in the United States and were being excluded from school participation or not receiving an education to meet their individual needs when PL 94-142 was enacted.

Setting Where Handicapped Children Are Served

Consistently from 1976 to 1979, the number of handicapped children served in separate schools and other more restricted environments decreased measurably. However, in 1980 the trend was reversed, with increasing numbers of handicapped children being placed in segregated, separate facilities apart from their non-handicapped peers (see Table 2) (U. S. Department of Education, 1982). When asked to explain the increased numbers of handicapped children in separate facilities, states reported to Special Education Programs (SEP) that several factors were involved: 1) reporting errors; 2) the local educational system is now serving children previously served by other state agencies (e.g., correctional facilities); and 3) parental pressure for placement in private schools.

Cost of Special Education

Increases in costs, attributed to the rising number of handicapped children receiving services and the personnel needed to serve them, are a major concern of legislators, school board members, administrators, taxpayers, and parents of school-age children. Because of schools' financial methods and accounting procedures, it is difficult to determine the exact cost of special education programming. However, special education finance studies (Rossmiller & Frohreich, 1979) have produced correlative findings demonstrating that: 1) the cost of special education varies considerably within any given category of handicapped condition; and 2) the cost of special education programming is not related closely to the quality of the program, nor is it a good predictor of student achievement.

In general, the cost of special education is about three times that of regular education, with average costs being approximately $1,399 per nonhandicapped student versus $3,794 per handicapped student (Reger, Note 1). During the current period of financial stringency, cost information is extremely important in order to most effectively utilize available dollars. The competition for limited resources inevitably will result in cutbacks for the educational community in general and services to handicapped children specifically. However, such competition is only intensified when separate services, and, in the case of severely handicapped students, separate facilities are maintained. If severely handicapped students are integrated into regular schools, and if their education is made the responsibility of regular school principals, then requests for resources may evolve into school-wide requests, and not requests based solely on the needs of a particular subpopulation.

Placement Options and Availability of Services

In order to more appropriately serve severely handicapped children, local education agencies (LEAs) should make alternative placements available to provide handicapped children with services that match their individual, structural, and related service needs. Severely handicapped students require a broad variety of intensive educational services. Unfortunately, these *services* have often been equated automatically with placement in separate facilities in a school district or in residential settings (Science Research Institute, International, 1981). Rarely is the portability of services for severely handicapped students considered without pressure from the courts or parents. Public schools should provide a continuum of alternative placements for severely handicapped students, with a strong emphasis on education in self-contained classes in the same schools as age-appropriate nonhandicapped peers, as well as planned interactions. If a true continuum of services were operational, and if services were considered portable, then examination of public schools throughout the country would be expected to show that: 1) in accordance with the integration imperative of PL 94-142, *most* severely

Table 1. Number of children ages 3–21 years served under PL 89-313 and PL 94-142, by handicapping condition, during school year 1980–1981

State	Speech impaired	Learning disabled	Mentally retarded	Emotionally disturbed
Alabama	15,079	18,373	34,840	3,961
Alaska	2,849	5,767	745	288
Arizona	11,247	24,423	6,592	4,959
Arkansas	12,117	16,303	17,449	535
California	95,177	149,094	39,714	30,178
Colorado	9,954	22,446	6,423	6,547
Connecticut	15,908	27,105	7,940	12,287
Delaware	2,085	6,460	2,405	2,687
District of Columbia	2,136	1,517	1,318	724
Florida	42,270	51,579	27,978	13,525
Georgia	27,541	31,823	30,021	16,395
Hawaii	1,369	7,527	1,807	402
Idaho	3,823	7,992	2,758	522
Illinois	80,480	71,711	51,626	32,094
Indiana	43,476	22,186	26,666	2,441
Iowa	15,782	25,771	12,643	4,025
Kansas	13,301	14,370	7,413	3,061
Kentucky	24,278	16,683	23,177	2,160
Louisiana	22,911	30,392	19,164	5,164
Maine	5,957	7,811	5,200	4,446
Maryland	26,443	50,041	11,060	3,445
Massachusetts	40,959	35,311	26,834	24,098
Michigan	48,937	48,925	29,882	19,618
Minnesota	21,189	36,448	14,239	4,503
Mississippi	14,847	11,223	18,593	369
Missouri	33,376	34,347	22,076	6,578
Montana	4,081	5,919	1,615	479
Nebraska	9,371	11,512	6,610	1,655
Nevada	3,022	6,011	1,217	449
New Hampshire	1,774	6,806	1,787	1,086
New Jersey	64,131	51,316	16,537	14,974
New Mexico	5,157	11,925	3,139	1,976
New York	41,994	44,550	41,675	45,797
North Carolina	26,347	40,830	39,986	4,550
North Dakota	3,148	3,624	1,809	252
Ohio	63,783	67,069	62,682	5,164
Oklahoma	19,379	27,253	13,372	689
Oregon	11,580	21,476	5,518	2,450
Pennsylvania	71,851	52,792	49,202	13,911
Puerto Rico	1,108	1,486	13,062	2,073
Rhode Island	3,368	10,333	1,974	1,166
South Carolina	19,174	17,887	24,941	5,256
South Dakota	4,993	2,512	1,260	330
Tennessee	32,339	30,355	21,945	2,814
Texas	67,702	130,772	28,608	13,463
Utah	7,369	12,879	3,194	9,698
Vermont	2,490	4,687	3,100	436

(continued)

Other health impaired	Ortho-paedically impaired	Multi-handi-capped	Deaf and hard of hearing	Visually handi-capped	Deaf and blind	Total
728	424	1,254	431	481	63	76,310
98	179	104	106	33	24	10,363
646	1,115	874	430	870	8	51,202
333	496	765	324	312	18	49,096
31,307	12,852	0	1,069	2,716	274	368,227
0	788	1,205	157	350	42	48,577
1,171	652	0	354	654	0	67,072
72	286	19	178	130	32	14,416
139	223	100	22	66	38	6,308
2,536	1,776	1,887	656	806	76	144,532
1,450	684	1,193	569	809	31	111,981
4	248	244	117	70	23	12,018
223	413	482	195	191	44	16,832
2,479	4,632	3,207	3,049	2,190	165	253,891
159	851	1,211	639	518	42	98,916
5	772	659	268	282	53	61,044
412	343	673	318	252	57	40,637
890	767	1,182	448	438	125	70,693
1,298	628	938	918	477	34	82,723
380	347	839	142	134	59	25,638
1,496	1,003	2,544	485	692	34	98,682
5,651	282	534	647	1,131	282	141,580
7	4,362	54	282	1,071	0	155,988
1,417	1,232	9	181	435	21	80,986
3	372	163	339	251	31	46,495
842	837	1,278	260	409	78	101,076
112	107	603	134	185	13	13,424
0	434	269	179	202	0	30,740
257	190	353	4	84	10	11,786
191	127	264	181	224	5	12,525
1,963	1,655	4,108	437	1,392	69	158,469
55	266	845	175	200	6	24,030
38,395	7,027	3,134	2,456	2,209	45	230,093
986	1,127	2,126	1,054	768	43	119,018
27	134	146	66	75	24	9,426
0	3,394	1,996	179	1,005	93	207,875
368	396	840	298	352	33	63,547
481	973	122	1,169	571	24	44,809
273	2,229	758	1,179	2,138	11	198,108
467	1,787	1,835	195	1,779	7	25,333
178	200	127	89	62	19	17,577
72	860	428	312	527	25	69,973
25	165	333	105	49	13	10,138
1,400	1,100	1,725	349	724	11	95,168
3,428	3,120	22,011	3,983	1,629	540	276,050
177	243	1,279	431	302	25	35,898
170	297	465	100	124	11	12,091

(continued)

Table 1. *(continued)*

State	Speech impaired	Learning disabled	Mentally retarded	Emotionally disturbed
Virginia	32,109	33,391	18,425	6,079
Washington	14,751	27,292	10,794	5,191
West Virginia	10,823	10,995	11,508	1,004
Wisconsin	16,986	25,628	14,668	8,575
Wyoming	3,100	4,947	1,050	767
American Samoa	3	108	69	0
Guam	444	346	919	65
Northern Marianas	0	104	11	0
Trust Territories	222	1,115	23	35
Virgin Islands	25	39	156	35
Bureau of Indian Affairs	869	2,393	612	224
U.S. and Territories	1,176,984	1,444,080	850,031	355,655

Produced by ED/OSE Data Analysis System (DANS), August 11, 1981.

handicapped students were being educated in age-appropriate integrated settings; and 2) a *small* number of severely handicapped students were being served in a variety of nonintegrated settings due to specific, occasionally temporary and extenuating personal needs not common to the majority of the severely handicapped population. However, since the vast majority of severely handicapped students are now served in segregated schools, then it can be assumed that public schools do *not* recognize that services are portable, and that the integration imperative is not being adequately addressed for this population.

Certainly progress has been made in providing services to handicapped children in general, as reflected in the work of administrators, teachers, and parents who are beginning to master the complex and challenging task of developing systems and plans that respond to the needs of such children. Yet, regardless of the overall progress, only one placement option, segregation, predominates for severely handicapped students. Although severely handicapped students are no longer typically educated in institutional settings, the implementation of PL 94-142 has done little so far to end the wholesale isolation of this population. Since public schools generally do not utilize a variety of placement options for severely handicapped students, it is tempting to conclude that placement is not individualized for these students.

Table 2. Number of handicapped children ages 3–21 receiving special education and related services by educational environments from school year 1976–77 to 1979–80

Types of Educational Environments	School years			
	1976–77	1977–78	1978–79	1979–80
Separate schools	212,632	181,361	149,678	212,021
Other	99,273	75,332	69,389	70,893

Source: U.S. Department of Education, Office of Special Education and Rehabilitative Services (1982).

Other health impaired	Ortho-paedically impaired	Multi-handi-capped	Deaf and hard of hearing	Visually handi-capped	Deaf and blind	Total
483	799	3,132	387	1,860	65	97,972
1,474	857	1,411	271	396	62	63,368
852	356	334	180	253	1	36,573
530	1,079	650	256	451	46	69,957
216	170	328	48	53	16	10,843
0	4	9	0	2	4	220
0	3	161	98	34	14	2,085
0	3	17	0	2	1	154
79	35	110	0	59	28	1,917
0	27	17	4	0	9	312
25	33	302	0	25	2	4,630
106,430	65,761	71,656	26,903	33,004	2,929	4,189,478

Summary of Problems

The concept of LRE has presented innumerable and far-reaching opportunities for the state and local education agencies. It is clear from the preceding discussion that the concept of LRE permeates the entire fabric of education under PL 94-142. The policies, procedures, structures, and attitudes of all those individuals involved in education are crucial to the successful implementation of the LRE concept. The problems associated with implementing the LRE integration imperative, along with potential solutions, are summarized below.

Problems:

1. Additional ancillary service staff may be needed.
2. Effective, well-planned inservice education will be needed for regular and special education personnel.
3. Due to lack of exposure, the community may see no need for (or may fear) integration.
4. Some buildings may require architectural adaptations.
5. Parents whose children have experienced only segregated education, with its presumed protective environment, may fear integrated settings.
6. In some states, policies, regulations, and funding patterns may present impediments to integration.
7. The high visibility of special education programs may result in unnecessary attention to simple problems that occur during transition to integrated services.
8. Due to the slow learning rate of severely handicapped students, their progress resulting from integration may be difficult to document within the time frame needed to convince school officials of the value of the approach.
9. Separate administrative structures for special education and regular education initially may impede joint efforts.

Solutions:

1. Comprehensive planning for integration at the state, district, and school building levels must be provided for.
2. The federal funding formula must be rendered consistent with and reinforce the implementation of integrated services within the states.
3. The principal participants in the transition to integrated services must perceive a uniform meaning and application of LRE.
4. States must identify and reinforce successful models of integrated services.
5. Active technical assistance for training and follow-up must be provided to districts by the states.

It is not enough for legislators, school board members, administrators, and teachers to be ideologically committed to educating handicapped children in the least restrictive environment. This commitment must now be translated into implementation strategies and plans that will result in effective education that meets the integration requirement of the law; that produces cost savings through better use of staff, space, and instructional time; and that reduces the need for extensive, unnecessary transportation arrangements.

ANALYSIS OF INTEGRATION PRINCIPLE

As noted earlier, the integration principle, as reflected in the LRE clause of PL 94-142, is basic to the provision of education for handicapped and non-handicapped students alike. The relevant requirements are as follows:

1. That to the maximum extent appropriate, handicapped children, including children in public or private institutions or other care facilities, are educated with children who are not handicapped; and
2. That special classes, separate schooling, or other removal of handicapped children from the regular educational environment occurs only when the nature or severity of the handicap is such that education in regular classes with the use of supplementary aids and services cannot be achieved satisfactorily (*Federal Register*, 1977, p. 42497).

Implementing the integration principle in field settings has proven difficult and confusing for the agencies responsible—that is, the state education agency (SEA) and the local education agency (LEA). Major areas of concern appear to be:

1. Confusion in reconciling LRE as a legal concept and LRE as an educational concept
2. Lack of standard practices in defining and describing the many facets of LRE that can serve as guideposts for implementation
3. Conflicting ideas between professionals, consumers, parents, and students about the meaning of LRE

Logic of Analytical Framework

In order to facilitate a better understanding of LRE, a framework is here delineated that helps to explain the problems associated with implementing the integration principle in field settings from the viewpoints of the various participants involved (i.e., legislators, school board members, administrators, teachers, community groups, parents, and students).

This framework is a systems approach, based upon the premise that LRE can best be defined within the context of comparing it with its bipolar opposite, segregation. As a systems approach, the framework assumes that knowledge observed and described within any component of the integration issue (i.e., subsystem) can best be interpreted and/or explained if one understands the whole system. Accordingly, the educational system is defined here as the total organization and structure of service delivery within a *state*. Each state service delivery system comprises the sum of a number of integrated parts that interact to produce desired results. In this way systems are unitary, interconnected, and purposeful.

The logical framework must include an understanding of the following three placement categories:

1. *Integration:* Provision of educational services to severely handicapped students that meet the minimum requirement of the LRE clause of PL 94-142, that is, the provision of individual education in regular schools with daily planned systematic exposure to and interaction with nonhandicapped peers.
2. *Neutral:* Placement of severely handicapped students in the same school as nonhandicapped students without interaction between the two groups.
3. *Segregation:* Provision of educational services to severely handicapped students that do not meet the minimum requirement of the LRE clause of PL 94-142, that is, the provision of individual education in settings including only handicapped students, without daily planned systematic exposure to and interaction with nonhandicapped peers.

It should be noted that the key factor in the *integration* definition is planned systematic exposure and interactions with nonhandicapped peers. As such, one could argue theoretically that a severely handicapped student could be educated in a segregated school but brought daily to a regular school or vice versa to meet the interaction/exposure criteria in the *integration* definition. In addition, from an interaction perspective one could argue that a placement that meets the *neutral* definition also meets the *segregation* definition. However, as a general rule, interaction with nonhandicapped peers is more easily achieved when severely handicapped students attend the same school as their nonhandicapped peers.

Logically Category 1, integration, represents the rational approach to integrating persons from a systems perspective, whereas Category 3, segregation, represents the irrational approach. Integration is envisioned as the most reasonable and rational approach to LRE, based upon its strong constitution, legal, and research foundation. (Gilhool & Stuttman, 1978; Talley, Elting, Chobot, Oliver, & Raimondi, 1979).

Identification of Participants

From this initial logical position of Category 1, the framework may be used to analyze and compare the direction taken by the various groups involved in implementing the integration principle in field settings. These groups include:

1. Clients—learners (severely handicapped and nonhandicapped individuals)
2. Consumers—parents
3. Community—taxpayers and patrons of the system
4. Professionals—administrators and teachers
5. Government—legislators and school board members

By studying the discrepancies in the meaning of integration for each group, problems associated with implementing the integration principle may be illuminated and possibilities developed for arriving at a consensus for rational action.

In the systems approach, the concept of "rationality" is seen as the underlying foundation for the integration principle; thus, implementing the integration principle is the rational response to the LRE clause of PL 94-142 for all handicapped and nonhandicapped children. As the rational position, it is both reasonable and desirable. Most individuals would agree that handicapped children should be integrated with nonhandicapped children to the maximum extent appropriate; however, the course of implementation as related to individual districts, schools, and children is a major source of conflict. In an analysis of child complaints by Special Education Programs (SEP), approximately half of the complaints received from October, 1980, to September, 1981, were alleged violations of PL 94-142 with respect to placement, the setting where children received a free appropriate education. Implementing LRE has been and continues to be a highly charged issue in states.

As mentioned above, Category 1, integration, is considered the rational approach, and Category 3, segregation, the irrational position from a systems perspective. Often an individual or group response taken alone or within a particular subcomponent of a system may be seen as rational, that is, reasonable and desirable. However, when viewed from the larger system context, it may be regarded as irrational. It is the hope of the authors that the logical framework presented here will assist those involved in the educational process to view their beliefs, roles, responsibilities, personal and professional behavior, and attitudes within the larger system context.

For example, from the perspective of a severely handicapped student (i.e., the client), one interpretation of integration could be a setting where the least number of physical barriers to participating in educational activities exists. The professional (e.g., administrator), however, may see this as an unnecessarily restrictive view, in that facilities may have to be modified or diversified to accommodate the full range of handicapping conditions. For some administrators integration may be equated with an undiversified facility that requires few alterations, on the assumption that if populations are required to be mixed then they must have the same needs. The point here is that what is viewed as restrictive is idiosyncratic with the group concerned and often is synonymous with the placement option that causes the most work, discomfort, or inconvenience for the group responding. For severely handicapped students and their parents, LRE is usually equated with a socially and physically barrier-free regular school because of the integration potential present through equal access to nonhandicapped students. For the administrator, LRE may equal any barrier-free school, including a segregated setting, since equal access to facilities is considered without regard for its correlated purpose of equal access to nonhandicapped students and normalized expectations.

Roles of Participants

Among the many participants involved in interpreting the integration imperative for severely handicapped students in the states are, first, the state governors, who usually control education by preparing budget proposals, approving bills on education, appointing state advisory board members, and by general administrative leadership. Legislators are also key participants, as they have absolute power under state constitutions to organize, structure, and maintain educational programs within their borders. Actions of legislators must thus be reasonable and consistent with state and federal constitutions. In the judicial area, judges interpret law passed by legislators. Decisions made in individual and class-action cases set precedents for interpreting the state's laws, rules, and regulations regarding severely handicapped individuals.

School board members are involved in directing the overall educational program by formulating policies and procedures, and approving personnel and budget recommendations. Since board actions must be consistent with state law, boards of education act as agents of the state in assuring that minimum requirements for mandatory education are met.

Superintendents are involved primarily in implementing the policies and procedures formulated and adapted by state boards of education. They are responsible for the day-to-day operations of the school system and act as instructional leaders for all staff. Increasingly, the superintendent as an instructional leader is involved in liaison activities with the community-at-large in order to obtain support for the educational program. The superintendent's "spokesperson" in each school is the principal, who implements board policy and procedures at the building level. Just as the superintendent is the instructional leader for the district, the principal is the instructional leader for the school. The role of the principal takes on additional importance in the coordination and quality control of instruction by virtue of his or her proximity to the classrooms and students. Teachers provide direct instruction to students who reside in the district, using teaching methods that are sometimes prescribed and at other times are left to the discretion of the teacher. Ideally, the instruction provided should be consistent with the curriculum adopted by the board of education, as described in the official curriculum guide for each respective grade level.

Other service providers, such as psychologists, speech therapists, occupational therapists, and physical therapists are involved in providing educational instruction and/or related services consistent with standards formerly approved by the state board of education. This group is significant when discussing appropriate educational services for severely handicapped learners.

Taxpayers/patrons are involved in the educational process by electing a governor, legislators, school board members, and, sometimes, superintendents who share an ideology consistent with their own. In some cases the taxpayers are asked to write and vote on bond issues that serve educational purposes. All taxpayers benefit from educational programs in local districts in varying degrees either directly or indirectly.

Parents, as taxpayers/patrons, are involved either directly or indirectly, in education. More importantly, parents as advocates for their children's welfare in both schools and the community, now and in the future, benefit directly from the opportunity for public education.

Students are involved as clients or direct recipients of instruction. If the curriculum is the intended plan for students, the students (or often in the case of severely handicapped individuals, their parents) must view the curriculum as that which is intended for them in their courses and classes. Implicit in curriculum and instruction under PL 94-142 is that children bring with them different experiences, knowledge, and skills that must form the basis for instruction, if instruction is to be truly individualized for that child. Therefore, a severely handicapped student's needs must be integrated into the general goals of the system's curriculum. In addition it must be recognized that beyond the written curriculum, children are the recipients of a host of unintended learning experiences in public schools, all of which become part of what the behavioral sciences call the socialization process for the child. It furthermore appears that the socialization process of public school education significantly facilitates students' successful participation in society as adults.

From the systems approach perspective, it is important to note that each participant has defined roles and responsibilities within that system. Operating policies and procedures define the type of interaction within and between organizations and participants at the local, state, and federal levels. Each system has both formal and informal levels of operation, with each participant contributing his or her unique knowledge, skills, experience, and attitudes. For the purposes of this chapter the ultimate goal or purpose of the system is that children, handicapped and nonhandicapped, be able to participate successfully in society in the communities where they reside (i.e., integration) and achieve economic independence to the maximum extent possible. For severely handicapped children this, at a minimum, means a genuine opportunity for education to be delivered longitudinally in integrated settings.

Relationship of the Participants

Two major assumptions regarding the relationship of participants significantly influence the implementation of the integration principle:

1. Successful implementation of the integration principle requires proactive responses by those in government and leadership positions at each level (i.e., local, state, and federal), including every service provider involved in public education (Gideonse, 1978).

2. The structure and organizational arrangements and patterns of the public education system directly influence the settings, types of services, and quality of staff provided to integrate children.

In spite of the legislation, regulations and policy statements currently in place in the states delegate the responsibility for implementing the integration principle to special educators and their staff, who are not in the proper position, and do not have the authority or organizational status to primarily influence the overall implementation of the integration principle. Never before has the need been more critical to seriously analyze and assist the current organizational structure and its impact on service delivery to handicapped students. According to the systems perspective described here, organization is defined as: the individuals in a system who perform distinct but interrelated and coordinated roles and functions to produce clearly articulated outcomes through communication, decision making, and mutual influence.

The pertinent participant relationships can be discussed by delineating their roles in terms of a system's policy position. Policy in this case is defined as: assistance in articulating problems, reviewing alternatives, and selecting the most appropriate course of action to solve a problem. Policy in its general sense serves as a guide in meeting a system's goals (i.e., programmatic statements for learners). Participant relationships are defined here in terms of four related policy position categories: 1) policy development, 2) policy implementation, 3) policy consumption, and 4) policy recipients.

Policy influences are not discussed in this section directly because it is the authors' belief that all categories influence policy in degrees dependent upon their organizational structure and arrangement. In its broadest sense, policy influences are better understood and explained under the heading of *politics,* discussed later in the chapter.

Policy Development

Legislators and school board members are most often referred to as policy developers. The relationship of the other participants discussed above is defined by the structure and measure of a group's influence. For example, parents, students, and community members elect and to some degree influence legislators. They also may participate in local board meetings. Increasingly, administrators and teacher organizations are attempting to maximize their influence. Policy formulation is decided by those with delegated authority by virtue of their position within the larger system. Decisions at this level have the greatest impact on the goals of education, particularly the implementation of the integration principle.

Policy Implementation

Educational administrators at the state, local, and school levels are delegated the authority to execute, administer, supervise, and coordinate systems policies and procedures adopted and approved by legislators and school board members. By virtue of their day-to-day involvement in the operations of the system, administrators could be said to have the greatest influence. Parents are involved to the extent that they participate in structured planning activities or attempt to resolve specific issues related to the future needs of their children, such as courses and classes. Parental involvement at this level is individual in nature and leads to resolution of issues that have minimum system-wide impact. If a group of parents is involved, the impact may be broader. However, it is at this level where future problems may be initially identified. The type and magnitude of the problem will determine the administrative group or groups—board members, legislators, judges—that will be required to solve the problem.

Policy Consumption

Taxpayers, patrons, and parents are included in this group, in addition to those policy formulators and implementors who are often concerned with implementation procedures and results, including cost, but who lack specific authority to carry out the system's roles and functions. As long as participants are satisfied with implementation, their involvement with developers and implementors is limited to routine interaction. When groups identify problems, action is taken between and among groups influencing policy and decision making. The power of these individuals or groups is measured by their relative ability to influence the system. Any single group can be influential, depending upon the stance taken by other groups. For example, parents often advocate more and better services for their children; however, the cost of these services sometimes causes other groups to counter these proposals. Policy consumption differences are usually resolved by legislators or boards of education.

Policy Recipients

Students, as the individuals most affected by the policies of an educational system, are most often identified as recipients. The goals of a school system are defined by student learning. The foundation for this learning is the formal curriculum that is adopted and approved by the board of education and that is also consistent with state laws and regulations. Many policies and procedures approved by the system are *enabling* policies, that is, they do not deal directly with learning but represent the means by which a system delivers educational services, certification of staff, and related services. Interestingly, students, although they are the primary recipients of the system, in general are perceived as having the least influence on the system because of the limited power they wield.

Summary

This section has presented a systems approach as a logical framework for understanding the integration principle from a total educational viewpoint. In reality special education is only a small part of the total system. It is critical, then, that the participants involved communicate their concerns regarding the integration of severely handicapped children with nonhandicapped children within the larger framework of education.

SYNTHESIS

Situational Context for Participants

This chapter has so far emphasized that problems associated with implementing the integration principle occur within the context of the larger system, in which identified participants at each level of the system have defined roles and responsibilities within the organizational structure. Organizations, policies, and procedures often define the interaction of the participants at each level. However, the system operates on both formal and informal levels, with participants contributing their unique experiences, knowledge, skills, and attitudes.

Descriptors of the System

The manner in which a system operates overall is dependent upon its key characteristics—as determined by the participants discussed above. These key characteristics, or descriptors of the system, are not exclusive of each other but are integrally related. The meaning of integration yields conflicting system characteristics, depending on the context and the participants' role. The characteristics are as follows:

1. *Ideology:* The body of ideas reflecting the social needs and aspirations of an individual or group.
2. *Politics:* The process by which society identifies its problems, reviews alternatives, identifies priorities, selects solutions, and allocates resources.
3. *Organization and Structure:* The system or method used to divide and assign work and the mechanisms to control and coordinate the activities of those who do the work.
4. *Organization and Structure of Special Education:* A structure subsumed under that of the larger educational system, but a unique structure that has evolved separately from regular education.
5. *Placement Settings:* The number, quantity, and kind of educational placements sufficient to meet the needs of all handicapped children who reside in the system. Multiple placement options must be available. Although placement decisions are made on an individual basis, placement in regular education settings is appropriate and preferred. Justification for removal from regular education settings is required. A system for serving children that effectively accounts for individual differences is implied; segregation is not implied.
6. *Availability of Services:* All services available to nonhandicapped students must be available to severely handicapped students. Special education and related services must be available to all severely handicapped children in accordance with their individual education program (IEP) reflecting their unique needs.
7. *Curriculum:* The formally adopted and approved statement of intended learning that the school district outlines for students in the system. Cur-

riculum statements are usually programmatic statements of the knowledge and abilities to which students should be exposed; they define learning.

8. *Instruction:* The teaching methods adopted and approved by the school board and used by teachers to influence student learning. Instructional techniques, programs, and practices are often defined at the district level. The degree of professional discretion regarding the modes of instruction is a current issue in the teaching profession.

9. *Learning:* Incremental changes in what the student knows, feels, and can do. If the teacher presents information a student already knows, the requirement for learning is not met. Implicit in this definition of learning is that instruction must be individualized for each student, based upon the skills the student needs in order to grow and become an economically independent member of the community.

10. *Accountability:* The method or procedure assisting system users to determine whether a system's goals are being met, whether a system's components are working together, and any problems that exist in serving clients. Accountability mechanisms assure answers to questions of who, what, how, and how much you know.

Remaining sections of this chapter use the systems framework to show, through situational contexts, how the various participants view integration and segregation. This analysis is based on the assumption that all behavior of participants is purposeful, but not always equally conscious (consciousness in this case implies a knowledge of the larger system as well as the antecedents and consequences of behavior in that system).

Before beginning the analysis, the role of segregation in the system needs to be clarified. Although there is general confusion surrounding the concept of integration, segregation can be viewed as the extreme opposite of any placement used to define integration. Segregation is absolute. The issue for us educators in the larger system is to define where we are in relation to the bipolar opposites, integration and segregation, and to begin to adjust our responses toward the more rational approach of integration.

It is possible to explore positions on the continuum from integration to the neutral position and then finally to segregation. The neutral environment can be constructed, as discussed earlier, as a position that merely removes the restrictions but does not accomplish integration through interactions. The neutral position assumes minimal effort on the part of participants, such as administrators and teachers and is not considered proactive (a requirement for integration, i.e., actively planned interaction). Integration requires comprehensive systematic planning efforts with the full support of leadership in all segments of the educational community. For integration to be fully operational, an approach must be defined that goes beyond neutral positions. In order to arrive at such an approach the following sections delineate the conceptions of integration that the various participants bring to the issue, based upon their context within the larger system.

Logical Framework Applied to Government Participants

Situational Context Implementation of the LRE is based upon a set of beliefs and assumptions central to our country's founding. It is only in the last few decades, however, that we have moved toward equal opportunity (integration) for all citizens, as reflected in legislative and judicial action. More recent action by governing bodies has made discrimination illegal and integration of social policy a goal in our human rights agenda. Passage of such legislation was prompted, and has been followed, by social unrest, with the schools a primary target of implementation policies. Although there is considerable agreement regarding the worthiness of the integration ideal, much disagreement exists as to the efficacy of implementing these social policy changes. Governing bodies (i.e., legislatures, boards of education) have generally overlooked that schools, as currently structured, are ineffective instruments of social change.

Meaning of Integration From the governing bodies' perspective, the integration principle as mandated in PL 94-142 assumes that the existing organization and structure of schools can and should function as the change agent. Integration policy alone, however, without proactive interventions, is not sufficient to meet the goal of normalized community participation and economic independence as a result of integrated education. Establishing the integration principle is certainly rational and appropriate, but given the assumption and operating arguments of the system, it is irrational to assume that the policy can and will be effectively implemented.

Characteristics of Integration The meaning of integration for government participants is clarified further by describing their involvement in the integration process for each major characteristic as follows:

1. *Ideology:* Governing bodies have documented the social needs of society at large and established programs for handicapped persons using laws, regulations, and rules affirming the integration principle. Such approaches can be considered rational from the governing bodies' point of view.
2. *Politics:* Governing bodies have been involved in allocating resources at all three levels in the system (local, state, federal). Given the competition among groups for the allocation of resources to resolve the problems may be considered insufficient in terms of the goal. However, from the point of view of governments, this is a rational outcome of the political process.
3. *Organization and Structure:* Consideration of the congruence of organization and structure with the integration principle does not routinely occur. Governing bodies typically mandate what should occur, not how it should occur. While, on the face of it, establishing a separate organizational structure for special education might be perceived as rational by governing bodies, a separate system in this case is incompatible with the integration principle and is therefore irrational from the viewpoint of the larger system.
4. *Placement Settings and Availability of Services:* Government participants do not usually consider the available placements and/or services in operation.

Once the integration principle is established, implementation is assumed. For governing bodies (policy developers) this is a neutral and rational response.

5. *Curriculum, Instruction, and Learning:* From the perspective of government participants, these matters are best handled by the appropriate professionals. However, recommendations are requested from professionals in the form of standards and are usually adopted and approved by the governing body at each level. From a government's point of view, carrying out the prescribed role is the rational response. However, without the mechanisms for accountability to determine how well the system operates in terms of student performance, this response could be neutral or rational depending on the consideration given to the problem from the viewpoint of the larger system.

6. *Accountability:* Government groups are involved peripherally in determining whether or not the social policies required are implemented effectively and as intended. Periodic review and hearings are the primary mechanism this group uses to determine accountability.

Logical Framework Applied to Professional Participants

Situational Context   The authors of this chapter accept that professionals (i.e., administrators and teachers), and particularly school administrators, are in the best position to support integration of severely handicapped students, not only because of their position within the educational structure but because of the formal and informal relationships they develop (Talley et al., 1979). Special education generally is viewed as a separate organizational structure within the school system. The extent to which regular and special education can be administratively integrated will directly affect the ability of the larger system to integrate students. As such, the educational structure mirrors a classic split in bureaucratic structure. Too often, administrators operate within the system in ways that reflect segregated decision making, segregated development of goals and objectives, and methods or processes of instruction (technology) that are not discussed between the groups involved and, therefore, are not fully understood (March, 1978). The result is ambiguity and confusion between the goals and practice of service delivery. Principals, teachers, and other service providers are responsible for translating laws, policies, and procedures into a coherent educational program for the children they serve. Yet, professional staff report spending considerable time reactively responding to administrative requirements and less time in planning educational programs that truly implement the integration principle. For example, scheduling problems often result in large groups of severely handicapped students being removed from schools and segregated in special classes for a large portion of the day (Rand Corporation, 1981). The outcome of efforts to implement the integration principle in schools appears to be fragmented and frustrating for all concerned because of a lack both of adequate planning and of proactive advocacy in school systems operation.

Meaning of Integration   Integration of severely handicapped students has occurred steadily, though slowly, as a result of PL 94-142. It appears that professional participants have underestimated the challenge of implementing the principle and have not faced it directly. The consequences of not confronting implementation directly, however, include the risk of dissillusioning and alienating parents of severely handicapped students in particular and the community in general. Placement services and procedures for decision making generally have been based on convenience and availability within the system, perhaps because organization and placement were not specified in the law. From the viewpoint of many professionals, the existing system remains acceptable and rational, even though all school systems clearly require changes to address the integration principle, especially for severely handicapped students. For teachers the meaning of integration is defined by the staffing patterns in the school, organizational arrangements of classes and courses, and the attitudes, knowledge, experiences, and skills of the teachers involved. If students' behaviors ''fit'' within the existing arrangement, then instruction and student/teacher action is considered rational by most teachers. Any variation from the existing arrangement is perceived as ''restrictive'' to most teachers and is therefore considered by them to be irrational. Severely handicapped students, whose unique educational needs fall outside the current boundaries of most systems, are, as a result, excluded from consideration within the existing options for integration. Actually the rational position would be one that requires knowledge of severely handicapped students' needs and provision of instruction to meet those needs, while providing such students equal opportunity to participate with all students (handicapped and nonhandicapped) in the system. For professionals, however, the basis for rationality is typically the *existing* system, not what the system is supposed to be/do. Many such teachers see their students as involved in a ''force fit'' that produces restrictive results for students. In actuality, far from restricting students, it is the convenience of maintaining the currently unjust status quo of the system that is at stake.

 Characteristics of Integration The meaning of integration for professionals is further clarified by discussing professionals' involvement in the characteristics below:

1. *Ideology:* Administrators and teachers alike profess agreement with the integration principle. This position is rational. However, there is disagreement within professional ranks over what integration means and how it should be implemented in the system. Without a focused definition and a system-wide plan for implementing integration, simple agreement with the principle is irrational from the larger system point of view.

2. *Politics:* The literature on education suggests that schools are nonpolitical. However, when politics is viewed as the distribution of power within and among organizations, schools become political ''hotbeds.'' In fact, administrators believe that schools are much too accessible politically to groups and other units of government who may have grievances against the schools (Talley et al., 1979). It is not unusual for teachers groups to nominate and support governing bodies that are sympathetic to their goals. Too often the goals of the weakest group politically (e.g., student/clients) are ignored in

favor of those who are politically powerful (Hollingshead, 1949). The goals of those who control are often unstated but implemented with consistency and precision. Subordinate behavior is rational from the professional point of view, while insubordinate behavior is irrational.

3. *Organization and Structure:* The organization and structure of regular education and special education, as described earlier, are separate. Any deviation toward integration would be considered irrational. However, the question is: Do the organization and structures that currently exist facilitate integration? Again for professionals, the rational position supports the existing structure, formally or informally, but not necessarily the integration principle. If the system's structure is contrary to the principle, then any change initiated in response to the larger system perspective would be considered neutral under the best circumstances, and probably considered irrational by most professionals.

4. *Placement Settings and Availability of Services:* Once again, the placement settings and services provided are defined in the context of the system. Professionals provide services and place children based on the existing system, that is, according to whatever is administratively available and convenient. In some cases, what is available and convenient may produce integration. This is true to the extent that the system is structured for integration and plans for service delivery are based on individual needs rather than categorical homogeneous grouping. Unfortunately, in most public school systems services for severely handicapped students are based on homogeneous groupings and delivery of services ultimately occurs in segregated schools. Therefore, unless professionals actively recognize that the existing system is irrational for the students, the integration principle will never be implemented for severely handicapped students.

5. *Curriculum, Instruction, and Learning:* For administrators the curriculum guide, instructional programs adopted by the board of education, and standardized testing programs represent rationality. For teachers, existing methods and techniques are usually considered the rational approach. What is taught in class is often not what is in the curriculum guide; what is tested for often becomes the curriculum. The results in terms of student programming is fragmentation at the school level (Rand Corporation, 1981). From the professionals' point of view their responses are rational. However, fragmented learning can only be considered irrational. From the perspective of the professional groups (administrators, teachers, etc.), the formal system, at this level, does not usually reflect the reality of what is happening.

6. *Accountability:* For professionals, accountability systems that do not address the outcomes of education and the effectiveness of the methods used to produce those ends must be considered irrational from the larger system point of view. However, the individual is subordinate to the system. If the system does not address accountability in the above way, then rationality and accountability are defined through the formal hierarchy dictated by the system.

Logical Framework Applied to Community Participants

Situational Context Sociologists portray schools as conservative reflections of their communities (Hollingshead, 1949). If community power structures are assumed to be adequately represented on school boards, decision making in the schools may be seen to reflect community values. The idea of integrating severely handicapped students is a radical one in this sense because it represents a significant change from previous and existing attitudes. Change in the direction of integration implies movement away from traditional values and is often automatically perceived as costing money, while the social and economic wastefulness of maintaining segregation for severely handicapped students is ignored. Moreover, integration may be seen as adversely affecting the power structure; thus, taxpayers may perceive their interests as threatened. This, in fact, may occur even though the governing structure approves of the social policy for integration. The rationality the community brings to the issues might be based upon the principles of enlightened self-interest; therefore, what is rational is that which serves the individual or group's self-interest. The history of racial desegregation in the United States suggests that school-based integration is more problematic for parents and other community participants than for the students themselves.

Meaning of Integration The attitudes of community taxpayers/patrons toward integration is conditioned by what they perceive it will cost them, not only financially but in terms of their current life-styles and beliefs. Therefore, integration's progress cannot be measured by mere agreement with the principle, but by behaviors that result in incremental movement toward integration in the system. A rational community response in this case could be support for a study of integration, or involvement in planning for integrated facilities and utilization efforts. No action in this case would be considered neutral; if, however, the result of no action is more segregation, the response would be irrational using the framework discussed earlier.

Characteristics of Integration The meaning of integration for community participants is further clarified by discussing the community's involvement in the integration process for each of the major descriptors below:

1. *Ideology:* For this group, the abstract principle of integration is both desirable and rational; however, depending upon the perceived consequences of implementation, responses vary in accordance with individual interest. If the response is inconsistent with the principle, it must be considered irrational.

2. *Politics, Organization and Structure, Placement Settings, and Availability of Services:* Placement settings for integration involve buildings and services to incorporate the needs of severely handicapped children and necessitate specialized staff, all of which cost money. To approve/adopt a principle of integration without allocating sufficient funds to implement it would be considered irrational. From the perspective of the community, the willingness to implement the integration principle is, to a degree, dependent upon the wealth of the community; that is, the level of services that would be provided by wealthier communities to achieve integration may be viewed as more

costly than segregation. In fact, as Stetson points out in this volume, integration clearly may be significantly less expensive. However, the wealth of the community may control the cost-related attitudes it brings to the issue, regardless of the reality of these costs.

3. *Curriculum, Instruction, and Learning:* For the community, economic concerns often predominate in local issues. Generally, the community is not involved actively in curriculum and instructional issues as a part of the comprehensive planning process. When it is involved, it generally defers to the professionals. Its acceptance or rejection of ideas is not always based upon what is best for the student, but rather the relative funding cost requirement. What then becomes rational to the community is responding to enlightened self-interest, based upon what is presented by the professionals.

4. *Accountability:* For the community, accountability is probably best described by what the schools are not doing, rather than how well they are doing what is required by state law and local policy. Taxpayers make decisions on the basis of what is known and what they are told. In this context, that is rational. However, unless the professionals present relevant accountability data on implementation of the integration principle, the community cannot make a rational response, simply because it does not have the information. In addition, the process does not allow the community to be effectively involved as a partner in the school's accountability mechanism.

Logical Framework Applied to Consumer Participants

Situational Context   Historically, the consumer participants, that is, parents of handicapped children, have been conditioned to distrust the general public, service providers, and social service agencies (U.S. Office of Education, 1978). Severely handicapped children have a long history of being rejected, of receiving inferior services, if any, and of being isolated from the public and the regular school population. In order that their children would no longer be denied services, parents organized and advocated laws that protected their severely handicapped children's rights to appropriate services, generally in separate educational systems. This trend was not only expensive but reinforced social and economic isolation from the general community. In some cases, when laws were passed adopting the integration principle, parents who fought for services in the past were, and still are, reluctant to give up the separate system. They fear that they will again have to deal with the ridicule, inferior services, and ultimately, rejection and isolation.

On the other hand, there is a growing body of parents who have experienced services for their severely handicapped children after PL 94-142 was enacted in 1975, and whose attitudes may be very different from those of their predecessors. Parents whose severely handicapped children started in integrated preschools may be especially receptive to the normalized expectations of integrated schooling.

Meaning of Integration   Given parents' attitudes as described above, the meaning of LRE is defined in terms of their handicapped child and their past experiences with the educational system. For parents who have fought hard for separate services, it is rational that they might prefer segregated placement. On the other hand, for parents who believe their children will do best in regular settings, it is rational for them to pursue any integrated option, that is, options that do not restrict their child's participation, especially where separate programs are the only current options. In terms of the larger system and implementation of the integration principle, it is irrational to expect that what is available or convenient is sufficient, even if the parent agrees. Rationality, in this case, requires the provisions of services and an educational setting consistent with what a child needs—this means regular interaction with his or her nonhandicapped peers. Parents are more likely to agree with professionals if the system adopts and implements procedures that serve severely handicapped children in integrated settings according to their unique needs and that furthermore actively involves parents in the process. Like other community members, parents can respond rationally to the system if the system is designed to produce outcomes consistent with the integration principle. Moreover, the system's rationality would ultimately be demonstrated in terms of student learning.

Characteristics of Integration The meaning of integration for parents can be further clarified by discussing their involvement in the integration process for each of the following major descriptive characteristics:

1. *Ideology:* For parents, agreement with the principle is rational. However, because of parents' past experience with the system, most new implementation efforts attempted by professionals are treated with skepticism. The rationality of the response may be dependent upon the manner in which integration is first presented—that is, to what degree were parents involved, and to what degree were provision of services and placement decisions based upon students' individual needs.

2. *Politics, Organization and Structure, Placement Settings, and Availability of Services:* Parents have consistently and effectively used the political process to obtain services for their children, including separate school systems. This response from a parental viewpoint is rational, even though in the larger sense it is inconsistent with the integration principle. Ironically, because some parents prefer separate systems, this may, in the long run, make it more difficult to achieve integration. Economic conditions are curently threatening the viability of separate systems, and may ultimately force integration. The challenge for all of us is to make the transition as comfortable and effective as possible.

3. *Curriculum, Instruction, and Learning:* Parents have been actively involved in effective programming of service delivery for their children in separate systems. This is a rational response. However, from the larger system perspective it may be neutral. A proactive rational response, consistent with the integration principle, would be to facilitate translation of what has been learned in a separate system into a fully integrated regular system.

4. *Accountability:* For parents, accountability is often simply a matter of how

well their child is doing in school. If they perceive that everything is going well, then usually no response or a busines-as-usual response is rational. However, if the context of the student's progress is in a segregated and therefore isolated setting, the response may be irrational from the larger system's point of view. Accountability, in this sense, would provide information on the child's progress toward the goal of successful participation in society and economic independence, as evidenced in part by interactions with nonhandicapped peers.

Logical Framework Applied to Client Participants

Situational Context Generally speaking, the educational context for a severely handicapped student has occurred separately and apart from nonhandicapped children and adults, except for the context of a handicapped child's family.

Meaning of Integration To discuss the meaning of LRE for severely handicapped children who have been isolated in separate schools, is to address their knowledge of life as they have experienced it. Primarily, their experiences have been with other handicapped children in settings apart from nonhandicapped individuals, other than professionals or family members. In this context, integration or LRE may mean simply the ability to get around, when, where, and how they chose to do so. From a severely handicapped student's point of view, this is rational. Due to lack of choice and experience, restriction may not be perceived as irrational. Any discussion of potential for learning, living, and working occurs within the context of the environment. Unfortunately, for many severely handicapped children, that environment means isolation from the larger society. It has been agreed that isolation, in and of itself, limits an individual's potential. The expectations that are set for severely handicapped students in segregated settings reflect the norm for the *segregated setting* rather than the norm for the *general population*. To be rational, the meaning of integration for severely handicapped students must be experienced and perceived in settings that approximate the norms for the general population.

Characteristics of Integration The following discussion of the integration process in relation to the following descriptive characteristics further defines the problem:

1. *Ideology:* For severely handicapped students, ideology is merely an abstract notion of social needs and aspirations. If the individual's aspirations do not extend beyond isolated settings, this presents a problem for society. Students, after all, represent a resource, and unused resources affect everyone, including the students themselves. More important, our society has a tradition of beliefs about the values and rights of *all* human beings. It is from our social tradition and system of beliefs that we derive our strength as a society.

2. *Politics, Organization and Structure, Placement Settings and Availability of Services:* For severely handicapped students, the services they receive, where they receive those services, and the organizational structure under

which they are served are matters that they have little opportunity to control. Such students, however, will help to determine the future of our society. Therefore, opportunities for successful normalized integrated participation and economic independence are vital if we are to remain viable as a society. That individuals are asked to act to assure the good of all in society is the implied social contract, and it is in this context that the politics of placement settings and of available services for educating severely handicapped children, consistent with the integration principle, prevails.

3. *Curriculum, Instruction, Learning, and Accountability:* For students, participation in courses and classes prescribed by law and policy is the rational response. The rationality of the system's response will be determined by whether or not those courses and classes facilitate successful, integrated participation in society and economic independence. Successful participation of severely handicapped children in larger society, has yet to be realized.

SUMMARY

The complexity and variety of the problems involved in implementing the integration imperative have created highly charged emotions surrounding the issue, at the same time that competition for limited resources has threatened the implementation activities associated with integration. This chapter has described the problems encountered, the people involved, the pertinent characteristics of their environment, and the points of view that may help explain their behaviors in various contexts. It is hoped that by better understanding participants' perspectives, a blueprint for action may be more clearly developed. We have attempted to redefine the LRE concept in terms of the people involved, the unique experiences that define their view of LRE, and the effects of those experiences on their lives, rather than simply affirming the legal obligation.

In its purest form, implementation of the integration principle moves toward a consensus of the conflicting rationalities that persons bring to the integration issue. However, the consensus must include the education and proactive mixing of severely handicapped students with their nonhandicapped peers; otherwise, conflicts between rationalities will continue to exist and the integration principle will be thwarted. On an optimistic note, the authors believe that adversity offers numerous opportunities. The challenge is in the will of the individual and society to seek out those opportunities. There is no one right and best answer; no single approach has been proposed here to resolve all the problems associated with implementing integration. Additional research in all areas discussed is needed. However, the direction that the research must take is clear—an analysis into the effectiveness of educating all handicapped and nonhandicapped students together. Beyond that, local education agencies need to develop specific solutions to bring about full implementation of the integration imperative.

REFERENCES

Brown v. *Board of Education*, 347 U.S. 483 (1954).

Campbell v. *Talladega County Board of Education*, 518 F. Supp. 47 (D.C.Ala. 1981).

Federal Register, August 23, 1977, *42* (163), p. 42497.

Fialkowski v. *Shapp*, 405 F. Supp. 946 (E.D.Pa. 1975).

General Accounting Office. Document No. IEP81-1. *Controller General report to chairman, Subcommittee on Select Education, Committee on Education and Labor, House of Representatives of the United States. Disparity still exists in who gets special education.* September 30, 1981.

Gideonse, H.D. Peer teaching and participation. In: J. K. Grosenick & M. C. Reynolds (eds.), *Teacher education: Renegotiating roles for mainstreaming.* Reston, VA: The Council for Exceptional Children, 1978.

Gilhool, T.K., & Stuttman, E.A. Integrating severely handicapped students: Toward criteria for implementing and enforcing the integrative imperative of PL 94-142 and Section 504. In: *Developing criteria for the evaluation of the least restrictive environment provision.* Washington, D. C.: State Program Studies Branch, Division of Innovation and Development, Bureau of Education for the Handicapped, U.S. Office of Education, 1978.

Hollingshead, A.B. *Elmtown's youth.* New York: John Wiley & Sons, 1949.

March, J.G. American public school administration: A short analysis. *School Review,* 1978, *86.*

Mills v. *Board of Education of District of Columbia*, 348 F. Supp. 866 (D.D.C. 1972).

PARC v. *Commonwealth of Pennsylvania*, 343 F. Supp. 279 (E.D.Pa. 1972).

Rand Corporation. *Study of special education services, Vol. 6: Age, handicapping conditions, and type of educational placement of the handicapped student population.* Santa Monica, CA: Rand Corporation, 1981.

Rossmiller, R.A., & Frohreich, L.E. *Expenditures in funding patterns in Idaho's programs for exceptional children.* Madison: University of Wisconsin, 1979.

Science Research Institute, International. *Local implementation of PL 94-142: Third year report of a longitudinal study.* Menlo Park, CA: Science Research Institute, International, 1981.

Talley, R.C., Elting, S.E., Chobot, R.B., Oliver, T.E., & Raimondi, S.L. *Education of handicapped students in the least restrictive environment: A review of the literature on preconditions, critical factors, administrative strategies and technical assistance.* Annandale, VA: J.W.K. International Corporation, 1979.

U.S. Department of Education, Office of Special Education and Rehabilitative Services. *Fourth annual report to Congress on the implementation of PL 94-142: The Education for all Handicapped Children's Act of 1975.* Washington, D.C.: 1982.

U.S. Office of Education. In: *Developing criteria for the evaluation of the least restrictive environment provision.* Washington, DC: State Program Studies Branch, Division of Innovation and Development, Bureau of Education for the Handicapped, U.S. Office of Education, 1978.

REFERENCE NOTE

1. Reger, G.R. *An analysis of special education cost in the state of Wisconsin.* Unpublished doctoral dissertation, University of Wisconsin, Madison, 1979.

Index